Paperweight

Also by Stephen Fry
The Liar

Stephen Fry

PAPERWEIGHT

HEINEMANN : LONDON

To my mother and father
... the most forbearing forbears

William Heinemann Ltd
Michelin House, 81 Fulham Road, London SW3 6RB
LONDON   MELBOURNE   AUCKLAND

First published 1992
Copyright © Stephen Fry 1992
Reprinted 1992 (seven times)

A CIP catalogue record for this book
is held by the British Library
ISBN 0 434 27408 9

Phototypeset by Falcon Graphic Art Ltd
Printed in England by Clays Ltd, St Ives plc

Contents

Introduction

Welcome to *Paperweight*. My first act must be to warn that it would be a madness in you to read this book straight through at one sitting, as though it were some gripping novel or ennobling biography. In the banquet of literature *Paperweight* aspires to be thought of as no more than a kind of literary guacamole into which the tired and hungry reader may from time to time wish to dip the tortilla chip of his or her curiosity. I will not be held responsible for the mental indigestion that is sure to be provoked by any attempt to bolt the thing whole. Snack books may not be the last word in style, but for those sated and blown by the truffles and *quenelles* of the master chefs in one kitchen, or flatulent with Whoppers and Super Supremes from the short-order cooks in the other, it may just be that *Paperweight* will find a place.

Perhaps, however, it will be the other end of the alimentary canal that furnishes us with a clue as to how to manage this book: its natural home may well turn out to be the lavatory, alongside *The Best of the Far Side*, an old Harpic-stained copy of *The Sloane Ranger Handbook* and everyone's cloacal favourite, *The Collected Letters of Rupert Hart-Davies*. It may be that each article of the book should have been flagged with a number or symbol indicating the length of time the article would take to read, that number or symbol corresponding with the health of a reader's bowel. In this way the reader could determine which sections to read according to his or her diet and general enteric condition. The whole book could then be got through without ever impinging on the customer's quality time. But whatever use you find for *Paperweight*, whether you do follow a lavatorial regime, whether you take the hint of its title and press it into service as a desk accessory, or whether you merely wish to deface the photograph of that disgusting man on the front cover, I wish you years of trouble-free, stain-resistant use.

To collect together the swarf of six or seven years of occasional toiling in the workshops of journalism and radio (an absurd metaphor and of a kind that *belle lettristes* do not seem to be able to avoid . . . how is writing articles even remotely like toiling in a workshop? Get to the bloody point) might seem like an act of insupportable arrogance. My only answer to that is to say that the publishing atrocity you hold in your hands is, in fact, an act of *supported* arrogance. It exists because over the years I have received many letters from readers and listeners asking if there might be made available to them some permanent record of the articles and broadcasts which I have so pitilessly inflicted upon an incredulous public – presumably with a view to threatening their children or using the resultant book as an accessory in some satanic ritual. *Paperweight* is, anyway, the consequence of such entreaties, I trust those responsible will profit from the lesson.

(What's all this 'there might be made available to them some permanent record' and 'the consequence of such entreaties'? Why do you have to descend to this greasy style traditional in Forewords? And where do you get off with all this mock humility? 'this publishing atrocity . . . I have so pitilessly inflicted'. Repulsive.)

My first forays into the kind of writing represented in this book (*Forays? forays?* What kind of word is that? Get a grip.) began in 1985 when Ian Gardhouse, a BBC radio producer of previously unspotted character, asked me to contribute to a programme of his called *Colour Supplement*. On or two of the broadcasts I made for this short-lived venture are contained in the 'Radio' section of this book.

Colour Supplement gave way to *Loose Ends*, on the first programme of which I introduced a character called Professor Trefusis. It was Ian Gardhouse's idea. The week before our first transmission, a real-life academic, it seems, had been appointed by the government to inquire into sex and violence on television. Gardhouse thought it would be appropriate for me to broadcast as that academic, delivering opinions on a medium with which a cloistered don would be completely unfamiliar. I came up with an ageing Cambridge philologist of amiable but sometimes vituperative character called Donald Trefusis.

I liked Trefusis. His advanced years and further advanced eccentricity allowed me to get away with spiked comments and straight rudery that would have been unthinkable if uttered in the normal voice of an aspiring comic in his twenties. Over the next two or three years I continued to perform Trefusis and his 'wireless essays', on *Loose Ends*. A generous, some might say over-generous (cloying mock humility again . . . though you'd call it *fausse humilité*, I bet), selection is included here. I also dragged up from time to time in the guise of Rosina Lady Madding, faded Society Beauty, until pressure of work forced me to retrench on so giddy an expenditure of time. (oh, give it a *rest*, will you?)

Apart from anything else, such spare hours as I had when not prancing about on stages or in TV studios were being taken up with writing a weekly column for the now defunct *Listener* magazine. Its new editor, the peerless Alan Coren (well, 'peerless' is all right I suppose . . . at least you didn't say 'that consummate good egg, Alan Coren') had hoicked me over from the books pages where I had been contributing occasional reviews for the literary editor, Lynne Truss. Some of those book reviews and a selection from the column itself are here reproduced in the section marked 'The Listener'. For the Christmas issue of 1987 I contributed a Sherlock Holmes story which I have taken the liberty of including too (what do you mean 'taken the liberty'? It's your bleeding book isn't it? Where's the liberty? *Really*). A brace of articles (you mean 'two') written for *Arena* magazine are collected in a Reviews and Oddments section, together with a couple of pieces I wrote for the *Tatler* under the editorship of that supreme figure, since sadly gathered, Mark Boxer. I have also included a few articles I wrote as television critic of the *Literary Review*.

The Listener changed publishers in 1989 and Alan Coren left, as did I. A little later the magazine folded entirely. (We're supposed to make a connection there, are we?)

A few months after this, Max Hastings, the amiable and modest editor of the *Daily Telegraph* (you like simply *everyone* don't you?) sent me a note one afternoon, care of the stage door of the Aldwych Theatre, where I was performing in one of the most significant flops of the season, a play called *Look Look*. He asked if I would consider a column for his newspaper. It so happens that a few months earlier I had changed, as a reader, from the *Independent* to the *Telegraph*. Although no Conservative, I found and continue to find myself more at home in the pages of that newspaper than in any other, so I agreed readily and happily (ooh, this *is* exciting).

For two years I wrote a column under the heading 'Fry on Friday', relinquishing the post in late 1991, under pressure of filming and writing work. It was an immensely enjoyable discipline, that of having to find the weekly topic, although there were times when I was writing ten times as many words a week, answering the huge number of letters that were flooding in from *Telegraph* readers, than it took to write the articles themselves. I dare say the great columnists of our age, the Waterhouses, Levins and Waughs would find my post-bag laughably thin, but for me the challenging, intelligent, friendly and sometimes not so friendly letters from readers proved one of the great surprises and delights of that period of my life. I may say that towards the end, my time crisis having grown to such frightening proportions, I found myself unable to answer a great many of the letters and take this opportunity to apologise for the perfunctory nature of any replies with which correspondents were forced to be content (what a *creep*).

The final part of *Paperweight* is the complete text of a play of mine called *Latin! or Tobacco and Boys*. I have included the programme note for its performance at the New End Theatre, Hampstead, which should explain the background to the piece. *Latin!* is I suppose the reason for my doing what I do. I wrote it during my second year at Cambridge. As a result, Hugh Laurie, who saw it at Edinburgh, asked Emma Thompson to introduce me to him in the hope that I might write with him for a Footlights revue. I have been writing with him, on and off, for the last eleven years and I hope to do so for many more yet.

I should like to record my thanks therefore to him, to Emma Thompson, to Alan Coren, Max Hastings, Ian Gardhouse, Ned Sherrin, Lynne Truss, Nick Logan of *Arena*, Emma Soames (*quondam editrix* of the *Literary Review*) and the late Mark Boxer. Thanks too to Lisa Glass of Mandarin Books for her patience and to Jo Foster for helping me to track down the *disjecta membra* of so many years. (You had to do it, didn't you? You *had* to end with a bloody Latin tag. What a *git*. And where do you get off with '*quondam editrix*'? Jesus.)

Stephen Fry
Norfolk, 1992

Section One

Radio

Donald Trefusis

This is the first Trefusis broadcast, from Loose Ends. *As explained in the introduction, it makes reference to a governmental decision to invite an academic to view a year's television and pronounce on whether or not the violence shown on our screens was harmful to the public and most especially, of course, the dear children of this country.*

VOICE: Dr Donald Trefusis, Senior Tutor of St Matthew's College, Cambridge, and Carnegie Professor of Philology, was asked by the government last year to monitor a large part of the BBC's television output, paying particular attention to scenes of violence that might disturb or influence young children. Here, he reports on his findings.

My brief, to inspect the rediffusion of violence in the BBC's television programming, was on the one hand appalling to an inveterate lover of the wireless, and on the other appealing to an avid student and chronicler of modern society, and on the other flattering to one who is – oh dear, I seem to have three hands here, never mind, suffice it to say that I approached the task with a glad, if palpitating, heart.

My predecessor on the Queen Anne Chair of Applied Moral Sciences[1] here always held that television, already an etymological hybrid compounded, as it is, of the Greek 'tele' and the Latin 'vision', was also a social hybrid, a chimera that awaited some modern crusading Bellerophon, athwart a twentieth-century Pegasus, to slay it before it devoured our culture whole in its filthy, putrescent, purulent maw.

I, however, essentially a man of the people, a man with his alert and keen young fingers very much on the thrusting, vibrant

[1]For some reason I seem to have introduced Trefusis as a Moral Scientist. It is later affirmed that he is a philologist.

pulse of our times, incline to no such intemperate view. For me television represents a challenge, a hope, an opportunity – or, in the words of T.E. Hulme, 'a concrete flux of interpenetrating intensities'. And it was with this high heart that I approached the duty my government had called me to do. In fact, when young Peter from the Home Office approached me for the task in the smoking library of the Oxford and Cambridge Club, I had to confess to him that I hadn't actually ever watched any television before. One is so busy. But Peter, whom I am proud to say I taught for the Classical Tripos in 1947, took the view that a fresh mind was what the problem needed: it was, therefore, with the confidence of ignorance and the blithe cheer of inexperience that I sat down to my brand new Sony Trinitron to sample the broadcast offerings of the corporation.

Violence, I need hardly remind a wireless audience, derives from the Latin word *vis* and its cognates, meaning strength. The violence I was briefed to hunt down, however, was a horse of a very different kidney. I shall keep you guessing no longer and reveal that what I saw shocked me to the very core of my being and disturbed me in a fashion that it is beyond my power to describe. Programme after programme violent, harrowing and potentially ruinous to the soft, impressionable minds of the young.

The first programme I chanced upon was entitled *The Late, Late Breakfast Show* presented by a – no, it is no part of my function here to descend to personalities and abuse – presented by a personage, let us say, that I would rather never see again in this or any other world. In this programme, violence was done to all the canons of decency, respectability, gentleness, courtesy, taste, humanity and dignity that I have striven all my life to uphold and promote. All were violated in ways too savage, too grotesque, too degraded to delineate. Such an obscene orgy of vulgarity, baseness and ignorance I hope never to witness again. The young mind is being brought up on the idea that self-advertising, huckstering loutishness is admirable; crude, unlettered bawdy at the expense of female dignity amusing; and puerile, banausic posturing and prankstering entertaining. Under the motto 'It's only a laugh' waves a banner of such shameful, irredeemable crudity that the imagination sickens. If this, I felt, is television, then the violence it is doing to the sensibilities of our young must be instantly halted

4

before it is too late. A subsequent stream of futile and insulting games programmes followed hard on the heels of this abomination: all week I was bombarded by violent filth. One programme consisting entirely of cut-up pieces of letters that viewers had had the impertinence to send up did such violence to this country's good name for literacy, intelligence, spelling, calligraphy, discernment and modesty that I feared I should faint clean away.

However, amongst this mire of violation, ruin and despair, some redeeming pearls did shine forth. From America, and from here, there were many programmes in which actors dressed up and pretended to be policemen or criminals and gave entertaining representations of fights and shoot-outs. Many a car exploded in a jolly and exciting fashion as part of this make-believe. I became particularly fond of a pair called Starsky and Hutch, who were forever simulating gun-fights and beatings-up. These merry, silly, romping fictional diversions were, as fiction always has been, and always will be, harmless, instructive and charming. I shall recommend they be left alone, as should be all drama and fiction. But the violence, the violence that attacks our young in the monstrous shapes I have already tried to describe, that I shall spare no effort to uproot, extirpate, decimate, annihilate and destroy.

Good morning.

Rosina, Lady Madding

The first of three monologues from Rosina, Lady Madding, *which appeared on* Loose Ends. *Imagine a voice not unlike that made by someone who speaks while inhaling.*

VOICE: Rosina, Lady Madding, at home at Eastwold House.

I live here alone in what, when I was a girl, was used to be called the Dower House. I suppose I am technically a dowager, though my son Rufus, the fourth earl, is not yet married. I love the country, it's very peaceful here. I am surrounded by photographs of my past. On the piano I have a photograph of myself dancing with David, the Prince of Wales – later of course Edward the Eighth and subsequent Duke of Windsor. David was a very bad dancer, always trod on one's toes, and I remember he once crushed the metatarsal bones in the foot of a girl-friend of mine – discreet lesbianism was fashionable at the time.

Here's a photograph of Noël Coward – darling Noël as we always called him. He was a very witty man, you know – it's a side of him not many people are aware of. I recall an occasion when I came onto the dance-floor of Mario's in Greek Street wearing a very daring frock, a frock that revealed more of my décolletage than was then considered proper – now of course I dare say it would raise nothing more than an eyebrow – but at the time it was very wicked. I came onto the floor and darling Noël came up to me and said 'Rosina' – he always used to call me Rosina – it is my name, you must understand. 'Rosina,' he said in that *voice* of his, 'Rosina, where did you find such an alluringly low-cut torso?' This was Noël's little way, you see.

The portrait above the fireplace was made when I was in Paris – Claude my husband was Ambassador in the late twenties.

I used to hold very literary parties at the embassy – Plum and Duff Cooper, Scott and Garrett Fitzgerald, darling Geoffrey Chaucer of course, Adolf Hitler and Unity Mitford, Gertrude Stein and Alice B. Topless, Radclyffe Hall and Angela Brazil – they could always be relied upon to attend. And of course O. Henry James Joyce Cary Grant. I remember F.E. Smith, later Lord Birkenhead of course, that's his picture there, just below the dartboard, F.E. used to say 'All the world and his live-in lover go to Rosina's parties' which pleased me very much.

Later when Claude and I went to India to take up the Vice-regency I met Gandhi with whom I used to play French cricket – he was awfully good at cricket, as a matter of fact: Claude always used to say, 'what the loin-cloth industry gained, the wicket-keeping industry lost.' Pandit Nehru was very impressive too, though if Edwina Mountbatten is to be believed his length was too variable for him ever to enter the ranks of Indian leg-spin immortals.

The large bronze statue of the nude male which stands on top of the synthesiser is of Herbert Morrison the Cabinet Minister. I use it to hang my bracelets on when I'm playing at the keyboard now. I spend a lot of time here in this room, remembering the past. Silly Poles Hartley, L.P. Hartley, you know, once said that the past is a foreign country, but I don't agree. The food was better for a start, and the people didn't smell. People often tell me I was one of a spoilt generation, rich, beautiful, idle, parasitical. It is true that I had every conceivable luxury lavished upon me during my life, met many famous and influential people, saw many exciting places and never did anything more taxing than organise large house-parties. But you know, despite that, if I had my time over again I wouldn't change a thing. Regrets? A few. I shouldn't have let dear T.E. Lawrence borrow my motor-bicycle. I'm tired now. Let me eat.

Trefusis's Christmas Quiz

VOICE: Donald Trefusis, Professor of Philology at the University of Cambridge, sets his famous Christmas quiz. Have pencil, paper or tape-recorder ready.

Human beings, who I must suppose make up a fair proportion of my audience today, are often immensely competitive in their ways. This is usually a quality much to be deplored and discouraged; clearly it is deleterious to the industrial and economic health of our country to have a large number of aggressive, competitive persons vying with each other for money or markets or whatever footling thing industrial figures do vie for when not taking up valuable compartment space in trains.

The competitive spirit is an ethos which it is the business of universities such as the one in which I have the honour to move and work, to subdue and neutralise. We talk often about our national malaise, which is not, as often assumed, in reference to our welcome immigrants from Malaya, but a description of the appalling and continuing trend of intelligent young men and women coming to universities and being encouraged to go into industry. Natural scholars, classicists and linguists are, from an early age, introduced to technology, management (whatever that is to be taken to signify) and commerce. We need look no further than that dismal circumstance if we are searching for reasons that may explain the decline of this country. How can this nation stand on its feet in the cut and thrust international sphere if it is unable to decline the middle mood of λυω or rehearse the argument of *Endymion*? A generation of citizens who buy red leather combination locked attaché cases and heated trouser presses while remaining ignorant of the metrical constitution of *The Faerie Queen* is not one ready to lead the world. However that is not the main text of my disquisition this day. I wished merely

8

to wash the background of my canvas with the foregoing colours from my palette of complaints before limning the foreground with the shapes and rhythms of my main composition.

For all that I rightly discourage adversarial attitudes amongst my students, at Christmas it is customary for me to set a small quiz. It is open to any member of the University who has, at any time during the previous twelvemonth, invited me to a Madeira and Biscuit party. Quite enormous international pressure has been put upon me to open this traditional little catechism to my listening public. The undergraduate prize, a chased filigree-work *étui* from the Second Republic, engraved with the winner's name and containing a small quantity of high-grade cocaine, has already been won, so I am afraid that I cannot offer the winner amongst you anything more than a signed copy of your choice of any of my published works together with a personally autographed edition of Mr Sherrin's latest amusing collection of humorous theatre anecdotes entitled *Larry's Such A Name-Dropper*.

The quiz is divided into two categories which I have named, rather aptly I think, Section A and Section Five. Section Five first, I fancy, for neatness. Prepare implements of scripture or instruments of magnetic sound registration.

Question 1:   What, please, have the following words in common: *almost, biopsy, chintz*? That's *almost, biopsy,* and *chintz*.

Question 2:   What have the Prime Ministers Lord Pelham and Lord Grenville to do with Lord Ickenham and Lord Sidcup? That's Lords Pelham and Grenville, Lords Ickenham and Sidcup.

Question 3:   What association does BBC correspondent Martin Bell have with the *Times* Crossword Puzzle?

Question 4:   What have poets Andrew Marvell, Philip Larkin and Stevie Smith in common, aside from their demises?

Question 5:   What have Poles and Staples to do with Shrimps and Wardrobes?

That was Section Five. Section A is the tie-breaker, and requires more creative effort from the competitor.

Question A: In twelve words devise a telegram to an imaginary Duchess whose *couchée* you are compelled to miss. It should be composed in a manner that leaves no doubt that you are skipping the engagement simply because you find her and her friends repellent, abhorrent and absurd.

Question B: Lean forward and touch each knee with the tip of your nose.

Question C: Wear bright, cheerful colours and adopt a sweet nature.

Question D: Where practicable, use a condom.

Question E: Be respectful to your seniors and courteous, charming and considerate to your juniors.

Question F: If you like popular music go out and buy five classical records and listen to them five times a day for a week.

Question G: If you like classical music go out and buy five popular music records and listen to them five times a day for a week and let's have no more nonsense.

Question H: Imagine that you are the defence counsel for Robert Maxwell. Try and persuade a jury that your client is not megalomaniacally insane.[1]

Question I: Write a poem in *ottava rima* on the subject of Halitosis.

There you are. This should present no problems for keen competitors. By way of encouragement I might say that four-fifths of my students achieved 98 per cent or higher in this quiz. The names of all successful candidates will be put into my crushed velvet smoking cap and one lucky name will be drawn out on Christmas Eve by the Provost-General In Ordinary of St Matthew's College, Sir Neville Soviet Mole.

---

[1]Had some trouble getting this past the BBC censor. Unusually for me, as you will see, this remark proved accurate and, if not prophetic exactly, at least resonant.

The very best of luck to you all, and if you have been, I'm glad you've stopped.

Answers to Section Five of Trefusis's Christmas Quiz

Really most gratifying and extraordinary response to my quiz. The answers were as follows: *almost*, *biopsy* and *chintz* are the only six-lettered words in the language whose letters occur without repetition in alphabetical order. Lords Sidcup and Ickenham have this in common with the quondam Prime Ministers Lords Pelham and Grenville – they were both creations of P.G. Wodehouse, whose given names were, of course, Pelham and Grenville. Martin Bell's connection with the *Times* Crossword is that his father Adrian, the writer and journalist, compiled the first ever *Times* puzzle. Andrew Marvell, Philip Larkin and Stevie Smith all have the city of Hull in common. Lastly I asked you for the connection between Poles and Staples and Shrimps and Wardrobes. L.P. Hartley wrote of course *The Shrimp and the Anemone* and his middle name was Poles, while Clive Staples Lewis was the author of *The Lion, the Witch and the Wardrobe*. There we are. I am happy to say that fourteen thousand of you sent in answers correct in every detail. The winner was a Mr J. Archer, of the Old Vicarage, Grantchester.

Jeremy Creep

Also broadcast on Colour Supplement.

VOICE: This week *Men At Work* talks to Sir Jeremy Creep, Principal of the London College of Architects in Rohan Point, Putney.

Architecture offers quite extraordinary opportunities to serve the community, to enhance the landscape, refresh the environment and to advance mankind – the successful architect needs training to overcome these pitfalls however, and start earning some serious money. I get all kinds of people from the schools and universities and my job is manifold and various. Firstly of course, it's visual. Young people use their eyes – to be a good architect in Britain today you need to do more than use your eyes, you must have them surgically removed. But you don't just have to be blind to be a modern architect, you must develop a lively sense of contempt for your fellow man, so early meetings with borough planners and council administrators are essential.

Next a carefully planned system of mind-direction seminars, as we like to call them. In these we show our students film of old buildings, old village communities, interviews with noted conservationists such as the late John Betjeman and His Royal Highness Prince Charles. By disseminating toxic gases and introducing mild electric shocks we induce a feeling of nausea, sickness and acute physical pain, which in time is associated with those images. Next we show film of large glass boxes, rough concrete towers and enormous steel girders, all the time stimulating the students with underseat vibromassage and soothing selections of Mozart, while they drink venerable clarets and smoke jazz cigarettes. By this means an aversion to old forms of architecture and a loving acceptance of the new can be effectively inculcated.

The observant amongst you will have noticed that earlier I have said that we remove our trainees' eyes and *then* show them films. I should of course have mentioned that an architect must be able to lie. He (or she) must be adept at lying in public fluently and easily. 'This building will stand for ten years', 'St Paul's Cathedral is ugly and needs to be surrounded with objects of beauty', 'This block of flats is built around human dimensions and needs', 'Architecture is first and foremost about people'. I doubt if even the most sophisticated detector would have challenged one of those statements, outrageous tissues of litanies of catalogues of farragoes of lies that they were.

A disturbing trend towards neo-Mannerism that has crept into 1980s office and council architecture has caused us to stiffen up our re-education programme lately and now it is common policy on presenting our diploma to the successful graduate to suck his brains out with a straw before allowing him to leave.

Le Corbusier, that most magnificent of architects (you see, not even a flicker on the polygram's needle there), once said 'A human being is a machine for living in one of my houses' and if Britain is to have a thriving, prosperous, happy, well-fed, well-paid, well-housed community of architects then those are the principles we must embrace.

Let me quote again, Sir Niklaus Pevsner this time, 'Building is the enclosure of space; architecture is the aesthetic enclosure of space.' In the library of my converted Georgian water-mill out here in Hampshire, I reach for the *Architect's Dictionary*, Volume One 'Asbestos to Balsa wood girders', and look up the word 'aesthetic'. I find this entry: 'aesthetic, obs. vulg. orig. unknown.' That could describe a modern architect couldn't it? Obs. vulg. orig. unknown. Obscene, vulgar bastard. Goodnight.

Trefusis Overdresses

Good hello to you all. I must state at the outset of this little talk, with frank, manly directness, that I am not a snob. Never have been, don't want to be. Robbie Burns and I, as so often these days, are in agreement, when we carol that rank is but the guinea-stamp and that a man is a man for a' that. Kind hearts, I am often heard to murmur to myself, when strolling about the ballroom at some omnium gatherum of the crested families of the realm, kind hearts are more than coronets and simple faith than Norman Tebbit. For all that, I am an old man with few fleshly pleasures left me, unless having my corns filed may be counted as sensuous and sybaritic, and it does give me pleasure, as the Season commences, to gad about the flesh pots of Society, cheering on the Varsity in the Diamond Skulls at Henley here, escorting a lissom sprig of the nobility to the Queen Charlotte Ball there. It is, I must own, hard to square my delight in these festivities with my Proudhonite-syndicalism on the one hand and my almost universal contempt for the generality of the upper classes on the other. The beauty of the events *eux-mêmes* is vitiated by the almost total foulness and self-esteem of those in attendance. It is hard to toss the contents of a half-pint mug of Pimms in the Stewards' Enclosure at Henley, for instance, without soaking one who is in total ignorance of the art of rowing. Unslip a rat in the members' stands at Lord's and you will start a score of individuals who couldn't tell you the first thing about cricket. But quite my favourite event of the Season is and shall remain Glyndebourne. Its preciosity and privilege notwithstanding, the smugness of those present aside, the awful luxury of the whole event discounted, this is a fine place to be. Imagine therefore my pleasure when, earlier this week, an old pupil of mine, now an international spy of growing reputation, invited me to meet him there to witness a new production of *La Traviata* directed by Sir Peter, Sir Peter, Sir Peter whatever it is.

I could barely stand still and let Glambidge, my gyp, tie my tie, stud my studs and brace my braces, so excited was I on the day appointed. I love to wear the full festive fig; an American girl once told me that it made me look kinda sexy and these things linger in the memory. My particular nightmare is overdressing, and Glyndebourne has at least the advantage of particular rules of dress. Black tie or nothing. Though I suspect nothing would be frowned upon, if not barred outright.

Glambidge and I arrived in good time to miss the first act. I shan't blame Glambidge, he drove that Wolseley to the limit. Unfortunately its limit appears to be nineteen miles an hour. Howsomever, we had five minutes to pass before the interval, minutes I filled inspecting the grounds and wondering at the particularly penetrating quality of fine cold driving summer rain. In due course the act ended and the audience filed out of the – well, the auditorium.

Ladies and gentlemen, mother, friends: imagine my mortification, picture my distress, conceive of my chagrin. That audience of opera-goers was dressed, each man jack or woman jill of them, in what I can only describe as the most appalling collection of day wear. The only black ties to be seen were those about the necks of the Front of House staff. My old pupil hastened up to me. 'Why, Professor,' he shrieked. 'Whatever are you dressed up like that for? This is the dress rehearsal – I thought you knew.'

I had come for the public dress rehearsal in evening dress.

Words, thousands of them, spin into my mind, some of them English, many of them culled from alien tongues; none of them, not a one, is capable of describing a scintilla of an iota of a shadow of a suspicion of an atom of a fraction of a ghost of a tithe of a particle of my horror, shame and pitiable distress. Of all the solecisms, gaffes, floaters, blunders and bowel-shatteringly frightful bloomers possible to make, I am fully persuaded that overdressing heads the field by a comfortable furlong.

Ichabod, ohimé, eheu, aïee! I dived like a kingfisher into the lavatory, slammed the door behind me and sat sobbing there for the ensuing two and a half hours. Every half-pitying, half-scornful look that had been cast me as I had flown into this sanctuary replayed itself in my tortured mind. They had all stared as upon some parvenu Armenian millionaire who wears bought medals at a British Legion dinner, or some *arriviste* mayor who sits even in his bath chained in aldermanic splendour. If only I hadn't told Glambidge he might drive on into Lewes to look up his wife who lives in a lunatic asylum just outside the town, I might have been able to sneak home even then. As it is I writhed in a lather of shame for the duration.

But now, in the cold light of reason, I am wondering if it is not possible that I over-reacted a little. Might a calmer man not have passed the whole misunderstanding off with a light laugh? Was I not being myself a little bit of a snob in attributing to others my own contempt for myself? If anyone was there, and saw me, perhaps they could write to me and relieve my mind.

Meanwhile, you have been patient. Many of you will wonder at my unhappiness and its irrelevance to real and earnest life outside, but the more intelligent will, knowing that there is an embargo on political talk at this electoral time, understand the subtext of my little reminiscence, and read the clear signals of its underlying allegory and know what to do about it. Onward and upward, heigh ho: if you have been, sit down.

Sidney Gross

Another extract from Colour Supplement.

ANNOUNCER: SIDNEY GROSS, tour operator for Sad People's Holidays, talks openly about his crime.

I think one of the great things about the kind of holiday that my company can offer is that it gives the chance for people whose IQ is between eighteen and thirty to have a really good time. Most of our holiday-makers are based out of Milton Keynes, Telford, Wales, Peterborough, Warrington-Runcorn – the kind of UK environment that has to advertise to get anyone to live there. We figure that the kind of person who thinks it would be nice if all towns were like Milton Keynes is the kind of person who is going to enjoy one of our packages.

We're interested in young, bright, attractive, good-time people, but they're never interested in us, so we have to make do with sad, old, desperate alcoholics and lechers who book themselves on one of our holidays in the vain hope that they might be able to go to bed with someone before they're fifty.

On our brochures you've probably seen the photographs of topless girls, hunky wind-surfing men and good-time couples playing beach games, and in fact it is perfectly usual for our holiday-makers to have exactly that kind of activity available for them to watch. On our islands, we arrange coach parties to the more expensive and fashionable beaches where they can spend all day watching young people having a good time from inside the coach.

I get absolutely fed up when people accuse Club Med IQ 18–30 of being a kind of licensed pimp. We have absolutely no kind of licence whatever. We don't need one. To those critics who claim our kind of holiday panders to the more revolting sides of human behaviour, that our holiday-makers are giving Britons abroad a bad name, I say look at our return-rate, look how many pleasure-seekers come back on our holidays again and again, looking for a good time. And who knows, on their third or fourth or fifth trip they might find one. We're in the miracle business.

APOLOGY:

Since that young, scabrous, wicked and irreverent piece was recorded the BBC has heard that Club Med IQ 18–30 has completely transformed the nature of the holidays it offers and people with IQs well over thirty are now admitted. We would like to apologise for any offence caused. We would also like to apologise for the use of the word 'squalor' and the phrase 'lowest common denominator' which have just occurred in this apology. Thank you.

Trefusis on Education

This one single broadcast for some reason attracted more correspondence than any other: I sent over a hundred copies out to people who wrote in asking to see the thing in print. Some nerve was touched, I suppose.

VOICE: Donald Trefusis is still on his lecture tour of the universities and women's institutes of England. This week has seen him in Newcastle, Exeter, Norwich, Lincoln and tonight, Nottingham. On his way between Norwich and Lincoln he had time to talk to his old pupil, Stephen Fry, whose parallel comedic tour has attracted widespread concern.

Hugely so to you all. Firstly I would like to thank the obliging undergraduate of the School of Mauritian Studies at the University of East Anglia in Norwich who so kindly retrieved my valise last night. I am sorry he had to look into it in order to discover its rightful owner, and I assure him the sum required in used banknotes will be left at the assigned place. I look forward to the safe return of the appliances.

Now, I'm particularly glad I caught you just now because I wanted very much to have a word about this business of education. I have visited so many schools, universities and polytechnics in this last week, listened to the tearful wails of so many pupils, students and teachers, that I feel I should speak out. As one who has spent his entire life, man, boy and raving old dotard, in and out of educational establishments I am the last person to offer any useful advice about them. Better leave that to politicians with no education, sense or commitment. They at least can bring an empty mind to the problem. However I would like to alienate you as much as possible at this time by offering this little canapé from the savoury tray of my experience. If you would like to kill me (and you would not be alone in that ambition) forget poison, expunge strangulation from your mind, and entirely fail to consider the possibility of sawing through the brake cables of my Wolseley, there is a much simpler course open to you. Simply creep upon me when I am least expecting it and whisper the phrase 'Parent Power' into my ear. Stand back and admire the effect. Clubbing cardiac arrest.

Parent power: schmarent power, I say. Don't misunderstand me, oh good heavens remove yourselves as far as possible from the position of not understanding me. Democracy and I have no quarrel. But on this head if on no other believe me, parent power and democracy are as closely related as Mike Gatting and the Queen Mother, and unless someone has been keeping a very fruity scandal from me, that is not very closely at all. Parent power is not a sign of democracy, it is a sign of barbarism. We are to regard education as a service industry, like a laundry, parents are the customers, teachers the washers, children the dirty linen. The customer is always right. Oh dear, oh dear, oh dear. And what in the name of boiling hell do parents know about education? How many educated people are there in the world? I could name seventeen or eighteen.

Because of course education is not the issue. 'Heaven preserve us from educated people,' is the cry. Ask Norman Tebbit, for whom a leering naked teenager in a newspaper is no different from a Titian nude,[1] ask him what education means. Ask the illiterate ghouls of Fleet Street or Wapping Street, or whatever unfortunate thoroughfare they now infest, what education is. A poem with swear words has to be banned from television or they will squeal for weeks.[2] They've dealt with the socialists in the town halls, now they want to turn on those clever people who mock them in their plays and books.

This new England we have invented for ourselves is not interested at all in education. It is only interested in training, both material and spiritual. Education means freedom, it means

[1] Tebbit had been reported as having made some such lovely remark that week.
[2] 'V' by Tony Harrison had caused something of a storm at the time.

ideas, it means truth. Training is what you do to a pear tree when you pleach it and prune it to grow against a wall. Training is what you give an airline pilot or a computer operator or a barrister or a radio producer. Education is what you give children to enable them to be free from the prejudices and moral bankruptcies of their elders. And freedom is no part of the programme of today's legislators. Freedom to buy shares, medical treatment or council houses certainly, freedom to *buy* anything you please. But freedom to think, to challenge, to change. Heavens no.

The day a child of mine comes home from school and reveals that he or she has been taught something that I agree with is the day I take that child away from school.

'Teach Victorian values, teach the values of decency and valour and patriotism and religion,' is the cry. Those are the very values that led to this foul century of war, oppression, cruelty, tyranny, slaughter and hypocrisy. It was the permissive society it is so horribly fashionable to denounce that forced America to back out of the Vietnam War, it is this new hideously impermissive society that is threatening to engulf us in another. I choose the word 'engulf' with great care.[1] Look at those Islamic cultures in the Gulf for moral certainty, for laws against sexual openness, for capital punishment and flogging, for a firm belief in God, for patriotism and a strong belief in the family. What a model for us all. Heaven help us, when will we realise that we know nothing, nothing. We are ignorant, savagely, hopelessly ignorant – what we think we know is palpable nonsense. How can we dare to presume to teach our children the very same half-baked, bigoted trash that litters our own imperfect minds? At least give them a chance, a faint, feeble glimmering *chance* of being better than us. Is that so very much to ask? Apparently it is.

Well, I'm old and smelly and peculiar and I've no doubt everything I said is nonsense. Let's burn all those novels with naughty ideas and naughty words in them, let's teach children that Churchill won the Second World War, that the Empire was a good thing, that simple words for simple physical acts are wicked and that teenage girls pointing their breasts at you out of newspapers are harmless fun. Let's run down the arts

[1] Surprisingly percipient for once . . .

departments of universities, let's string criminals up, let's do it all now, for the sooner we all go up in a ball of flame, the better.

Oh dear, listening back I can't help feeling that some of you may have got the impression that . . . well, it's only because I care. I do care so very much. And when I'm away from home and see how poor and ignorant a people we are, well it upsets me. I think I should take one of my slow-release capsules and perhaps snuggle up with an Elmore Leonard and a warming posset. If you have been, I wonder why.

Trefusis and Redatt

I gaze grumpily from my window this morning and my heart straightway melts at the sight below: I see along the river banks those harbingers of spring, tossing their heads in sprightly dance, decked out in their bright oranges and yellows, dancing and bobbing and waving – the tourists. It's not in me to be miserable when I know that I am sharing the planet with creatures who wear fluorescing nylon anoraks and Argyll check knitwear.

At this time of the year it has become something of a ritual with me to devote a day to sorting out my papers: I file my correspondence, bring my scrap-book and commonplace books up to date and hire a skip to take away all the letters I have received during the past year from credit card companies. I deal with what is prettily called junk mail yearly rather than as the occasion arises because instead of simply throwing it away I like to return it direct to the companies who sent it me in the first place. What Mr Visa or the Messrs Diners Club think about receiving a large consignment of shiny paper from me every year I have no idea, they haven't done me the favour of communicating their opinions on the subject. If their feelings in any way correspond with mine then I suspect that they are wildly irritated by the proceeding. I cannot imagine that a credit card employee would be any more interested in buying an ear-ring caddy or onyx wine cooler than I am, for all that there may be space for up to three of his or her initials upon the lovingly crafted surfaces of those objects.

The real joy of my spring clear out, however, is the letters. I enjoy a wide and varied correspondence. I am currently engaged in an epistolary war of attrition with philologists and structural linguists all over the world. There is a certain Professor of Melanesian languages in Penang with whom I have been arguing by letter for thirty years about the root of the simple Papuan word *redatt* which, as some of you may know, means 'unlikely to take part in evening games'. A useful word and one that reflects the greatest credit on the Papuan people. As a person who is very far from being *redatt*, delighting in all manner of parlour entertainments, I have found that the simple explanation of the word to members of a houseparty will make them all much less likely to refuse to participate in whatever diversion I may wish to set up towards the end of the day. This is an important point about language. Most people who do not like to engage in after-dinner games and sports in some measure hold themselves aloof and consider, with a distressing hauteur, that they are somehow above the sportive frivolities of other men. To be told that their measure has been taken by a race thousands of miles away, whose life style might be imagined to be far less sophisticated than their own, is somehow galling to such persons. That a simple people has dared to distil a dislike of evening games into a word, that is too much for them. The unsporting persons are not after all fascinating or alluringly enigmatic – they are simply *redatt*, unlikely to take part in evening games.

And so at Easter time I would like to take it upon me to unburden myself of another word. Rather rare, it comes from an old Urgic dialect of the tundra, used in the fourth century by the Lappish community that settled near Helsinki after the great Herffteld thaw of AD 342. The word is *Hevelspending*, it is a noun and it means 'the gasp made by one who, walking in the morning, smells spring in the air for the first time after a long winter'. We in Britain have a word 'mugger' that means exclusively 'one whose profession is to stop others in the street and forcibly to relieve them of their possessions' and the Lapps have a word meaning 'the gasp made by one who, walking in the morning, smells spring in the air for the first time after a long winter'. *Hevelspending*. Do you know sometimes, ladies and gentlemen, it may just be the wild anarch in me, but I can't help wondering whether perhaps – oh, I don't know. Still, that's just the contemplative mystic in me, I suppose.

As the bright sunlight pushes spring through the coloured panes of my old window as I talk to you now, I note that there are tears running down my silly shining old face, flowing through the channels of flesh and dripping from the chin onto the waxed wood of the table at which I sit. We have words for this weakness too, senile lability it is called, the tendency, on contemplating ideas like Spring and Home and Friendship, to weep like a child. Oh dear, I'm so old, so silly. Shallow persons talk of staying young, but they miss the terrible beauty and awful splendour of being old at heart. Heigh ho, if you have been, well there you are.

Sir John Raving: Cricket & Golf

Sir John Raving, Sports Editor of the New Spectator, *talks again.*

I want if I may, and since I've paid good money for this air time, I don't see why I mayn't, to take you back in time, ooh, four hundred or so years. I want you to imagine two shepherds, one of them is English and we shall call him, because we are imaginative and interesting, Thomas Burgess. The other is a Scot, and his name shall be Ian MacAllister. So, Thomas Burgess and Ian MacAllister. Shepherds twain, with good flocks to superintend and hundreds of miles separating them. They both have that rare gift, a sense of fun. Other shepherds, friends of theirs, are too dull ever to feel boredom. They are able to stand there with a glassy look in their eyes watching their sheep till the cows come home . . . oh, well, you know what I mean. But Thomas and Ian need entertainment to brighten their lives. Let's take Thomas first.

One day, a sunny day in mid-summer on the rolling Hampshire downs which are his home, Thomas takes the leather ball it has ever been the solace of an idle hour for him to play catch with and tosses it to Gregory, his rather stupid son. 'Gregory,' he says, 'I'll stand in front of this 'ere wicket-gate and I want you to throw the ball at me.' So saying he strides to the gate and flourishes his shepherd's crook, or 'crooket' as they called them in those parts. Gregory flings the ball at his father. Whang! Thomas swings the crooket and strikes the ball lustily, sending it flying over Gregory's head. Gregory trots off in pursuit. Thomas meanwhile gets some straw from a bail and twists it into smaller little bails which he places on top of the gate. 'Right,' says Burgess, when his son has retrieved the ball, 'have you another go, my lad. Try and hit the wicket-gate. If you hit the gate and knock off them bails a straw, I'll give thee the crooket and thou canst have a go at the gate thyself.' All afternoon Burgess defended that wicket-gate with his crooket. Such was the depth of his mind and his skill at games, that by evenfall, in the pub at Hambleton, he was already arguing with Gregory about whether or not being struck on the legs in front of the wicket counted the same as the ball actually hitting the gate and dislodging the bails and whether the leg-glide was as pretty a stroke as the cover-drive. The first, and perhaps greatest, innings in cricketing history had been played. The great game was born.

Meanwhile, in Scotland, Ian MacAllister's friend Angus was moodily swatting a stone along the ground with his crook when Ian stepped up to him. 'Angus,' he said, a strange light shining out of his eyes, 'you ken yon trusker, away down the brae there?' 'I beg your pardon,' said Angus. 'You know the rabbit hole over there in the valley?' repeated Ian. 'Oh that, aye,' said Angus. 'What of it?' 'Weel,' said Ian, 'I bet you a pound I could get that stone into that rabbit hole in fewer strokes of the crook than you could.' 'Yeah?' said Angus. 'Yeah!' said Ian. And the bet was on.

It was a royal battle. Angus moved his head on his first shot, put too much shoulder into his action and sliced the stone straight into an exposed scar of sand in the hillside. 'Oh bunker!' said Angus. Ian fared no better, hooking his drive clean into a tinkling burn that ran in dead ground below. 'That'll cost you a stroke to get out,' Angus ruled smugly. After twenty-four strokes Ian tapped the stone into the rabbit hole to win the bet. There was a fraught pause. 'That was nivver the stone you started out with,' said Angus. They halved the hole and started again, making for another rabbit warren three hundred yards away. And so the day wore on till after eighteen holes they were all square and friends again. They christened their game golf, because they were Scottish and revelled in meaningless Celtic noises in the back of the throat.

Two shepherds from two different countries. Two games with their crooks. And in these sporting 1980s I only want to say this. A game is a good thing. Golf is a game, cricket is a game, snooker, tennis, football, rugby and association – they are all games. Poker, Scrabble, Boggle, chess and backgammon are also games. There is no generic difference between them. The only difference is that the first set of games are usually played out of doors and involve physical exercise and expertise, the second can be played sitting down and involve only mental agility. Sport, on the other hand, is a different thing. Running about a track is sport, lifting heavy weights and rowing along rivers and throwing javelins and hammers and cannon-balls, hitting people in the face with your fist and bicycling round a stadium – those are all sports. They certainly aren't games. And what I want to say is – games are good, indoors or out of doors, involving brain power, or muscle power, wit or skill, games are good. They spring from the minds of men and women who want to entertain themselves and express their delight at life. A sport, such as weightlifting or running, is to a game, such as cricket, what a knobbly-knees competition is to a Shakespeare play. It's interesting that some people possess huge amounts of muscles or speed, just as it's interesting that they have particularly knobbly knees. Interesting, but not life. So let us have games not sport. That's all. If you have been, good afternoon.

Trefusis on Exams

And a very good to you. We come to that time of year when the young people with whom I make it my business constantly to surround myself here at Cambridge dive off to their several rooms, bury themselves in wet towels and cold coffee and try in one week to stuff into their elastic heads that which should have been slowly oozing and seeping in over a period of three years. Much tummy-rubbish is talked about examinations by those who know little of them, so perhaps I, as a setter and marker of examinations, should tell those of you who might still be of the opinion that they are difficult or important or indeed easy and unimportant something about how good results may be achieved without the tiresome interference of knowledge or application.

To the young person starting out on an academic career I would say this: education prepares you for life, it is therefore incumbent upon you, in order to succeed, to cheat, copy, steal, paraphrase, adopt, adapt and distort. I enjoyed distinct academic success at this University on the basis of two essays. I presented them for my Lower and Higher school certificate, reproduced them for my Cambridge entrance – and was awarded a scholarship thereon – again I regurgitated them for the Part One and the Final examinations of my degree. At each succeeding grade I introduced longer words, stole quotations from newer authors and redressed sentences according to prevailing academic fashions and tastes. But in essence my entire academic reputation and position rests on nothing more substantial than the achievement of memorising a handful of rather banal, second-hand essays. It is a monstrous overestimation of the wit and percipience of the examiners to suppose that they – 'we' I should say – are capable of in some fashion 'seeing through' the facility, triteness and falsity of candidates such as myself. If a case is well put, with style and flair and dash, then we award it a First or an Upper Second.

Therefore I would urge any examinees listening to me to look at their most successful essays and calculate how best the first and last paragraphs of them might be polarised and aligned to give the impression of answering any question that the exam, on the day, may pose. Lest I be accused of leading the young astray or be sued for heavy damages for causing disastrous results, let me say that it takes a certain brand of deceitful and cunning intelligence or at least a sound grasp of the technique of examinating to understand the universal applicability of one's own work and how to dress it convincingly for a gullible examiner: unless you possess these qualities it is better for you to grind away in the approved fashion with honest blood in your veins and diligent industry in your hearts.

'So unfair!' you chorus. But look around you, look! There are the men and women with money and power. It is precisely that brand of sly, manipulative, exam-passing deceit that they exhibit in the real, grim and earnest world that they have created beyond the pleached groves of academe. Are these persons honest and diligent, do they strive for truth? No. Our examinations reflect and feed a world stewed and sunk in corruption and moral obloquy. The smart, the plausible, the adaptable and the specious, they are the ones who 'get on'. Therefore I urge you, if you share my disgust with this brilliantined and smarmy world – abolish our examination system so that superficial, feckless and facile brains like mine are scorned and stout hearts and candid minds like yours or your children's are venerated. As long as we allow the kind of cogent and presentable detritus that breezes through academic life to walk into influential and powerful jobs then our national soul is tainted.

How can anyone be surprised that Oxbridge graduates so often achieve great political and financial renown? First by passing exams into our universities and subsequently by passing out they rehearse the cheating and swindling that passes for achievement in the wider world beyond that their academic forefathers prepared for them.

But now, I shall have upset my colleagues and confrères: it is, you will not be astonished to learn, not generally liked when one of their number exposes their secret to the world. Fortunately for them the world is so much in their thrall it seldom believes or takes notice.

Now, leave me, I have a whole pile of papers to mark. Top of the list the offering of a man I am sure will rise to the premiership of this country in a brace of decades. See how he starts: 'If Kraus's moral shadings are not to be believed, an ethical vacuum exists in pre-structural linguistics: only grammatarian wishing and philological phantasy can fill so gaping an aesthetical lacuna.' Purest drivel, but an obvious First. I wrote the book from which he paraphrased that very sentence. Flattery will get you everywhere. If you have been, at once.

Trefusis is Unwell

I am sitting in bed this morning, speaking into a BBC recorder, my head more full of undesirable fluids than the Cambridge public swimming baths. The weather seems to have permeated my old lungs and tubes to a most deplorable extent. Friends have been most kind, many have rallied round with patent specifics. I think it safe to say that I have drunk more possets, neguses, toddies and warming tisanes this week than any other man of my weight in the county. The Emeritus Professor of Moral and Pastoral Theology was even enough of a poppet to lend me his flannel pyjama suit, a thing of beauty in confident vermilion, so I feel quite the thing.

I am given to understand that this year is Esperanto Year, indeed have received enough Esperanto Propaganda through my letterbox to convince me of the fact. Esperanto is an amusing attempt to make Spanish sound elegant, and as a philologist people assume that I must be implacably opposed to it and to other hothouse cultivated languages: Volapük springs to mind.

Languages are like towns: they must grow organically and for good reason. Esperanto is like a new town, Telford or Milton Keynes; it has, linguistically speaking, ample walkways, spacious parking, rational traffic flow and all the modern amenities: but there are no historic sites, no great towering landmarks: there is no feeling that mankind has grown and lived and worked here, shaping the architecture according to necessity, power or worship.

The English language, however, is like York or Chester or Norwich or London – absurd narrow twisting streets that strangers are so lost in, no parking, no velodrome: but there are churches, castles, cathedrals, customs houses, the remnants of old slums, and old palaces. Our past is there. But not just our past, these cities are not museums, they contain the present too: estates, office blocks, contraflow cycle paths. They are living things, towns and languages. When we speak English, the old of the King James Bible, Shakespeare, Johnson, Tennyson, and Dickens is uttered in the same breath as the new of advertising and *Blankety Blank* and *Any Questions*. In our language the Barbican Centre stands near St Paul's.

Not so for the French of course, who have fouled things up most awfully; the reason that all but the most banal people are agreed that Paris is an absurd and pointless city is that it has not really changed in over fifty years. No tall buildings are allowed within its centre. It is the same city that people rightly loved in the nineteenth and early twentieth century, when it was truly ancient and modern. Now it is just ancient. The ridiculous French language is controlled and regulated too: words are proscribed or approved by a board of academicians roughly equal in understanding to a not very bright pencil-sharpener.

Now of course the Esperantists don't argue that everyone should speak nothing but Esperanto, merely that it is a natural choice of second language, just as no one is suggesting that all towns should really be like Milton Keynes. Milton Keynes just happens to make an ideal conference centre and Esperanto makes an ideal conference language. And in this sad world there is a great deal of conferring to be done. People who have never read a book in their lives have a dim idea in their heads that it is clever to argue that because there are no great works of literature written in Esperanto it is therefore a bad language to learn. Makes no sense. May as well argue that no one should live in Perth Australia because it has no palaces or abbeys; it's beside the point, snobbish and illogical – but then that's what most people are, isn't it? Perth is busy building its own palaces and abbeys.

I am an old man full of mucus, whisky, honey and lemon, but I have enough belief in the present and hope for the future to say by all means let us learn Esperanto and let us confer in it in Milton Keynes. Now, leave me, I must curl up in my Cambridge bedroom with a new edition of Cicero's *De Legibus*. If you haven't been – achoo!

Trefusis on Boredom

VOICE: Donald Trefusis, Prince Miroslaw Professor of Comparative Philology at the University of Cambridge, extraordinary fellow of St Matthew's College, visiting fellow of St Oestrogen's, Copenhagen, and newly appointed dialectician-in-residence at Selfridges, speaks with enchanting candour.

Magnificently so to you all, and not without becoming splendour. Do you know, it's a funny thing but that little muscular twinge seems to have sorted itself out. I can now raise my arm clear above my head. The next step must be to get the arm attached to the shoulder again and then I shall be as right as . . . as right as rainy ninepence in a trivet. But I really mustn't complain: what does anything matter as long as I have my wealth? You can't put a price on wealth, can you?

We have a few moments in hand, so I would like to waste your time with a rather rambling and unstructured discourse on a topic which I know is dear to the hearts of many of you out there, as you lie in bed, drive to the shops, sit in the kitchen, splash about in the bath, rummage around in the potting-shed, dangle your rod over the river bank or, who knows, sit fishing – rewind and delete the inappropriate descriptions – and that is the subject of boredom.

My dear mother, in her singing days, was a very busy and popular opera star: the roles she undertook in Milan, New York, Paris, Bayreuth and London as a leading tenor left her very little time for her young ones. I remember she told me once, while she rehearsed the part of Wotan for what was later to become known as the famous Stupid Production of *Die Walküre* at Chalfont St Giles, that only boring people could ever be bored. She was always saying things like that: unutterably tedious woman that she was.

But, my loves, when one thinks about it, and strangely, even when one doesn't, what on earth *is* boredom? Is it a pathological condition like pain, that warns against idleness? Is it a psychological disturbance like clinical depression? Is it perhaps an emotion akin to guilt or shame? Is suspense the same as boredom? When we wait for a late curtain to rise in a theatre, is that feeling of frustration boredom or impatience? I wonder. Well, as you don't seem to be answering yourselves, I shall have to undertake to anatomise boredom for you. It is a diverting and capricious paradox typical of this whimsically established world of ours that those who can most profit from this disquisition, namely those most prone to boredom themselves, will already have turned off their wireless in their *ennui* whereas you, long-suffering listener, all cock-eared absorption and interest that you are, probably do not know what boredom is.

Well, let us take an instance. I am implausibly bored by travel. Not being able to control a motor vehicle, Bendish my driver takes me everywhere, and I sit beside him, listlessly eyeing the landscape – how did Morgan Forster phrase it? 'heave and merge like porridge', that was it – as we stir it with the Wolseley. The inaction, the passivity, I find impossible. I would rather watch Gyles Brandreth dry. I think it is something to do with not being in control. The life of a passenger is not pleasant. I become fractious, captious and bumptious, morose, sullen and froward. It occurred to me one day, when slumped in just such a lard of torpor and woe, that to be inactive in one's life as I am inactive in my car must be as close as one can ever get to hell on earth without actually moving to Oxford. Children are easily bored because, in the wider sense, they are never at the wheel. To be unemployed, I shuddered to myself, is suddenly to be retranslated into childhood. One is fed, one is housed, one is generally speaking cared for, and I should jolly well think so too, but the wild racking boredom of it. It would be like an endless M25. Orbiting about the lights, but with no power to jerk the wheel and pilot oneself whithersoe'er one required.

Recently, however, I conquered in-car boredom by devising amusing games which give me purpose and distract Bendish from the unpleasantness of Sierras trying to park in his exhaust pipe . . . why is it always Sierra drivers? Perhaps the angle of the head-rests in that make of automobile closes off nerve signals to the brain and causes some kind of mental retardation . . . however, chief of the diversions with which Bendish and I beguile the time is called Mattishall. In this game one of us becomes Mattishall, a clever international spy disguised as a leading figure in the world of the arts. The other plays the part of Melvyn Bragg and must attempt to discover by interview who Mattishall is pretending to be. 'Mattishall, Mattishall,' Bendish might say – and really he does a most passable impression of Mr Bragg – 'Mattishall, Mattishall: who would you say has been the greatest influence on your creative life?' 'Well,' I might reply, 'when I was twelve I was taken to see an exhibition of neoplasticist art in Belgium containing manifesto De Stijl works by Mondrian and Schumacher: this was formative.' 'Ah,' Bendish might say, guessing a little too early, 'you are Michael Jackson.' And so we proceed, until such time as he divines that I am really Colin Welland or Delia Smith or whoever it might be. Such fun. But then I know the car will soon stop and I will be master of my fate again.

Well, what could be fluffier? I've been reading the late Mr Ellmann's chokingly brilliant biography of Oscar Wilde and have decided that each day of my life I shall coin a new epigram, so that one day people will quote me in pubs, launderettes and lavatories the world over. My epigram this week is about compromise. Compromise, my dear Marquis, is a stalling between two fools. A stalling between two fools – don't you wish you had said that? If you have been, go back to sleep.

Trefusis on Hating Oxford

*At this time, as you might be able to infer, Oxford was looking for a
new Chancellor, Sir Harold Macmillan (Lord Stockton) having died.
The Boat Race was due to be rowed on this particular Saturday.*

I have received so many letters from you on one particular subject
that I feel compelled, albeit reluctantly, to address it today. Mrs
Quanda Earnshaw, Miral Blackstock, Tindy Welmutt and Bruden
Wamp all ask the question directly: Why did I not stand for, run
for, sit for or otherwise put myself up for the Chancellorship of
Oxford University?[1]

Aptly enough, today sees what a Wodehousean magistrate
was pleased to call the annual aquatic competition between the
universities of Oxford and Cambridge, in short the Boat Race,
and I feel it appropriate to outline my reasons for failing to apply
for what the *Daily Telegraph* called 'this most prestigious academic
position' and the *Express* 'the role of supremo at Britain's top snob
posh university'.

I am, as those of you who have ever listened carefully to my
little wireless essays before now will know, a most tolerant and
sweet-natured person. Gentle, slow to anger, constant, docile and
biddable. I am also, as those who have listened between the lines
should be able to testify, a Cambridge man. I have no chauvinistic
or overzealous attachment to Cambridge. Anyone who has lived
and worked within a large institution, whether it be the BBC, the
army, a school or large hospital, will know that cream and scum
alike rise to the top; that blundering, hopeless, blinkered, purblind
and ignorant incompetence inform the actions and governance of
such places at all times. That bitchery, cattery and rivalry frustrate

[1] It was eventually Sir Roy Jenkins who was appointed to that office.

co-operation, good fellowship and trust. What, then, can explain my towering, blind, irrational hatred of Oxford and all things Oxonian? Let me instantly qualify this: I number amongst my best and firmest friends alumni and members of Oxford University. Some of the most upright and splendid people I know are qualified to put M.A. (Oxon) after their names. Yet this burning, implacable detestation. Wherefore. Am I simply mad?

Well, let us attempt to examine the differences between our two oldest universities. 'Cambridge produces martyrs,' was a popular phrase, 'Oxford burns them.' This in reference to Cranmer, Latimer and Ridley, Protestants burnt in Oxford under Mary Tudor. Cromwell was a Cambridge man, Oxford a Royalist stronghold in the Civil War. Almost every significant prime minister in our history has been at Oxford, up to and including Mrs Thatcher. Trinity College, Cambridge alone can claim more Nobel Prizes than France, Germany and Italy put together. Rutherford, Isaac Newton, Hewish, Crick and Watson, an awesome scientific heritage to match Oxford's political. Keynes was Cambridge, Oscar Wilde Oxford. Warm, surreal Terry Jones Oxford; logical, ruthless, sarcastic John Cleese, Cambridge. Cuddly Dudley Moore Oxford, spiky Peter Cook Cambridge. Nedwin Sherrin Oxford, Jonathan Miller Cambridge. Is a pattern beginning to emerge for you? There is a streak of moralism, stern logic, rigour and discipline in Cambridge. Perhaps the weather, the cold Ural winds howling across the fens broken only by those icy stone fingers pointing up at the East Anglian skies. There is a softness about Oxford, a hedonism, something to do with the green Thames, the gentle valleys that break west into the roll of the Cotswolds. Oxonians are small and dark and slow drawling, from Wales and the south and west, Cambridge sires a race of tall, gabbling, lanky lighter-haired men and women. Stand Douglas Adams or Bertrand Russell next to A.J. Ayer or John Betjeman and you will see the difference at once. Many of you will be saying, 'but I like the sound of Oxford, green, pleasant, mellow, fun-loving. Cambridge seems to be peopled by monks and mathematicians. We would rather the decadence of Wilde to the rigour of Milton.'

Ah but. We have plucked out and looked at the great products of each institution. What do such traditions do to the generality of graduates? These great medieval towns are there to educate are they not? As a teacher I can only abominate a place whose history instructs its students that the prime ministership is theirs by right, that luxury and sybaritic pleasure and a kind of grand world snobbism are permissible or even natural. Cambridge with its humanism and tolerance, its methodologies and system, may, at its extremes, turn class smugness into treachery and self-hatred, but in the end I would rather have taught a traitor than a prime minister.

Enough madness. There really is no reason left in me. Hatred is irrational, how can I hope to rationalise a disgust and a contempt? Suffice to say that I shall be wearing light blue all over today and hoping for a second successive victory on the tideway.[1] I shall return you to Oxford's favourite son Nedwin. If you have been, you've only yourself to blame.

[1]It was not to be. The Dark Blue buggers won it and have done every year since.

Trefusis on Old Age

I can't remember what the cause of my absence was. It is probably as Trefusis says.

Hello. It's very comforting to find myself back behind the microphone again after so disturbingly long an absence. My apologies for relinquishing the old Saturday morning stand go to those of you, particularly Mrs Bertilde Medicine of Homerton, who like to use my voice on the wireless to threaten their children with. The reason for my spell away from this space is a submission to a really rather virulent bout of laziness, which was complicated by a further recurrence of the old indifference and chronic indolence which afflict me from season to season. I'm almost fully recovered now, though still subject to moments of apathy and idleness. It's a problem old flesh is heir to. When you arrive at my advanced mileage it is surprising how almost nothing seems to matter any more. Forty-three years ago I crossed two continents and three mountain ranges in order to obtain an original manuscript of the Sanskrit Ranahabadat for which I paid half a year's stipend. Only yesterday I spilt a mug of the regular seven o'clock Low Fat Instant Horlicks all over those sacred pages and my only concern was with the waste of milk. *Plus ça change, plus c'est complètement différent.*

Yet there are those older than me, oh yes. The President of the United States of America can give me two years. It is customary amongst thrusting, urgent young comedians, commentators and the like to represent him as a silly, dithery old man incapable of sentient articulation or rational thought. It is of course so easy to mock. At least I find it easy. It's *difficult* to mock sane, intelligent, honest people, but it is almost childishly simple to mock hare-brained, senescent pithecanthropoids like America's Chief

Executive. He really is a monstrous old dotard, isn't he? But then you see this is what happens if you invest power in the old. Can you imagine a personage such as, for instance, myself organising economies or representing nations? It is a laughable notion, and yet I have twelve and a half times the intellect, humanity and wisdom of Ronald Reagan. That doesn't stop me from being a cretinous old idiot and a full stick short of a bundle, mind you. But that is pardonable, indeed it would be an essential quality, a *sine qua non* in a politician: my abiding sin, and what completely disqualifies me from being able to hold high office, is that I simply do not care. And it is quite apparent that this lethargy, this supreme indifference also afflicts Mr President. He frankly could not, in Rhett Butler's endearing phrase, give a damn. This quality is charming in the old so long as they do not wield authority: in my case it results in a fine, free insouciance in my attitude to form-filling, tax paying, traffic regulations and micturational control. In the case of Reagan, however, it manifests itself in such startling incidences of floutings of international law, decency and protocol as have recently been witnessed in his hideous, mad dealings with Iran.

It is alarming to realise that the man with the most power vested in him on God's shining earth is almost certain to care more about whether or not passing his morning motion is going to be more or less painful than it was last time, than he does about the wicked immorality of his administration in its attitude to neighbouring countries. It really won't do. How can it do? It can't, of course. It can't do. No, of course it can't. Stands to reason.

The American people seem to be very fond of the old darling, however, which buffets me back and forth between hope and despair. Despair because it is quite evident that our generally pleasant species has little time left and hope because it is clear that should I piddle down the staircase or fail to pay my yearly taxes I will be able to apologise in a voice shaky with emotion and get clean away with it.

Well, it's March and there's no escaping the fact, March is bath month. Time for Andidge, my gyp, to fill the tub and soak away the dirt of another year. People ask me why I take a bath in March every year and I reply that it would be unhygienic and insanitary not to. But before I leave I must take this opportunity to reply to Nilyard Standeven of Archbishop Browning's School Wisbech who asked me if I would like to address his school on an improving topic. I have two disquisitions, Mr Standeven, and should be delighted to deliver either to your academy, they are the Doric Particle In The Later Fragments Of Menander (with slides) or Nitroglycerine: A Practical Course For Beginners. Take your pick and let me know before the Second Sunday in Lent. Meanwhile all of you, if you have been, hello.

Trefusis's Obituary

VOICE: Dr Donald Trefusis, Regius Professor of Philology at the University of Cambridge and Extraordinary Fellow of St Matthew's College, has been thinking about death.

There used to be a curious convention in the electric cinema, deployed to convey the passage of the years. Deciduous calendar pages peel and blow away, fluttered by the gale of time. Like so many kinematographical fancies, this one has lodged in my own mind and at the turning of the year, there always flashes upon my inward eye the picture of a great white leaf stamped 31st December 19x peeling off to reveal 1st January 19x+1. Sometimes, the image is clear enough for me even to read the motto beneath the date. This New Year's maxim, for instance, was 'Kindness costs nothing', a rather peculiar little lie – I have no idea whom they were trying to fool with such nonsense. However the passage of time, the annual January gas explosions and the death of liked ones have contrived to put me in morbid mood.

When a Fellow passes away, I mean Fellow in the technical sense here, at this College, there is a tradition that the only obituaries published by the University or faculty magazines and periodicals are those written by the deceased his or herself. It is the business of a Fellow, from the moment of election, constantly to update such a notice, against the possibility of an untimely gathering to God. It occurred to me, given the rubbishy and hypocritical outbursts made on the demise of Harold Macmillan by prominent nonsenses all over the country, that you might like to hear my current obituary, updated last October before the publication of my *More Ionian Particles*. I hope it might set you about a similar task and let my own words on my death serve as a model of their kind.

The philological establishment was set about its ears last night by the cruel snatching away at the early age of seventy-four of one of its brightest lights, Donald Neville Scarafucile Packenham-Sackville Trefusis, who died peacefully in his sleep/fell into the River Cam/ate a botulistic scallop/was foully murdered by a bookseller/took his own life/was electrocuted by wetting his bed with the electric blanket still switched on/fell into an acid bath . . . delete where appropriate.

It is hard in a few words to sum up the life achievements of this extraordinary man. Of his published output we need only say that the fourth edition of the *Cambridge Philological Bibliography* (ed. Trefusis) devotes twelve pages to his extended works alone. Of his character we need only say that he was as reviled, scorned and despised as any pure academic.

Born to a life of Edwardian splendour in 1912, the only son of Lady Dolorosa Sackville-Packenham and Herbert Trefusis the lepidopterist and amateur comedian, Trefusis was educated at Winchester and St Matthew's College, Cambridge, where he read Mathematics, becoming Senior Wrangler of his year in 1933. An early interest in Philology was consolidated when, after work on cryptanalysis with Alan Turing in 1939, he was invited to join Hut 8 at Bletchley Park in Buckinghamshire at the outbreak of the war to assist the team set up to crack the German Enigma codes. His breakthrough on plug-board equivalency helped ensure the total and reliable decryption of German naval transmission traffic throughout the war.

But in 1946, his St Matthew's Fellowship still kept open for him, he returned to Cambridge with a new interest in Philology and Structural Linguistics that was to absorb him for the rest of his life. Mathematics became only a secondary interest, though its techniques enabled him to devise his famous Fourier analysis of embedded sentence structure in 1952, when he discoverd the simple equation 'theta is greater than or equal to gamma-shriek over upsilon, where theta is a preconditional morpheme predicated by the sentence complement phi'. This opened up a whole new field in linguistics, enabling Trefusis to learn seventeen languages in six years, to add to his already impressive polyglottal store of twelve fluent and thirteen reading languages. His knowledge of seven Vietnamese dialects proved invaluable to the ultimate victory of the Vietcong over America. Indeed his work for International Communism, both as spy and as recruiter of agents for the Soviet Union, China and his beloved Bulgaria, cannot be overestimated.

To those who knew him and worked with him, Trefusis was catty, rebarbative and treacherous. He gladly let fools suffer and it is said of him that his impatience and intellectual conceit was almost Oxonian in its breadth. He believed, however, in students, teaching for forty years with undiminished pleasure. His hatred and contempt was reserved entirely for his colleagues and for journalists, whom he would often go out of his way to kill. He married, in 1943, Dagmar, the daughter of Sir Arnold Baverstock the noted child-molester.

In 1986 a new career opened up for him as popular wireless essayist on BBC Radio, where his laboured pedantry and contrived acidity won him a new, unlettered audience. It is perhaps the ordinary Briton who will be most affected with delight by his passing.

The death of Donald Trefusis leaves a gap in British academic life that is easy to fill. Application to St Matthew's College, King Edward's Passage, Cambridge.

There! Simple, manly and refreshingly dishonest. May I suggest that you resolve to write such a piece about yourselves this year? It will save your family and friends the pain and embarrassment of having to make up lies themselves. If you have been, I don't see why not.

Trefusis Nibbles

The Regius Chair of Comparative Philology in the University of Cambridge, which has been filled by my round, ample and spreading nates for the last fourteen years, was instituted by King Edward the Seventh in the year 1903 to further, as the Charter rather endearingly phrases it, 'the better understandment of tongues around the Empire'. A question often raised, I believe in querulous and envious tones, in the Senior Combination Room of St Matthew's College, is how my little wireless essays, such as the one you are just about to stop listening to, can in any way be said to contribute to the better understandment of anything. It was therefore with some pleasure that I received yesterday, *grâce à* the producer of this programme, something closely touching the bailiwick and purview of my professorial chair. It was a copy of the new *Collins Cobuild English Language Dictionary*. The handsome, leatherbound, exquisitely tooled despatch rider who delivered the book at the London address where I have been staying recently as a guest of the Bloomsbury Carpathian Exiles Theosophy Circle made me ponder once more on the strange obsession within London of delivering everything by motor bicycle. Whenever I favour the Metropolis with a visit I find it impossible to talk on the telephone to a Londoner without somehow agreeing that something should instantly be delivered to me. I spoke to my publisher yesterday for example. Within five minutes he had offered to bike over a cup of coffee, two mint imperials and a clipping from this month's *Which Radio Pager*. But I meander from the gravamen of my discourse. The panniers of one of the many riders who visited me yesterday were weighed down by the new *Collins English Dictionary*: the purpose of this substantial and awesome volume is to provide clear, readable definitions of modern English vocabulary for the learner. It is all rather fascinating.

The editor-in-chief, Professor Sinclair, has excluded words which he claims have no current circulation in speech. Thus the verb 'percuss', as he has been publicly explaining, is refused admission, it being argued, I think perhaps fairly, that English speakers rarely if ever talk of percussing things or of themselves being percussed. What is notable however is the style of the definitions. We are all used to a terse, stripped language in our lexicons and it is interesting to peruse a dictionary where full sentences are given. Let me follow this dictionary's example and, instead of telling, let me show. I shall compare Chambers, usually regarded as the best modern concise dictionary, with this new Collins. I take a word at random like 'nibble'. Chambers has this to say.

Nibble, *v.t.* to bite gently or by small bites; to eat a little at a time – *v.i.* to bite gently; to show signs of accepting as an offer, or of yielding, as to temptation (with *at*): to find fault – *n.* the act of nibbling; a little bit – **nibbler**; **nibbling**. – *adv.* **nibblingly** [origin obscure; cf. L.G. *nibbelen*, Du. *knibbelen.*]

Collins is altogether more relaxed, not to say saucy, about the whole thing.

nibble, nibbles, nibbling, nibbled. 1 If you **nibble** something or **nibble** at it, 1.1 you eat it slowly by taking small bites out of it, for example when you are not very hungry. EG *Just nibble a piece of bread . . . She nibbled at her food.* 1.2 you bite it very gently. EG *She nibbled my ear lobe playfully.* 2 When a mouse or other small animal nibbles something, it takes small bites out of it quickly and repeatedly. EG *They like to nibble at their food throughout the day . . . It was nibbling a carefully chosen leaf.* 3 A nibble is 3.1 an act of biting something gently or quickly. EG *A few licks and nibbles quickly put him off.* 3.2 in informal English, a light meal which you eat when you are in a hurry or when you are not very hungry. EG. *Do you fancy a nibble?*

Well, Collins ignores the wider possibilities of nibble taken up by Chambers, the sense of accepting, or being about to accept, a challenge, a piscatorial metaphor unless I mistake, drawn, I say, from the enterprise of fishing, but otherwise they seem to be in agreement. Though what Collins means by 'a few licks and nibbles quickly put him off' I would not venture to guess.

That tells you something about the style of the work. What of its content? How modern is it? Well, Chambers recognises the word naff in its sense of naff off, but Collins doesn't give it house room. Collins does have an entry under 'street credibility', however, Chambers has none. An odd definition from Collins. 'If someone says you have street credibility or street cred, they mean that ordinary young people would approve of you and consider you to be a part of their culture, usually because you are modern and fashionable rather than old-fashioned; an informal expression made popular in the 1980s'. Many political nuances have been glided over there. But perhaps that is understandable. What is more surprising is that they would allow a foreigner to make free of words like 'blighter' without warning them that they have a jocund and far from street-credible smack to them. Chambers is happy to admit that blighter is a word customarily used in a playful manner, but Collins is more serious. 'Someone you refer to as a blighter is someone you do not like, or who you feel has done something wrong.' You see you can't do it, you can't collect, mount and stuff words and hang them like trophies. However pretty the display case, a butterfly pinned against a card is not the same as a butterfly in flight. Perhaps the next *soi-disant* modern dictionary will have scratch and sniff sections to help with the flavour of words. But I'm very much afraid that foreign students in Cambridge will this term be uttering cries of 'I say, stop it you beast' and 'Have you bounders no street cred at all, dash it?' I do hope so.

And to Cambridge I must away now. London doesn't suit me. I can't keep on installing new wirelesses in my car for ever; thieves will have to look elsewhere. There is a limit to my patience. And now the producer has just biked over a message (the verb 'to bike' I notice is not included in either dictionary under advisement); the message tells me that I have gone on long enough. Well, rather than bike my ending to you all individually, let me use the speed of the airwaves to say, if you have been, I'm most awfully pleased.

Trefusis and Rosina

In which Donald Trefusis and Rosina, Lady Madding, recall a night of love that never was.

Donald Trefusis first:

If I were asked to remember one evening above any others it would be that evening in June when, just down from Cambridge, I attended one of Jaquinda Marriott's extraordinary *salons* in Kerdiston Square.

Jaquinda, who had the most fascinating ears in Europe, was something of a mystery. Married to Archie Marriott, the sportsman and Shadow Chancellor of Oxford University, she was said to come originally from the Hungarian royal family, although all of us suspected her of more humble origins. It is certainly true that the birth records of one Mabel Blifford were destroyed in a fire in 1924 just six months before Jaquinda appeared on the scene. But whatever her provenance there was no doubting the perfection of those ears and the splendour of those *salons*. She collected people of talent rather as some people collect children from school – every day. Pianists, painters, poets, statesmen, novelists, princesses, even oboists were gathered together under those lovely, pendulous lobes and bidden to attend her *levées* and talk and play and smoke.

The *soirée* to which I refer was her second of the Season and I arrived late owing to an argument with a cabbie. He had advanced the claims of Baron Corvo as a novelist over those of Capt W.E. Johns and this I could not allow. When at last I extricated myself the party was in full swing. Ivor Novello and Cecil Beaton were wrapped in deep yellow *crêpe de chine* in the hallway, reciting passages from *The Old Curiosity Shop* in Danish,

49

a fashionable pastime amongst the younger dandy set at the time. Minty Havercuck, the Duke of Montreech's young bride, in a devastating flounce of Berlin silk, talked animatedly to Malcolm Lowry and T.C. Worsley, whose dancing seemed in its heat and frenzy to stand as a kinetic symbol of our mad decade, as it rushed headlong towards destruction in perfect 5:8 time.

But all these sights receded into background mist for me as I beheld a young girl whom I had not seen for four years. Rosina Bantwigg, the younger and by far the second most lovely of the celebrated Bantwigg twins. She stood, her hands behind her back, her head cocked like an inquisitive librarian, listening to John Gielgud teach Sacheverell Sitwell how to time a joke. Oblivious to everything else, the ragtime music, the Prime Minister's feeble impression of Vesta Victoria, Unity Mitford's moustache, Cardinal Halloran's swimming trunks, I gazed on this enchanting creature hungrily. She turned for a moment and saw me. A bright smile lit up her face as she approached. 'Why Donald,' she said, 'how perfectly delightful.' The voice, the image, the smile are fixed now in my mind like stars in the sky. They pilot me through life, they are my one fixed point, the paradigm to which all else in my universe must strive. At that point, I rather injudiciously jerked my head back, shut my eyes and vomited all over her. The heat, the tallow, the hemp, I don't know what it was. Without stopping to look back I hurried from that room and out of that life for ever. She married Tom Madding of course. Never saw her again.

Rosina, Lady Madding, remembers the same evening:

Because of my connection with the Kirkmichael family – my grandmother, the Marchioness Gloweravon, was born the Lady Vyella Kirkmichael – I was afforded from an early age a glimpse of English drawing-room and country house society, before the Second War drew a thick black-out blind across that world and extinguished its brilliance for ever. It was that privileged *entrée* that so positively endorsed my already strong feelings of adolescent crypto-syndicalist anarcho-Marxist neo-Buddhist Presbyterianism. A mordantly cynical young hound I might have been in the 1930s, but even I, in my gauche rejection of all that my family stood for, could not fail but be captivated by the beauty, the charm and the effulgence of those relics of the century's golden Edwardian summer, whose brightness and warmth shone all the more strongly through the sombre gloom of a depressed decade.

Of course, my favourite parties were those given by Jaquinda Marriott in her London residence in, I think, Kerdiston Square. She called them *salons*, they weren't of course. No hair-dryers.

I remember one such evening in the May or June of 1932. Everyone had to come dressed as a paradox. Bertie Russell came as the group of groups which is not contained within that group: I came as Achilles, with my sister Castella as the tortoise. I felt most sorry for G.K. Chesterton who came as the answer to the question 'Is this a question?' and was ignored for the whole evening. It was a lovely summer's night, I was nineteen, the world was at my feet.

But every Eden contains a viper and the canker in the apple of this evening took the shape of the foul Brandelia Cawston who dedicated herself to spoiling my evening. She mocked me, trod deliberately on the train of my thought, dropped ash in my glass and yawned whenever I spoke. She had never liked me and she was doing her best to provoke me into vulgarity. And then, while I was listening to Osbert Sitwell teach Laurence Olivier how to do a German accent, I spotted young Donald Trefusis across the room. My heart missed a beat; here was the now tall and comely youth whom I had hero-worshipped to abstraction when I was still in pig-tails and sheep's ears. Brandelia Cawston spitefully pinched my arm. A glance at Donald told me that he had seen this and taken in the whole situation. I excused myself from Olivier and Sitwell and, followed by the odious Cawston girl, approached Donald. He jerked his head back and, reading his intentions perfectly, I stepped smartly to one side to allow him to puke all over the wretched Brandelia. Never was I more delighted. I had not seen anyone look to such disadvantage in society since Edgar Wallace's toupée caught fire in Cap Ferrat in 1924. I turned to thank my bold rescuer, but he had vanished, leaving not a wrack behind. I never saw him again. I think of the dear man always, wonder what became of him. Life can be so cruel. Let me wrestle now.

Trefusis Accepts an Award

This is a record of Trefusis's only television appearance. Here he accepts the British Press Guild's award for Best Radio programme or somesuch.

Heaven bless you, I must confess that I find all this light a little distressing, I dare swear my eyes will accustom themselves to the glare in time. It really is no wonder that television persons look so monstrously stupid. I now know that it is the blaze of electric light which lends that dead, hopeless look to the eyes. I'm wandering from the point. Where am I? Awards. Prizes.

Well, I am sure that the British Press Guild, or whatsomever body has offered this wireless trophy to us, did so with the very best intentions, but I am bound to remark that I think it is a terrible mistake. I am sure I have no wish to offend any of the officials responsible, and I have no doubt that we are all deeply sensible of the profound compliment paid us but I must reasseverate: you have made a foul blunder. I am far from saying, you must understand, that we do not *deserve* this accolade. I have no doubt that our little broadcasting feature is no more beastly than any other that smutches the airwaves. Indeed on occasions we create moments which can only be described as golden in the intensity of their excitement, the freshness of their vision and the vigour of their insight. Nonetheless I stand by my view that to embody this worthiness in the form of an official award spells death, confusion, disaster and ruination. Let me delineate my reasons.

I have a dread fear that awards serve only to encourage recipients into a state of bumptiousness and self-conceit that can only be considered alarming to persons of sense and tone. *Loose Ends* is transmitted in the morning, 10.00 of a Saturday. Wise persons, honest persons are abed at this time. If not precisely under the blankets at least they have got no further than the breakfast table. The nervous system is steadily adjusting itself to the horrors of daylight and loud noises. Picture the hideousness, if you would be so kind, under such circumstances, of a bumptious, self-satisfied Nedwin Sherrin. A man whose saving grace is his detachment, calm, modesty and discretion of demeanour transformed into an animated, confident and self-satisfied clarion. It really cannot bear thinking about. No, I must apologise, but this airy, glib distributing of prizes may unleash forces upon the airwaves that we will all come to regret.

What great works of literature did Kipling produce after his Nobel Prize? None. He was too busy sitting at home, glowing with pride and burnishing his silver cup with the cuff of his sleeve. Prizes must come not as an encouragement to continue, but as a valediction, a closing encomium, a farewell tribute.

You have meant well, ladies and gentlemen of the British Press Guild, and we all thank you, at another time I would have been prepared to be excessively fulsome in my thanks, even to the extent of kissing each and every one of you full on the lips for an embarrassingly long time, a privilege of the old. As it is I fear I must temper my gratitude with wariness. No, really these lights are getting to me now. In a moment I will achieve the dull, glazed look of a dead halibut or a live weatherman. I sense a migraine and a filling sinus. Time, I fancy, to press a cologne-drenched handkerchief to my temples and lie down. If you have been, thank you for stopping it.

Trefusis and the Monocled Mutineer

The BBC had just screened Alan Bleasdale's The Monocled Muti-
neer, *a drama based on the so-called Mutiny of Etaples during the
First World War. The screening had caused howls of protest from
some quarters. It coincided with the appointment of Sir Marmaduke
Hussey as Chairman of the BBC.*

VOICE: This morning, on his return from the island of Crete,
Donald Trefusis, Regius Professor of Philology at the University
of Cambridge and Extraordinary Fellow of St Matthew's College,
turns his waspish attention to the political storm arising from the
appointment of the new Chairman of the Governors of the BBC.

Waspish? What do you mean waspish? Really these boys who
do the announcing have the most peculiar ideas. Waspish indeed.
Hello. As most of you will already have read in this quarter's edition of the *Neue Philologische Abteilung*, that noble *vade mecum* of
the linguistically concerned, my excavations into the origins and
splendour of the Minoan dialects of Ancient Greek have just
been completed, and have been compared in their size, scope
and sweep to those more material digs made by Sir Arthur
Evans at Knossos. Just some of the reviews of my work: 'A job
of daring reconstruction and imaginative revivification', *Language
Today*. 'Professor Trefusis has cast a new light on Greek particles
and their antecedents', *Which Philologist*. 'I shall never look at the
iotal slide in the same way', *Sparham Deanery Monthly Incorporating the Booton and Brandiston Parish Magazine*. But my work has
earned as much condemnation as praise. 'Left wing nonsense,'
writes Ferdinand Scruton in *The Times*. Of that I say little. I may
only observe that the chain I wear about my neck as I speak has
depended from it a medal of the Eleutherian Order First Class, a

token of appreciation from the Cretan people worth more to me than all the academic plaudits that I have no doubt will be mine before the sycamores have quite shed their last golden leaves onto the fast flowing waters of the Cam. Ah yes, to be home in russet England is something indeed.

Crete is a wine to be sipped with pleasure only for short periods. Without, it must be said, the steadying influence of the BBC's World Service to keep a rein upon my reason, my stay on that incomparable island would, I make no doubt, have been insupportable. The despatch of news, information, music, drama and imbecility from Bush House to Kalathas was unending and inspiring. But one oft repeated theme on the short wave commentaries never failed to catch my attention. Imagine my horror to learn of the presentation of a dramatic series on the television in England while I was away, called, I believe, *The Molecule Mountaineer*, by a Mr Alec Bleasdale. Unless I vastly mistake the matter a dramatist has distorted history to suit his own vile political ends. My father happened to be at Etaples on the fateful three days in question and there is no question but that what has since been described as a revolution was merely an incident in which a private hesitated for a fraction of a second before carrying out an order to shoot himself. So great was the discipline, loyalty and affection for their officers of the British fighting men during that glorious war that this trivial act of hesitancy seemed like gross insubordination besides the norm of instant obeisance and respect that prevailed amongst the cheerful, eager-to-be-senselessly-slaughtered soldiers at the Front: a small blemish that marred the beautiful truth of Tommy's constant patriotic wish to obey in all things the noble, wise and strategically brilliant officers who led him. And now some ghastly playwright has tried to make something more of it than that. The government has rightly stepped in to intervene. My prayers are with the new Chairman of the BBC. His first duty, as I see it, must be to burn all tapes of, and prohibit any future productions of, the twisted plays of that arch propagandist and historical liar, William Shakespeare. For too long have the radical lunatics running the television centre got away with encouraging such pseudologous, canting and doctrinaire mendacities as the *Tragical History of King John*, *King Richard III*, *Kings Henry IV*, *V* and *VI* in all their false and lying parts. As any historian will tell you, there was no hawthorn bush at the battle of Bosworth Field under which Richard III's crown did or did not roll. He never said, it is my duty to inform you all, 'My horse, my horse, my kingdom for a horse'. Shakespeare MADE IT UP. IT WAS A LIE, a dreadful, propagandist lie to please the fashionable place-servers of the day. I trust Mr Marmalade Butty will prohibit all performances of this frightful bearded playwright's works in future. 'Why', as my great predecessor in the Chair of Philology at Cambridge was used to ask, 'why are all the clever people left wing?'

Some of the more sensitive amongst you will detect a note of teasing irony in my voice. Of course you are right. Really it is beginning to look as if I cannot turn my back on Britain for a moment without ghastly interfering ignorant imbeciles meddling in things they quite simply do not understand. The idea of a politician being able to tell the difference between history and fiction is grotesque in the extreme, they cannot tell a drama from a jar of pickled walnuts or a work of art from a moist lemon-scented cleansing square (such as Olympic airlines very thoughtfully provide for one's facial laving after an in-flight supper); the thought that they can be trusted to do so is absurd, preposterous and hideous. Fiction, it appears I must tell stupid people everywhere, is pretend, rather like politics. If every fiction masquerading as fact, whether it be revoltingly jingoistic or never so crassly iconoclastic, were to be anathematised then it is not only copies of Shakespeare and Milton and Dickens and Joyce and Shaw that would be flung on the pyre but every recorded utterance by every human being. For as a philologist I am in a position to tell you that language is a lie. Yes! Language itself. A stone is a stone, the word 'stone' is not a stone, it is a token, a linguistic banknote that we exchange to indicate the idea of a stone. It saves us the trouble of having to haul one out of the ground to show our interlocutor what we mean.

Whether the assemblage of fatuity, prejudice, hatred and fear that constitutes the British public (those not listening at the moment) and the instruments of its political will understand the economics that regulate the supply and exchange of these linguistic banknotes or not – and fellow linguists will forgive my rather mechanistic pre-T.E. Hume approach – is immaterial.

Oh, gentlemen, ladies, all – the lies, the futility, the unreason, the folly. If you want repression, censorship, hypocritical moralising and propaganda on your televisions then go and live in America. There! I'm tired now, my thighs and hams are taut from the flight from Iraklion, I must visit my buttock masseur at Addenbrookes: a splendid man – he leaves no stern untoned. If you have been, goodnight.

Trefusis Blasphemes

VOICE: Donald Trefusis, Professor of Philology at the University of Cambridge and Extraordinary Fellow of St Matthew's College, presents another in a series of his widely noticed 'Wireless Essays'. On this occasion he speaks in angry and scandalous vein on the subject of Blasphemy.

'The woods decay,' shrilled Tennyson, 'the woods decay and fall.' As we approach the season of no light, no sun, no warmth, no leaves, no joy, no green, November, as Hood with archetypal paranomasia liked to phrase it, my mind turns to eternal Verities. His Lordship, the Bishop of St Albans, a prelate in a long line of book-burners and anathematisers, has seen fit of late to damn, castigate and otherwise consign to the great bonfire a charitable venture entitled – and I find this hard to credit, but my young friends here at the University assure me that it is so – *The Utterly Utterly Merry Comic Relief Christmas Book*, a work of many hands whose proceeds are to be sent to Africa and other places that have most need of material assistance this Yuletide.

The laws of blasphemy, like those of treason, still go unrepealed in this great free land of ours. Blasphemy, like treason, had its uses in time of tyranny. To question in the smallest detail the obvious lies upon which the power of Church and State was founded might have caused the whole house of cards to collapse. A chain of mendacity is only as strong as its weakest link. It was blasphemy to suggest that the world was millions not thousands of years old, treason to wonder whether the king was just and good. The Church and State fed lies to their subjects for centuries and needed the kind of laws that Stalin showed himself expert in to keep the truth at bay.

But what, we are in a hurry to ask, are blasphemy laws doing in Britain now, and what does the episcopacy think it is doing attempting to invoke them? The Church has no power over our lives any more, which is something in the nature of a blessing for those who do not enjoy red-hot pokers or iron thumb-screws, so whom is a blasphemer threatening when he makes light of a religion? Not God, who, it must be faced, as inventor of laughter and creator of all things is quite big and strong enough to handle a joke without some humourless cleric springing to his defence. No, blasphemy only threatens those whose faith in their religion is weak, whose beliefs in it are insecure. A lifetime's commitment to a church is a noble thing, and those who embrace their faith with strength will find that the sniggerings of the unfaithful glance off them harmlessly; but those who doubt it, or who have allowed the glory and the politics of rank and favour within the Church to mean more to them than their faith itself, then they certainly will quiver with baffled vanity and scared outrage at every joke or squib.

'But people, the ordinary faithful, are offended by crude comic blasphemies,' voices are raised to tell me. Yes indeed. But what of *my* religion? I am a lover of truth, a worshipper of freedom, a celebrant at the altar of language and purity and tolerance. That is my religion, and every day I am sorely, grossly, heinously and deeply offended, wounded, mortified and injured by a thousand different blasphemies against it. When the fundamental canons of truth, honesty, compassion and decency are hourly assaulted by fatuous bishops, pompous, illiberal and ignorant priests, politicians and prelates, sanctimonious censors, self-appointed moralists and busy-bodies, what recourse to ancient laws have I? None whatever. Nor would I ask for any. For unlike these blistering imbeciles my belief in my religion is strong and I know that lies will always fail and indecency and intolerance will always perish. The starving of Africa might also be pleased to reflect that a public denouncement from the pulpit is as effective a booster of sales as a two million pound advertising campaign.

Oh I'm too old to care. Let these hideous cassocked apes raise the tyrannical ghosts of dead statutes, let them clap their warty hands over the mouths of those who would speak, let them be consumed by their own vanity; the leaves have fallen quite from the immemorial elms, a watery sun strikes feebly the stones of the college courts and I have a bassoon lesson in half an hour. If you have been, bless you.

VOICE: The BBC would like to make it plain that, however decent or logical or true they may be, the views of Donald Trefusis are those of a sad, laughable and monstrously opinionated academic, and we dissociate ourselves from them entirely. Except for the bit about Stalin. That was all right.

Trefusis on *Any Questions*

As an intemperate and passionate listener to the wireless I was very surprised to hear that certain persons have been pestering the good officers of the British Broadcasting Corporation and demanding to be allowed to be heard on that oldest of sound arenas *Any Questions*. Do you know the whole story?

There is a frightful programme on the Home Service called *ThrowUp* or *Feedback* or *HowlRound* or some such drivel. It's one of those monstrous ideas that can only emerge from the dripping caverns of the mind of the criminally insane or the Oxford educated. It seems to exist entirely for those unconscionable members of our society who demand that the wireless should be some kind of genteel hermitage upon which the language, idiom and vitality of the real world never impinges. These poor afflicted creatures spend their time with an ear against the speaker counting occurrences of the word bugger. If I had a large amount of money I should certainly found a hospital for those whose grip upon the world is so tenuous that they can be severely offended by words and phrases and yet remain all unoffended by the injustice, violence and oppression that howls daily about our ears. The only advice I would give anyone who loves the wireless is to write in each time you hear a drama or a comedy that compromises on language. How can I listen to a play that is supposed to be a reflection of real life where characters say nothing but 'bother' and 'dash' all the time? It is a grotesque offence to the integrity of art. Unless you are heard the gibbering lunatics will carry the day. However, this is really by the way.

Feedback is a Radio 4 programme and therefore is naturally a kind of sanctuary for the mentally deficient – you mustn't think I'm biting the hand that feeds me here, I happen to know that the small but charming audience for my little wireless essays is composed of none but the judicious and the wise. I am aware that none of you has ever written in to complain at the phrase 'bloody bastard', you're not insane. Most of the *Feedback* audience, however, *is* insane. Quite appallingly potty. Barking mad to a man. Imagine then the length, breadth, depth and height of my dismay on hearing that from amongst this audience was to be culled a pool or well or reservoir of potential guests on *Any Questions*. Two hundred of the ripest bedlamites in Britain have written in to be considered for the post of Ordinary Person On the Panel.

We have to thank for this barbarous notion a deluded soul, a forlorn stumbler in the darkness of unreason, who wrote to *Feedback* complaining that the politicians, authors and financial rapists who usually comprise the bench are not representative of the wide world. 'Let us hear the voice of the common man' is the cry. How you could get more common than Peter Marsh, Gerald Kaufman or Edwina Curry or other such ghastly confections I should be very interested to know. However, the motion has been carried and certain persons will soon be heard on the programme.

Any Questions is one of those institutions designed to provoke anger and precipitate apoplexy across the kingdom. If you see a purple-faced person shouting and screaming at a wireless set then there is a better than even chance that it is *Any Questions* that is exercising them. It is astonishing how articulate one can become when alone and raving at a radio. Arguments and counter-arguments, rhetoric and bombast flow from one's lips like scurf from the hair of a bank manager. But the BBC in its wisdom provides a remedy. *Any Answers*. It is there to prove precisely how much more worthless, even than a politician's views, are the opinions of the wireless-listening public. That is where to go if you wish to embarrass the intelligent members of your family by discussing concepts you barely understand, like law and order and morality. It is to *Any Answers* that you turn when you want to deliver yourself of your prejudices and hatreds. *Any Answers* will be an important document for future generations, when they seek to examine the decline in literacy, courtesy and understanding that finally propelled the twentieth century into an abyss of selfish individualism and unneighbourly aggression. But *Any Questions* has a more immediate function.

We live, my dears, don't we, in a democracy of sorts. A democracy is a means whereby we channel our contempt for our fellow man into a lively scorn for those elected to represent him. Kindly men and women accept invitations to appear on *Any Questions* to absorb the hatred that would otherwise spill onto the streets. We know who these people are, we pay them handsomely for their sacrifice. They come to stand for the intemperate views that are killing our country. If we dare to replace these souls with ordinary people I fear for what may happen. I know that if I were driving my Wolseley around Cambridge and I happened to hear some lawyer or housewife talking about moral fabric or the family unit I should very likely swerve onto the pavement and massacre a dozen family units there and then.

No, no, it's too dangerous. Let the maniacs continue to write their letters and let the public men do the speaking. I must hand you back to London now and leave you with this public maniac. Nedwin.

Trefusis Goes North

At the time of broadcasting, the 'North–South Divide' was au courant. Trefusis muses on the subject after a trip North:

Hello. You notice that I say 'Hello' rather than 'Good morning'; that was a tip from young Alistair Cooke, because you never know with the BBC, do you, when you are going to be repeated? The World Service for instance may decide to transmit me to Zimbabwe in the evening, or to Malaya at midnight. We broadcasters must arm ourselves against such possibilities, and so we say 'Hello'. Perceive that I don't say 'Hello everybody', because it is perfectly possible, however unlikely, that not everybody is listening. And I don't say 'Hello my lovely darlings' in case any of you are driving as you listen to this, it would be easy to swerve off the road after so shamelessly provocative a come on. And so 'Hello' to you.

I want to address today a totally illusory subject, which is to say I wish to discuss something that simply doesn't exist. In my capacity as Saussurian Visiting Lecturer to the University of – well, I shall name no names here, let us call it the University of North Yorkshire, I had cause this week to visit a large Northern city to deliver myself of a talk on Mauritian dialects and their relation to Melanesian aphatic sign systems. Never having been further north than King's Lynn before I set out with some trepidation. I had decided to make a few days of it and visit Leeds, Bradford, Barnsley and even venture west of the Pennine chain and pop in on Manchester and Liverpool. One thing I knew, there is no such thing as a North–South Divide. The *Daily Telegraph* told me so, as did the *Mail* and the *Express*. No such thing. I can only conclude that it is a coincidence that Northern towns have parades of boarded up shops and streets where, rather than bustling prosperously, the citizens hang morosely about on street corners with nothing to do. A coincidence that grocers' have half empty shelves, that the only full emporia in the High Streets are betting shops. A coincidence that the North breathes poverty, neglect and despair where so many Southern towns ooze comfort, prosperity and confidence. A coincidence that a party of Eton schoolboys visited Newcastle the other day as part of some kind of A level Social and Urban History course and the story made the evening news on television. I am not a sceptical man but I shall read the *Telegraph* that the Senior Combination Room of my college still insists on taking, with rather more care in the future.

Am I to advance a sentimental view of the North after such a brief glance about it? Did I find the people more friendly, kinder, simpler, straighter, stronger and truer? I am glad to say that I did not. Some were disposed to be amicable, some disposed to favour me with looks of such deep loathing that the glass in my spectacles came close to melting. Most Northerners struck me as people like any other. Others just struck me. They're only flesh and blood, how can I blame them? A strange, windy old man wandering vaguely about their streets, his tweed, his gait, the very angle of his stoop shouting centuries of Southern privilege, it must have been insupportable to them.

The North seemed to me to be like a restaurant kitchen which still uses an old coal range and cold room and tries to compete with a kitchen that has microwave ovens and deep freezes. A blacksmith's forge on a motorway. Here is Southern Britain showing that fortunes can be made out of making money and offering services and there is the North still trying to make *things*. But our castle down here is built on sand, their meaner dwelling is built on rock. Their neglect I sense is real, our prosperity an illusion. But then the aim of politics has always been to keep a grip on fantasy.

Why is he West Wittering about South and North, you ask? I pay politicians and journalists to spout specious and facile lies about society, I don't need jumped up old monsters like this Trefusis idiot to add to the problem. Well mayhap you're right, so I shall leave you.

As I look out of my window I see the gales whipping the surface of Father Cam into little wavelets that feather their way upstream bearing windblown twigs along on a winding course away from the parent trees from which they were so rudely snapped and I think that perhaps we are twigs wrenched from some great mother oak, bobbing and ducking in the stream of exigency until we reach the ocean of evidence. And then the thought occurs that I'm an old and silly man who should know better. If you weren't: goodnight.

Lady Madding Again

VOICE: STEPHEN FRY went along to Eastwold House in Norfolk, to visit Rosina, Lady Madding, the Dowager Countess of Brandiston.

I hope you don't mind sitting in here, at my age you get rather fond of draughts. I know you young people feel the cold terribly but I'm afraid I rather like it. That's right. Yes, it *is* nice isn't it? Though I wouldn't really call it a cushion, Pekinese is a more common name for them. No, well never mind, he was very old – just throw him on the fire would you?

Parties? I don't know *why* you want to talk about parties. I'll try to remember for you. Ah! Now, you see that photograph there . . . there, on the table, next to the skateboard? Noël Coward. I didn't mix with him very much, he was a little . . . what we used to call a 'little Strachey', that was our code word. But I liked him, oh I liked him very much. We were in Paris once, I remember, where my husband Claude was attached to the British Embassy, well he was attached to the British Ambassador as a matter of fact, Rupert Davenant, everybody was. We gave a party in our house off the Pont Mirabeau. Noël came, Christian Dior, Bournvita Chanel, Pablo and Rosie Casals, indeed as F.E. Smith remarked, there were too many candles and not enough moths. Molotov was there from the Russian Embassy, you know, and Eric Satie and Jean Cocteau. Jean and Molotov had been asked to leave Maxim's earlier in the evening for upsetting the diners with their Edward G. Robinson impersonation and I asked Noël if he didn't think this was an absolute riot. 'Not a riot, Rosina,' he replied in that way of his, 'they were only asked to leave – in a riot a Molotov Cocteau is usually *thrown*.' Well of course I screamed with laughter. It was so funny, you see. And I remember another occasion when I gave a party at my house in Dereham Square, Queen Mary came, and Queen Dagmar of Denmark, Noël was there and Goldsworthy Lowes Dickinson and E.M. Forster and Guy Burgess and Queen Tsatsiki of the Hellenes. 'Look at you, Rosina,' said Noël, again in that way of his. 'The Queen of Society, in the Society of Queens.' Everyone screeched, I may tell you. Yes, help yourself to sugar . . . Mm, I think you'll find it easier if you just use your fingers. Those coal tongs are a little dirty. Mm? Oh that, that's a nude study of Brian Close, the Yorkshire and England cricketer. I have hundreds of copies. I keep them for the Scouts to polish when they come bob-a-jobbing.

My husband Claude died seventeen years ago and Bobby succeeded to the title. He was only ten. Kit, my other son, he's a furniture restorer in the East End of London somewhere. I hardly ever see him. If he isn't stripping a dresser or French polishing a tallboy then he's usually at work on his furniture. You know what they say, if at first you don't succeed, you're not the eldest son. My daughter Mawinda is an actress, you may have seen her. She's the girl who says she can't believe any powder could get that nightie clean without boiling. We're all very proud. Though I have no idea what a nightie is. Something poor people wear I suppose. But there was tremendous competition for that part, you know. They say Judi Dench swore she'd tear Mawinda's eyes out, she was so jealous. Really? Well I'll call Crith, he'll show you out. You must call again, it's so pleasurable to sit and remember. I'm having a party tomorrow night as a matter of fact, can I persuade you to – ? Everyone has to come dressed as a famous character from history. Ned Sherrin's coming as himself. Oh, do you know Nedwin? I can tell you a very funny story about him. Do you know the lingerie shop in New Bond Street, well, I was about to go in there one afternoon when –

SHERRIN: Unfortunately that's all we have time for from Rosina, Lady Madding, as we have to get on with the next item, which is . . .

Trefusis's Postcard From America

During the early summer of 1986 I went to America, where Me and My Girl *the musical was being rehearsed prior to a Broadway run. Trefusis sent back a number of Aural Postcards:*

VOICE: Donald Trefusis, Emeritus Professor of Philology and Fellow of St Matthew's College, Cambridge, is in America at the moment. He has sent back some of his impressions of a country he is visiting for the first time.

Yes, well, hello to you all back home. To think of you all folded in England's green bosom, thousands of miles away, while I am here in this thrusting virile forest of concrete and glass, baffles my mind and threatens to unseat my reason. I find it hard to obey the instructions of the very kind young sound engineer and speak in a normal, level tone of voice. If I am shouting, I apologise, but it is as much excitement that causes me to do so, as the feeling that you are a whole Atlantic away from me.

I am here, as those of you who read the *Neue Philologische Abteilung* will be aware, for a conference on the migration of the forward labial, here at Columbia University, New York. Without getting too technical it concerns itself with the influence of the Hispanic plosive on American English, a field in which I have been counted something of a specialist.

As this is the first time in my entire life that I have been outside Cambridge, you can imagine that I have suffered something of a fright over the past few days. Culture shock is I believe the terminus technicus employed over here to describe the massive sense of derangement and abstraction one feels. I can hardly believe that a whole other planet could afford as many surprises as this single taut, urgent city.

The first thing to tell others who have not visited this island conurbation is that the buildings here are very tall. Oh yes. Enormously tall. Simply very, very high. This is a fact. They just go up and up. Even as I speak I am on the twenty-first floor of a building, and still not yet a third of the way to the top. When examining Persian palimpsests of the Cyprian dynasty on the *sixth* floor of the University Library in Cambridge I was wont to succumb to spasms, so you can imagine the painful and embarrassing scenes and remonstrations that resulted in the lift when I first essayed this building. I have vertiginous seizures just thinking about it. This extraordinary height of the buildings informs the skyline, as you will readily imagine. The result, really most surprisingly, is one of astonishing beauty. I must also tell you that the taximeter cabriolets, or taxi cabs as they call them for short, are coloured a gay and vivid yellow, not unlike a spring mimosa, that lends a seasonable splash of primrose to the place. I assume that they change colour throughout the year, red for autumn, white for winter and perhaps a cerulean blue for summer. Ah, no, the young engineer on the other side of the glass partition here is shaking his head. Clearly yellow is a settled thing.

Now, to my speciality. They say 'specialty' here. The iotal elision, as we philologists call it, is not uncommon. They also drop the final letter 'i' from aluminium and deliver the word as aluminum. And who is to say them nay? One of the commonest subjects for discussion here is stress. It is talked about all the time. They appear to have established a causal relationship between stress and diet, which is very fascinating to me. I must say I am enchanted and encouraged with America's interest in my discipline, in England most people seem not to consider philology or linguistics from one day to the next. But stress is certainly a talking point here. Take, for instance, Hong Kong. They say *Hong* Kong, which always seems to imply that there is another kind of Kong which they are anxious not to confuse with that of the Hong variety. *Hong* Kong. The stress on the first word. There is a proprietary blend of instant coffee you may know called Maxwell House. At least that's what we call it. Maxwell House. Here it is called *Maxwell* House. A much less even stress. They somehow believe, though, if I am to believe the newspapers, that this stress problem is caused by smoking and lack of exercise as much as anything else. I had always understood that it was simply a result of the transhistorically separate development of British and American English and the Yiddish influence, as in *chicken*-soup. I have a great deal yet to learn.

A gentleman approached me in the street earlier and asked, 'Have you got a light mac?' to which I replied, truthfully, 'No, but I've got a dark brown overcoat.' The reward for this candour was a bloodied nose. I think I am going to have to study the customs very much more closely before I dare venture out onto the streets again, alone. Thank you for listening.

If Mrs Miggs is tuning in, as she promised she would, Don't forget to dust the books, Mrs M, and remember that Milton's worming tablets are on the tantalus beneath the Cotman etching in the study. You have to hold him down on his back and prize his jaws open to get them in. You may take next Tuesday off. Goodbye everyone.

Postcard Number Two

Donald Trefusis, Emeritus Professor of Philology and Fellow of St Matthew's College, Cambridge, continues his stay in New York.

Disastrous happenings! Calamitous events! Dear me, where to begin? I spoke to you last week, of my initial excitement with New York. I must confess that I have now begun to find life in this thrusting virile city a little fatiguing. My address to the philologists of Columbia University went very well. It was on the origins of the lazy 'r' in English urban dialects. I demonstrated the generic similarity between the Cockney's lazy 'r' as in 'Round the ragged rock the ragged rascal ran' and the Brooklyners, as in 'Round the ragged rock the ragged rascal ran'.[1] This caused quite a sensation as you can readily imagine. Since that academic triumph my time became much more my own. I began to explore New York with great enthusiasm and interest. Such an ethnic gallimaufry. I ventured south, or down-town as they say here, this week, with fascinating and ultimately catastrophic results. I made towards Canal Street, to one side strikes Mott Street and Chinatown, a really extraordinary area. It is as if one had walked through a tear in the fabric of the time-space continuum and transported one-self directly to Hong Kong. Streets and streets of Chinese banks, restaurants, supermarkets, toyshops. But cross Canal Street and *eccolà*! We are in Mulberry Street and Little Italy. At this table Joe Bandano died in a hail of bullets. In this restaurant Louis Farnese was filled with lead before he had a chance to finish his zabaglione. Into this gutter trickled the blood of Vito Matteole,

---

[1]Clearly you have to imagine the sound here. Not quite 'wound the wagged wock', but gesturing towards it.

72

the famous bel canto tenor, after succumbing to a nose-bleed.

Such geopolitical compression is unnerving. After a lifetime in Cambridge where all types muck in together, Leavisites living down the corridor from structuralists, phenomenologists using the same launderette as Hegelian dialecticians, I find this ghetto life something of a confusion. The choice of cuisines was so bewildering that I thought it safest to hail a taxi and go in search of a steak and kidney pudding. I took down the following conversation in Trefusian, my own phonetic shorthand, I find it an invaluable way of recording street scenes and bodega conversation.

'Okay bud, get in, where d'you want to go? Restaurant? Sheeze, what kind a restaurant? You want Italian? French? Indian? Japanese? Mexican? Thai? Chinese – we got Chinese Dim Sum, Chinese Szechuan, Cantonese, Mandarin, Vietnamese, Korean, we got Indonesian, Polynesian, Melanesian, you want Czech food maybe, a nice Schnitzel with polychinkas? Russian we got. Hungarian? Bulgarian? You like Cajun food, maybe? – that's Louisiana, New Orleans – you know gumbo and jambalaya? Good Cajun restaurant on 26th and Lexington. African food you like maybe? Canadian? Scandinavian? You tell me, I'll take you there. What's that? English? The hell you say. An English restaurant? What you talking? Ain't no such thing. Whoever heard of an English restaurant? There's a New England style restaurant on East 19th and Park. But English I never heard of. Sri Lankan, Yugoslav, Malayan, Argentine sure – but English? You gotta be kidding.'

A blow to national pride indeed. I was persuaded by this gentleman of the etiolated labials and baumannised vowels that Greenwich Village would be the most likely place in which to find an English restaurant, were such a thing to exist, a hypothesis which he frankly doubted. I told him that there were plenty of such establishments to be found in England – or in Cambridge at least, I have never ventured outside of Cambridge until now – but I fear he suspected me of being intoxicated. I was set down in Washington Square, a circumstance that could only delight. I stood in the middle of this bustling concourse and stared up at the houses around me, trying to imagine which one it was that so inspired Henry James to write his great novel *Washington Square*.

My reverie was broken into by the approach of a large black man who spoke to me in a language that I could not understand. I tried what little kitchen Swahili and restaurant Matabele I knew, but to no avail. The man kept repeating the words crack, coke and dope. In exasperation I pretended to agree with him. No sooner were the halting words of assent out of my lips than a package was placed in my hands. I blinked in surprise and uttered words of protest and remonstration. This was too kind. But from out of the dark, unseen hands were suddenly laid upon me and something hard, cold and metallic clicked about my wrists. 'Okay punks, you're both busted.'

I am speaking to you now from a police station, or precinct house, here in Greenwich Village, where I have been formally charged with the illegal possession of cocaine and cannabis. My black friend has denied any connection with the large quantities of these narcotic materials discovered on my person and has stoutly maintained that I was trying to sell them to him. The police seem to be aware of my academic standing and intellectual accomplishments for they have constantly referred to me throughout our interviews as 'Wise Guy', the compliment is growing thin, however, and I yearn for liberty.

I am being pressed to quit the microphone now, and must leave you. Mrs Miggs, if you are listening back home, don't panic. Go to C staircase and tell Professor Steinitz of my straits, he is a lawyer and will have ideas. Otherwise, continue to feed Milton and dust my collection of petrified Danish pastries. Next week I shall try to broadcast again. Meanwhile love to all.

Postcard Number Three

VOICE: Donald Trefusis, Emeritus Professor of Philology and Fellow of St Matthew's College, Cambridge, sent us his postcard from New York last week informing us that he had been taken into custody by the New York Police Department, arrested and charged with peddling drugs in Washington Square. Professor Trefusis has just sent us this postcard.

Heavens! A week of great events and excitements. When I was a child, adventure stories for boys always had at least one chapter headed 'Alarms and Excursions'. Such a title would suit this morning's postcard well. When I left you last week, I was ignominiously empenned in the city gaol of the Greenwich Village precinct of the New York Police Department, enduring the tart insults of Captain Donahue. I had been wrongly arrested and charged with possession of cocaine and cannabis resin and attempting to distribute the same for profit. It transpires that Washington Square, where the arrest took place, is one of the centres for drug bartering in New York City. The man who had pressed the narcotics upon me in the dark, a gentleman by the name of Winston Millington, continued to deny all knowledge of them. I had been left holding, as it were, the baby.

Those who know me well, and indeed those who can claim only slight acquaintanceship with me, would chorus indignantly at such ill-usage, they know that I am not the narcotic type. My first and last experimentation with serious drugs took place in my hot youth, when, in a moment of madness, for which I still reproach myself, I assisted my friend Professor Lehmann in his effort to synthesise a drug which would enable the user to leap great heights and accomplish astonishing feats of physical endurance. I tested the drug for him and was apprehended by the University Proctors clambering on the roof of Great St Mary's singing 'Where Will the Dimple Be?' and 'My Very Good Friend the Milkman'. As I explained to the good police captain, that is the whole history of my life with drugs. I took down in Trefusian, a phonetic Pitman's of my own devising, the conversation that took place between us.

'Don't come it with me, wise guy. I know you're into this right up to your shaggy eyebrows. The crack operation in New York is growing out of control.[1] We knew there was a mastermind behind it. You got careless and took to the streets yourself. Listen, punk, I got no time for people like you. You ever taken a look at the results of your operation? Go down the subways, down the alleys. There's kids there weighing a hundred pounds, stomach cramps, dying a slow death because of mothers like you. You make me tired. This crack we found on you, 90 per cent pure cocaine. Those rocks kills, mister. And I'm going to bang you in the hoosegow so long by the time you come out your clothes will be back in fashion. Now, how about that statement, you mother.'

'Officer, how many times must I tell you that I haven't the faintest idea what you are talking about. I am not a mother. I have never been a mother, I have no intention of ever becoming a mother. I am completely innocent, and demand to see the English ambassador.'

And so the conversations wore on.

Fate, however, rescued me. Winston Millington's apartment had been routinely searched as had been my hotel room. In my hotel room they found nothing more offensive than a foxed and well-thumbed copy of Schopenhauer's *Die Welt als Wille und Vorstellung*. In Millington's flat however they uncovered enough cocaine to service Hollywood for an afternoon. Tons of the substance.

'I dunno what to say, Professor Trefusis. I guess I owe you an apology. You're on the level after all. My advice is steer clear of areas like Washington Square. How can I make it up to you?

[1] At this time almost no one in England had heard of crack: it was only just getting out of control in New York, with disastrous results as we all now know. Crack is cocaine baked in an oven with bicarbonate of soda: the resulting crystal is called a rock and is smoked in a glass pipe.

Listen, you interested in seeing New York? Tell you what I'll do. How'd you like to come round in a patrol car with me tonight? See the real city? Whaddayasay? Least I can do.'

I didn't confess to Captain Donahue that my greatest interest, as a philologist, was not in seeing the town, but in hearing more of his fascinatingly attenuated vowels and delayed fricatives, and consented readily.

That journey will form the substance of my next postcard. Meanwhile I wish to thank all of you who sent in messages of good will to me. I found it all most sustaining. Particular thanks to F.G. Robinson of Glasgow for the bubblegum and words of support. Thank you Nedwin Sherrin for the Black Forest Cherry cake, you must have dropped one of your nail files into the mixture, which the police confiscated, I have it now and will return it to you when I get home.

Meanwhile, Mrs Miggs, the crisis is over. New York is suddenly very friendly again. Stroke Milton for me and remember to Pledge the Second Republic escritoire in the study. Love to all. Mr Sheen will do if we've run out of Pledge.

Postcard Number Four

VOICE: Donald Trefusis, Emeritus Professor of Philology and Fellow of St Matthew's College, Cambridge, continues to report on his visit to New York. Last week, under arrest for drug-peddling, he was exonerated by police captain Donahue who offered to make up for his wrongful arrest by taking him out one night in his patrol car and showing him New York from a busy patrolman's point of view.

'Okay, Prof, you sit next to me, and we'll hit the patrol. We'll be around the Stuyvesant Square region tonight. Now, it could get dangerous here, so whatever happens, you stay in the car. An average night, I gotta deal with firearms, kids on angel dust, everything. Angel dust? It's a drug. The kids get high on it and believe me it gives them the strength of ten. I'm not kidding, I've seen a kid dusted up, it took twelve of my men to hold him down. You see that gun there? The stubby little thing on the floor in front of you? Right, that's like no gun you've ever seen. That's a stun-gun. It gives the punks an electric shock, stuns 'em. The only way we can deal with them. It's dangerous though, can kill a guy with a weak heart. What can we do?

'Hold on, there's the radio. That was the precinct, putting out a general call, disturbance on Stuyvesant Square south, sound of shooting. Ten four, control, car 59 in the area and responding. Put on your seat belt, Professor, we'll be jumping lights and driving fast.'

You can imagine my excitement. To be here, as a Professor of Philology, sitting right next to the most fascinating fricative I have ever heard. He had a way of squeezing his 'r' sounds that wasn't quite a rhotacism, that I found thoroughly satisfying. 'Patrol', not exactly 'patrol', and not exactly 'patwol'. The secret lies in the softened, half-voiced dental 't' sound that precedes the 'r'.

We arrived in Stuyvesant Square to discover a Mexican shooting pigeons. He just wanted to eat. However the NYPD, as the police here call themselves, take a dim view of fire-arms being loosed off in densely populated urban areas, and soon Pedro was in the back seat, under arrest. This was a marvellous opportunity to test a theory I have about the intonal relationship between Mexican Spanish and Afrikaner Dutch. I took down every word he said in Trefusian, my patented phonetic shorthand.

'Gee, I'm sorry mister, but I was so hungry. You gonna book me? I tell you now, I am illegal immigrant. I have no green card. But if you send me back to Mexico I will be killed. My brother-in-law, he is a big wheel in Acapulco, he kill me. I beg you, just let me go. Keep my gun but let me go, I will cause no more trouble I promise you.' I couldn't but interrupt.

'I say would you mind very much repeating the word "gun" again, there was a very interesting "u" sound, there. My name's Donald by the way.'

'Captain, do I have to share the car with a loco? He want me to say the word gonn? What kind of gringo you got here, Captain, what he do wrong? He kill someone?'

'You hold your tongue there, Spick. That's Professor Trefusis, he's a friend of mine. Uh-oh. There's the radio. Someone holding up a liquor store down the street. Ten four car 59 on the scene and responding. Jesus, there's three of them. Car 59 requesting immediate back up. Stay in here you two.'

Three frightful young hooligans in balaclava helmets were emerging from an off-licence. They had shotguns in their hands and had already fired at the captain as soon as he sprang out of the car door. The windscreen shattered and Pedro and I felt that it would be safer on the street than marooned in such a sitting target.

'Professor get the gonns from the car, quick. You take the electric stonn-gonn, I'll take the magnum.'

'You two get back in the car. Let me handle this on my — '

An ugly shot rang out and Captain Donahue grabbed his leg. Pedro fired twice and two of the robbers fell to the pavement. A wailing of sirens in the distance indicated that help was at hand, but one of the criminals was at large, still armed, screaming Hispanic obscenities from his cover. I moved noiselessly on my stomach, giving thanks to what I had previously thought of as wasted years in the South Cambridge Cub Pack. As I eased forwards I heard the sound of rapid, irregular breathing. I took a deep breath myself and called out in firm, clear tones:

'Now then young man, you drop that ugly weapon and come out with your hands in the air, at once, do you hear?'

A flash of savage white teeth in the darkness was all I could see, a grotesque clicking of metal all I could hear, as the crazed villain cocked his shotgun. I leapt forward and pressed the trigger on the strange device I had taken from the car. A buzzing and crackling of electricity and a dull, sickening thud as the last of the robbers was on the ground, unconscious.

Pedro and I sat with Captain Donahue in the ambulance as we rushed him to St Timothy's hospital.

'Guys, I don't know what to say. Pedro, I'll see you get a medal for this, and as for you Professor, hey you . . . '

'Hey you, you, you! Wake up there! You think this bus is a hotel for the night or what? Wake up! This is the terminus, you gotta get out here. Come on, move it!'

Dear me, such dreams this city inspires. Such dreams. Love to all.

Section Two

Reviews & Oddments

The *Tatler* and Sex

*This article was commissioned by Jonathan Meades, now a cel-
ebrated restaurant critic and documentary-maker. At the time he was
a features editor under Mark Boxer at the* Tatler *magazine. He was
compiling a Christmas feature which consisted of Things That People
Didn't Do. He rang me up asking if there was anything I didn't do.
Gavin Stamp and Brian Sewell and others were contributing articles
on why they never watched television, drove cars, went on holiday,
and so on. The only thing I could think of that I abstained from utterly
was Sex. This little article has sorely tried me since. Every time I am
interviewed I am asked about my celibacy. Every time someone writes
about me they (quite justifiably I suppose) complain that I'm 'always
going on about' my sexual abstinence. All my fault. For the record, I
remain as pure as I was when I first wrote this article, which was in
1985.*

Lord Hailsham, you may remember, sent letters to important people in Cabinet earlier this year telling them he strongly disapproved
of 'having sex'. Quintin and I have had our disagreements over the
years – we could never agree about John Denver, for instance –
but on the subject of sex we are as of one mind.

I haven't – and I can't speak for Hailsham here – had sex
for four years. This didn't begin as a conscious embrace of the
positive virtues of celibacy, nor was I forced to make myself
unavailable because no one wanted me. Less an oil-painting and
more an oil-slick I may be, but I think that if I wanted intimate
carnal congress I could find it without paying. I gave coitus the
red card for utilitarian reasons: the displeasure, discomfort and
aggravation it caused outweighed any momentary explosions of
pleasure, ease or solace. A simple calculus of felicity.

Sex does not enrich or deepen a relationship, it permanently

83

cheapens and destabilises one. Everyone I know who is unfortunate enough to have a sex-mate, joy-partner, bed-friend, love-chum, call them what you will, finds that – after a week or two of long blissful afternoons of making the beast with two backs, or the beast with one back and a funny shaped middle, or the beast with legs splayed in the air and arms gripping the sides of the mattress – the day dawns when Partner A is keen for more swinking, grinding and sweating and Partner B would rather turn over and catch up with Mike and Psmith. Dismal weeks follow. A finds it difficult to meet B's eye any time after 9.00 in the evening, B announces in a nonchalant voice that he or she is 'completely bushed' just so that A will know that 'it isn't on tonight' and, before they are a month older, nasty cracks appear.

I yield to no one in my admiration of the erotic capabilities of the human body. The contemplation of the erotic is a joyous frame in life's rich comic strip. But let it not be supposed that there is anything erotic about coition. A walk, a smile, a gait, a way of flicking the hair away from the eyes, the manner in which clothes encase the body, these can be erotic, but I would be greatly in the debt of the man who could tell me what could ever be appealing about those damp, dark, foul-smelling and revoltingly tufted areas of the body that constitute the main dishes in the banquet of love. These zones, when interfered with, will of course produce all kinds of chemical reactions in the body: the blood will course, the breath will quicken and the heart will pound. Once under the influence of the drugs supplied by one's own body, there is no limit to the indignities, indecencies and bestialities to which the most usually rational and graceful of us will sink. And, my dear, the *smell* . . .

Let's face it, we have outgrown the functional necessity for these lusts. There was a time when Man did not connect the act of intercourse with the production of babies. It is, after all, a very long-term cause and effect. There is no obvious reason to suppose that a penetration one summer leads to a baby next spring. And so in the past we *had* to keep rogering blindly away all the time and Dame Nature was kind enough at least to make it spasmodically pleasurable. We have inherited this instinct to rut as we have inherited other instincts once necessary for survival: the instincts to fight and quarrel and frighten and conquer. But these vestigial urges have no place in a rational, intelligent community that can determine its own destiny.

I concede that it is healthy to remember and respect our origins and the duality of our nature, but we still have eating and sleeping and defecating – these are far less under our control and serve to remind us quite painfully enough of the physicality and baseness of the flesh that houses and imprisons our great creating minds. We have no need of the moist, infected pleasures of the bedroom to humiliate us more.

Besides, I'm scared that I may not be very good at it.

Books Do Furnish A Room

Some book reviews written for the Tatler *here. Written, with typical cowardice, in a disguised persona. Perhaps because I was afraid of the possible revenge of Baron de Massy to whom I was extraordinarily unkind. I still have a copy of his book* Palace, *however, and I really think my opinion was fair. Hating critics as I do I include this to show my hypocrisy or, if I wanted to be kinder to myself, to show that I know how foul critics are because I've been one myself.*

Williver Hendry, editor of *A Most Peculiar Friendship: The Correspondence of Lord Alfred Douglas and Jack Dempsey* and author of *Towards The Brightening Dawn* and *Notes From A Purple Distance: An Ischian Memoir*, casts a loving eye over some June publications.

I pluck two books down from the reviewing shelf, autobiographies the both: here is *Palace* by Baron Christian de Massy, sprig of the house of Grimaldi, and here *The Beaverbrook Girl* by Janet Aitken Kidd, fruit of the Beaverbrook bough.

Massy, nephew of Prince Rainier of Monaco, shows us a photograph of a crumpled Ferrari from which he emerged unscathed. *The state of my Ferrari after it had slid 150 yards on its roof. I don't know how I got out of this one*, quips the legend beneath. *Scuba diving with plastic surgeon Ivo Pitanguy, Brazil, 1977* needs no comment from me, nor I think do *Back from Africa with the repaired Alfa Romeo* or *Mamou and her notorious terriers in front of the castle.* Here is a wild, exotic world: peopled by exciting, glamorous personalities! The scene shifts hectically from Monaco to Gstaad to Beaulieu, Brighton and Paris and then back again, in a mad helter-skelter of parties, press-launches and nightclubs, to Monaco! How right was Scott Fitzgerald: they are not like us these people; they converse freely with motor-racing champions, glossy magazine editors and the manufacturers of ski bindings! We can only gape with wonder as Baron de Massy spins his tales. We chuckle at the impish devilry which inspired him to name his dogs Cocaine and Cannabis. We sigh with envy at evenings which, as often as not, seemed to finish off at nightclubs where McEnroe, Gerulaitis and Borg were seen to be present! Here is more *chic*, *élan*, *panache*, *diablerie* and *esprit* than could be found at the cosmetic counter at Boots. But what of the man's prose?

> From the salon we proceeded up the grand staircase to the ballrooms, where I saw Gunter Sachs and his wife, Mirja, Jackie and Helen Stewart . . . I also saw Cary and Barbara Grant, the Sinatras, Gregory Peck, Ava Gardner, David and Hjordis Niven, and the Niarchos family. Others there were Marc Bohan of Dior, Madame Artur Rubinstein, Maurice Druon and Edgar Fauré of the Académie Française, the French stage and screen star Marie Bell, the Rothschilds, Edmond, David and Guy, and their wives, and the Duke and Duchess of Orleans. The Duke of Huescar, the son of the Duchess of Alba, was wearing his black ceremonial uniform slashed by the blue cordon of Isabella II of Spain. A Scottish relative of ours was dressed in the family tartan and kilt.

Note there the details of dress: he misses nothing, this one. But there is cunningly wrought narrative too. We learn how one night Salvatore Dozio (he arrived newly rich at Monaco having made over $100 million from 'various mysterious dealings'!!!) bet any of his four Rolls Royces against the author's one Ferrari that a man they spotted in Régine's was Ringo Starr. Massy knew the man to be Adrian, Mr Starr's manager, but accepted the wager and chose as his prize a bottle green Corniche with beige leather seats! Salvatore, a good loser, toasted the victor with Louis Roederer Cristal champagne! Such style! But like all great stories this one is tinged with tragedy. For Massy soon learnt what it meant to drive such a car. Once a woman spat upon the vehicle, on another occasion its sides were scraped! Signs of envy were everywhere. And then – *comble de malchance!* – sour old Uncle Rainier reported to the officials that his nephew possessed a Rolls

Royce whose customs duty had not been paid and he was forced to sell. But our hero, with touching spirituality, reveals that he felt little regret at the car's passing out of his life: it had been fun to own, but it meant nothing to him. Remarkable anecdotes of this quality fill Baron de Massy and Charles Higham's book. Here is that marriage of style and content we look for in all great writing. A shatteringly vulgar and worthless life captured in shatteringly vulgar and worthless prose. A must.

What of Mrs Aitken Kidd? A formidable lady indeed. We see one photograph entitled *An important win in combined driving at the Hickstead driving Derby* and another dubbed simply *Painting in my studio at Slythehurst*. We are in the realms of parody here surely. Slythehurst? But look at some more pictures: *Proud owner of the Vega Gull, a fast, good-looking aeroplane* and *Marriage to Drogo Montague, son of the Earl of Sandwich, at Caxton Hall* and further explanation from me is unnecessary. Artist, sportswoman, débutante, and pilot. A rich life. She was born to money, position and eminence; she enjoyed wealth, beauty and accomplishment and yet, I cannot help but feel, if she had her time all over again she wouldn't change a thing.

What else is on my shelf this month? Virago have produced *The Female Malady: Women, Madness and English Culture, 1830–1980* by Elaine Showalter. This is a good work of serious feminist scholarship, and as such, I am sorry to say, unlikely to appeal to my readers. That is your problem, not that of the book. See how hard on you I am! Elaine Showalter intelligently examines definitions of female insanity in relation to historical attitudes towards women. Chapter Two is entitled 'The Rise of the Victorian Madwoman's a circumstance which alone is worth the entrance money of £6.95.

I hope Eleanor Bron will forgive me if I quote a little from *Pillow Book* (Methuen £4.95), the arrival in paperback form of her engaging collection of thoughts, reminiscences, axioms and observations. From Phil on *The Archers* one day she heard this noble line: 'Did those lambs get off to the abattoir all right this morning?'

She also collects her own thoughts under headings. We have things that make you appreciate men ('a lover who presents you with a huge cardboard box halfway through lunch, in which are packed thirteen china rhinoceroses'), difficult things ('doing reaction shots as Mary, Mother of Jesus, to a Crucifixion which was filmed three days before you arrived') and frightening things ('the baying of an audience before a charity show in which the Monty Python Team is appearing'). An entrancing little book.

Three Forms of Sudden Death (and other reflections on the grandeur and misery of the human body) is the work of F. Gonzalez-Crussi (the kind of surname that these days I would urge any young writer desirous of instant publication to adopt), who is an eminent Professor of Pathology. These essays on physiology use the author's knowledge of anatomy and disease as a platform from which to discuss mortality, the universe and the human mind. Works of upper-middle-brow scientific philosophy are all the scream at the moment; a breadth of reading, a shrewdly accessible use of crispy technical words and a wealth of macabre anecdote combine to force an impression that wise and true things are being asserted. It may be that close inspection reveals that this is not the case, but it is fun being fooled. I was reminded of Primo Levi's excellent *Periodic Table*, the conversation book of many an Islington and Fulham dinner table, my young friends tell me.

The Ludlumesque machismo of the prose style of *The Kidnap Business* (Pelham Books £13.00) is most depressing. This is the world of 'the stake out', 'the drop' and 'clean phones', written in the style which has made Dick Francis and Frederick Forsyth their fortunes, taut, wiry, sparse, spare, lean, tense, wry. Such a style first made an impression because it was considered in some way 'journalistic', while journalistic writing of the kind embodied in this book now seems to go out of its way, in its turn, to imitate thriller prose. This is how the book opens: 'Outside, the traffic poured towards the Rome suburbs. Inside, the office was unremarkable.' The effect is to fictionalise fact by adopting the outworn stylistic tricks of those who attempt to factualise fiction. I hope that makes sense. Reading back, I see that it does. Good.

I have nothing to say about Alexander Walker's *Vivien* (Weidenfeld & Nicolson), a biography of Vivien Leigh, other than that it seems to be very good indeed.

I also feel free to heap praise on Roy Kerridge's *People Of Britain* (Robert Hale, price n.a.), admirably lacking in preciosity, and free from that snobbism, prejudice or sentimentality one might, perhaps unfairly, attribute to *The Field*, the magazine which saw the first publication of much of this enthusiastic and good-hearted gallop around the British Isles.

Historians will be pleased to hear of the publication of *Charles I and Oliver Cromwell: A study in contrasts and comparisons* by Maurice Ashley (Methuen £13.00) and of Christopher Hibbert's *The Grand Tour* (Thames Methuen £15.00).

I wish I could report the publication of my collection of janderisms, *Way Up On Poop Deck (and other clippings)*, but Something Has Gone Wrong at the printers. I think you have enough books to be going with for the time being.

The Annotated Father Brown

Here, from the books page of The Listener, *is a review of a very strange book indeed:*

The Annotated Innocence Of Father Brown: G.K. Chesterton, Edited by Martin Gardiner, Oxford University Press, £12.95

This is a very odd[1] book. A heavily annotated[2] edition of Father Brown? I picked up my review copy a bewildered[3] being. So bewildered that the large question mark suspended above my head cast a dark shadow over the opening pages, making concentrated reading almost impossible. Has the Oxford University Press gone mad,[4] I wondered. Or perhaps Father Brown is being set for A Level these days. Why on earth should the simplest and purest detective stories ever written need annotation? The answer, and it is by no means a satisfactory one, is to be found in Martin Gardiner's introduction. He notes that the Sherlock Holmes canon has, over the years, attracted hundreds of works of mock-serious scholarship as well as inspiring the foundation of many groups and societies – he mentions the Baker Street Irregulars, more of that later. But, he complains, 'Nothing like the Baker Street Irregulars has been formed around the Father Brown canon – five books of short stories plus several tales not in any of the books. *I find this surprising.*' My italics, and if I could have them printed in red ink, I would. Surprising? If Mr Gardiner's launching pad for this book

---

[1]'Odd' Peculiar, rum, strange.
[2]'Annotate' 'To add notes to, furnish with notes (a literary work or author)' (*Oxford English Dictionary*).
[3]'Bewildered' Baffled, perplexed, puzzled, all of a doo-dah.
[4]'Mad' Potty, bonkers, dippy.

is genuine surprise at such a circumstance, then surely we are in for a rough read.

The use of the word 'canon' seems to me to be the giveaway here. The Sherlock Holmes stories constitute a canon, the Father Brown stories do not. I feel qualified to speak on this subject having been in my time, as a schoolboy, the youngest member of the Sherlock Holmes Society of London. For a few thrilling, mad, exultant years I lived and breathed Sherlock Holmes to the exclusion of all other lives and oxygens. I could recite huge passages of the text, remember dates, details, names and incidents as if I had actually been by the Great Detective's side during each adventure. Which of course I had, for Watson had taken me there. We can all picture those lodgings, seventeen well-trodden steps up from the ground floor, the patriotic initials V.R. shot in bullets above the fireplace, the tobacco-bearing slipper, the shelf of commonplace books. We all know Holmes with his pipe, his violin, his lens and his cocaine, and Watson with his thick English neck and those twin legacies from the Afghan Wars, the trusty service revolver and the bullet wound that still twinges when the weather turns. We all know that hundreds of letters a year are still sent to Mr Holmes at 221B Baker Street[1] and that for some odd reason, only a little to do with literary merit or deep psychological insight, Sherlock Holmes lives, independently of his creator, as few fictional characters before or since have lived. But what is Father Brown? A dumpy figure in a shovel hat. He has no chronology, no place, no paraphernalia, no details. Chesterton is sovereign in his kingdom, the two are inseparable. What is canonical about those five books of short stories? How many letters a week does Father Brown receive in 1987?

Holmes lives by detail, his criminals leave palpable traces in the world, traces from which the analyst can infer and deduce. From facts, from taxonomy, from concrete evidences Holmes can build up the picture of a crime. Father Brown approaches it from quite another direction. From his knowledge of man, his sin and his soul, Father Brown can extract the particular. It is amusing to

[1] 221B Baker Street currently houses a main branch of the Abbey National Building Society. A Building Society is a large financial institution providing mortgages for lenders and low rates of interest for investors.

treat the Sherlock Holmes stories as real history, the verisimilitude of the style is a help here, and any inconsistencies can be attributed to Watson's fogged memory rather than the author's carelessness. It is the details that fascinate us with Holmes, with Father Brown it is the generalities. Small wonder that, on reading, the little priest appears to exist in a vacuum, a universe away from those cluttered Victorian rooms in Baker Street.

The inspiration for this misguided annotation of *The Innocence Of Father Brown* is Baring-Gould's *Annotated Sherlock Holmes*. It may as well have been Enoch Powell's edition of Thucydides' *Peloponnesian War*.

Well, I have suggested that there are no apparent grounds for the scholiast to interfere with Father Brown, but has Mr Gardiner at least tackled his subject with glee or wit or learning? I am sorry to say that I do not think he has. This is not all his fault. He is an American,[1] not in itself prohibitive of any of the foregoing qualities, far from it. The alert may have deduced his nationality already ('You know my methods, Watson. Apply them') from his reference to the Baker Street Irregulars.[2] Unfortunately, however, he seems to have annotated the text expressly for his fellow countrymen. A lot of footnote space is therefore devoted to explanations of where Hartlepool,[3] Highgate,[4] Putney,[5] Bond Street[6] and suchlike places are, and which famous literary people once lived in them. And I wonder how many of you will need to have 'Boxing Day'[7] or 'Father Christmas'[8] glossed? Do you not

[1]Native or resident of the United States of America.
[2]The Baker Street Irregulars (named after Holmes's army of street urchins) is an American Sherlockian group. An Englishman would more naturally have cited the Sherlock Holmes Society of London. 'Brilliant, Holmes!' 'Meretricious.'
[3]Hartlepool is an eastern seaport town in the county of Durham.
[4]Highgate is a northern suburb of London. Samuel Coleridge and Andrew Marvell were among its famous literary residents.
[5]Putney is a London suburb on the south side of the Thames. The poet Algernon Charles Swinburne was one of its famous literary residents.
[6]London's Bond Street is noted for its elegant shops and fine art galleries, and for such famous residents as James Boswell and Laurence Sterne.
[7]The first weekday after Christmas, apparently.
[8]The English name for Santa Claus and not, as you might think from the name, a kind of Romanian chest harp.

know what a 'rook'[9] is, or an 'old buffer'?[10] I appreciate that a number of Americans might be sent into paroxysms of puzzlement over such opaque anglicisms, but this book is being published in England and offered to an English public. Mr Gardiner also makes a number of mistakes in his glosses. He does not quite appreciate the significance of the phrases 'two-pence coloured', for example, or 'sewn up'. Stratford we are told is 'a railway station east of London'. And does Westminster really 'contain Hyde Park'?

Mr (or possibly Dr) Gardiner is apparently a 'world famous' writer on mathematics and science and he loses no opportunity to denounce fringe religions or to introduce into his footnotes anecdotes from the life of Einstein. Certain passages are drawn to our attention as being 'arresting, beautifully worded sentences' or 'marvellous paragraphs', but otherwise Chesterton's literary style is not discussed.

Try as I might I cannot understand why this edition is being presented to the public. Chestertonians will possibly appreciate the bibliography at the back of the book, but there is little here that they will not already know. For the rest of us there is a smartly printed edition of twelve magnificent stories, one or two undoubtedly absorbing glosses (I particularly enjoyed a discursion on the history of Sunny Jim of Force Wheat Flakes fame) and a great many irritating and irrelevant ones. Chesterton once observed that angels can fly because they take themselves lightly. If you happen to see a book soaring majestically around the countryside in the near future you can rest assured that it won't be *The Annotated Innocence Of Father Brown*.

[9]The rook is an entirely black variety of European crow, smaller than a raven and a trifle larger than a jackdaw.
[10]'Old buffer' means simply a chap or fellow – 'usually expressing a slight degree of contempt' (*Oxford English Dictionary*).

Arena

This was written for Arena *magazine.*

Nine out of ten readers who expressed a preference have said that articles in men's fashion magazines which open with the words 'When I was at Cambridge' are unreadable and horrid. The world has sorrow enough without adding to it reminiscences of crumpety, crusty, punting days on the Cam. But I know you'll forgive me if I risk it because what I have to say may well rock the foundations of the British Establishment, give the Attorney General a substantially unpleasant headache and profoundly alter the way we think about day-wear for the over-forties.

When I was at Cambridge it was, naturally enough I felt, my ambition to be approached in some way by an elderly homosexual don and asked to spy for or against my country. Some undergraduates wanted to be 'noticed' by post-Structuralist lecturers and invited to contribute to *Strategies of Difference*, the English faculty's quarterly in-house deconstruction and semiology magazine, others were keen to tell the world about their loving relationship with God. Others yet were interested in the idea of doing some of the sex they had heard so much about at school. There were those who wanted simply to be left alone and develop and grow as human beings, those who mucked about in rowing-boats and those who trailed teddy-bears along the ground and called each other 'my dearest lovely old dear', though I'm happy to say that those last were quickly mopped up at the beginning of each term by small, highly mobile assault teams armed with American army flame-throwers. Cambridge isn't Oxford, after all. But I, I simply wanted to be recruited by a begowned whoopsie from whichever extreme of the political spectrum. My wish was granted: more of that later.

We all know about the English obsession with spying. It has been calculated that more ironic remarks, more acerbic observations and more balanced, sober appraisals have been made by *Spectator* journalists on that very subject than even on the amusing topic of the rise of the left-wing clergy. Something deep in the English character leads us to want more than anything to live deceitful lives; perhaps it is something anal. Perhaps not. It may be our world lead in irony that creates in us a craze for deception and guile, it may be our highly developed sense of world disgust. It is apparently true that if a Frenchman is approached by a member of his government and asked, while on holiday, to deliver a certain package to a certain address for a small sum of money and the undying gratitude of the Republic, he will tell the functionary in question to go and boil his head. British consulates in every neck of every wood in the world, however, are daily besieged by Englishmen who beg to be used as couriers, dead-letter postmen, lamp-lighters, sleepers, moles or honey-trappers, for a free trial period, no job too dirty, no demand too obscene. We all believe we qualify as *The Perfect Spy*.

I can trace my own mania for covert operations back to when I was twelve and Straker-Nesbitt passed me a note during double maths. It was a searing June, I remember. A childhood June. It seemed as though the only cloud in Gloucestershire was the cumulus of chalk swirling in a shaft of sunlight that streamed through the classroom window and lit Mr Dobson's bald head as he squeaked simultaneous equations on the green-board. I decrypted Straker-Nesbitt's note on my one-time pad or 'rough book'. The message was clear. Unequivocal. Bald. Direct. Shocking in its glaring obviosity. It smote me like a smiting thing. 'Hearne is in love with Martineau. Pass it on.'

I did not pass it on. Throughout that cruel June I patiently 'turned' Straker-Nesbitt until he himself was in love with Martineau, paid Jackson-Spragg to *pretend* to be in love with Martineau and personally refereed the fight in which Straker-Nesbitt broke Jackson-Spragg's arm and was expelled. That evening I went to bed with Martineau myself.

The spying virus had invaded my blood, my senses, my identity. Identity? I *had* no identity. I was a stand-up chameleon, an onion of lies, each new skin a deeper deceit. The original skin, the truth, had been peeled off and discarded years ago. In the assize of daily life I could as easily be God's advocate as the Devil's: everyone's friend, the enemy of all.

In the second week of my first term at Cambridge, however, I was just another frightened, self-regarding young thing who hoped that Heffers bookshop hadn't run out of copies of *Sir Gawain and the Green Knight* and that if MI5 or the KGB were going to move, it would be soon. I had a tea-pot, an Elvis Costello record and a coffee-grinder. In case I was going to have to pass as left wing, I wore jeans – very unfashionable in those punk years. Should it be that I had to move freely amongst the establishment, I wore a tweed jacket and old-school tie. Sneakers on my feet, a Barbour round my shoulders, I looked like the living result of a game of pictorial consequences.

Dr Sir Rannald Seward made his move at a 'Tea Party Against the Cuts' on Scholar's Lawn.

'And you are Fry?' he said, stabbing the table with his fore-finger and catching a crumb which he transferred to his mouth with practised ease.

'So they tell me,' I replied with a sorrowful half-smile that hinted at nothing and promised everything.

He patted my groin. 'And what do you think of Nicaragua?'

'I've not met. Is he in this college?'

I saw him again a fortnight later at an Early Music concert to raise money for SWAPO.

'Ah, Fry. I didn't know you were fond of Monteverdi.'

'It's a beautiful country and the Americans have no right to try and destabilise it,' I said with passion.

'Come to my rooms tomorrow for tea. Bring a cat.'

To my surprise there were seven other freshmen of my year also present at the tea-party. I noticed with a thrill that we all dressed alike and that we all shared the same shifty, awkward look of *voyeurs* caught in the act of peeping through a hole in a bathroom wall. We didn't talk much. Apart from anything else my cat didn't get on at all well with the turtle, the Dandy Dinmont terrier, the guinea-pig, the Roman snail, the Shetland pony, the sea-lion or the Marino ram brought along by the others.

'Gentlemen,' said Seward at last, above the din. 'Take those animals into the other room and come back. I have something to say to you all.'

When all was still he spoke again. 'You eight have already caught my attention this term.'

Sixteen lips puckered into eight unsightly smirks.

'Look at yourselves. Who are you? Confused and uncommitted, vacillating and shiftless: snivelling public school boys looking for street credibility. Or are you rancid bourgeois upstarts trying to pass yourselves off as aristocrats? A smelly old man asks you to tea and tells you to bring an absurd animal. You do it. You don't question his sanity, you simply do it. He impertinently rubs your bottoms and you say nothing. You have no confidence, no belief in self, no sense of belonging to the world, no interest in humanity, no understanding of who you are.'

I shifted uncomfortably. This didn't sound like a recruitment speech.

'I have no doubt you will stay as you are. You won't change a thing about yourselves.'

Ah, that's better, I thought. He seems to be giving us our orders now.

'You will spend your three years at this place in a crass mental jelly. You will commit yourselves to nothing, engage yourselves in nothing, believe nothing, feel compassion for nothing and have sympathy with nothing. History will march on: cities will fall, nations will starve, the world will turn. But you will be no part of it. If you are ever questioned you will echo the prevailing clichés of the moment, but reveal nothing of yourself. You will go out into the world, get your jobs in advertising, industry, the City, education. You will live and behave as if this tea-party had never happened. You will be asleep. Fast asleep. Think about what I have said. Now get out.'

These were tough commands. He wanted us to live apart from, yet within, the world. We were to be sleepers. How did he phrase it? 'You will commit yourselves to nothing, engage yourselves in nothing.'

Well my generation has done as it was told. We have blown with the wind and lackeyed the varying tide. I must admit that after three years of it I grew impatient to be contacted, to be awoken and used. I don't want to belabour you with the technicalities of the 'tradecraft', as we spies call it, but in the end you must *become* your cover, think it, breathe it, believe it. A lot of deep moles actually become unusable after too long because they assume their fictional identities so perfectly that they either forget or recant their original purpose. Not me, I hope. Not my generation. We are made of pretty strong stuff. When the call comes we'll be there. Until then, we'll take the *Daily Mail*, we'll investigate the advantages of endowment mortgages and no one will ever guess that we are really seething with passion, vitality and enthusiasm. Just don't keep us waiting *too* long or the world will have gone by and we'll have missed it.

The Book and the Brotherhood

Also reviewed in The Listener.

The Book and the Brotherhood. Iris Murdoch. Chatto & Windus. £11.95

Iris Murdoch. I've always admired that name. The iridescent, dilating bloom of 'Iris' and the honest, moral authority of 'Murdoch' inspire such perfect confidence. And what titles she finds to place below that excellent handle! She must look down the list and glow with pleasure: *The Fire and the Sun*, *The Nice and the Good*, *The Red and the Green*, *The Servants and the Snow*. What a shame Thackeray got there first with *The Rose and the Ring*. And now we have *The Book and the Brotherhood*, perhaps the best title yet. I'm not being flippant: titles are very important to writers, and to readers too. The words of this title pound like distant drums in the mind as you read, just as they pound in the minds of the novel's characters as they live.

Partly fed by Oxbridge literature, partly by hazy images of some Platonic Academy, I went up to my university aware that I might work my way into some holy circle of friendship; whether the Apostles or some more local and informal sodality I didn't know, but Anthony Powell and Simon Raven, Iris Murdoch herself and countless biographies had prepared me for the belief that university affords opportunities for special friendships – not pairings, but a wider, sacred circle, within which any number of pairings may be made. It never quite happened for me: friends I found, and have kept, by the dozen, but there is no definable *coterie*. I was aware of it happening for others and am peripherally associated with a number of different fraternities which have lasted the lustrum that has elapsed since my graduation. The peculiar feature of these groups is their self-consciousness – they have named themselves as a circle; once that is done a group dynamic comes into play that binds them somehow to watch over each other for ever. They are aware of the ideal of the Academy and feel obliged to attempt to live up to it. They have created their own college, which lasts beyond the ambit of their undergraduacy, and of which they are all fellows. It is a life fellowship.

The members of the Brotherhood in Iris Murdoch's novel are fellows of just such a private college, one which has lasted three decades. We meet them at an Oxford commem ball, and a confusing fifty pages that is. Close on a dozen characters we have to become acquainted with, and that involves a great deal of turning back and checking up. Which one was Gerard? we ask ourselves. Was he the one who? – oh no, that was Gulliver. And was it Lily or Tamar who is Violet's daughter? And who exactly is Violet anyway? Did Gerard once live with Jenkin or Duncan? Or both? And what decade are we in? The young people at the ball are favouring dark blue frilly evening shirts, so it can't be the present day. But it is. Iris Murdoch is a little behind the times with young people's fashions. Does she really think it possible that a rock band might exist that is called The Treason of the Clerks? Fair enough, she can't be a novelist, a Plato scholar *and* a DJ.

By the end of that evening we are a little clearer. It is well worth the effort. Iris Murdoch's central idea, the plot, is a terrific one, which she must have been delighted to hit upon. This brotherhood of Oxford men and women decided in the hot flush of their left-wing youth to commission the hottest and leftmost-winged of their number, Derek Crimond, to write a book. A work of political philosophy, neo-Marxist social economics, we are not quite sure what form it was supposed to take, *they* are not sure. At that time they had graduated, were doing well in the Civil Service and Diplomatic Corps, felt guilty that Crimond, in staying closer to their ideals, was unable to afford the time to write his great work and so they self-consciously formed a *Gesellschaft* on the Rilke and Musil model that would support Crimond in his work. But that was years ago. Crimond still draws the salary, but not a paragraph of his book has appeared: besides, the rest of the group have moved steadily away from those radical positions into soft socialism and outright liberalism. Crimond has stayed as pure as ever, an advocate of violent revolution, terrorism even. As devices for studying the meaning and motions of intellectual integrity, friendship, betrayal and trust through time, the Brotherhood and its dreaded Book are ideal. How can the shining silver ideals of the Academy and Holy Friendship survive the corroding realities of the social, sexual and political world that sublunary adults inhabit? The grubby truths of adultery (Crimond for a second time steals the wife of poor Duncan Cambus), post-adolescent hysteria, suicide, even murder, besiege the hallowed citadel.

The device allows a subtle and complex world of symbol and mythical iconography to play teasingly with the narrative: books, towers, water, blood, the moon and death form a Major Arcana of images that implicate Wagnerian, Hellenic and Freudian legends of *Blutbruderschaft*, renunciation, runes, oracle and eroticism.

The story is compelling and the characters absorbing. How likely it really is that any book might be written which could change the world or even raise a brief eye-brow of interest in the 1980s is a moot question (if Crimond was preparing a television series or a pop album then perhaps the Brotherhood would really have something to worry about), but we are prepared to believe, for the purposes of the novel, that the Book *is* a threat. Crimond, who broods over it all like an obmutescent winged avenger, scaring the living daylights out of his friends, is really successful only when off stage, which he is most of the time. The other characters talk a great deal, and reveal their different histories, but are not sharply defined or 'rounded' in that good old-fashioned Forsterian sense. It may seem odd to say that this doesn't matter in a 'realistic' modern novel, but it doesn't, nor do the occasionally stilted and melodramatic passages of dialogue really concern us. The plot and the ideas and the 'concrete flux of interpenetrating intensities', as T.E. Hulme sweetly phrased it, propel you into a real world with as much force as any novelistic techniques of realism. As usual, Iris Murdoch writes better men here than any male novelist that I am aware of is capable of writing women. The oddest feature of her Brotherhood is their humourlessness, old friends can set each other laughing at any minute: the *Crimondsgesellschaft* don't appear to have laughed together for years.

It is impossible with Iris Murdoch not to suspect, guiltily, that there is some closely structured Platonic argument lurking beneath the contemporary drama and that, in not detecting it, one has somehow missed a point. Certainly this is a wonderfully structured novel, moving through three seasons with pleasing balance and delicate internal patterns and rhythms, but it is not a crossword puzzle, nothing is hidden or archly disguised. The writing is always lucid and poised and fluid. Her prose reminds me of water: always propelled by the gentlest energy, connecting with itself in dozens of different ways, absolutely clear and effortless: resonating not with a boom but a tinkle. That kind of flow can move rock more powerfully than dynamite. Some of the passages of description, Gerard's childhood grey parrot, skating in a meadow at sunset, are as beautifully written as any prose can be today, linking physical description and personal developments with extraordinary touch. In a novel about the bonds that attach people to ideas, ideas to people and people to each other and about the blood that flows in and between them, such absolute passages serve to bind the ideas and the people of the novel, through art and language and image, to the truth that the life of the mind subserves the life of the soul. Intellectual and political absolutism is defied by the perfection of imperfection. This is a substantial moral and artistic achievement. Oxbridge people with Oxbridge troubles perhaps, but that is Iris Murdoch's milieu, and need be no more irrelevant than Jane Austen's Regency parsonages or Chekhov's decaying Russian estates.

A Television Review

For a short time I was the television reviewer for the Literary Review, *a magazine now edited by Auberon Waugh, but previously the responsibility of Emma Soames.*

Here is a selection of monthly reviews of television, written – for the large part – for an audience who abominated TV.

A short word about Noel Edmonds: **No.**

A long word about Noel Edmonds: **Unconscionable.**

Noel Edmonds is, himself, a fine and good man, kind to furry animals and tidy with litter. His and his producer's contributions to *Comic Relief* cannot be overestimated. But – and oh, how it pains me to have to be honest – there is a dark side. He lends his name (the Noel, incidentally, has long puzzled me: ask anyone unfamiliar with the man to look at him and guess his forename and they will – China Street to a Lombard Orange – hazard at Graeme, Bryan or Rodney or, at longer odds, Andy or Mike; never Noel.) to the grisliest entertainment that television currently offers.

Mr Edmonds started life as a disc jockey, his life in the public eye that is. No doubt for years previously he toiled unseen as a disc stable-lad, mucking out the studios and so on – it's a tough school. But it was as a disc jockey that he first achieved fame. And as a disc jockey he was no more horrific a personality than his job demanded. That's pretty horrific, certainly, but many others in that line of work exceed the limits of their professional duty with a zeal nothing short of disgusting. From disc jockey to children's television presenter is a short step. A step forwards intellectually and financially. Noel took it nimbly. *The Swap Shop*, over which he genially presided, was a great achievement on the part of the BBC. Early Saturday mornings had suddenly, with the cult success of *TISWAS*, become a furious battleground in the ratings war. *The Swap Shop*, tidier, more responsible, more acceptable to middle-class parents, in short, more *BBC* than its rival, was a big hit. Noel projected himself as a friendly older brother, slightly racy, slightly cocky, slightly frivolous, but certainly a Good Thing. Then some nameless poltroon had the idea that those qualities might appeal to an adult audience. What became of Chris Tarrant's like ascension to the world of grown-ups (*OTT, et al.*) is a matter of painful broadcasting history. Tarrant is now, *Oh how the wheel becomes it!* a disc jockey for a local radio station . . .

Noel's foray however seems, at first glance, more successful. He has yet to fall from grace. But the programme he presents now, *The Noel Edmonds Late, Late Breakfast Show*, BBC1, Saturday evenings, is, in the words of Professor Donald Trefusis, 'puerile, banausic posturing and prankstering'. The evil lies not in its content, sickening as it may be, but in its style. The very qualities that made Edmonds so perfect a children's entertainer make him a perfectly appalling adult one. The show is a *Swap Shop* version of all those ghastly 'people are so interesting' programmes which LWT inflict upon us in wave after wave, *Game For A Laugh, People Do The Funniest Things, Surprise Surprise* – there's a new one every month. *The L.L.B.S.* has a competition to find 'Mr Puniverse', Golden Egg Awards for the funniest blooper, blunder, fluff, corpse or gaffe on television, or even, God save us all, on home videos. Members of the public have jokes played upon them while being watched by hidden cameras, the giggling Noel and a frightful studio audience. The dignity of womankind is set back at every turn by revolting innuendo and nauseating lechery. In the name of populism and jolliness non-conformity is mocked, and contrived eccentricity encouraged. It is as if the world has been taken over by a student bar and its rugby club. Cars, beer, Samantha Fox (whoever she may be), soccer and the Royal Marines, these are the gods of the show. There is no joyous Dionysiac revelry, no antic misrule – just flatulent, graceless slobbery and smirking.

I have just risen, sobbing, wasted and drained, from watching Frank Capra's *It's A Wonderful Life*. Nothing strange about that. Anyone with half a heart will be unable to rise from that film in any other condition. What is strange is that the time is now precisely 5.15 on a Thursday afternoon. When all is said and done, the single most important reason for the invention of television is that it continues to allow generation after generation to get to know films that they would otherwise have little opportunity to see. If you want an explanation of all the nameless horrors of our age you need look no further than to the television stations that can put out *It's A Wonderful Life* at half past two in the afternoon and *The Noel Edmonds Late, Late Breakfast Show* peak time on weekend evenings. If the network companies can be likened to public libraries, and I don't see why they can't, then we are dealing with establishments that keep all the good books tucked away in a small, inhospitable garret in an annexe to the main building and fill the main shelves with Robert Ludlums, Barbara Cartlands and tattered comic books. 'But that's what the people *want*.' Of course it is. It's a self-fulfilling prophecy. Such works are so much easier to find, so clearly marked and catalogued; the librarians are so keen to supply them. Send Noel back to Saturday mornings and present a James Stewart or Gary Cooper film in his place every week until his brutalised audience has some humanity put back into it.

In an *Omnibus* documentary about Hancock, Patrick Cargill, seated stiffly in an arm chair like Velasquez's Pope Innocent X, told a story of how thrilled Hancock was to be working with 'real actors' (after Kenneth Williams and Bill Kerr, I suppose) when he had the privilege of playing opposite Cargill in *The Blood Donor*. 'I remember he said to me, "when you play a doctor, Patrick, you really *are* a doctor".' Thus is a dreadful myth propagated, the myth that actors are 'good at comedy'. If the television companies have a funny script they will, like as not, search for an 'actor' to play a part in it. Timothy West, Robert Hardy, and Donald Sinden are all actors. Good ones. They have played tragedy and comedy on the legitimate stage and on television with great success. They have also tried light entertainment and succeeded in being about as amusing as a bomb in a primary school. The reason seems to be that as soon as they are in front of a studio audience they stop being actors (the very purpose for which they were hired) and try and become music hall stars. Subtlety flies out of the window, closely followed by timing, control and credibility. Watch John Cleese, Rowan Atkinson, Tony Hancock, Rik Mayall or Tracy Ullman and, however grotesque their characterisations, however manic their performances, they always retain a grip on reality. Watch Donald Sinden in *Never The Twain* or Robert Hardy in *Hot Metal* and all you can see is waggling eyebrows, camp intakes of breath and furious, embarrassing mugging. Patrick Cargill in *Father, Dear Father* was as guilty as any of them. Hancock to him was Stanislavsky to Vincent Crummles.

The return of Joan Hickson as *Miss Marple* to our screens is exultantly to be welcomed. I have seen no performance lately so exquisite in its subtlety and detail. Every bird-like inclination of the head, every little exclamation and every gentle inspection of an interlocutor's face is a revelation. More episodes are being made even as we speak. Forget the creaking plots and self-conscious Englishness of the settings. That magical performance is all.

I have no doubt that everyone who watched Jonathan Miller's production of *Così Fan Tutte* late in March will agree with me that special television productions of opera are greatly to be encouraged. That magnificent French production of *Le Nozze di Figaro* some years ago with Dietrich Fischer-Dieskau and 'Kiwi' Te Kanawa paved the way. Close-ups and closed-lipped singing bring opera alive in a way that can more than compensate for the loss of live excitement. The only drawback with this *Così* for me was the singing in English. Call me old-fashioned, purblind, hidebound, reactionary and out of touch if you will, but I believe that one of the great advantages of being born English is that one can hear the world's greatest opera in a language other than that in which one asks strangers the way to the lavatory and orders deliveries of coal. However literate or musical the translation, opera in English always sounds like Gilbert and Sullivan. Most libretti are horribly commonplace and I feel very sorry for Italians and Germans who listen to Da Ponte and Wagner and cannot hear the pretty rhythms and alliterations of their two beautiful languages for the banal meaning they also convey.

You might be interested to know that there is a lawyer currently operating powerfully within LWT whose job has been to censor material from the programme *Saturday Live*. Here is a list of some of his decisions:

You can say the word 'erection', but not the word 'dick'.
You can refer to a character's sexual prowess by describing

him as being able 'to come in pints', but you cannot say the word 'bastard' ('basket' is sufficient).

Genitals and breasts can be blown up live, but pig's intestines are not allowed to be seen.

You can point your bottom at the screen and break wind, but you cannot pretend that a prop motor car belongs to Jeremy Isaacs ('a Channel 4 Executive' is acceptable).

You cannot mention the disease thrush or the issue of advertising 'female hygiene' equipment on television but you can crack a joke about the Space Shuttle disaster.

You can show a man putting his fingers into a liquidiser which fills with blood, but you cannot say the word 'Horlicks' ('malted milk' will do).

You can say the word 'turd' but not the word 'sodding'.

Well now, it is possible that *you* can find a rationale behind those decisions, but I'm blowed if I can. I had thought that the law was a parliamentary and practical codification of notions of right and wrong. Either someone somewhere has some very strange notions about right or wrong which this lawyer is faithfully representing, or the man has personally taken it into his head to dictate his own peculiar (and if I may say so, *very, very* peculiar) ideas upon the television-watching public. Either way, I think we should be told. I understand the same man has something to do with LWT deciding to withhold a report on the Hell's Angel who 'died' in police custody, a case for which the new and startling legal precedent of a coroner's inquest being considered *sub judice* was created. If lawyers start taking over executive and artistic decisions in television because of management's fear of men of the stamp of Winston Churchill MP then we might as well all go to bed and pull the sheets over our heads.

Adolf Forster

'Music is the deepest of the Arts and deep beneath the Arts,' someone once said. Forster, I think, though it may have been Hitler. I read *Mein Kampf* and *Two Cheers For Democracy* in the same week and I still keep muddling them up. Whatever. Music is certainly deep beneath what the universities call the televisual arts, or what a man on *Question Time* (now greatly diminished by the return of Robin Day) called 'the most immediate media'. The *Handbook Of Rhetorical Terms* calls that an oxycretin.

Now, I hope I have as tolerable an ear in music as the next man. You can give me the tongs and the bones any time, and I'll be as happy as Larry the sandboy and as right as a rainy trivet. *Any* time, but not *all* the time: I like a good cose too. Unhappily, the art of the spoken word on the wireless is now confined to a rapidly deteriorating Radio 4 and a newly self-conscious BBC World Service, with the odd illuminating talk on Minoan Clitoris Cults still sandwiched between concerts on Radio 3. And we're lucky. In America and Europe broadcast conversation has been extinct for years. Television is going the same way. I'm not just talking about the All Music Channels that have sprung up in Europe and America, nor the proliferation of music (especially pop) programmes on television, nor ghastly Euro-aberrations like the incompetent and vulgar Night of a Thousand Satellites that so outrageously deprived us of an episode of *The Human Jungle* on 21 June this year. I'm talking too about the great sickly wash of music that is poured over every drama, every entertainment, every documentary now broadcast. It is more than a little vexing to see an otherwise splendid documentary such as *Letters From A Bomber Pilot* (Thames) marred by an over-emphasis on Glenn Miller, or, to look at it from the other end, to hear motif after motif of Wagner's *Ring* being vulgarised and abused by inappropriate association with E.M. Hitler and the Nazis. Specially commissioned film and television music, however, is quite unexceptionable: no one can mind associating the *Miss Marple* theme with Miss Marple, or 'Tum, di dum, ti tum diddy-tum tum' with *Dallas*, but I'm damned if I'm going to associate 'When I'm Sixty-Four' with Barry Took, or Mozart's 'Musical Joke' with show-jumping from Hickstead: it may not be a very funny joke, but it deserves better than that. Television advertising, of course, is an even worse offender: who can hear '*O Sole Mio*' without thinking of a Cornetto? Bach's Suite No. 3 in D without thinking of Hamlet cigars? The Largo from Dvorak's 'New World' Symphony without conjuring up a picture of Hovis being baked in a cobbled Northern town plum spang in the middle of the Old World? Great testaments to the Art of Persuasion, as advertising now calls itself, but a bit of a bummer for the composers in question.

I've been stuck in what Adolf Forster would call my 'lebensraum' all summer, watching the fight for the Ashes. There is no doubt that Ian Botham, 'the Both.' as Mike Brearley used to call him (to rhyme with 'cloth', not 'sloth'), has provided the best and most exciting television this country has seen since the Clee made *Fawlty Towers* all those years ago. But the Both. is the despair of Tom, Richie, Jim and Ted in the commentary box. Pavilioned in splendour and girded with praise, he spits great strings of spittle all over the pitch, he chews gum, he laughs when he fails, he PUTS HIS HANDS ON HIS KNEES when he stands in the slips, if you please, he streaks his hair with gold highlights and he is well on his way to becoming cricket's first millionaire. For poor old Tom and Ted and Trevor and Fred – the Grave, the Dex, the Bail and the True – who played, if one is to believe them, in the days when you were lucky if you emerged so much as a thousandaire at the end of your career, it's all a bit much. They may not have earned big money, but really speaking, as Tom Graveney would say, they did play the game properly, classically, intelligently. And now, watching Gower's XI, they just cannot help themselves. They carp, they cavil: they pick, they niggle. Only Big Bob Willis, who has just joined the commentary team, is indulgent. He knows, none better, what it's like having these frightful old wiseacres whingeing on while one is trying to play. I hope he watches when the BBC show old test matches from the Trueman, Graveney, Dexter, Benaud, Bailey era during intervals for tea or rain. For *what* do we see? HORRIBLE CHEST-ON BOWLING ACTIONS! BADLY SET FIELDS! DROPPED CATCHES! BATSMEN PLAYING ACROSS THE LINE AND BEING BOWLED ALL OVER THE PLACE! LEG SIDE LONG-HOPS BOWLED TO OFF-SIDE FIELDS! FANS INVADING THE PITCH! It's all there in black and white. Damn these silly men! Damn their impudence! Damn their vain, crabby, resenting spite! Is this what comes with age? Please God may I never be old like that.

But cheer up. No one could be less petulant, crabby or resentful than Don Henderson's retired policeman, who can be seen on Wednesdays on ITV in *Bulman* (Granada). He has been joined by the wonderful and cheerful Siobhan Redmond. Together they roam the streets of Manchester and Chorlton, pretending that they are in London. They are helped by one recurring London bus, some cunningly placed *Evening Standard* news stands and talk of 'blags', 'manors' and 'liberties'. Still, as Noel Dyson said in Ronald Frame's *Paris* (filmed in Glasgow), one of the new season of plays on BBC2, 'If you don't have imagination, what *do* you have?'

Brand X

'I love to lose myself in a mystery,' Sir Thomas Browne confesses in *Religio Medici*. I know what he means. There are few more enjoyable pastimes than snuggling up with a good murder. But such mysteries are penetrable, they are 'susceptible of rational explanation' as Sherlock Holmes might say. Holmes, incidentally, is currently to be seen in a marvellous new incarnation on ITV every week, played by Jeremy Brett, who has overcome the fact that as a young man he was, to use a phrase of Anthony Burgess's, 'adventitiously endowed with irrelevant photogeneity' and is now, in his maturity, acting magnificently. In the current series we have been treated to 'The Copper Beeches' and 'The Greek Interpreter', in both of which 'all of my friend's remarkable powers were needed'.

Sir Thomas Browne's most famous adventures also required considerable thought; 'The Affair Of The Siren's Song' and 'The Name Achilles Assumed When He Hid Himself Among Women' (Hilda, as it turned out) prompted him to remark that such cases, though presenting features of some interest, 'are not beyond all conjecture'. But I know of a problem, a twentieth-century mystery, which would appear to be beyond all hope of unravelling, and which would surely have taxed the Masters themselves. The question is this: What is the name of the substance that sloshes about inside the heads of television programme controllers in this country? It must *have* a name. It may even have a use yet undiscovered, as an animal feed possibly, or a replacement for glycol in Austrian wine, and I know for a fact that administrators of public swimming baths in this country are looking for a cheap substitute for the chemical that turns red when introduced to urine. Whatever thousand and one valuable things about the home this strange compound may help its owner do, thinking is not one of them. There must be a name for the stuff, or what's a language for? So until that last dark truth is revealed to us I shall call it Brand x, though there are those cruel enough to suggest that it is Brand y (the Cognac or Armagnac varieties) which is the real cause of the trouble.

Brand x it is that causes millions of pounds' worth of ship to be spoiled for veritable ha'p'orths of tar. A good example is the aborted *Rates of Exchange*, a planned filmed version of the Malcolm Bradbury novel. A script was written (originally an economical script, I might add, made more adventurous and expensive at the insistence of the producer), actors were signed, rehearsal rooms booked and the enterprise was afloat and within sight of the channel (BBC2 in this case) and all bode fair, when the plug was pulled, the rats fled and the vessel was summarily scuppered. The venture was too expensive, therefore it had to be called back. Not, 'I'm afraid we're going to have to reduce the cost', but simply, 'you're fired.' The result of course (because of money already spent on the commission of the material and the reconnaissance of the locations and the subsequent paying of compensation to the actors who had been contracted) was that the BBC was hundreds of thousands of pounds out of pocket with no saleable or screenable product to show for it. That's Brand x. A new kind of madness that I never got with my old cerebral tissues.

Brand x it is that causes the corporation and the independent networks to sit on millions and millions of pounds' worth of past programmes and resolutely refuse to show them. To be fair, it is partly the fault of unthinking television journalists who snidely refer to 'repeats' as if they were a nasty stain on their corduroys. What's *wrong* with repeats, for Grade's sake? If a thing's worth sitting in front of once, it's worth sitting in front of twice. No one wants to see a diminution in the number of new programmes on television, but surely everyone wants to see past editions of *Monitor*, re-runs of *Mission Impossible* and repeats of *Monty Python* and *The Forsyte Saga*? Brand x has already seen to it that some priceless hours of television have already, criminally, been wiped forever, and no longer exist in any form; John Fortune and Eleanor Bron's brilliant and innovative *Where Was Spring*, for example, is now nothing but particles of loose magnetised ions floating in the ether. Of course it is true that actors' repeat-fees revert to a higher percentage after a certain period and repeating consequently becomes more expensive, but not enough to deny us these pleasures. The solution, as my predecessor[1] on this column has said before, is to create a Repeats Channel. All it takes is a spare frequency. I am sure obstacles lie in the path, but who, at this moment, is bothering to think about clearing them? When comes a glittering Siegfried to wrest the hoard of unseen treasure from these clumsy Fafners?

Talking of shining heroes, the final contest for the Ashes at the Oval raised another difficult problem. How is it that Peter West, one of the most experienced men in television, is still so indescribably incompetent and uncomfortable in front of a camera? How can it be? People come into television every year from other walks of life: take Bob Willis, Bob Wilson, James Hunt and Richie Benaud. In these sportsmen-turned-commentators we might expect a stilted delivery and a nervous manner, but within a month these men and many like them become a hundred times more coherent, relaxed and at home when facing the lens than dear old Peter West, who has been on our screens now for over twenty years, over thirty in all probability. How come? Goodness knows I wouldn't have it any other way, but – purely out of interest – how is this? He gulps and swallows and brays, he splutters and dips his head and blinks; in interview he leaves embarrassing pauses between questions and interrupts with embarrassing remarks during the answers. It's incredible. Take my own case: I am incapable of producing a tuneful note from my throat – it is a source of almost inconsolable grief to me, but I live with it and I remember never to appear on television in concert singing with Placido Domingo. But if, and I say this with all due humility, some crackpotted producer did insist on employing me in such a capacity, I dare swear that after twenty-five years I would by now be known as the Norfolk Nightingale and have hospital wards and express trains named after me and plaster casts of my tonsils in every museum in the land. *Übung macht den Meister*, as they say in Germany, and *Arbeit macht Fry ein Meistersinger*. But twenty-five years seems to have left

[1]Richard Curtis, co-writer of *Blackadder, Not The Nine O'Clock News, The Tall Guy* and creator of Comic Relief and Red Nose Day.

poor Peter West as hopelessly, blissfully, thrillingly inadequate as when he started. A real blow for the opsimath.

But, to return to the question of repeats, some things *do* improve with age. BBC2 is re-running *Star Trek*, a programme of remarkable quality. To introduce the series, they screened an American programme called *Memories of Star Trek*, in which Leonard Nimoy, Mr Spock in real life, showed how he personally was responsible for thinking up all the character traits and mannerisms that made Spock one of the great fictional creations of our times. It appears that the Vulcan salute derives from a rabbinical gesture that worshippers at synagogue are forbidden to watch. The celebrated Vulcan neck-pinch allows Leonard Nimoy to incapacitate foes without running about and rehearsing complicated fight sequences.

At its best *Star Trek* says remarkable things about civilisation: the object of the quest of the *Enterprise* is to discover what civilisation means. A typical adventure will examine the problem of being an intelligent creature, a creature of advanced understanding and knowledge (not a problem likely to beset television controllers as we know), and of being at the same time a creature of passion, of dark, turbulent desires. We are constantly being shown the fight between Apollo and Dionysus that Nietzsche saw as being at the centre of Greek tragedy.

One *Star Trek* episode culminated with Jim turning to McCoy and gesturing to the flight screen: 'You know, Bones, out there someone is saying the three most beautiful words in the Universe.' Do you know what those words are? You might think that they would be, revoltingly, 'I love you', and in nine out of ten television programmes they would be, but not in *Star Trek*.

CUT to McCoy looking quizzical and raising one eyebrow. CUT back to Captain Kirk, still looking out of the window, an almost wistful expression on his lovely face. He tells us the words. They are, simply, '*Please. Help me.*' MUSIC. END CREDITS.

That's television.

Don't Knock Masturbation

A character in Christopher Hampton's *The Philanthropist* once urged: 'Don't knock masturbation. Masturbation is the thinking man's television.' So now we know what you thinking men who don't watch television are up to. And indeed we know what you are. It is to you that I address myself this week. Why don't you watch television? You really should, you know. I have devoted this week to providing you with a starter's course in television which I urgently recommend you follow.

Firstly a few words of exhortation. I cannot pretend to know your reasons for not watching television, but I hope I can persuade you that they are insufficient. If you haven't got a colour set, a monochrome will do, and if you haven't got a monochrome, then God bless you.

I think it was Rilke, and I have to confess that I am far too lazy and far too low on the correct works of reference to be able to check (perhaps you could let me know), anyway if it wasn't Rilke it was Kraus (Karl, I would think, not Alfredo), and if it wasn't either of them it was somebody else, who said: 'A book is like a mirror, if an ass peers in, you can't expect an Apostle to peep out.' So let it be with television. If an ass watches television he will watch good television in an asinine way and bad television in an asinine way (I can never remember which emperor it was that built the Asinine Way, I rather think it was Heliogabolus). I happen to know that none of you is an ass and am sure that after reading this and following my course you will be watching television with the same keen, intelligent ardour with which you already pursue the thinking man's alternative.

So, television is like a mirror in one respect, but in its active function it has often been described as a window: a window on the world. In some ways it resembles the old bow window of

White's Club, St James's, during the Regency. Sitting elegantly and looking through that funny dimpled glass, the wise *Beau* could find out all he needed to know about who was in town, with whom and why. The latest fashions would be paraded before his eyes, the latest town-whispers and society *on-dits* confirmed under the scrutiny of his disbelieving quizzing-glass. The special properties of that particular window afforded an excellent all round view. But, glass being what it is, he was not only the watcher: he soon became the watched. For the window fast became famous and all manner of people, some of them quite definitely not of the Upper Ten Thousand, would take long detours to go and see who that day was sitting in the window looking out. It became impossible to decide if the world looked *out* of the window or if the world looked *into* the window. On which side of the glass was this world of which the window afforded such a good view? Or was the glass itself the world? Those on each side thought that what they were looking at constituted the spectacle. Only the window knew which was which, and it wasn't telling. To add to the confusion, from some angles the glass reflected the viewer back on himself, and from others the funny dimples and the wide convex angle of the bow gave such a distorted view that it was impossible to believe any of it was real at all.

Television is the same. Of technological necessity, the only thing the world can watch on a television screen is the world that has been watched by television cameras. Which is the real eye, the camera that watches the world or the eye of the world that watches the television? How very sophistical it all is. As they used to say on a television programme that used hidden cameras a great deal: 'We're watching you, watching us, watching you.' It's also true that we're watching them watching us watching them. You'll need to say those sentences aloud a few times to make any sense of them, but it's worth it because it says a great deal about how active a thing television watching is and how reflexive the communication that takes place.

The first programme I would recommend to you, bearing this quality of television's in mind, is *The Marriage*, a 'fly-on-the-wall' scrutiny of a young couple's betrothal and early wedded life. But we don't watch it because we are interested in this particular couple: that is the last reason anyone could choose, unless they were in some way related to them. We watch it, with strange fascination, because we want to see how people behave when they are being watched. Ghoulish? Possibly. Voyeuristic? Obviously. We want to see what happens to two people (as normal as rice-pudding when the series started), ardent volunteers as they were, when their private life is minutely and impertinently probed by a television producer and his crew and 12 million ordinary people like themselves. More importantly we watch it because we want to know what happens to *us* when we participate in so gruesome a spectacle, which is what we do when we tune in. If we watch it actively and honestly, haughty disdain for such revolting proceedings will not be the reaction, nor will be snobbery at the poverty of the taste, imagination and mental life of the ordinary people of this country . . . although it would be hard for those feelings to be too far away. I watched *The Marriage* at first because I knew millions were watching it and finally because I knew I liked watching it and I wanted to find out why. I still don't know.

Know thyself. Don't watch television because it's 'well done' or 'well produced' or 'interesting'. *The Marriage* certainly has no more merit than any other programme as 'Television' in the telejournalist's sense of the word. Watch it because *you* are interesting, well produced and well done.

All in all, it is necessary to watch for no other reason than that most people do. As a reader of the *Literary Review* you are, of course, a student of the human heart and a researcher into the human mind. If you were a student of Shakespeare you would study what his audience read, watched and spent their days doing. The people in the world around you are living their lives with the Colbys and with Nick Ross and Terry Wogan, with Grange Hill, Blockbusters and The Tube, with Captain Furillo, *Vorsprung Durch Technik* and David Icke, and you don't know what a single one of those things really means to us. A massive frame of reference, a whole universe of discourse is utterly closed to you and I believe that you are the poorer for it.

And aside, quite aside and apart from television as a social phenomenon, an historical text to be read, there is – there really is – television as an (albeit infrequent) creator of works of art and a frequent transmitter of works of art from other media: music, painting and, predominantly, cinema: television as a teacher, traveller, biologist, doctor, natural historian, contemporary historian and repository of knowledge, trivial and quadrivial.

So, your list of things to watch. Begin one weekday morning, with BBC's *Breakfast Time*. It may be a wrench to leave John Timpson and Brian Redhead, but do it anyway, just for one morning. Change channels frequently to TVAM and note the superiority of the BBC's lighting and design. But note also the smugness and cosiness of the BBC, a *Daily Mail* next to the *Sun* or *Mirror* of ITV. Imagine millions of people also watching with you and picture what their reaction to these horrific programmes might be. You needn't watch breakfast television again, unless there is another Brighton bombing or similar sensational early morning news story.

We will leave the afternoon alone, I'm assuming you work for a living, although I do know that there are some poets amongst the readership. Afternoon television is about to have big money spent on it, but for the moment it consists largely of Australian soap operas and women's magazines which certainly repay close investigation, but only when you are more familiar with your new toy.

But do watch *Blockbusters* on ITV, 5.15 weekdays. Yes, every weekday. Bob Holness chairs this quiz programme for adolescents and it is simply compulsive. It has created a whole new hotly contested scheduling time: the pre-evening-news slot, as they call it. It will tell you a great deal about how our adolescents are being educated, just as *University Challenge* (some ITV regions, various times) will tell you about our undergraduates. *Blockbusters* is exciting and enthralling – it also ends *in media res*, sometimes in the middle of a question, which is too thrilling for words.

You must watch *Wogan*, terrifying as the prospect sounds. The man is a hopeless interviewer and appears to be a ridiculous egotist, but you will find out who is doing what and who is popular and interesting in this world that you have finally decided to inspect.

Yes Prime Minister is middle-class, middle-aged, middle-brow. It is held up to be the acme of current situation comedy, where *The Young Ones* was the acne. Give me spots any day. Of course *Yes Prime Minister* is clever and witty and well-performed and written, and of course I would hate to miss a single episode, but it will never be seen as a landmark in the history of television comedy, as *Fawlty Towers* was, or *The Young Ones* or *TW3*; it will never really be remembered. I am aware that my view is treasonable.

I, Clavdivs, luckily for you, is being repeated. You've read the Graves novels, now see how television can adapt and adopt, adeptly. Magnificent writing from Jack Pulman, brilliant acting from nearly every single person in the huge cast. This is one to watch simply for satisfaction.

The last recommendation is for you to watch the *Channel 4 News* at 8.00 p.m. They broadcast at the best time and in the best fashion, you'll find yourself watching regularly.

That's it. Just try all those programmes in one week, that's all I'm asking. The following week, take ten evening programmes at random from the TV magazines, I *mean* at random. And watch them from the beginning: it's no good starting to watch half way through. You wouldn't read a novel starting at chapter nine. If it's been on for five minutes, you've missed it. If you give them that chance, I guarantee you will find excitement, filth, pathos, amusement (horrified and enchanted), nonsense, brilliance and absurdity in abundance. In short you will see and share in humanity to an extent that is not possible in any other way, because you will see all humanity, not just your friends and coequals, but those you hate and those who hate you, those you find beautiful and those you find disgusting, people cleverer than you, and people who never knew what you forgot when you were twelve: people, events, possibilities and fictions that make up and are made up by an institution, an organism, a public event that until now you have always shunned. Come on down!

Cricket, Lovely Cricket . . .

Those of you not frightfully interested in cricket will probably want to skip this: reviews for The Listener *of a whole crop of cricketing books.*

Leslie Frewin (ed.): *The Boundary Book, Second Innings: A Lord's Taverners' Miscellany of Cricket* (Pelham Books) £14.95

Matthew Engel (ed.): *The Guardian Book of Cricket* (Michael Joseph, Pavilion Books) £14.95

Christopher Lee: *Nicely Hurdled, Sir! Two Centuries in Prose and Poetry* (Elm Tree Books) £7.95

Peter Haining (ed.): *LBW Laughter Before Wicket!: 100 Years of Humorous Cricket Short Stories* (Allen & Unwin) £10.95

Bob Willis & Patrick Murphy: *Starting With Grace: A Pictorial Celebration of Cricket 1864–1986* (Stanley Paul) £14.95

Don Mosey: *Botham* (Methuen) £9.95

Simon Barnes: *Phil Edmonds: A Singular Man* (The Kingswood Press) £9.95

Frances Edmonds: *Another Bloody Tour: England in the West Indies 1986* (The Kingswood Press) £9.95

For every kind of person there is a kind of cricket; for every approach to life there is an approach to cricket and for every kind of cricket and every approach to cricket there is published, more than twice a week, a cricket book. Eight of these are under advisement now. Of the eight, five are anthologies or miscellanies of one kind or another, two are biographies of active players and one is the tour diary of a cricketing wife.

The Boundary Book: Second Innings is perhaps, of the anthologies, the one I would recommend as the volume most worthy to sit alongside the Harpic, the Haze and the *Spitting Image Bumper Giles Book Of Alan Coren's Holiday Misprints* in any good lavatory. The selections are of precisely the required brevity and variety for any healthy and agreeable session in the Smallest Pavilion. Indeed, there is more variation in spin, flight, pace, length, drift, trajectory and line than even John Emburey in top form can produce. There are cartoons, memoirs of great cricket figures, a wonderfully seamless flow of reminiscence of forties cricket from Harold Pinter, a riveting article on left-handedness, lyric poems of impossibly maudlin self-indulgence, a *Private Eye* parody of the Bodyline television series, a C.L.R. James appraisal of Bradman, alone worth the gate money, and dozens of photographs, fragments, musings and ravings from such diverse contributors as Simon Raven, Lord Olivier, G.K. Chesterton, Peter Ustinov and Umpire Harold 'Dickie' Bird. At £14.95 (the proceeds from which are donated to the Lord's Taverners' charity for disabled children and young cricketers) this wonderfully produced collection, a brilliant successor to Leslie Frewin's original Boundary Book, is the volume I would most want to find in the cricket bag I hang hopefully at the end of my bed every Christmas Eve.

The Guardian Book of Cricket, edited by Matthew Engel, the finest, fairest and funniest cricket journalist we have, is another excellent collection. Engel has assembled from the archives of the *Guardian* cricket writing which covers the game from 1826 to the present day. He has had gold to work with. A newspaper that can boast Cardus, Arlott, Keating, Woodcock and Engel as regular long-serving cricket writers and, as occasional contributors, James Cameron, Alistair Cooke, Jack Fingleton, Michael Frayn and C.L.R. James, can well justify immortalising its ephemera. Rather than giving us one long chronological survey he has grouped the writings intelligently into subjects. I was reminded of E.M. Forster's novelists, different generations all working in the same time and place. Within a few pages we can read match reports of Jessop's 1902 and Botham's 1981 Tests, which show us just why the two are so often compared, and, in a salutary chapter headed 'The Game's Not The Same', we are shown that the same kind of drivel about the Decline of Cricket was being written in 1904, smack in the middle of the Golden Age, as is being written now. *Plus ça change* . . .

LBW: Laughter Before Wicket! and *Nicely Nurdled, Sir!* both, as you can see, have exclamation marks after their dreadful titles. This tells us something about the rather twee attitude towards cricket both anthologisers share. Christopher Lee (the BBC's Defence Correspondent) ruins for me an otherwise excellent (though brief) selection of cricket writing (a great deal of which has been seen before) with irritating and monstrously prejudiced interpolations: 'I discovered that The Game was a bond . . . (he insists on calling cricket 'The Game') . . . there was a common cynicism towards the antics and sometimes the motives of the professional game. Many cricket followers are reactionaries, which is no bad thing, except that modern players are not reactionaries.' Balderdash. I shall never listen to Mr Lee analysing Superpower Summits in quite the same way again. 'In proper cricket, that is cricket kept in sight of chestnut and church spire . . . ' So cricket in sight of factory chimney, palm-tree or mosque is improper cricket, is it? Thank heavens 'The Game' is bigger than some of the small minds that write about it.

LBW is a rather tame collection of 'humorous' cricket short stories. To qualify for inclusion the authors had to have played cricket at some time in their lives, not a particularly strenuous condition to satisfy. P.G. Wodehouse who opened the bowling for Dulwich as a schoolboy contributes, not surprisingly, the best story, whose hero meets a schoolgirl who knows about cricket:

> It surprised him in a vague sort of way that a girl should have such a firm and sensible grasp on the important problems of life. He had taken his sister to Lord's one summer to watch

the Gentlemen v Players, and she had asked him if the sight screens were there to keep the wind off the players. He had not felt really well since.

Starting With Grace is a collection of photographs mostly garnered and marshalled from the holdings of the BBC Hulton Picture Library. A good, general text by Bob Willis and Patrick Murphy accompanies photographs of cricketers from Grace to Gower. As a pictorial history it is pleasant enough, but as I don't own what one might call a proper coffee table, I wouldn't really know what to do with it once I had had a good look through. There is an appendix of statistics on players past and present, but to keep it for that purpose would be like buying a car because you need a spare radio.

Don Mosey, known as the Alderman to those who listen to Radio 3's *Test Match Specials*, would not, I am sure, claim to be a Cardus, but his biography of Botham does contain some dreadful inelegancies: 'scant luck', 'goodly quota', 'He visibly bristled'. Nor can sentences like 'There was beautiful weather for the whole of that Test and it was good to see a huge crowd in a ground which is not usually the best for support on such occasions' encourage one to believe that this was a book which took a very long time to write. More disturbingly, this is a biography that actively dislikes its subject. Two lines in a biography of Ian Botham to describe his bowling performance at Edgbaston in 1981! Two lines! Hundreds of pompous paragraphs on 'the relationship between press and players', pages on how much better a bowler Trueman was, pointlessly smug attacks on anything modern from pop music to hair-styles, foolishly ignorant and ill-considered remarks on the problem of sport and politics, but two lines on Botham's match-saving five wickets for one run in 28 balls! If he wanted to write a book expressing the glory of the past and the decay of the present then he should have done so, but to foist his miserably small-minded and platitudinous views on the kind of cricket lovers for whom Botham is as much a hero as Compton and Trueman ever were to previous generations is nothing short of disgraceful. His patriarchal clap-trap about Botham failing to heed the warnings of his headmaster and his setting poor examples to the young is of a piece with this kind of remark: 'On any normal day they (the police) were faced with the virtually impossible job of trying to maintain law and order in an increasingly undisciplined society where, it seemed, an agitator or nut case had only to cry "police brutality" to have the allegation plastered over every front page and TV screen in the country.' Botham may not be a saint, there may be interesting things to write about the press in modern cricket, heroes may have a responsibility to their public, but this nasty little book does nothing but drag the debate down into the squalid English regions of snobbery, self-righteousness and cant.

Phil Edmonds: A Singular Man, on the other hand, is a delightful biography of one of cricket's most delightful players. Intelligent, amusing, aggressive, ridiculously brave, athletic and scornful, Philippe-Henri Edmonds has enriched Test and County cricket for more than ten years. Simon Barnes, a witty and fair-minded journalist, has chosen as a central pivot for the book Edmonds's awkward personal and professional relationship with Mike Brearley, his Test and County Captain for many years, the ramifications of which are presented in a sane and balanced manner from both points of view.

For a gloriously insane and unbalanced view of modern English test cricket, however, we look to Phil Edmonds' adoring wife, Frances, whose *Another Bloody Tour* is as refreshing to the reader of worthy, masculine cricket literature, as a tray of interval drinks on a hot afternoon. It is true that she could wear her learning a little more lightly. The overuse of sixth-form words like 'emarginalised' and 'apotheosised', not to mention unglossed tags in several of the foreign languages in which Mrs Edmonds is fluent, encourages the reviewer to be more bitchy about abuses like 'practiced' failing to be snapped up in the proof-reader's slip cordon, than he would otherwise like. But this compound of tart gossip, garlicky character assassination and coy insinuation is utterly irresistible and an excellent addition to any bookshelf. There is good sense here too. Compare her analysis of the West Indian attitude to Graham Gooch's sporting links with South Africa and Don Mosey's ludicrously naïf nonsense on the subject. The flannelling fool first. Many feel, Mosey says, that cricketers like Gooch 'had done nothing more reprehensible than pursuing their careers . . . by taking up winter employment where it was offered.' He goes on to call the deputy Prime Minster of Antigua 'a tin-pot, two-penny ha'penny politician'. 'Gooch was the latest pawn to be used in the sinister game of chess being played out by political grand-masters, and he did not get the support or anything like the support he was entitled to expect from his employers.' Frances Edmonds, however, says this:

> The cankerous tendrils of apartheid are deemed to contaminate any sportsman who has played there. Who should say whether this is right or wrong? In the West Indies it is simply inevitable. It remains part of the world where it is dangerously ingenuous to think of cricket as a mere game. Caribbean cricket forms an integral, probably even a predominant part, of a complex social, political and philosophical nexus, a web from which it is totally indivisible . . . international sportsmen would do well to understand it . . . Go to South Africa by all means. Take the loot. But let's muster the imagination to realise that some people are bound to object.

A breath of fresh air to blow away the cobwebs that have clung to cricket writing for too many years.

Bernard Levin

Such impudence in one so not particularly young. Again, for **The Listener.**

Bernard Levin: *In These Times*, Jonathan Cape, hardback, £10.95

I have to confess right here and now that my feelings upon being called upon to review an anthology (and it is Levin himself who says that these volumes are collections of pressed flowers, and we all know that an anthology is, if it is to be taken *au pied de la lettre*, nothing more, nor indeed less – and who would have it otherwise? – than a posy or, *mutatis mutandis*, nosegay – though no doubt the gentlemen who busy themselves with instructing us how to live and speak would have words to say, nay, shriek, on the subject of how gay or otherwise the nose may or, come to that, may *not* be, for as sure as eggs are graded ovular Euro-units there will lurk in some dank council cupboard a malevolent creature whose only joy in life is to tell us that 'nosegay' is now proscribed, look with a spot I damn it – of flowers, and if you, having followed the wild and twisting path of my clauses to a successful conclusion, can sight, in the purple distance, the welcoming beacon that promises an end to this parenthesis, then Levin is the writer for you – five hours of reading Levin and the plain English sentence is only a dimly perceived memory, if I can just find my way out of this clause, I will join you – ah, θαλαττα, θαλαττα, I choose the Attic double ταυ, note) are not unlike that of a schoolboy on being called upon to write a report on his schoolmaster.

It is the fashion amongst persons of rank and tone within the world of journalism and what is loosely called the 'media' (I once heard television described as 'an immediate medium', *o tempora o mores, eheu fugaces*, I'm going to run out of Latin tags and literary allusions before the season is quite out, *pace* Lady Bracknell) to mock Mr Levin with scorn. There is too much passion there, too much commitment, too much *enthusiasm* for the blasé denizens of the Street of Shame to handle. I may as well state at once that over the years I have found my views on such trivial subjects as the real threats to human freedom today and the existence of free will diverging more and more widely from those of Mr Levin, but that has never stopped me from lighting on any printed word of his with a glad cry, for the man writes like an angel, like a devil, like one whose connection between thought and word is absolute. His zest for life, his affirmative view of humanity, his belief in that simple, obvious truth that were you to lob a copy of the Sunday edition of the *New York Times* out of the window anywhere in the world, the chances are at least 90 to 1 in favour of it KO-ing a *good* person, a decent person, a friend (P.G. Wodehouse, to whom Levin's prose owes a great deal, and I am sure he would be the first to admit it – Levin that is, not Wodehouse, Doctor Sir Pelham was too modest, and anyway he has long since been gathered to God – used, when in town, to solve the problem of the long walk to the post-office by the simple expedient of tossing his letters out of his window: his belief that the average human, finding a stamped and addressed letter on the pavement, would naturally pop it into the nearest pillar-box was never once, in decades, shown to be unfounded) have always struck a chord with me. Too few voices today are raised in chorus of that splendid truth.

In These Times is the fourth collection of Levin's writings; it contains his personal selection of two years of regular feature-writing for *The Times* under the heading 'The Way We Live Today' and book reviewing for the *Observer*. In an uncharacteristically pompous introduction he notes that over the years he has found himself returning more and more to three 'themes': Freedom, Responsibility and Art.

In his condemnation of tyranny the world over his language is that of the Byron of *Don Juan*, entertaining, excoriating, unremitting and savagely comic. His column has often been used to raise individual cases of injustice, torture and inhumanity, particularly of course behind the Iron Curtain, and no one could have anything but praise for his tireless efforts on behalf of the abused and enslaved in all wicked regimes. This volume contains some of his very best articles about such cases, appalling stories of injustices in Lithuania, Russia, Czechoslovakia and South Africa.

But the real bee in the bonnet that Bernard Levin has been sporting these last seasons, and its buzzing informs the majority of his articles whatever their pretext, is that of Individual Responsibility. Levin's brand of libertarianism is founded upon an absolute belief in man's direct responsibility for his actions. Free Will Exists! is the message that is semaphored in massive gaily coloured flags from every rise and knoll in the Levin landscape. This may ultimately be the truth, but to erect it as an Ultimate Truth from which all penal and social systems, all politics and economics should flow is to proclaim a way of dealing with our fellow man that may fall short of the ideal.

Such is the zest of his argument that any organisations or movements that set out to put right deficiencies and imbalances provided by birth or weakness of will or human folly are contemptuously dismissed. Animal liberationists act not from a love of animals but from a hatred of mankind, from

an unbearable rage at the very fact that there is a universe and that we are in it, for good or ill, along with the animals. I noticed, for instance, the satisfying relish with which nuclear disarmers describe the impending holocaust and its lakes of molten eyeballs, its forests of instant skeletons, its mountains of roasted flesh.

Come, come! Tush! Not to say, faugh! Levin has 'noticed' elsewhere that the most 'strident' feminists are the ugliest. He, a man so sensitive to the corruption for political ends of connotational language, uses words like 'moderate' and 'extremist' as his tennis balls, to be struck and bandied which way he will.

All his unworthy observations, loaded language and fraudulent attributions of malignancy to what, let's be frank, turn out in the end to be anyone or anything left wing or liberal, will only infuriate those who think and act differently (while they may often ultimately believe congruently) to Mr Levin and will only cause smug satisfaction in those who share his politics and social obsessions. But the latter will get all the satisfaction they require from the Scrutons and Butts and Mounts who litter the same features page of *The Times* as Mr Levin, but whose poisonous effusions contain not one scintilla of an iota of a suggestion of a millionth part of the wit and learning and humanity that are contained in even his most enragingly illiberal pieces.

But I can and do, and recommend that anyone else should, ignore differences and welcome common ground. Above all there is the writing, just sit back and enjoy the prose of our best living newspaper writer.

The Satire Boo

A review for The Listener *of books on satirical institutions.*

Tooth & Claw: The inside story of Spitting Image by Lewis Chester. Faber & Faber. Paperback. £3.95

Inside Private Eye by Peter McKay. Fourth Estate. Hardback. £9.95

If there is one cow more sacred, one tradition more revered, one taboo more respected than another in this country it is that of The Great British Satirist. From Chaucer to Ingrams by way of Dryden, Swift, Dickens and two world Waughs we are proud of those dirty, snarling and untameable dogs who will as readily tear the throat out of the innocent as the guilty. But this is the age of T-shirts, video cassettes, international residuals, coffee-table books and spin-off merchandising. The fatuous categorisations of today determine that 'satire' means no more and no less than 'topical comedy'. In this quarter of the twentieth century, therefore, satire is respectably big business and strictly defined. Satire is a comforting reminder of what a tolerant, democratically self-scourging nation we are. For this reason sackings and crises within *Private Eye* are considered as newsworthy as Asian earthquakes, and a victim's opinion of his or her *Spitting Image* puppet as fit for the tabloids as a pop star's heroin habit. The satirists rapidly become the establishment and their organs pillars of it.

This is reflected by the publication of two books that 'take the lid off' our two most prominent and revered satirical productions, the above-mentioned *Spitting Image* and *Private Eye*. Enough words have been processed on the nature of the *Eye* for any feeble analysis of mine to add greatly to the store of diskettes on the subject piling up in editors' offices up and down the land. We know that it is public school, prurient, prudish, homophobic, anti-Semitic and cruel. They know it better than anyone. The Great Bores Of Today cartoon in their 500th anniversary addition showed a Bore reciting just such a list of dreadful vices. Whether the *Eye* is really, as Sir James Goldsmith claimed, 'the pus leaking from the wounds of a sick society' or, in Quentin Crewe's words, 'a healthy pimple on the skin of an exuberant nation' probably depends upon whether, like Sir James Goldsmith, you are a pompous litigant being made a fool of in public by men cleverer and wittier than yourself, or whether, like Quentin Crewe, you are a well-paid writer and artist happily relishing the spectacle. Peter McKay's book *Inside Private Eye*, written from the point of view of a long-term contributor and professional hack, claims to provide an insider's view of, to quote the blurb, 'what goes on in those writ-strewn offices where the imperious Lord Gnome presides over the unruly band of wags who pen his organ'. As such it will unquestionably be of interest to a percentage of the *Eye*'s alleged one million readers.

The book contains an immensely useful glossary of 'Eyespeak'. At last I know why Alec Douglas Home is always referred to as Baillie Vass, why Victor Matthews is called Lord Whelks and who the Beast of Bouverie Street is. Having mentioned the gossip content and this valuable glossary, I suspect I have mentioned the only things of value in the book. That it is written in the kind of prose journalists especially reserve for this kind of work, you will naturally expect. It is a kind of Dick Francis style: 'Dempster then made what was generally believed afterwards to have been a crucial mistake', 'His face now white with anger, Hislop rose to speak', that kind of dreary piffle. The book is also awash with repetition; we are twice told who 'Beachcomber' was and within a couple of pages there are two reminders that the Earl of Arran's weekly *Evening News* column was 'eccentric'; P.G. Wodehouse is twice rendered as P.J. Wodehouse, which can only lead one to believe that McKay dictated the book and has a not uncommon oral 'J', 'G' problem, or that he is devastatingly illiterate. I think we should be told.

But these are minor carpings. My essential problem with the book is that it seems to me totally to misunderstand the reason for the *Eye*'s popularity. McKay says of the readership, 'they read it because it strays over the border of what is permissible and tasteful in its attempts to peer beneath the public face of the rich and famous.' Drivel. They read it for one reason and one reason only: because it is funny. When it stops being funny they will stop reading it. *Journalists* may read it because it strays over borders, takes off lids and peers into things, the *public* reads it because it is the only regular funny periodical readily available in Britain. *Punch*, described by Forster over sixty years ago as mere 'suburban sniggerings', has changed only to the degree that suburbia has changed. Whether Ingrams has stepped aside to make way for young Ian Hislop, his successor to the editor's chair, in order to carve out a new readership less interested in the affairs of the Anglican church and the wicked deeds of industry and press barons, or whether, as McKay believes, he has not really stepped down at all, but set up a puppet, time will tell.

The book wastes too many pages telling us things we already knew from Patrick Marnham's *The Private Eye Story* or Ingrams's own *Goldenballs* and too few telling us how an edition is really produced or what goes on in the rooms where the jokes are thought up. McKay has clearly never been present in those rooms; we hear of the laughter bellowing out of them and can only picture poor McKay sucking his pen in an outer room wishing that he too was funny like Ingrams and Waugh. He might also wish that he had their gift for prose.

Lewis Chester, author of *Tooth & Claw: The inside story of Spitting Image*, is also a journalist, with books on Onassis, Jeremy Thorpe and Beaverbrook to his credit. This is an outsider's view of the four or five years that have led up to *Spitting Image* becoming an established success.

You might be tempted to ask why such a book has been written so soon. Certainly *Spitting Image* is very successful, but who is going to want to read 150 pages telling us how it got that way? Fluck met Law, you will say, they worked on magazines and things for a bit and then they thought (or someone else thought) they should make a television programme with their models brought to life by puppeteers. Script writers and impressionists were hired, a pilot was made and the series began, very shakily at first, but gradually improving in quality until it all became very popular and much loved. The programme was sufficiently naughty to get a lot of publicity because of the outrageous way it portrayed the Royal Family, but now it is so respected an institution that a member of the Royal Family attacking it today would scarcely seem less outrageous. End of story. That's what *you* think. In fact nothing was that simple. The book heaves and shivers with tales of back-biting and bitching. Since the idea was first floated the entire project seems to have been an extremely grubby affair: the in-fighting, sackings and lust for financial stakes in the enterprise have, I am reliably informed, been if anything understated. This takes some believing.

It seems that before a joke had been written or a puppet made, the various protagonists were already arguing about who should have what slice of the notional pie. There is certainly a great deal too much financial detail in the book to interest me, whenever I see words like 'equity' and 'share-holding' I fall fast asleep, but these words seem to have meant everything to the half dozen or so producers and managers of *Spitting Image* and Chester goes deeply into the business.

A television company, as anyone who has ever gone near one can testify, is an enormous contrivance designed specifically to cock things up. Television executives are never really happy unless they can go home to their wives or husbands in the evening and tell them that they have successfully obstructed or fouled up a project. This aspect of the *Spitting Image* venture comes across nicely. For the first series the producers and director were forced to edit a £3 million programme from a van in a car park. The first programme had to run short because all Royal Family material was ordered to be excised for fear of offending Prince Philip, who was due to open Central TV's Nottingham studios the week of transmission.

Tooth & Claw has been published as a paperback by Faber & Faber and will appeal more to those interested in deals, arrangements, financial bickerings and political bitchery than those interested in the creation of a funny programme. There is a table of contents listing chapters whose headings are ludicrously unhelpful: 'The Bad-Mannered God', 'The Naughty Mandarin', 'A Nasty Passage', 'The Lunch Break' and 'Getting it on the Stick' are five examples out of twenty-four. There is, annoyingly, no index. I would hardly describe the book as an ideal stocking-filler for the average *Spitting Image* viewer, but I would heartily recommend it to anyone foolish enough to be thinking of embarking upon a large television project.

Child of Change

A review of the autobiography of a remarkable man. So much Gorbachev's man that it will be interesting to see how he develops in the new Russia. He, of course, is not Russian. Kasparov's real name, Weinstein, betrays his Jewish origins, while his home town, Baku, is now part of an independent republic struggling with huge ethnic problems.

Child of Change: by Garry Kasparov & Donald Trelford

From the time *homo ludens* crawled from the primeval slime of spillikins and strip checkers and first stood and called himself a man, the sixty-four squares and thirty-two pieces that define the limits of chess have exerted a powerful fascination over the species. There are, as chess players and George Steiner are fond of remarking, more possible positions in chess than there are atoms in the universe. The chances of dropping a tray full of ball-bearings on the floor and their falling in such a way as to spell the phrase 'Little Scrotely welcomes careful drivers' are greater by far than those of two identical games ever being played. And what skills does the game require? The average master is easily capable of playing a game blindfold. Grandmasters have been known to play fifty games simultaneously without a sight of one of the boards. All decent players can remember any one of their serious games and many of their hundreds of ten-minutes blitzes. Such prodigious feats of memory argue that to do well at chess does not demand the usual intellectual faculties, unusually developed, but instead a special freakish facility that may as well be called an abnormality. Only music and mathematics share with chess the phenomenon of the child prodigy: Mozart's famous trick of remembering an entire requiem, various mathematicians' ability to calculate cube roots in their head are all of a piece with the weird gifts of the grandmaster. It is traditional for the public to satisfy themselves that such gifts must result in deficiencies in other areas: in order to keep in a single head tens of thousands of games, positions, openings and tactical ploys, in order to analyse twenty or thirty moves ahead in dozens of permutations, in order to close out a vast auditorium and the noise of the world and involve oneself purely in the fields of force that pulsate between the wooden men on the board, in order to do all that, surely it must be necessary to relinquish a little humanity? We remember that at school the chess team was largely composed of bum-fluffed, spotty, be-anoraked creatures with the social grace and wit of Nicholas Ridley on a bad day and console ourselves with the thought that chess is a game for wimps and weird brain-boxes.

I have to disappoint you if you believe that this is really true of chess. All those exhausted clichés about 'winning' and 'going for it' and 'psychological preparation' that sportsmen of all kinds inflict upon us are as much a part of the grandmaster's vocabulary as the sprinter's. Chess world champions are distinguished by a terrifyingly powerful will to win. The photograph on the front of Garry Kasparov and Donald Trelford's semi-autobiography of the current world champion, shows the awesome sight that meets the man who dares to sit down and challenge Kasparov's mastery in chess. Huge, thunderous brows, a stubbled face whose shadows point to five o'clock by half past nine in the morning, shoulders hunched forward in murderous anticipation. How clear the mind of an opponent must be, how strongly the forces of will and purpose must flow in him not to lose to this horrifically virile and energetic mental athlete before the first pawn is pushed.

It is deeply satisfying to know that chess is not somehow 'played out'. The great Capablanca thought he had mastered all its mysteries when he suddenly faced Alekhine in 1927 and lost. New ideas will always refresh the game. By objective Elo ratings Kasparov is the strongest player who has ever lived. 'Strong' is the word chess players use, not 'clever' or 'cunning' or 'brilliant' or 'gifted'. Although those qualities may be necessary, it is the strongest man who wins. Perhaps that is why, despite 100 years of organised tournament play for women, men still dominate chess. Over and above the advanced sense of spatial dynamics and transformational geometry which is revealed by scientific experiment to be better developed in men than women, chess calls for supernatural qualities of competitiveness and aggression – it was men, after all, who invented the game. All the tactical, analytical skill in the world will not help you if, when sitting at the board, your nerves and your killer instinct are weaker than your opponent's. Chess is an art, not a technique: like a batsman or an actor, a player may inexplicably lose form one day. Despite all his mental gifts, all his knowledge, the player may be deprived of that blend of concentration and confidence that alone can allow the creative impulse to flow. An artisan or a technician can master their material, the artist and the athlete cannot.

Garry Kasparov emerged in the late 1970s as one of the most gifted chess prodigies in human history. The story of *Child of Change*, which I have to say straight away is the best chess biography I have ever read, and I've ploughed through a few, is not really the story of Kasparov's chess development; in fact the nuts and bolts of chess itself, his mastery of tactical and positional theory and his education in the praxis of the game are rarely attended to, although key games are usefully recorded in an appendix for the enthusiast. This is more the tale of how Kasparov single-handedly took on the Soviet and world chess establishment in order to earn what he and most chess observers saw as his natural due, the right to face his fellow-countryman and arch-rival Anatoly Karpov in single combat. Kasparov's constant claim is that if it were not for Gorbachev and *glasnost*, he would not be world champion today.

Bobby Fischer the author of 'modern' modern chess is effectively author of the whole saga. His refusal to defend his world title against Karpov in 1975 gave Karpov the championship without ever having to fight for it. Karpov's position restored to some extent wounded Soviet prestige and, in the last days of Brezhnev, Karpov, the 'good boy' of Russian chess, party member and line-toer, created an inner clique who clung to him like barnacles to a rock. He guaranteed them money, cars, foreign travel and they were not about to let anyone take that away from them. Kasparov's emergence like a bolt from the blue threatened their security: he wasn't supposed to have come on so fast. Indeed, Kasparov first learned that his compatriots weren't keen on encouraging him when he was directly told: 'We have one world champion, we don't need another.' But Kasparov wasn't interested in that, he was interested in chess. If he was the best, then he should win. Obstacle after obstacle was placed in his path, but he learnt how to use politics too, playing the pride of his home town politicians in their local boy's achievements against the Karpov lobby in Moscow.

The peculiar satisfaction in all this to chess enthusiasts is that Karpov's style of play reflects the wider historic elements of the story, he is cautious, positional, classically pure. Kasparov, as befits the child of *glasnost*, the pioneer of the new Russia, is dashing, daring, cavalier, complex and surprising. The two greatest living players are seen to play for the future of Russia itself.

I will not spoil the story for you by re-telling the central drama of Karpov and Kasparov's first world championship match and the shameful part played in it by Campomanes, the General Secretary of FIDE, the international controlling body of chess, it is as extraordinary as any sporting crisis from Bodyline to the boycott of the Moscow Olympics and deserves to be read in context.

It may be that *Child of Change* is a little ungallant about Karpov, who is surely a chess genius; perhaps Kasparov's outrage at the treatment dealt him is a little too self-righteous, but I am convinced by the whole book. For the observer the battle lines are clearly drawn and Kasparov emerges from this excellently written and structured autobiography as a solid gold, genuine hero. His endearing fondness for Lermontov and Vissotsky (new to me, but extensively quoted), his passion for chess, the high doctrine of the game he preaches and his extraordinarily well-balanced approach to it suggest that only success can spoil him. He is rich, handsome, young, fantastically popular and terrifyingly talented. He is a good sportsman and a literate and intelligent observer of life and society. He loves his homeland and seems to be playing as active a part in its reconstruction as any citizen within it. Only a contract to sponsor Adidas turbo chess-sneakers or the Sony 3-D Low-Fat Chessman could prevent him from becoming one of the most significant Russians of the age. The Child of Change may well grow up to be the Man of the Moment.

Agony Cousin

A short bash writing a column for the Daily Mirror *is represented by this foolish article.*

Stephen Fry in his restless search to undergo every experience on your behalf became an Agony Cousin for a week. Here are his answers to letters on topics as far ranging as subjects that are about one thing and other subjects that are about something completely different:

Hello! In this life, it is well known, you should try everything once, except incest and country dancing. This week I'm having a stab at being what I like to call an Agony Cousin. I had a full postbag this week, all the more so for being stuffed with letters. But this experiment only lasts for this week, so please don't send me *your* problems!!! Okay? Great! Thanks! Oh, and bless you. Much appreciated. That's the way! Mm, I should say so. Blimey, yes!

Dear Cousin Stephen, What's happening to my body? I am thirteen and a half and I have begun to notice changes in me and in my feelings to others. What *does* it mean? Yours, Slightly Puzzled

Dear Slightly Puzzled, Pull the other one. You know perfectly well what's happening inside you, you just want me to write a reply that includes the word 'genitals' so you can have a good dirty giggle over it. I only deal with genuine problems here, if you want smut turn to Marje Proops.

Dear Cousin Stephen, My girlfriend, whom I love very much,

is unable to satisfy my appetites, and I have started going to restaurants behind her back. I am terrified that if she sees me eating in a strange place she will end our relationship. Should I tell her before she finds out? Yours, 'Hungry'

Dear 'Hungry', There's more to a relationship than just plain eating you know. Of course for the first few weeks, food and mealtimes will be the most important thing you have between you, and you'll spend all day at the table together exploring each other's tastes and range of cooking styles. But if a relationship is to last, it's important you learn to find interests outside the kitchen. If she can't satisfy you at the moment, perhaps it's because you aren't telling her what you really want and need. Buy a cookery book, there are plenty available, showing a variety of cuisines that may be more to your taste. Happy stuffing!

Dear Cousin Stephen, To settle a bet, could you tell me whether Norwich City have ever won the Littlewoods Cup? My friend says they haven't, but I think they won it four or five years ago. Yours, 'Wanting-To-Know-Whether-Or-Not-Norwich-City-Have-Ever-Won-The-Littlewoods-Cup'

Dear 'Wanting-To-Know-Whether-Or-Not-Norwich-City-Have-Ever-Won-The-Littlewoods-Cup' – Hold on to your hat, you're *both* right!!!!!!! Norwich *did* win the Littlewoods Cup – or League Cup as it then was – but then the next year they didn't, and they haven't won it every single year since. Almost a record, rather like 'Ebony And Ivory', which was almost a record too.

Dear Cousin Stephen, Mr Dawlish – he's our Headmaster – says I have to do a double Maths period every Tuesday morning, but I hate Maths and it clashes with *Neighbours* the Australian soap on Daytime TV. Can you come round and shoot him in the head so that I can get off having to turn up? Lots of love, Dennis.

Dear Dennis, I wish I could help you, but you have a duty to go to school. I know you teachers don't get paid enough but there are lots of children relying on you to help them get through their exams, so buck up and get teaching.

Dear Cousin Stephen, I'm an unemployed Indoor Bowls Commentator and last week I found an original painting in my attic. It's signed by Van Gogh and I've had it valued at twenty-five million pounds. Do you think I should sell it? The painting goes so well above my mantelpiece that it would be a shame to get rid of it. My wife thinks I am potty. What do you advise? Yours, 'In a quandary'

Dear 'In a quandary', At your age certain changes take place in your body. New hairs start growing and your voice begins to crack. It's all perfectly natural and needn't upset you unduly. I am returning the photograph and yes, it is a strange shape, but then we all come in different shapes and sizes. I have to confess yours is the first one I've seen that looks like Esther Rantzen.

Well, that's all I've got time for this week! Next week I'll try my hand at negotiating with Gorbachev to try and rid the world of nuclear arms! Who knows, the week after that I might be in *your* town! Look out!!!!

Lots of love

Cousin Stephen

Lord's: The Great Lie

This was commissioned for a book called My Lords!, *a compendium of writings on the HQ of cricket.*

Lord's! The very word is an anagram of 'sordl'. The Headquarters of Cricket. The acre or so of green velvet nestling in the warm folds of St Johnners Wood. The acre (itself an anagram of 'hectare') that is girlfriend, mistress, mother, casual boyfriend, sergeant major, nurse-maid, father-confessor and one-night stand all rolled into one. All rolled into one by the heavy roller of memory, on the square of reminiscence; that square that slopes slightly at one end assisting the deviating swing of recall that causes the ball of thought to cut away from the norm of reality and catch the outside edge of fantasy that is snapped up by the cupped hands of fate.

Lawks! 'Each article should be crisp and to the point, elegant without being too elegiac and firmly rooted in first-hand personal experience.' There's a thing. I fear that in my opening paragraph I may just have been guilty of overstepping the mark. In these austere times the purple Cardus gets shown the yellow card. Time to crispen up. My first-hand experience of Lord's began as second-hand experience when, an engaging youngster with important new strains of impetigo and hair that could oil a Harrow-sized Stuart Surridge Special, I picked up *Psmith In The City* by P.G. Wodehouse. This masterly work, after *Ulysses* and the invention of the electric under-duvet, quite possibly the most important achievement of the twentieth century, contains a scene in which Mike Jackson, last and greatest of the cricketing Jacksons, is called upon to make up the numbers at a Lord's cricket match. Keats had a dash at explaining what he felt like when first peeping into Chapman's Homer, he said that he felt like some watcher of the skies who sees a new planet swimming into his ken: the experience, he went on to relate, wasn't so very unlike that of fat Cortez standing to the west of the Darien Gap and looking at the Pacific for the first time. I've not read Chapman's Homer. Don't ask me why: pressure of time; always been meaning to; never quite got round to it; promise it's first on the list for my next holiday, etc. etc., but I can assure you that *Psmith In The City* caused feelings in me by no means dissimilar to those which animated the bosom of John Keats.

'Lor!' I said to myself. From that day to this Lord's Cricket has exerted the most powerful influence over my being. But there's many a slip 'twixt wicket-keeper and gully. The influence has been, let us be quite clear about this, an entirely fantastic one. Let me attempt, in my fumbling way, to explain. Imagination, Iris Murdoch once remarked, in that way she has, is a creative force that comes from the individual soul: fantasy, she went sternly on to asseverate, is a non-creative force, it comes from the imagination of others. My fascination with Lord's is a result entirely of the fascination of others. There is a literature, a lore and a pre-selected attitude to Lord's already in place. That is what I have been seduced by.

Lore! That is what has done it. Let's be honest. It's a cricket ground less beautiful than many – Worcester and Adelaide spring to mind as more charming venues – whose place as an English cultural icon owes much to the eccentricity and absurdity of its foundation, the weirdness of the cricketing Lords who determine the laws and direction of cricket from its Long Rooms and Galleries and the heraldic peculiarities that surround the institution, Old Father Time, the irrelevant 'Marylebone' appellation of the society that uses the ground as its club room, the grotesque flame-like colourings of that club, the preposterous jacket-and-tie rules, the necessary spectre of spotted dick and starched nannies that is raised by the ground's 'Nursery', oh a hundred other wild and wonderful details that serve to create a flavouring and an atmosphere that is consonant with our Law Courts, our Constitution, our Royalty, our great Universities, public schools, gentlemen's clubs and other dotty splendours. 'What is your idea of heaven?' 'The Saturday afternoon of an Ashes match at Lord's.' 'What is your idea of hell?' 'The M25 on a Tuesday in February.' Lord's proffers an attainable paradise whose joy is entirely tribal. We are *told* that Lord's is heaven, it's our Heaven, a British heaven. If you can't accommodate this view of the place then you are seven kinds of stinker. Those are the laws.

Laws! Cricket has laws, not rules, and I'm prepared to obey them all. I'll be subversive, imaginative and independent three hundred and sixty days of the year, creating my paradise and my own sodalities; but when it comes to cricket I join in the common fantasy. I sit watching the white Druids waving their ju-ju sticks and I worship at the common shrine. For five days I *belong* to this silly country with its silly vanities, injustices, bigotries and cruelties. The whole crowd of spectators are my friends and we share a common secret, a common advantage over everyone else on the globe. I say to myself 'I'm *here!* To my left there's the famous clock, to my right the famous score-board, on the famous field are the famous players and I am part of the famous crowd on this famous first day of what will be this famous match.' I'm playing the game and I like it. Like Mike Jackson I'm playing at Lord's. I'm playing at being English. It's ludicrous, but then that's what ludicrous means: playing the game. I once sat next to Mick Jagger watching David Gower make a hundred against Australia. Can't get no greater satisfaction than that, now can you?

Lords! It isn't in London, it's in the mind, the collective unconscious of the British, like the Old Course at St Andrews and the village fête. Lord's isn't cricket, it has little to do with the multiplicity of physical talents and tactical thinking that make up the game, a game better expressed on a beach in Barbados or coconut-matting in Colombo. Lord's is an opportunity for a certain kind of Englishman to leave the world of edge-of-town shopping and Trust House Forte Conference Suites and dive head first into a beautiful, shameless, disgraceful, delightful and ludicrous lie.

The World Service

Another article written for Arena *magazine.*

This is London. *Ta diddy dah, di tah diddy dah, dah diddy dah, ti dah diddy tah. Yum tum tum-tum, tah tiddy tum tum, tum tiddy tah tum, tiddy dum dum, di diddy dum dum-dum, diddy dum dum-dum, diddy tum dum, tum tiddy dum dum.* Dip. Dip. Dip. Dip. Dip. Deeeeep. BBC World Service. The News, read by Roger Collinge . . .

The warm brown tones trickle out of Bush House like honey from a jar: rich and resonant on the Long and Medium Waves for domestic listeners or bright and sibilant on the Short Wave for a hundred million Anglophone citizens of the world for whose benefit the precious signal is bounced off the ionosphere from relay station to relay station, through ionospheric storms and the rude jostling traffic of a hundred thousand intrusive foreign transmissions, to arrive fresh and crackling on the veranda table. Oh, to be in England, now that England's gone. This World Service, this little bakelite gateway into the world of Sidney Box, Charters and Caldecott, Mazawattee tea, Kennedy's Latin Primer and dark, glistening streets. An England that never was, conjured into the air by nothing more than accents, march tunes and a meiotic, self-deprecating style that in its dishonesty is brassier and brasher than Disneyland. A Mary Poppins service, glamorous in its drab severity, merry in its stern routine and inexhaustible resource: a twinkling authoritarian that fulfils our deepest fantasy by simply staying, even though the wind changed long ago.

Ooh, I love it. It is my guide, philosopher and friend, the plaything of an idle hour and the study of an earnest; it is the cat on the lap of my days. Since I was twelve the wireless in my bedroom has been permanently tuned to 648 on the Medium Wave. If we are to believe the monstrous wicked nonsenses who make their money out of detecting trends and writing banal and obvious books about them, then listening to the World Service makes me a Young Fogey as surely as if I wore an eyeglass, joined The Travellers' and pretended never to have heard of Mick Jagger. They're wrong of course, these Creeps Unveiling New Trends and Images Every Season (there must be a simple acronym for them somewhere), there is nothing fogeyish about the World Service or those who listen to it. It is true that, to the casual listener, the news readers and announcers sound as if they are wearing dinner-jackets, but that is more a function of the need to speak slowly and clearly through unreliable frequencies and into the ears of non-native English-speakers, than an indication of its nature and style. The World Service is much more important than the quaint vestige of a vanished world that the Facile Analysts of Recent Trends In Eighties Society would like it to be.

So what is it, this World Service? Well, it is the chief English-speaking product of the BBC's External Services, which weekly broadcast thousands of hours of programming around the globe in scores of different languages.
Cripes, that must cost quite a wad. As is well known, the External Services are funded, not by the licence-payer, but by the Foreign Office.
Lawks. Yes indeed. The English-language World Service provides a continuous stream of broadcasting, something akin to our own Radio 4, and it is to this service, just one of so many, that we refer when we say BBC World Service.
Well, thank you. Not at all, anything else you want to know?
Don't think so. Fine, I'll —
Oh yes, is it all spoken word broadcasting then, this BBC World Service? By no means. Edward Greenfield presents a Classical Record Review, Paul Burnett a weekly top twenty chart programme, Bob Holness, Central TV's cult Blockbuster super-presenter, offers an MOR dedications slot called *Anything Goes*, Richard Baker presents his *Half-Dozen* once a week and there are lots of small features on opera, the musical, ballet, and choral music. In

addition there are regular programmes on Country Music and Folk, Tom Robinson fronts a new music feature —

Yes, yes, I've got the idea, you don't have to go on about it. I dare say I find out the rest in the Radio Times. Ah, well, that's just where you are wrong, my proud young beauty. There is a strange conspiracy afoot which goes out of its way to make it as difficult as can be to find out programming. It used to be almost impossible for a resident Briton to get hold of a copy of *London Calling*, the World Service listings magazine. The service was for the World, not for Britain. If one managed to pick up the signal at all, it was good fortune, not design, and it is still difficult to get good reception west or north of London upstream of the waves as they flow to Europe.

I suppose it paints a pretty rosy picture of Britain, being funded by the FO? I have tried as hard as I could over the years to detect any hint of overt or covert pro-British or anti-communist propaganda, bias or slant in the output of the World Service and failed. It really does seem to be as dispassionate and disinterested as it is possible to be. Indeed the grimmest portrait of Britain I have ever been offered outside *Duty Free* was I think that presented by a recent World Service programme on the now celebrated North–South Divide. Bitter interviews with Sunderland schoolchildren and South Eastern politicians pulled no punches whatsoever. Goodness knows what kind of picture of Britain the liverish ex-pat in India, the Canadian businessman, the Indian farmer, the Colombian coca-leaf exporter or the Australian corporate raider would have got: a truthful one, I suppose. Perhaps the only programme one could call remotely partisan is a funny little feature called *New Ideas*, the notion of which seems to be to plug new British inventions.

You said, rather pompously I thought, that it was akin to Radio 4. How akin? The similarity to our own Radio 4 is apparent the first time you listen. A large number of broadcasting staff from the BBC's domestic services is employed to present regular World Service programmes. Malcolm Billings, Margaret Howard, Chris Kelly, Benny Green, John Tidmarsh, Dave Lee Travis, Renton Laidlaw, these will all be familiar names to the audiophile. Actual Radio 4 programmes and plays can be heard: *Just A Minute*, *The Goon Show*, *My Music*, *Brain of Britain*, *Letter From America* and hundreds of others have all been given a global airing. But there is plenty of original programming too: *Meridian* the daily arts magazine, *Outlook*, the daily news and features programme, *Letterbox*, Margaret Howard's look at listeners' letters, *Radio Newsreel*, *Sports Roundup*, *Book Choice*, *Network UK*, *Europa*, *Short Story*, *The Merchant Navy Programme*. These and many others, including prestige dramas, are special World Service programmes, designed exclusively for the overseas listener.

Prestige Dramas? What do you mean 'prestige'? Oh I don't know. It means dramas that have got Michael Hordern in them, I suppose.

Lumme. Er, can I go now? Yes, yes. Off you trot.

You see the glory of the World Service is that, like Radio 4, it provides the last great outlet for the Spoken Word. The dominance of literary people and 'literariness' in the world of communication leads us to forget that radio is a more 'natural' way of communicating than print. Poetry and story-telling were the invention of non-literate societies. Printing effectively processed, packaged, distanced, controlled and modified the message. The oral tradition, the practice of using our voice and our language to do more than simply ask the way to the lavatory or complain at the loudness of the music, is under threat. Throughout the world, radio is simply a way of broadcasting news and music; television is fatally concerned with images, actions and spectacle; books have retreated into a ghastly world of awards and snobbery, and the drama – well, the drama has for some years been the preserve of the middle-brow, middle-class, middle-aged ironising articulately around a book-lined set.

But, by some freak of history, we happen to have a blooming domestic and external broadcasting station whose business is to talk to us. All we have to do is listen. The Good Lord gave us two ears and only one mouth, my dear white-headed mother used to say, before I got rid of her and acquired a younger one, more in keeping with my own tender age.

Am I being unpleasantly racist when I observe that Americans, who have no proper spoken word radio station, have virtually no auditory faculties either? In the past an American's ears were used to keep his spectacles on; with the universal adoption of the contact lens, it is probable that evolution may well phase out his ears completely over the next hundred years or so.

Who is telling the world stories, communicating ideas, fantasies and impressions? Who is instructing, entertaining, alarming and soothing us with the spoken word? Only Radio 4 in this country (and that at the price of having to soak up the toxic waste of mad listeners' letters and telephone calls) and only the World Service of the BBC across the globe. I do not believe that this is any cause for jingoistical rejoicing, however. If it were the Voice of America, the United States external service, that was of high quality instead of the World Service, then I would listen to that instead. As it happens, the Voice sets new standards in dreary propagandist nonsense. And so we are fortunate that, by historical accident, it is this country that holds the torch – and the great advantage of that is that no matter what part of the world we are in we can always get the Test scores.

Section Three

The Listener

Naked Children

As I was sweating away over the weekend with planks of wood and chisels trying to recall the principles of school carpentry, a friend called in and asked me just what the hell I thought I was doing. 'I have a hi-fi and nowhere to put it,' I said, 'and there comes a time when you have got to make a stand.'

And how right I was. There is a psychological crisis facing humankind which seems to have gone largely unnoticed: it is a crisis that strikes at the heart of what we are and what relationship we establish with our own souls.

When I was young, really very young indeed, absurdly young, quite tiny in fact, my doting parents used to photograph me. On summer days, in the exuberant simplicity of my youth, I would slip out of my clothes like a salmon and sport brightly and nudely on the green. In my confiding innocence I would wave at the lens, turn somersaults and delight in the fresh, unspoilt loveliness of life. Like most master criminals, my parents were then content to wait. The years passed and I entered that gangling, shuffling, blushing age which any day now I hope to leave. I began to bring friends home for inspection and to drink wine and talk languidly about neo-plasticism and the national characteristics of the Germans with a blend of informed tolerance and modest percipience that would have made Socrates sound like John Selwyn Gummer. Just as it would begin to emerge that I was clearly the most fascinating and urbane figure of my age and weight in the county, the air would suddenly be thick with photographs whose obscene frankness and intimate detail would cause even the most hardened child pornographer to clutch the table for support. When you've seen in detail a nude infant doing a backward somersault you know why clothing exists.

As friends stared glassily at photographs of me and the strange little barnacle that in those days passed for my organ of generation I tried to explain that the child they were scrutinising was not me. This was the biological as well as the psychological truth. Every cell in my body had by that time been replaced. P.G. Wodehouse's typewriter comes to mind as a model of this important phenomenon. He bought his Royal in the 1910s and used it right up to his death. But by then every part of it had been renewed: the chassis, the platen, the roller, the keys – everything. Was it still the *same* typewriter? Am I the same person? The philosopher's axe is sharper than Occam's Razor.

I was at least spared that new dimension of humiliation suffered by those whose parents used movie cameras and now squeeze their video camera triggers at anything that pops its head up. The BBC have decided that 'Attic Archives', as it calls the records of these crimes, are suitable matter for broadcast. Aside from the aesthetic horror of having to sit through those saturated Ectochrome blues and greens and experience the cheap melancholy of the sun and smiles that lit young flesh now long corrupted I am worried about the psychic dislocation that photography engenders. For thousands of years the only way a human being had of inspecting himself was to stand in front of a glass of some kind. This had the advantage of being 'live action', as it were. Go in front of a mirror and raise your right hand. Your reflection will do the same (always excepting that you are Groucho Marx, of course). We are masters of our own bodies, we control them. The one who looks out is the same as the one who looks in. But since the cine camera we have had this independence taken away from us. This is one of the many horrors of watching yourself on television. You see yourself with an odd expression on your face but try as you might you cannot remove it. This is a problem, by definition, only suffered by those born into the moving-camera age. The subject on the screen is not the one watching. You have been de-centred. You are capable of a self which can move, think, speak and affect others and over which you have yourself no control. This is a profoundly disrupting nightmare and goes a long way towards explaining some of the neurotic crises of identity that characterise our century.

For a few men and women, in Anthony Burgess's handsome phrase, 'adventitiously endowed with irrelevant photogeneity' to make a career out of being seen on screens is one thing. They're good at it and well paid for the howling insanity such a process inevitably provokes. But to encourage all mankind to split the atom of self is foolhardy in the extreme. Besides, as an Equity member, I'm not sure I like the idea of everybody getting in on the act.

The Family Curse

I don't want to waste your time by devoting this precious page, which is after all a fair-sized sliver of Canadian tree, to a discussion of Clause 28 or 29 or 30 or whatever number it might now be. You're a decent human being: you are as embarrassed to be living in a country which can have stained its statute books with so spiteful, repulsive and nauseating a collection of bigotries and lies as I am. The horror of it all should not be ignored or forgotten, but I prefer to move away from a specific lament to remind you that the tenor and thrust of the Legislation (if such a slimy smear swabbed from the epicentre of Satan's anal ring can be dignified with the name) is to criminalise the promotion of homosexuality as an acceptable equivalent of family life. Family life, family values, decent normal family, family fun, family shopping, family leisure. The word is used these days much as the word 'Aryan' was used in Germany during the 1930s. Anything that isn't Family is 'unfamily', and anything that is unfamily is unrepresentative of the joyful majority. The ruthless condemnation of unfamily values is therefore a populist democratic imperative.

Family schmamily, I say. What is it with us at the moment that this word should be transmogrified into a shining banner borne 'mid snow and ice that will lead us into a new golden age? It can hardly be a defence against the rise in the crime rate. After all, something like eighty per cent of murders are domestic in origin, child molestation and physical abuse are almost entirely family crimes and I believe there is only one recorded case of incest being practised outside a family and that turned out not to be incest after all.

It seems to me that if we are going to control thought in this country, and that would appear to be the intention of our wise, loving and humane masters, then some sort of Bill to forbid the promotion of family life would be timely and appropriate.

There is a programme on BBC2 called *Weekend*, the foulness of which is hard to communicate. Like any 'family' programme, whether hosted by Noel Edmonds or Frank Bough, it seems at first to be nothing more offensive than a celebration of Pringle knitwear, with elements of a Fred Perry sports-shirt parade. If only it were so innocent. It is in fact an apotheosis of the Family. The idea of the programme – harmless, indeed laudable, at first glance – is to provide information about weekend events around the country, or UK as they call it. The grisly side of the whole undertaking is that a 'typical family' is selected to try out some 'leisure activity' at one of the hundreds of 'heritage amusement happy parks', 'family fun centres' or 'activity theme happy fun, fun happy leisure happies' that are using up valuable space that could otherwise be devoted to less noxious enterprises, like the construction of fast-breeder reactors or Union Carbide factories. This 'typical family' spends a day at the Gehenna of the programme's choice and comes back to give 'points out of ten'. Safety of course is a prime consideration: is the activity theme play area adequately supervised? Does the netting of the wildlife and environment habitat centre, or 'zoo' as we call them in this country, have little pointy bits that might snag Jason's 'LA Rams' sweatshirt? All these things must be taken into consideration.

I cannot convey to you the sense of overwhelming misery that sweeps over me when I watch this and other horrors unfold. Marks & Spencer, for instance, are going 'edge-of-town hypermarket' because, according to a spokesman, 'family shopping' is where the future lies. Fond of my family as I am, and none could be fonder, I know for a fact that had any such procedure been regularly practised during my childhood I should have become a 'Family Massacre At Sainsbury's Checkout' headline before my tenth birthday.

Children want privacy from their parents, parents from their children. Independent and alternative interests, often parricidal in their nature or meaning, are essential. Parents shouldn't like their children's taste in music, clothes, television or friends and *vice versa*. At least they shouldn't *have* to, or be expected to. Nor should we be expected to like our government's taste in values, moral outlook and foreign policy. You won't huddle me into a great Christian national family that doesn't talk to queers, expects the sick and disabled to receive charity and gives a good thrashing to anyone who dares to cheek our policemen and soldiers or asks too many impertinent questions.

Obedience, compulsion, tyranny and repression are family words as much as love, compassion and mutual trust. It rather depends on the family. I wonder which sort of 'family values' we most readily associate with our government? Well, I don't really wonder: it's all too plain.

A Glimpse of The Future

TWENTY YEARS' TIME
Continuing our occasional selection of extracts from The Listener
as they appeared twenty years ahead. This week an article from The
Listener *in June 2008.*

**The infamous spy Simon Mulbarton speaks from his cell
in Wellington, New Zealand.**

Yes, I had gone up to Cambridge in '79, and it was there
that I became a Thatcherite. I know it sounds extraordinary
now, but you see it was very much the fashion. There was a
tremendous amount of unemployment, recession, racial tension
in those days, and a lot of us undergraduates were naturally
ardently cynical and passionately realistic, and so we drifted
into monetarism, Friedmanism, and some of us into outright
Thatcherite/Reaganism. Remember, too, we had the great cause
of the Falklands War to rally behind: a lot of older undergraduates
flocked to join up, it was like an ideological battle-cry for us to
defend the overdog. You have to understand the atmosphere of the
times, you see. There were a lot of very influential unintellectual
dons there, Casey, Cowling, Roger Scruton, pillars of the establishment and columns in the *Salisbury Review* – Thatcherism was
very much in the air amongst us more unthinking students. We
read a lot of Paul Johnson and Ferdinand Mount, and their new
ideas of grabbing what you can for yourself, letting the market
control things, squashing the trades unions and so forth, had very
great appeal to a new generation of selfish young people frightened
at the prospect of not getting a job. Some of us had even visited
America, under Reagan, who had been elected earlier, and we were
inspired by what we found there – you have to understand that this

was before it became apparent that the man had completely lost control of his senses – it all seemed so simple and appealing.

I was first approached by someone from the CIA in 1980, I remember, during my second year up, at a meeting of the Disciples Club, an élite gathering of top right-wing students. We took it in turns to read the others a paper: the *Mail*, the *Express*, *Sun* – whatever: some of the more extreme members were of course quite unable to read. Anyway, I was approached by a don from Peterhouse who had been a Washington man for some years and he asked me if I'd be prepared to work for the CIA. I agreed readily.

I had never made any secret of my right-wing allegiance, and when after Cambridge I was accepted into the Foreign Office, I think they were perfectly well aware where my sympathies lay. I began feeding my various Washington contacts with information straight away. I never thought of myself as a traitor. After all, the Americans had fought on our side during two world wars. They had been our allies. We owed them that. We owed the same thing to the Russians, of course, but that isn't how we looked at it. America was the great white hope of greedy capitalism, and we believed in it. I thought that in being pro-American I was serving Britain's best interests.

Obviously it's very easy to see now, with hindsight, that I was completely misguided, but remember that it wasn't until the early 1990s that we began to grow disillusioned with Thatcher and Reagan and saw what really lay behind their appealing façade. By then, of course, it was too late for those of us in deep cover. There were many of us, some very highly placed members of key establishments: the BBC was riddled with right-wing anti-intellectuals, we'd had one man working for years on staff selection. Fleet Street was seamed and honeycombed with us, and as for MI5 . . .

They worked to try and persuade the public that the Soviet Union was a wicked enemy and America a benign friend. You'd think we might have had difficulty explaining away the invasion of Grenada, the propping up of El Salvador, the attacks on Nicaragua, and some of us did find all that hard to swallow, but people still flocked to our cause. America was pumping Britain full of cultural propaganda, you have to understand. Our moles in the media helped convince the British public that wanting to get rid of nuclear weapons was naïve, whereas the belief that possessing them would somehow permanently guarantee freedom from destruction was not naïve, and on the whole they managed it. Ironic as things turned out.[1] Of course they are all dead now, so they can't answer for what happened.

I was in New Zealand, ostensibly for the Foreign Office, in fact trying, on behalf of the CIA, to destabilise an absurdly naïve anti-nuclear government, when it all happened, so I was rather lucky. In a thousand years or so, when it's safe to go back to the Northern hemisphere, the records of those years will be intact. As I say, we really did believe that we were doing the right thing. And after all, that's what matters, isn't it?

[1]Doesn't seem that impressive a prediction in the light of What's Happened In Eastern Europe, does it?

Friends of Dorothy

I have recently had the honour to be involved in two rather colossal and heart-warming events both of which, for one reason or another, have been more or less ignored or patronised by the squalid lobsters who scuttle on the floor of our society, which is to say the press.

The first was a fairly gigantic stage show at the Piccadilly Theatre which aimed to laugh contemptuously at the vicious little squirts behind the infamous Section (*quondam* Clause) 28. The *Standard* which, for those fortunate enough to live outside London, is as grotesquely partisan a newspaper as is permissible without actually dropping pretence and coming out as a Tory party broadsheet, and which was as responsible as any other organ for the very piece of legislation under advisement by consistently overplaying the infinitesimally small sums of money laid out by Labour councils and the GLC to unhappily named 'Lesbian Theatre Co-operatives' and the like, contrived studiously to ignore the evening, managing to find on the following day only a story about some deranged Tory who thought the Clause needed to be 'strengthened'. The show was designed specifically to 'promote' homosexuality within the (doubtful) meaning of the Act by having works performed which were exclusively by gay writers, playwrights and composers. Obvious names like Auden, Shakespeare, Wilde, Tchaikovsky, Orton, Britten and Marlowe and perhaps more surprising names (to some) like Edward Lear, Saint-Saëns, Noël Coward and A.E. Housman contributed the material. The performers included many 'straight' artists and musicians, like Dames Judy Dench, Joan Plowright and Peggy Ashcroft and names like Tom Stoppard, Simon Rattle and Paul Eddington whom it vastly annoys members of the raving right to see associate themselves with such causes. Surely that nice man from *Yes Minister* can't want nuclear disarmament or sexual tolerance? It is a short step from that kind of annoyance, the kind of 'why are all the clever people on the left?' whine, to statements like 'actors should stick to acting'. This – coming from illiterate Yahoos and slobbering drunkard hacks who can barely thread a piece of paper through a typewriter, let alone stop to be charming, humane and friendly to their fellow citizens, yet daily imagine themselves qualified to mouth off any piece of bile that occurs to their dulled senses – seems a bit rich.

The second entertainment with which I was involved was altogether a vaster and more trumpeted affair. This was the great Wembley birthday party for Nelson Mandela. My own reaction to this centres chiefly around the acute embarrassment felt at the fact that my microphone didn't work properly for the first minute or so of my 'set', as we rock and rollers call an act. One can add to that the curious circumstance that while even Margaret Thatcher has been resolute in her calls for Mandela to be released and for apartheid to be dismantled, the preponderance of the press continued to present the thing as some kind of anarcho-Stalinist rally.

The question as to when P.W. Botha, whom the whole world recognises to have no mandate to rule the peoples of his unhappy republic, agrees to renounce violence and his control over an aggressive army and police force, seems irrelevant to feature writers in that same *Standard* whose television reviewer seems to be the only journalist on the paper with both sides of the brain connected. A feature headlined 'The Biased Broadcasting Corporation' seems to me to cast doubt on the sanity of the entire sub-editorial staff.

Cromwell, Éamon de Valera, Menachem Begin, Nasser, Ortega, De Gaulle, Mugabe, Shamir, Castro, Kenyatta – these are just a few names of statesmen (not all of them first choices for a cosy bedmate, I grant you) who began life as 'terrorists', as 'men of evil with whom we will not talk'. The tyrants they supplanted were in all cases, I contentiously claim, worse rulers of their people than their successors and are rightly represented now as 'terrorists' themselves.

But those who choose, even in a celebratory act, to believe in the democratic spirit, are denounced as 'naïve' at best and 'sinister' at worst. *The Times*, whose only intellectual accomplishment aside from its crossword and parliamentary sketch-writer is the bewildering variety of ways it manages to dispraise the BBC in a manner that promotes its proprietor's wretched satellite system, attempts a lofty condemnation of these galas. The events are 'trivialisations' of 'affairs too complex for pop-singers' minds to grasp'. What complexities these are and how a *Times* leader-writer's mind is capable of grasping anything other than the fact that broadcasting in Britain must be 'opened up' we are not privileged to know.

History, fortunately, will forget these banausic and irrelevant gnats, but not before thousands more die screaming in South Africa under the premiership of a man who is freedom's friend as much as Margaret Thatcher is Dorothy's.

For those of you who do not know what a friend of Dorothy is: ask a policeman or one in five Tory MPs.

Thatcher on TV

Margaret Thatcher – and let's face it, there are no two finer words available with which to begin a sentence, their power to draw the reader in is matchless – demonstrates a weird human paradox which charmingly exemplifies the hopeless chiasmal symmetry of polar oppositions. For in the case of M.H. Thatcher, the right-wing press make much mention, in her defence and towards her glory, of the circumstance that she is, in their belief, the most detested and vilified politician in living memory, this they say proves her worth and significance. The left-wing press, or at least, such of it as there is, makes quite as much of the fact that she is the most lauded and deified leader of modern times, a fact, they are convinced, which clearly highlights her evil. Each wishes to prove, by pointing up the extreme reaction of the other, the supreme importance of the woman: in the one case her importance as a force for good, in the other as a force for ill.

With my own views on the chintzy, lacquered creature who governs our state, I do not wish to burden you. Of Lady Bracknell, Jack, in *The Importance of Being Earnest*, remarks 'she is a monster, without being a myth, which is rather unfair'. Our Prime Minister is probably a myth without being a monster, which is unfairer by far. I dare say she is socially and privately as charming a person as ever one could meet, but the myth is as monstrous as can be. If only it were the other way around.

Well that's what I *would* have said, before I heard a rather disturbing story about her, since confirmed by other sources. It concerns an occasion when a television crew came to record an interview with her, quite early on in her premiership. An interview with someone like her is designated, by documentary production teams, a 'Grade A Priority Assignment'. On such assignments certain personnel are doubled: electricians, sound recordists and so on. On the day of this interview Mrs Thatcher, taking a look at the large number of people around her, asked in what I am assured (by a Tory as it happens) was a far from friendly voice, whether or not it was really necessary for there to be so many people employed on a single interview. This government's publicly expressed wish to 'do something' about overmanning in the television industry, tells us what was in her mind when she asked this question. Aside from the sheer arrogance and impoliteness of all but stating outright in their presence that you suspect fellow citizens of being sponging passengers, hitching a free ride on the back of luxurious union-enforced regulations, her petulant question shows a great lack of imagination.

Anyone who has ever had any dealings with film or television crews, especially on location, will know that the key element is time. Lighting takes a great deal of it. Film and video cameras are vastly inferior to the human eye and, if subjects are not carefully and skilfully lit, the resulting picture is inferior. I can well imagine the outcry in the press and Tory Central Office (if there is any difference between those two charitable foundations) were Mrs Thatcher to be shown underlit, overlit, or lit so as to make her look sinister, fat, dirty, ill-nourished, mad-eyed, apoplectic or any of the other deceptive conditions bad lighting can impose. Within a television studio where purpose-built lights can more rapidly be controlled, it is a fairly simple matter to light for an interview. But Thatcher is Prime Minister, her time is, one must assume, reasonably valuable. As far as television interviews are concerned the mountain is usually willing to come to Mohammed. Ten-kilowatt lamps do not hang in vast numbers from the ceiling in Downing Street. Hence the larger than average crews assigned. But apparently, at least on this occasion, the Prime Minister was quite unable to see any of this, all she saw was an opportunity to make a waspish remark about overmanning, so alienating a large group of people who were excited to be in her presence and keen to take up as little of her time as necessary.

I don't want to make too much of this event, we all have bad days, naggy, catty days, and I am not arguing that this event proves once and for all that the woman is a shrieking Medusa, but I would say on the general subject of staffing levels, that those who use the phrase 'overmanning' seem mostly to prefer money to people. A Chinese restaurant that employs forty waiters doesn't make us angry – the profits are lower but they get by, they provide for their family and serve the customer all the more quickly. But when it comes to public service industries, just 'getting by' becomes inadequate, and providing for our wider family at the cost of lower profits, unthinkable. And so we remain hard-pressed, over-worked, and – socially – underlit.

Sock Fury

I am angry. I am really angry. I am so angry I can barely go to the lavatory. I am fuming. I don't think I've ever been crosser. If you poured boiling jam down the back of my neck, set fire to my trousers, defecated on the back seat of my car and forced me to stare without blinking at the cartoon of myself that accompanies this article I couldn't be more furious. Hopping mad about sums it up. The reason for my ungovernable fury is simple to relate. I've lost my sock. The one I had intended to put on this morning. Its twin languishes alone on the floor of my bedroom, denied the awesome privilege of sheathing my right foot because of the immortal cheek of its wayward brother. I've had to find another pair. To put the lid on the whole sorry business I spilt coffee granules all over the kitchen floor. These two appalling catastrophes have combined to push my blood-pressure up so high that there is some danger of my sustaining a severe nose-bleed.

Now, I'd be the first to concede that in the cool, clear light of logic there is nothing bowel-shatteringly significant about these two incidents. I dare swear that in a day or two I will have forgotten all about them. Well, give it a week. What is so infuriating is the *fact* that I am incensed by two such nugatory, not to say trivial, hiccoughs in the life of one who generally speaking doesn't have too much to kvetch about. You see, a human being has only a certain amount of choler to expend and I have a horrid feeling that I could never, ever, in my life be more angry about anything than I was fifteen minutes ago when I ransacked my room in search of this blasted benighted god-forsaken bloody sock, which even as I write is probably laughing itself sick behind the wainscotting or wherever it is that the foul thing has chosen to hide. And it won't do. Whatever strange moral, ethical or evolutionary purpose anger was designed to serve, getting batey about errant footwear can't be said to come anywhere near the top of the list. Yet I swear that if you were to attach an irometer or crossness sensor to my brain its needle would shoot straight to the red line where the dial reads 'Danger. Extreme Overload. Evacuate' quicker than a rabbi from a gnu.

The same is true of happiness, of course. If I were left a billion pounds by an eccentric tycoon, asked to open the bowling for England, given a new cartoon for my *Listener* column, offered the chance to perform the topping-off ceremony on a new multi-storey car park built in Nicholas Ridley's back garden, I should of course be madly, deliriously, absurdly happy. But not any happier than I was when, at the age of eleven, I discovered a ten-shilling note in the pocket of an old pair of shorts. Certainly no more ecstatic than when I was taken by mother, aged six (me, that is, not my mother: she was significantly older), to see *A Hard Day's Night*. I simply do not possess the capacity to feel any greater joy than that which lit me from within when Rolf Harris gave me his autograph backstage at the Britannia Pier, Yarmouth. Any simple felicity gauge would back up my claims.

So what price the world? If I tremble with rage at a mislaid gentleman's half-hose or wriggle with pleasure when a bearded Australian writes his name on a ticket stub, what have I left in the emotion-bank for genocidal injustice or universal peace? It's no good trying to imagine that those who suffer torture and cruelty and poverty feel exactly as if they've lost a sock, only it happens to be a very beautiful sock, with wonderful clocks and an attractive heel-panel, because it simply won't wash. Well, with a modern powder at today's lower temperatures and a little liquid fabric conditioner it'll come up lovely as a matter of fact . . . what I mean is that the argument doesn't cut any ice.

Am I then to assume that my life is so empty, my existence so vapid and barren, my mind so shallow, facile and unsympathetic, that the only event capable of engendering wrath in me is the loss of a small, foot-shaped tube of cotton? That really is a ghastly notion. If I thought it was true I would have to end it all. But what kind of a suicide note could one leave? 'Realised that my anger about the sock was unjustified and proved me valueless. If it is found amongst my effects please have it stuffed and mounted and presented to the nation as a warning to others.' Not much of an epitaph is it?

I suppose I'll have to fill in my credit card mail-order catalogue and send away for . . . 'The Sock Caddy, available in executive green or boardroom burgundy and personalised with up to one of your initials. Two tough, weather-resistant, distressed leather trays that provide twenty-four hour, round the clock protection for your socks. We call it the Bedroom Friend.'

But imagine waking up to the sight of such a thing. I'd be livid.

Wimbledon Horror

Somewhere in England there lives the git whose aural graffiti (unless some philanthropic dubbing mixer decides otherwise) will permanently mar the taped record of this year's men's singles finals at Wimbledon. He is the vandal who never tired of bellowing 'Come on Stefan' at precisely the least appropriate moment during the stormy, unpredictable course of that excellent match. His verbal daubs incited contrasting screams of 'Come on Boris' which provoked yet more variations upon the original theme until it sounded as if a million macaws had been let loose in one part of the Centre Court and meant to have it out with the four million assorted kookaburras and cockatoos who were being horribly raped in the other. The giggling, prating, graceless home-counties hooligans responsible for making these vile, barbarian ululations are horribly mistaken if they imagine either that a) Edberg is in any way edified or Becker becalmed by the erotomaniac squeals and pithecanthropoid bellows of their brain-damaged supporters, or that b) viewers across the world separate these acts of yelling barbarism from the less physically destructive but more publicly cursed rampages of British fans across Europe that the yelling tennis fans no doubt join in smugly condemning as disgracefully injurious to our reputation abroad.

It is a bizarre fact that the more widespread and accepted the cliché the less basis in truth it is likely to have. The prime example of this is the hoary old lie that most clichés have a basis in truth. It seems to me that clichés are a despairing attempt to create a truth by insisting upon one, rather like the bar-room braggart's boasts of Don Juanism which reveal nothing more than bedroom inadequacy. Take for instance clichés about the British. 'The British are tolerant.' Pooh. What other developed democracy has such a ridiculous and squalid history of intolerance? From the imprisonment and roasting of heretics, witches and poachers, to the censorship of literature, art and television: from St Alban through Wilde, Joyce and Lawrence I think we can point with pride to as grim a catalogue of intemperate, bigoted repression as any nation on earth. The much vaunted British love of the countryside? What price the green belt in the acid-rain-inducing dustbin of Europe? Where be your hedgerows now? Your pimpernels and water meadows that were used to set the poets in a roar? Those who speak of the great British breakfast would perhaps be surprised that bacon and eggs with toast or tea have been consumed for ages in other countries too, without any sense from the partakers of those collations that they were doing anything other than tucking into the great Danish breakfast or the great Rwandan breakfast or the great New Zealand breakfast. If our history of bear-baiting, pit ponies and ejected Christmas puppies can honestly be called a great British love affair with animals then the average praying mantis and her husband are Darby and Joan. And those hideous, screeching, baying howls from hell that yearly destroy Wimbledon argue that the British are imbued with a sense of justice and fair-play about as much as Hitler was full of a spirit of coy playfulness. The best legal system in the world? Do us a favour.

Quoting Doctor Johnson is the last refuge of the scoundrel, so I will desist. I am no hater of Britain or the British, but as someone somewhere once said, 'a patriot loves his country: a nationalist hates everyone else's.' We would have so much more cause to love this place if those much bandied clichés really did hold water.

But I do love this country, as Cordelia loved Lear. All the Gonerils and Regans who protest such a vast, sweeping, unthinking love seem to be doing the least to make it a place worth living in. Shouting that we are tolerant does not make us so: claiming without the slightest knowledge of other countries that this institution or that tradition within Britain is 'the best in the world' only serves to make us look ridiculous. Yelling and screaming at tennis players while they try to play seems to me to make Wimbledon even more miserable than the one clichaic fact about Britain that really does, as it were, hold water – the weather.

Saying Fuck

I am not sure whether Norris McWhirter would care to add to his *Guinness Book of Records*, after due verification and controlled testing by Roy Castle, the improbable claim for an all-comers British Record that I am about to make. I believe, and am open to refutation from those who know better, that I have said the word 'fuck' on television more times in one sitting than anyone of my age and fighting weight in the kingdom. It may be that McWhirter in his capacity as leading light of the libertarian organisation into which he pours his splendid energies will find this a frivolous and disgraceful record. It would make a semantic nonsense of the British Freedom Association (if that is its correct style and title) should he actually disapprove of people saying the word 'fuck' on television, but then people more wicked than he have made a nonsense of meaning in the name of freedom, so I wouldn't be particularly surprised.

The details of the meeting which saw the lowering of Kenneth Tynan's old record are important. The conditions were ideal for such a bold attempt: a live, late-night discussion programme hosted by, if memory doesn't betray, Roger Cook and Susan Jay, familiar to viewers everywhere. The venue was the Central TV studio complex in Nottingham. The studio audience was composed of students and pensioners. Fellow discussioners included Michael Bentine, Ben Elton, John Lloyd (the TV producer, not the tennis player – nor indeed the ex-editor), Hugh Lloyd, self, Barry Cryer and scriptwriter Neil Shand. The subject under advisement was comedy.

The producers presented the thing as a vicious war of words in which old and new comedy were to tear polemical strips off each other. 'The battle lines are drawn up for the war of the comics' bugled the introductory script, much to our surprise. If it weren't bad enough that Ben Elton should reveal a genuine love and admiration for Eric Morecambe, Laurel and Hardy and Tommy Cooper, what should happen but that Barry Cryer should lavish praise on Rik Mayall, Rowan Atkinson and Elton himself? This was as adversarial as *Stars on Sunday*.

The subject of shocking language arose. A few comments were made on either side and then I was asked to comment. I tried to remember from my reading of a transcript of the famous trial, and crediting him duly, what Richard Hoggart's argument had been when defending the language of *Lady Chatterley's Lover*. We have simple, direct words which describe human functions like eating and sleeping, the argument ran, but when it came to reproduction, we only allow ourselves to use on the one hand cumbersomely medical and latinate phrases like coition, copulation and coitus or, on the other, hideously twee and periphrastic euphemisms like 'intimacy', 'love-making', 'carnal knowledge' and the rest of it. The same applies to our inability to find a simple word to describe the act of expelling waste solids through our bottoms: evacuating, passing stools, doing number ones, defecating and excreting all rather hedge around the business, as it were. The word 'shit' doesn't. This circumlocution and sanitisation argues a guilt and an embarrassment about these physical processes which is surely unhealthy. If we came upon a culture that felt a sense of shame about breathing or yawning and insisted upon using alternatives like 'inhale' and 'pandiculate', I think we should believe it odd. How much odder that we should find sex dirty and wish linguistically to disinfect it?

If television and radio and the magazines all used the word 'fuck' as a matter of course, expressly *not* as an expletive or expression of abuse or frustration, but in its real sense, I really would not be surprised if we did not end up a healthier nation for it. If school teachers describing animals talked about the way in which they fucked rather than 'the mating process', if barristers and judges used 'fuck' in court cases where penetration is an issue, instead of relying on those strange forensic phrases 'intimate contact' and 'physical relationship', if parents used it when explaining reproduction to their children, then a generation would grow up for whom the word held no more mysterious guilty terrors and strange dirty thrills than the word 'omelette'. What would that do to the sex crime statistics? Were we to have taboos about the word 'kill' or the words 'maim' and 'torture', however, it might perhaps be healthy: cruelty and homicide are things we really should be ashamed of.

Anyway, what with one thing and another, I found myself using this word 'fuck' and its many cognates about eighteen times in three minutes, smashing all known records out of sight. Susan Jay's eyes glazed over slightly and her left knee wobbled a little, but all in all she withstood the blast like a game professional. What proves the thesis, for which I take no credit, is the fact that Central TV logged no complaints about that edition of the programme.

There is nothing shocking about the word 'fuck': what shocks is that we find it shocking. That's a coitus of a worry. In fact, it scares the fæcal solids out of me.

Worse – By Design

We live, as did Lady Bracknell, in an age of surfaces. Our problem is compounded by the sorry fact that surfaces are not what they were. Is it formica, or is it false formica? Is that a real mask? How true is that lie? Is this a genuine nose? I suppose it is partly the fault of our age's entrapment within two modes, the visual and the literary, both of which need, for their effect, to keep a firm grip on fantasy. Take *The Listener* and its pretty new costume. Does the design reflect the real identity of the magazine, or does it create a new identity that the readership and contributors, given a fair following wind, will eventually catch up with? I don't think you have to be vastly cynical to believe that the latter case fits. The image is the fact. The literary mode that infects us may be considered to be on a higher plane, but is equally false, and therefore equally true. A book is judged, not by its reference to life, but by its reference to other books.

In railing against the spectacular as extruded by television, film and this new world of 'design' that threatens to engulf us, the literary-minded elevate the book and the written word to a degree of aboriginal reality that is as absurd and dishonest as claiming that the trouble with computer games is that they stop people watching television. Writing and books are technology: they happen to be older than sit-com, that's all. They are as responsible for creating styles and reflexes of thought and expression as any commercial or Hollywood blockbuster. Don't get me wrong: books are great and good, but a thoughtless snobbery that respects them as totems and pathways to enlightenment, truth and Vedic happiness in themselves is dangerous and deluded. There is a technology, younger than books perhaps, but older than television, that gives us access to a much more genuine form of human intercourse than reading a false literary language or watching spectacular images. I'm talking about the technology that gave this very magazine its name. Wireless telegraphy, the radio broadcast.

At a time when the spoken word is forgotten in the rush to design a new masthead for a magazine or devise a new video technique for a young person's TV show it is worth considering the proposition that radio, to paraphrase Forster rather horribly, is the deepest of the media and deep beneath the media. I'm talking about speaking radio of course, not music stations.

Radio suffers from one tragic defect, however. It isn't cool, or sexy, or whatever quality it is that gets people in brasseries excited. Design is sexy, books and magazines are cool, music is both those things. But a human voice in intimate contact with a listener is considered as cool and sexy as a barn owl.

I don't know what it will take to interest the Groucho Club, *Blitz* magazine and logo designers in radio. For all the above-mentioned reasons it is necessary for them to be interested in it before the public will be, for design and style comes first. Radio 4 can't change its masthead and typeface to make itself appear suddenly more interesting: its independence from that kind of design manoeuvre is, after all, what makes it so interesting in the first place.

My fear is that some fearful gink from a place calling itself The Logo Factory or something equally foul will approach the controller of Radio 4 and persuade him that there is some way he can smarten up the 'image' of the station and before we know where we are it will be a *Network* 7 of the airwaves. By their own terms anything as styleless as the Home Service falls into a category entirely of their own devising which is variously called Old Fogey, Young Fogey or Institutional Dreary. If you accept that lie, then you have to accept the greater lie that something needs to be done about it. If you are persuaded to believe that the silver birch is insipid and 'bad design' (whatever that much bandied phrase may mean) then you can soon become persuaded that the time has come to spray it gold.

Oh dear, I do sound appallingly old fashioned, don't I? But of course I don't *sound* anything, this is a written article, not a spoken. So it's a lie. I've hidden behind phrases and words that delude and ensnare. If I was talking you could tell exactly what

I meant. Perhaps *The Listener* should redesign itself again. As a tape cassette. I can see the sleeve. The word 'the' in ITC Bookman Bold oblique, the word 'listener' in a sort of Stack Helvetica with torn paper effect. Could work, Marcus what do you think? I'll get Cyprian and Zak onto it and fax something over to you . . .

Christ

I'm not much of a theologian, but I know my St Ignatius from my Ian Paisley – my Loyolists from my Loyalists as you might say – and can spot the difference between a Pelagian and a gnostic at fifty paces. I am puzzled however, I must confess, by this problem of offence. I am referring of course, as who isn't these days, to Martin Scorsese's new film *The Last Temptation of Christ*. I would like fully to understand the objections to it. As I am not a Christian it may be held that it is not my business to understand or comment on the doctrines of the faithful, but I do not believe that it is excessively perverse to ask why the opportunity to watch the latest film of one of the most important and obsessively moral film makers of the last twenty years might be denied me.

I am not overstating the case when I describe Scorsese in that fashion. I remember an interview he gave to Melvyn Bragg, years ago now, during which he was asked what he thought his films were mostly about. Sitting there, low in a preview-cinema seat and blinking like a timid *curé*, he replied, without hesitation, that they were about sin and redemption. I thought of *Boxcar Bertha*, of *Mean Streets, Taxi Driver, Alice Doesn't Live Here Anymore, Taxi Driver, Raging Bull, The King of Comedy*, as remarkable and serious an *oeuvre* (as we cineasts like to call them) as any director could lay claim to and I sort of understood his point. Whatever else these films may be, they are not populist, commercial trash. They are as close as Hollywood ever gets to 'serious cinema' these days.

What upsets those who, like me, have not seen the film but have only heard tell of it, is, I believe, a scene in which Christ has some kind of erotic fantasy. I gather that the picture does not make light of his suffering, mock him, underplay his achievements or present him as anything other than the impassioned Son of God that Christians believe him to be. It does that which art does best: it shows a human being to us, just as Shakespeare showed us Antony and Cleopatra, with more regard for human truth than for historical.

This is particularly appropriate in the case of Jesus Christ for, as I understand it, his triumph on earth rests on the fact that he was fully a man. God, the argument runs, abdicated all his divinity and made himself one hundred per cent flesh. He ate food therefore, he wept, suffered, slept, went to the lavatory and in all other ways sustained the thousand natural shocks the flesh is heir to. Christians have no right, if they accept this story, to rail at God and say 'you don't know what it's like, being a human', the Christian story is all about God showing that he did find out precisely what it was like, and thereby offering us an opportunity of salvation. I think it is a magnificent story: humane, profound, fascinating and complex. That I don't happen to believe it is essentially my problem, it's not something I'm proud of or ashamed of. That the Church that grew from it has so signally failed to live up to its promise is no reflection on Jesus. As Cranmer said, there was not anything by the wit of man devised that was not in part or in whole corrupted. But the point, the whole point, of the story is the remarkable paradox of a divine humanity. If Christ was not in real pain when on the cross then the story is meaningless. Any God could *pretend* to be in pain, this one apparently paid us the supreme compliment of *really* suffering.

But now he is in heaven, on the right hand of God the Father and moving about us as the Holy Spirit. He looks down on cruelty, on savagery, on murder, tyranny and pain. These things cannot occasion him pleasure – nor can they his children. Then how can it be, by dint of what measure of tragic insecurity and doubt can it be true, that so many of his followers and worshippers make more fuss about a film that attempts honestly to examine the fullest human dimension of his life on earth than they do about the daily pain and viciousness that goes on around them? If God genuinely believes that an attempt to portray him on screen as a full human being is a greater sin than the million other injustices that pervade our globe then we're in real trouble. If he doesn't, then why is it that the only time Christians band together as a force to be reckoned with is when they wish to censor and condemn?

I repeat, I am not a Christian, and when journalists of the shining human qualities of Paul Johnson attack this film on behalf of the 'one and a half billion Christians' on earth, as he did recently in the *Daily Mail*, I beg to be excused from that number. It may then be said that this denies me the right to comment on Christian feelings. That may be true, but if we are going to return to a theocracy which proscribes certain productions of art and writing I would ask Christians to become as exercised by injustice and cruelty as they are by heterodoxy. That's all.

I am saddened by the full knowledge, which any writer or broadcaster will understand, that this article which I have been at pains to make as inoffensive as possible (God will forgive, I hope, my disinclination to join in the twee convention of spelling his personal pronoun with capital aitches) is bound to provoke from professors of Christianity personal letters to me of a ferocity and bile that those who have never dared to write about religion in public would scarcely believe. Why the adherents of the gentle and extraordinary Christ who died on the cross two thousand years ago should be so intolerant of those unfortunate enough not to have embraced his doctrines I do not know, but if Martin Scorsese has offended God then I am sorry, and I am sure Mr Scorsese is sorry too.

All I ask is that I be allowed to see this film. If it makes a mockery of Christ then I will condemn it. If it makes a mockery of bigots I will praise it. To the heavens.

Bikes, Leather and After Shave

I don't know what has happened to me recently – some kind of hormonal change perhaps – but there is no doubt that I have altered quite significantly over the past few months. I am a changed man. Perhaps Virgo has once more been rising in the fifth house from the left, not counting the tobacconist. I don't think it can be the male menopause, not at thirty-one years old, and it can't be my mid-life crisis, I had that at twenty-seven. Well, let me unload the facts and you can judge for yourselves. There are three key alterations, three hiccoughs in the epiglottis of my life to which I would draw your attention.

Item: on or about the middle of February this year I started wearing leather jackets. Nothing strange about that, you might think. But if I tell you that on or about the *beginning* of February this year I would have been the first to lay substantial bets against my ever being seen dead in a rubbish skip wearing any such thing, you might give pause. I have never, ever, in all my born daze even considered myself to be anything remotely resembling a simulacrum of a thought of a shade of an approximation of a suggestion of a suspicion of a leather jacket kind of person. I never held anything against those who did wear them, you must understand, but I knew Golden Bear bomber jackets in distressed goat and Harringtons of supple calf were simply not me. I was Mr Dunn & Co., barely able to walk past Simpsons of Piccadilly without a Daks floor-walker rushing out and trying to hire me as a mannequin. Tweed and cords and stout walking brogues for me and if they were called the 'Balmoral' or the 'Blenheim thornproof', then so much the better. But suddenly it's chinos, Bass Weejun loafers and creaking leather jackets. Peculiar.

Item: on or about the end of February this year I walked into a shop in the Euston Road and rode out of it half an hour later on a motor-bike. Again this may not strike you as worthy fodder for an episode of *The Twilight Zone* but once more I have to assure you that nothing can have been further from my mind a fortnight earlier. Cars I love, can't have too many of the things, but motor-bikes? I had never stood astride one in my life until that afternoon and there I was wobbling out of the shop and into one of the busiest roads in Europe while the salesmen held their breaths. Knowing what I now know I would never have done anything so fatuous, but then I never would have known what I know now had I not. What Hardy would have called one of life's little ironies. The kind of little irony that can lead to you being scraped off the road with a spoon. A cousin of mine who was a casualty surgeon in Manhattan tells me that he and his colleagues had a one-word nickname for bikers: Donors. Rather chilling.

The astute connecting thinkers amongst you will believe that there is some connection between the twin purchases of leather jacket and motor-bike. Perhaps you are right, but it was all subconscious, I had no idea when I bought the jacket that I would shortly be buying a bike, and it only occurred to me when I was on my bike that it was a good thing that I was wearing a leather jacket, because the 'Blenheim' may well be thorn-proof but it is a lot less sliding-across-rough-tarmac-at-30mph-proof than good leather.

Item: on or about the middle of April this year I bought from a chemist a bottle of after shave and a bottle of *eau de cologne*. Again hardly fit material for Ripley, but the fact is of the three events I still find this the weirdest. I mean, *after shave*? Me? I could more readily have pictured myself dabbing pig's urine on my cheeks than *Le Vétiver de Paul Guerlain*.

So there you are. I throw myself on your judgment, like an adolescent, with the question – What is happening inside me? What do these changes mean?

The most obvious answer, I suppose, is fear or lack of confidence. When I was young I went round looking as old and tweedy as possible because I wasn't happy with my youth and now that I am crawling lumpenly to the grave I act and dress like a Romford teenager. Fine, I can take that. But given a fine education and all the advantages attendant upon my upbringing and good fortune in life, I am forced to ask the questions: what access to universal truth do Romford teenagers have that I do not that enables them to act young when they are young and put away childish things as they attain man's estate? Where do I obtain this secret, is it in the *Next Directory*, is it available in *eau de nil* and can it be delivered straight away? Because if I carry on at this rate my friends in ten years' time, such as I will then have, will have to get used to the sight of me in a sailor-suit rattling down the street on a tricycle.

But for the moment it can at least be said that I smell quite nice.

You and Your Toffee

I was listening the other day to *You and Yours*, Radio 4's answer to a question that no one has yet bothered to ask. I am sure that Consumer Programming, into which category *You and Yours* proudly falls and sprains its ankle, provides a useful service and I have no doubt that the world is full of enough sharks, cowboys and pirates to satisfy almost every genre of Hollywood film, and yet whenever I do focus my ears on that extraordinary twenty-five minutes of unleavened dough I find it harder and harder to smother a scream.

The edition I found myself listening to had uncovered a scandal which centred around a new kind of toffee, an appetite suppressant as it happens, but for all that nothing more nor less than an ordinary toffee. It appears that when one or two of 'our researchers' ate this toffee – and I do recommend that you sit down before I go on, what I have to unfold is a tale of commercial cynicism and criminal negligence the like of which you will never have imagined, it will shock you to the very core of your being – they found that the toffee consistently **STUCK TO THEIR TEETH AND WAS REALLY JOLLY HARD TO CHEW!** It's quite true. In one case it even removed a filling. Can you imagine it?

It seemed to me monstrous that they could only allow this fascinating story of skulduggery and exploitation on an international scale a nugatory ten minutes of air time. I wanted to know more. Could it be that there had been no clear *warnings* written on the side of each toffee explaining that excessive mastication could cause a not-to-be-desiderated adhesion to the surface of the molars? It may be that the toffees have sharp edges which could easily cause Baby to bump into them, sustain a sharp contusion, go into an infant frenzy and set fire to the house? What about the wrappings? I have an awful feeling that Baby could tie them together into a primitive noose, throw them over a beam and hang himself. And that, as we know, could easily have someone's eye out and come up in a very nasty bruise indeed. Do the toffees have a safe, wipe-clean surface, in case Baby decides to play with them in the vicinity of a dog-mess? And on a more sinister note, is it possible that although they retail at 36 of your earth pence each, they only cost something closer to 35 pence to make, and that the manufacturer is actually making a profit out of them? At the very least I think we should all be demanding a full and open enquiry. Some kind of legislation is surely in order too.

I mean, what is it all about? Are we now a nation of such dozy, helpless incompetents that we have to be warned about a blasted toffee? I have tried one of these ruddy confections: fairly tasty, reasonably good at dulling the edge of the appetite and available in a convenient hand-bag size. Otherwise the thing is basically, *mutatis mutandis*, a toffee. Fewer calories perhaps, but nonetheless one of God's honest toffees. I have eaten chewier, have wrecked my snappers on tougher. Do we really need an earnest journalist to imply in his tones of suppressed excitement and outraged propriety that somehow the thing is a cross between thalidomide and an unshielded Stanley knife? I beg leave to doubt it.

A category of broadcasting journalism is invented: Consumer Affairs it calls itself. There is valuable work to be done. If the world is being flooded with teddy-bears whose eyes are held in place by rusty spikes then I suppose we should know about it. In the sixties Braden and Rantzen and others performed a valuable service. Ministries were set up, British Standards devised, consciousnesses raised. The tragedy is that it all made such wonderful television and excellent radio. For wicked as humanity is, in all kinds of subtle and horrifying ways, its wickedness in the field of manufacture and purveyance of substandard or hazardous itemries does not extend far enough to fill up the dozens of dedicated Consumer Programmes that now cram the airwaves. A juicy story of iniquity and shoddy practice will be snapped up by Roger Cook or Esther Rantzen months before poor old *You and Yours* will get a sniff of it. So they are left with toffees that actually have the temerity to stick to your teeth and kettles which might scald you if, when they are full of boiling water, you hold them upside down over your head. Consumer Programming has practically legislated itself out of business.

Caveat emptor is a noble maxim, but here is another: *quis custodiet ipsos custodes?* Who shall protect us from consumer protectors? How is it that *Which?* magazine, one of the pioneers of the noble movement we have been discussing, is more guilty, perhaps even than *Reader's Digest*, of that very brand of junk 'you may have won £200,000 pounds in our prize draw Mr Stippen Pry' mailing, and tacky, huckstering paper-wasting from which consumerism was surely invented to protect us? A nasty case of gamekeeper turned poacher if ever there was one. I shall be forming an independent production company that will produce *Them and Theirs* the watchdog of the watchdogs. A panel of testers will be examining *Which?* magazine and organs like it. If I find that it uses nasty old metal staples to bind its pages together, well, they had better look out, that's all.

Christmas Cheer

Something festive, they said. Something a thousand words long and festive. It's Christmas, you see, and the cry is for something . . . well, not to put too fine a point on it . . . something *festive*.

Christmas is a time for saying that Christmas is a time for doing things that one should, frankly, be doing anyway. 'Christmas is a time for considering people less fortunate than ourselves.' Oh, and July and April aren't, is that it? 'Christmas is a time for forgiveness.' We should be vindictive and beastly for the rest of the year? 'Christmas is a time for peace on earth and good will towards men.' Let us therefore for goodness' sake concentrate during the rest of the year on bellicose malevolence. Piffle-bibble.

I would hate to be considered an old Scroogey-trousers, the spirit of Christmas courses through my veins, softens my heart and hardens my arteries in as full an Imperial measure as those of any man of my age and weight in the country, I hope. So how, merry pink-nosed reader, shall we be Christmassy together, you and I? I like to think of this little column as a brassière, or do I mean brasserie? Brazier, possibly. All three! A column that lifts, separates, supports, serves excellent cappuccino and crackles merrily with sweet-smelling old chestnuts. And the oldest chestnut of all must be the adage that Christmas is a time for children.

Grrrr! That's what I used to think of Christmas as a child. Likewise, Waaah! The intolerable, aching suspense of it, the terrible monstrous disappointment of it! (You see I'm even succumbing to a Dickensian rash of exclamation marks! A Merry Eczemas rash of explanation marks, I suppose.) Christmas to a child is the first terrible proof that to travel hopefully is better than to arrive. It is impossible in adulthood to recapture the same kind of wriggling excitement, clammy anticipation and fidgeting desperation that one felt as the little cardboard doors of the Advent calendar swung open. I am told by the diminishing members of my acquaintance who still indulge in sexual intercourse and other corporeal rummagings and pokings that to watch a partner undress or to climb stairs towards a carnal assignation can invoke approximate sensations of tingling thrill, but I beg leave to doubt such claims and shout 'humbug, hooey and humgudgeon' at them. Only Christmas to a child can do this. Again, much like sex, the event ends with a sad, flatulent realisation that these things are better imagined than enacted, better anticipated than performed. A realisation that is brought fully home when the final horror of Christmas comes screaming hot from hell. The Thank-You Letter.

As a child you grasp Christmas to your bosom with joyous wonder and then ask, puzzled and crest-fallen: 'Well here it is, what do I *do* with it? This is Christmas Day, but what's different? Everything out of the window is normal, I *feel* the same, I *look* the same. Where's Christmas? Where's it gone?' Where indeed? It was never there, but in the mind.

Part of the problem, of course, is that spirituality keeps creeping into the festivities. Indeed it seems to be getting more and more religious every year. One yearns for a return to commercial values, to put a bit of the materialism back into the season.

There is a story that St Augustine persuaded an English king to turn Christian when sitting with him in a great hall having a Christmas feast – it wouldn't have been called a Christmas feast, it would have been called a Yuletide wassail, I expect – it was a big winter do, that's the point. As was common in those days before Magnet and Southern sliding patio doors, the party was going with a swing. A great fire crackled in the log, a great log crackled in the fire, and a log fire crackled in the grate. All was glee and revel. The only ventilation provided took the form of two holes high up on either end of the roof.

Of a sudden, or 'suddenly' as we say in England, a bird flew in through one of the holes in the wall, fluttered about for a bit and flew out through the other. The King, we shall call him Boddlerick, because I have no idea of his real name and have not the faintest intention of hauling my great corse up the stairs to look it up, who was accounted something of a philosopher, turned to Augustine, his strangely berobed and behaloed guest, and said unto him these words, in this wise: 'Behold, strangely berobed and behaloed guest! Is not our life like that of this poor bird. From the dark and howling void we came, cast suddenly into a world of colour and warmth and light, of music and mirth and merriment, briefly to flutter our baffled wings in alarm, only to be pitched back into the eternal cold and dark again?'

A good analogy, you'd have thought. Worthy of Jonathan Miller himself. But Augustine was having none of it. 'No, no, sire, majesty, liege,' he countered, 'you have it entirely the wrong way round. Our lives are dark passages in the stream of light that is God's love. To those who know God, through the window is Paradise.'

Instead of telling Augustine not to be such a silly old ninny and to get another skinful of rude mead and another eyeful of rude dancer, this fat-headed king liked what he heard and fell bell, book and candle for the whole funky Christian groove thing. This country and its Christmases have been damned ever since. Because, from that wretched day on, the world and its colour and music and light are things which we have had to write crawling thank-you letters to God for until we die. As little children sprawled before the lap of Father Christmas Almighty we cannot even enjoy the gifts of the world without guilt, shame, terror and gibbering gratitude.

So bog off St Gussie and roll on Boddlerick, say I. It's cold and dark and loveless outside, and this is as good as it ever gets. So let's feed the poor now, because their reward is *not* in heaven, let's drop ash on the carpet, slob around in our dressing gowns, mull wine all day long, watch television lying on our tummies, forget our thank-you letters to granny and God and have a ripping good time.

But let's not do it on Christmas day. Let's do it every damned day, for ever and ever Amen.

Predictions for the Year 1989

Welcome to what I hope will be a very engaging year. It's obviously a little too early to let you know exactly what's going to be happening in the world over the next twelve months, but I can tell you that it will be very much the mixture of old and new that you have come to expect from the prestigious and stylish eighties, blending traditional appeal with modern convenience. The only hint I will give you is not to throw away those back-issues of *The Listener*. Kindling is going to be pretty rare next winter: I know December '89 seems a long way off, but it's best not to take risks with one's body warmth. Otherwise Fauvism, as predicted, is set to make a come-back, the career of Anita Harris is going to be radically reassessed and Derek Jameson will suffer from a slight head cold in mid-August. The only particularly dark cloud on the horizon will be Tony Meo's continued run of bad form at the snooker table. But don't worry Tony! September looks like a winner as you take a fresh look at your stance and re-examine the rhythm of your cuing arm – the left arm in your case, of course. On the pop front, House music will continue to lose ground to the more fashionable Garage sound, which in turn will give way, in mid-June, to the Patio beat and thence, by October, to Garden music which will be followed, with any luck, by Down The Drive music and, eventually, A Very Long Way Away Indeed music.

Well, don't blame me, I have a column to fill. And if a columnist has a single solemn duty, it is to make predictions for the New Year. The problem with this sacred charge is that, in my experience, the only consistent and predictable thing in the world is randomness and weirdness. All I can bank on is that the coming year will yield fresh conflicts and calamities that will transform previously obscure peoples and nations into household names, produce novel bacilli and viruses that, like herpes, will be on everyone's lips by this time next year, and precipitate new catastrophes and disasters that will keep yet budding more bereavement counsellors in work well into the nineties. In short, we will continue to be astonished by the future.

If there is anything remarkable about the world and us race of humans, if there is a single marvellous and extraordinary fact in the universe it is this: we *find* existence remarkable, marvellous and extraordinary, despite its being the only condition we have ever known. Let me try and explain. If you brought up a baby in such a way that everyone around it took their clothes off in the dining-room, thrust soft fruits down their trousers in the kitchen, licked the walls in the sitting-room and jumped up and down screaming the word 'fwink' in the bathroom, that baby would grow up without ever finding such procedures in any way peculiar, until, that is, said infant discovered that these were far from normal practices in other households. As far as hearth and home go, we accept what we are given.

But when it comes to what Douglas Adams so rightly designated Life, the Universe and Everything we can do nothing but boggle. If we had all originated in a cosmos where things were ordered differently our amazement would make sense, but what we have and all we have ever had is the given state of things, what Wittgenstein, when relaxing, liked to call The Case. We have experienced no other possibility, yet we find it surprising (for all the world as if we had just arrived from Zegron 5 where time travels backwards, traffic jams are unknown and matter can be created at will) that music exists, that there are orchids which smell of rotting meat just to attract flies and that ewes are delivered every spring of frisky little lambs. Why are we gobsmacked by a state of affairs that is all we have ever known? Why are we so like Noël Coward's Alice, who, on observing the beasts of the field, remarked 'Things could have been organised better'?

The capacity to imagine other worlds and universes beyond our experience, the ability to question the cruelty and inanity of God and the feeling that we can enrich our lives just by taking a stick and sharpening it without having to wait for evolution to give us horns, claws or quills, these characteristics underlie every improvement we have made over nature and every harm we have inflicted upon it.

1989 will, I am sure, be a year in which the wise will continue to question our value, as climatic and environmental disasters accelerate and the affluent West becomes ever more desensitised to the suffering of the struggling two billion whose lives are most whirled into chaos by the wind that we are sowing. The January columns of future years will open by assessing our species' chances of surviving the year.

Nevertheless I am optimistic. For while we and we alone are primarily responsible for the critical state the world finds itself in, we and we alone are *aware* of it. And as long as we wonder, as long as we hold images of better organised universes in our heads we cannot perish.

So a Happy New Year to All Our Readers. It's a wonderful life.

The Talker in *The Listener*

I have always been rather curious about the titles of newspapers and periodicals. This is because I have a strange and mildly diseased mind. If, that is, I have a mind at all. When I was at University the man whose proud duty it was to direct my studies, inspire my soul and fine me for vomiting in chapel without a chit from the Senior Tutor, used to say that I had no mind whatever, or at least that my mind was nugatory. 'Your mind, Mr Fry,' he would say, 'is nugatory.' For a long time I was too proud to look the word up in a dictionary and believed he meant that my mind had the consistency of Montelimar, that chewy sweetmeat which takes its name from a southern French town famous otherwise for its manufacture of cigarette papers. What he did mean, as most of you will know, was that my mind was negligible: which, to save others amongst you a tiresome consultation with Chambers, did *not* mean that my mind was capable of transforming itself into a piece of female nightwear, it meant that there simply wasn't that much of it. You will readily understand that I was not best pleased by this intelligence and the aspersions it cast upon mine.

Came a garden party during the course of my second year when, maddened by cider, vodka, lemonade, Benylin and *triple sec*, I asked the man why he thought me so stupid.

'I do not think you stupid,' he said, 'at the moment you are certainly stupid: stupid with wine and jazz cigarettes, but usually I find you more than ordinarily alert and nimble-witted – for an undergraduate, at any rate.'

'B-but, Dr Name-Withheld-For-Legal-Reasons,' I yipped, 'you said that my mind was nugatory.'

'And so it is, you crapulent young fool. You have a terrible mind, really quite terrible, I don't know when I ever encountered one so bad. But you have a very reasonable brain. Most capable.

I, on the other hand and for what it may be worth, have a most excellent mind and an atrocious brain. Only a fine mind, after all, could appreciate such a distinction. The Name-Withheld-For-Legal-Reasons's have always had fine minds, the Yorkshire branch of the family excepted.'

I thanked him briefly for his explanation and, having rushed to the Senior Tutor to obtain the relevant docket, was soon puking happily in the choirstalls with renewed confidence in my noddle.

So there you have it: someone mindless is addressing you this day. I have no doubt that the regular gang of old muckers who heave themselves to my stall every week will have reached that conclusion long since, but newcomers have every right to be warned. However, the shadows grow long and I must return to the gravamen of my text. I said earlier that I find newspaper titles interesting: it seems like an age ago doesn't it? We've been through so much together since then. But we can pick up from where we began, I hope.

These titles: how appropriate are they? Does the *Observer* observe to a greater extent than the *Spectator* spectates? In what manner does the *Sun* shine that distinguishes it from the *Star*? Is it precisely the effulgent rays from both these organs that the *Mirror* busies itself reflecting? And over what does the *Guardian* stand such jealous guard? Is it better to be a Listener than a Clarion or a Bugle? And was there something in the very titles of the *Morning Post*, the *Daily Sketch*, the *Daily Graphic* and the *Herald* which contributed to their decline? These are not such vapid musings as, at first and probably second and third glance, they appear. The title must, presumably, denote some kind of intention. Are we no longer interested in graphic sketches and trumpeting heralds and buglers? What would *you* call the national newspapers and magazines?

The Times is perhaps the most appropriate: it has a quite eerie knack of tagging along with the *Zeitgeist*, though whether this will continue under present management when current Toryism has its day, remains to be seen. The *Telegraph*, under its old editorship, was rightly named: there was indeed the smell about it of the kind of commercial stationery which used to include in its heading the 'Telegraphic Address'. Now, however, the new broom, with its faintly embarrassing sponsorship of American Football and its student pull-outs and young people's cut-out-and-keeps, inclines one to believe that it should change its name to the *Fax*. The *Sun*'s lunacy must qualify it for a deed-poll change to the *Moon* and the *Spectator*'s strange and violent espousal of right-wingery everywhere leads me to feel that it has succumbed to the same disease that afflicts spectators in other spheres of activity, giving it the right to call itself now the *Hooligan*.

But these are idle rambles on the strand of time (four titles there, you note) and your own musings will be apter and brighter. I shall leave before I start to bore, I would hate you to think that the soft, voluminous folds of *this* periodical should now go under the name the *Talker*.

Ad Break

I always feel that I'm skating pretty close to the wind when I talk about advertising. I am no stranger to the world of radio and television commercials. It was with some amusement that two weeks ago I read an article by Robert Robinson in which the glabrous sage remarked: 'It is extremely unlikely that anyone reading this has ever been asked to do a voice-over for lavatory paper.' And would you believe it, on the facing page stood a grey wall of turgid piffle written by someone, *viz* myself, who had been asked to do just that very thing! What the odds are on periodical next-door neighbours both being hired for their ability to talk about the length, softness, absorbency and strength of a bog-roll are, I wouldn't know. They are probably similar to the odds against someone of complete ineptitude and absurdity making it to cabinet rank in a great democracy. And yet, as we see in the case of, say, Paul Channon, these things do happen. And while on the subject of botty-tissues and the hawking of them, I have always wanted someone to have the courage to do a sparse, spare, stark commercial for them, of the 'Kills all known germs – dead' kind. 'Andrex: for wiping your bottom with.' Or, 'Dixcel: it wipes your bottom – guaranteed.' But perhaps the world isn't ready for that.

On my involvement with the world of advertising I blow hot, cold and luke-warm. Sometimes I feel like a naughty old whore who's no better than she should be and at other times I think to myself, as Orson Welles did: 'Well, Toulouse-Lautrec did posters: Auden wrote copy for the Post Office – it's a noble tradition.'

But now I wonder. A set of newspaper advertisements has been appearing in our public presses over the last few weeks. The origin is the Midland Bank, an institution second only to this periodical for its fame as a listener. The Lord alone knows who they've been listening to lately, the ghost of King George III, I shouldn't wonder, but they've come up with 'three new bank accounts for three new kinds of customer'. The full-page advertisements for these new services took the form of questionnaires asking you to identify yourself as either a Vector person, an Orchard person or a Meridian person.

'Can you programme a VCR machine without getting four solid hours of Ceefax?' is the first question addressed to those who might be wondering whether (without having known it for all these years) they are a Vector person. 'Would you take out an overdraft to go to a friend's surprise party in San Francisco? And maybe live without carpets to buy a CD player?' 'Is the amount of plastic in your wallet spoiling the cut of your designer suit? If you've nodded to yourself while reading this, call us free . . . &c.' Well now, this is bizarre. You don't have to be an expert semiologist or observer of British society to guess at the kind of customer they are after with these questions. But then nor do you have to be an exp. sem. or obs. of Br. soc. to know that exactly that kind of customer would, rather than 'nod to himself', be the first one to vomit quite profoundly all over the newspaper, or at the very least, laugh himself into some kind of nervous spasm. So we must assume that the bank is in fact after the customer who would *like* to be the kind of person who has friends who hold surprise parties in S.F. But if that's true the bank is in trouble because it will be enrolling frighteningly sad and unwell people who in all probability will plunge themselves into terrible debt by stuffing their designer suits with plastic in order to spoil their cut, and going without carpets so as to be able to install CD players. And Vector people shouldn't deny themselves carpets: they need them. And they need them on their walls too: padded.

An Orchard person, apparently, spends Sunday helping the kids build a tree house, is an expert with a shopping trolley and would drum up a protest against a new motorway cutting through their town without expecting their photograph in the local newspaper. This is just babble from the hospital bed. The Orchardese are represented by a photograph of a Sunday lunch with a twee salt pot and carving set. Help me, I fear I shall go mad.

The last category is the Meridian type of person. 'Do you know the difference between the Dow Jones and Inigo Jones? Do head waiters know your name? Do you care about famine? And send donations, by covenant, without having your arm twisted?' Now this is sick. I'm sorry but it's sick. If the advertising industry is attracting people who can write this kind of excrement without irony then all is lost, fly the country. Their minds need some kind of soft, long, absorbent paper which will wipe them clean. I would be happy, if Robert Robinson isn't available, to do the voice-over for such a tissue for free. It would be in the noblest tradition of public service broadcasting.

Absolutely Nothing At All

Journalist friends tell me that columnists are allowed to write one *column of this nature* once *in their lives. Hum.*

This week I am not going to write an article, for the sad and lonely reason that my brain seems not to be working today. I hate to short-change you, but that's it. Nothing to say. For those of you reading who've never had to sit down on a weekly basis and provide 850 gleaming words of discursive prose for an imperious martinet of an editor who is expert with single-stick, fencing foil, field gun and combat sarcasm I may tell you that it isn't a breeze. A breeze is one of those things which it most specifically never is. It may be that you couldn't care a busman's burp what it is or isn't. 'It can be a breeze,' you reason, 'or it can be a hurricane. Of what possible interest can that be to us? We pay good money for these words and we don't give a monkey's god-daughter what pain the production of them may cost.' I suppose you're right, damn you; you're hard but you do have a very good point. After all, I should be most surprised if, as I was tucking into a packet of Abbey Crunch biscuits, Mr McVitie were suddenly to appear on my door-step and give me a solid quarter of an hour on how hard they were to bake, what agonies of composition the devising of the recipe gave him and how unappreciated he and his army of skilled pastrycooks were. Yet I am morally, if not contractually, obliged to give you your eight hundred and fifty whether you want them or not: and if I am going to have the impertinence to harangue you in the first place I might as well harangue you on the painful topic of how hard it is to think up subjects for haranguement.

My 'copy', as we scribblers call it, is generally required to be handed in for marking by Thursday morning. I speak to you now on a Wednesday evening, my brain emptier than a camel's bladder. My usual course is to trawl the newspapers for matter which enrages me. How many times has Kenneth Baker used the word 'standards' and 'values' this week and how many times has he used them in a sense comprehensible to speakers of the English language? Has Paul Johnson blinded the world with the shining love of his vision, depth, insight and humanity once more? Has the government been Up To Something? It sounds a tadge pompous, as if I'm a sentry on patrol guarding the gates of decency, but I have to start somewhere. Today I've drawn a blank. Nothing seems to have angered me at all either in print or on the television screen. The only really remarkable occurrence was that of the writer to *Points of View* who ended her letter to Anne Robinson with the phrase 'Ta muchly' which caused a strange shudder in my bowels and small green and red lights to dance in front of my eyes, but that soon passed. Perhaps something in my own life can be turned artfully into a sustaining 850-word parable that will amuse, enlighten and entertain? A van driver reversed into the front of my car crushing it like an eggshell this morning. I barked my shin on a table leg at 3.24 p.m. and I dropped a potato behind the sink at 7.50 where it is likely to remain for all time. John Donne could knock that little list of cataclysms into a pretty decent sonnet that would overturn the government and beckon in the thousand-year reign of Christ, I expect, but it's beyond my powers.

When the newspapers fail to yield fitting subject matter, it is surely time to pace the room like a caged tiger convolving great thoughts or to amble down the road on a letter-posting mission in order to clear the head. This latter course often works, which is surprising as it is the clearness of the head which is the problem in the first place. But today nothing: nix, zilch, sweet zip dang-doodley zerosville Idaho. Tennis players have elbows, house-maids have knees, writers just have blocks. I have to believe that I am not alone, otherwise life would be insupportable. Presumably the day dawns which sees Roger Woddis bereft of an idea – I have yet to see any evidence of that day, I am glad to say, but it must dawn. Does Bernard Levin have seven bottom drawers that he providently filled in the fat months so that the *Times* readership is fed during the lean ones? Who can say?

Well, my long day's task is done and I am for the night, as Cleopatra almost said. Eight hundred and fifty words of empty logorrhoea. I just hope you don't feel cheated. I can console myself with the knowledge that until Douglas Hurd has steered his abominable Criminal Justice Bill through Parliament I have the right to remain silent without your drawing any inference from that silence.

I have nothing to say and I've said it.

The Young

I was very worried the other day to read in the *Daily Mail* – the fact that I was reading the *Daily Mail* at all is worrying enough, you'd be right to interject at this point – that today's young people are apparently money conscious, job conscious, less likely to 'drop out', more likely to conform, more intolerant of homosexuality, less interested in drugs and have a greater sense of the importance of the family than their predecessors. This is disturbing news. Have things really got as bad as that? You needn't worry too much, the *Mail* was merely projecting its own sordid fantasies onto a batch or raft of quite harmless research figures that had fallen out of some statistician's computer. But then that's the *Daily Mail* for you. In many ways it is the worst newspaper in the land because somewhere in its image it has left room for us to suppose that it is a class up from the dirty tabloids. It relies on the laziness of the young estate agent or accounts executive who knows he should be buying the *Independent* – but it's a short train journey into work after all, and those big pages take a lot of unfolding, so what the hell, let's pick up a *Mail*.

If there is one thing against which the *Mail* stands as four-square as a wretched snotrag of a paper can stand at all, it is what we might call the Liberal Conscience. They won't stick it at any price. I'm an old-fashioned sort of bloke myself. I think young people should spend a great deal of time being outrageous, stoned, riotous, carnally experimental, kind, unworldly, angry, generous, sceptical, unselfish, anti-family, anti-government, anti-power, anti-money, antihistamine, anti-just about everything the established world represents. Being young, in fact. But that's the traditionalist in me. I have no particular objection to being dis-agreed with on this one and can sometimes bring myself to look at a nineteen-year-old in a suit and tie without actually laughing myself sick or being reminded of that brutal description of Leonard Bast, the young City worker in *Howards End* who 'had given up the glory of the animal for a tail-coat and a set of ideas'. You can call me anything you like for housing these strange doubts. But one thing I won't be called is trendy. Yes, I may well leave myself open to being described as left wing: certainly I will allow that I have liberal views on Nicaragua, feminism, gay rights, nuclear weapons, the environment, the Health Service, the Third World, greed, trades unions and whatever else might be calculated to win a few columns of gibbering nonsense from George Gale or Roger Scruton. Call me a Communist, a subversive, a weirdo, a useless excrescence, a faded relic of a failed generation. These are things open to debate. But for goodness' sake don't try and pretend that there is something trendy about it. If you want to know what is trendy and what has been trendy for ten years now at the very least, it is an implacable opposition to that liberal conscience: if you want fashion, look at the concerted effort in seven eighths of the press to discredit any manoeuvres towards debate on the subject of capital, the family and the notional norms of this island now.

There is one area of the world where a shining example of respect for the family, patriotism, tough punishment of criminals, morality and a sense of religion as part of national life is being set and that, of course, is in Iran and its sister Islamic countries. It may be that by smothering the possibilities of debate, by creating a climate in which doubt is discredited as 'trendy', 'faddish', 'communist' or just plain mad, we are on course to create a western version of Islamic fundamentalism that will see us refighting the Crusades before the century is out. I, in my fluffy, trendy and silly old way, rather tend towards hoping that we don't. But one thing is certain, the jehads against the Bishop of Durham, gay people, union leaders, Prince Charles, and anyone else who dares pop his head up above the parapet and wonder what the hell we think we are doing won't enrich this strange and wonderful country of ours by one penny, but will tend towards impoverishing it utterly. The recent budget may have stopped the brain drain, but the high taxation on conscience and doubt is encouraging a soul drain that is surely going to prove much harder to reverse.

Such hysterical paranoia in one so young? I know, I really

am most dreadfully sorry. I'll be seeing blues under the loo next. Perhaps I'm wrong, perhaps there is a graceful tolerance in the newspapers that I have overlooked, perhaps there is a drop of water amongst this rock. I'm unconventional enough to hope so.

Me & A Stapler of My Own

A regular *Listener* feature.

This week author and broadcaster Tom Murley.

Tom Murley first burst into the public domain with his appearance in the Observer's *'Me And My Cuff Link Caddy'. Other appearances quickly followed, including 'Inside My Bathroom Cabinet' for the* Sunday Telegraph, *the* Mail On Sunday's *'Cousins' column (with his cousin Leslie) and 'Things I Wish I Had Known Yesterday' for the* Sunday People *magazine. He lives in Kensington, Hampstead, Muswell Hill, Surrey, Camden, Putney, Gloucestershire and Suffolk (and Salisbury if being interviewed for* Wiltshire Life).

It's a Rexel *Pagemaster*. Shabby now, I suppose. A little battered and scratched, like me. My family laughs at me for hanging on to it, they can't understand why I don't throw it out and buy a newer, smarter model, but somehow I've retained a certain fondness for the thing. Marina (my wife of thirty years) says it means more to me than she does, and I suppose to some extent that's true, though she'd kill me for saying so. Perhaps that's why. This old stapler wouldn't kill me for anything. It's more of an old friend than a stapler. It forgives me my odd moods, my caprices and never exhibits a trace of jealousy. It just goes on being a stapler. That's a comforting, dependable thought somehow.

I bought it in an old stationer's in Gower Street in my first year at UCL. Four shillings and ninepence and thruppence for every fifty staples. I use it for attaching pieces of paper together.

You simply square up the sheaf and put it between the jaws of the stapler. Being right-handed, I like to use the upper left-hand corner, that way I can easily turn from one sheet of paper to the next without the top sheets obscuring my view of the lower ones. There's a small plate on the bottom jaw; it's on a swivel. You turn this plate with your thumb (or finger) and when you use the stapler each staple will be splayed outwards rather than closed in on itself. I've never really understood what one would use this feature for, but it's nice to have the option.

I met Marina, oddly enough, in a small café just outside the very stationer's where the stapler was bought. We married two years later and have three children, Jacinth, Barabbas and Hengis. When we bought our first flat in West Hampstead, just off West End Lane, when Marina was very pregnant with Jacinth, the stapler came with us. Marina told me that there wouldn't be room for it, but somehow I found a space in my desk, and there it has sat ever since, though we left West Hampstead years ago.

I rise every morning at 5.00 (two hours earlier than Jilly Cooper) and wake up Marina and the kids. Breakfast is usually Cretan honey with a little unpasteurised kumis and a nectarine (twice as nutritious as Freddy Raphael's breakfast and three times as exotic as Shirley Conran's). Then I run round the park/common/heath. I've taken to Danish Navy exercises. Not many people have heard of these, which is why I do them. They consist of stretching and breathing exercises indistinguishable from the same stretching and breathing exercises that everyone has been doing for a hundred years but you have to wear a towelling *thmarjk* or 'tracksuit' to do them in, so I get four more people every morning laughing at me than Laurie Taylor does.

Then it's down to work. I like to dictate first drafts to myself (Marina gave me shorthand lessons for Christmas in 1968) and I take down my dictation on a Phillips and Drew narrow feint school exercise book, using a B2 pencil. I like the soft darker lines of a B2. I write on the left-hand side only. I then like to do revisions on the right-hand side in an old Waterman's 'Invicta', writing only on alternate lines. This is four times more complicated and pointless a way of writing than Simon Raven's method. I take that text and transfer it onto a 70 megabyte IBM mainframe computer which Barabbas gave me for Father's Day last year. This is sixty-five million more bytes than Len Deighton has available on his word processor. I always write standing up, at an old credence table I bought from a sale of the fittings of St Michael and All Angels Church, Islington.

I work in ten-minute bursts, in between I go for long swims. I built our swimming pool myself, to my own design. It is shaped like the Burmese symbol for eternal serenity, which is a rectangle. The Nepalese symbol for eternal serenity is an endless knot, so perhaps it's as well I gave up my interest in Nepalese religion when John Fowles started getting interested too: if my swimming pool was shaped like an endless knot I wouldn't be able to count lengths so easily. The pool is filled with Evian water – chlorinated tap water is bad for the lymph glands – heated to 70°F.

Then it's dinner round the stapler. I skip lunch (unlike Kingsley Amis and Anthony Burgess). If the kids are home from school we'll play some word game or talk about what they've been up to during the day, I think these moments can be important. I don't watch television, I think it destroys the art of talking about oneself. Then a Taiwanese fruit bath and bed. I sleep on the right, the stapler on the left. Marina has a separate bedroom. I'm not quite sure why.

Next week: Traveller and poet Millinie Bowett in the feature 'My Press-on Towel and I'.

Give Us Back Our Obfuscation

There was a time when you could hardly open a newspaper, especially a *Times* or *Telegraph*, without coming upon an article, written by some guardian of common sense and plain thinking, which railed at the jargons and periphrastic prolixities of trades unions, sociologists and the bureaucracies. Sesquipedalian circumlocution was frowned upon. What used to be called roundaboutation was mocked and fleered at. The argument, which always flowed over a current of individual libertarianism, was that the uneducated, posing mandarins of the corporate state dressed up their wicked intent in an attire that hid the dwarfish and deformed shapes beneath. A ruthless pogrom against 'meaningful situations' and 'on-going scenarios' was established. *Private Eye* ran a column exposing the more pungent examples of such language that occurred in the public prints: Philip Howard, Michael Leapman and Bernard Levin, with varying degrees of wit and purpose, highlighted in *The Times* moments of the obfuscatory logorrhoea and gobbledy-gook weasel verbiage that was threatening to unseat their reason. In keeping with the Jovian rumbling that writers for that newspaper still like to imagine informs the tone of the Thunderer, the shining intent of language is for them to inform with clarity and precision.

I am sure that a great deal of good was done by these apostles of lucidity. A DHSS document that is impenetrable or equivocal insults, confuses and oppresses. What interests me however is the feeling I have that these outbursts can be seen now as part of the late seventies movement that prepared the way for She Whose Court Shoe Ribbons Peregrine Worsthorne and Roger Scruton Are Not Worthy To Tie. I am not suggesting for a moment that the strategy was deliberate, just that those Don Quixotes who tilted at the windmills of State, Socialism, the Town Hall and the University Sociologists believed language to be a crucial battleground. The modes of utterance which they ridiculed were typically, therefore, those of state institutions: the rhetoric of social science and left-wing orthodoxy. 'To purify the dialect of the tribe' was the mission, to return to the Addisonian virtues of common sense and plain-speaking.

But it isn't so simple. The word 'stone' is not itself a stone, it is a kind of promissory note. If I use it, I will not be asked to fetch a stone to show what I mean, for the meaning of that particular word is generally understood, just as producing a banknote does not require me to go to Threadneedle Street to fetch the sliver of gold that the note promises to deliver. But were I to use the word 'stone', in its sense of a measure of weight, in America where they count weight in pounds, then I would have to convert it for them before I could use it, just as I would have to convert English money there before I could spend it. A common understanding is clearly a prerequisite to the use of linguistic currency.

But the language of what T.E. Hulme called 'the capital letter moralists', referring to those who were free with words like Justice and Reason and Virtue, assumes a common understanding of fundamental aims, beliefs and ideas which there is no evidence to suggest exists. Common sense and a common view of the world may well have been possible in the eighteenth century, but we know, or ought to know, better by now. For all its infelicities and inelegancies, the language of the sociologist or the left-wing historian is carefully politicised to take account of the fact that a neutral use of words like 'equality', 'freedom' and 'decency' is quite impossible. Those who tried to understand the world therefore devised quasi-scientific jargons which might well produce phrases like 'meaningful relationships within an on-going familial context' but which (unless you are such a donkey as to think the phrases are used to impress, when they so manifestly fail to do so) at least strive for an honest *de*notation of phenomena shorn of dubious *con*notations. But when today's politician or guardian of public morals use words and phrases like 'ordinary decent people' or 'morality and family life' or 'moderate thinking' they are using words that have no more foundation in universal truth than do the propaganda buzzwords of Nazism, Communism or Christianity.

We take pride, or used to, in the plurality of our society, in its elasticity and tolerance. As we retreat politically and socially into more rigid structures, so the politicians take on a language of common assumptions and unchallengeable assertions. Returning to the banknote metaphor, a whole economic system is being built on a fundamentally unsound and illusory standard: there is nothing in the bank but dogma and declaration.

I am not so sure, after all, that I do not prefer the phrase 'notionally limited scope for action within wider ambits and prescribed social parameters' to the word 'freedom'. At least I know where I am with it.

Compliant Complaint

This business of complaining. It worries me terribly. Part of the problem is that I have a rather snazzy alarm clock. I have abandoned the square pot of tea and spit in the face of boiling water that I was treated to by my old Goblin Teasmade and turned my back on the bleeping reveille that morbidly reminded me of those cardiographic blips that threaten to straighten out into a single tone, and have embraced with fervour a black box that contrives instead to jerk me from the dreamless with television. I know it's a shameful luxury, but what with my secret diplomatic missions in the daytime and duties as a volunteer neurosurgeon at night, morning television is the only chance I get to peer into the magic eye. Don't be too disgusted at my sybaritic lifestyle but the programme that usually evaporates the honey-heavy dew of my slumbers is called *Open Air* which begins at nine o'clock, goes away for a bit to make way for *Kilroy* and other such fantastic aberrations and then returns to sweep up the mess it's made, round about eleven thirty.

Open Air is a weird charter for the mad people in this country. That this island is heaving and groaning with barkingly deranged citizens no one can doubt, what is so worrying is that they are given licence to parade their bizarre delusions on a daily basis. Take the snooker problem. Anyone with a mind to read the ratings can see at a glance that the World Professional Snooker Championships yield BBC2 just about its highest viewing figures for the year. In other words, snooker is remarkably popular. A great many people like it. Millions and millions. For seventeen days the tournament is covered by the BBC, chiefly on channel 2. And then for weeks afterwards people who probably watch ten minutes of BBC2's normal output in a week write, telephone, fax and telex the BBC complaining that there is nothing but snooker on television, which aside from being a downright lie, seems to me to be a perfectly dismal and hopeless observation. Do they imagine that the BBC are going to throw away their chance to show an immensely popular sporting event just because Mrs Edith Plackett and a few hundred others don't understand the rules and don't want to watch it? You can bet your socks that half of those who gripe at snooker are glued to their sets during Wimbledon fortnight. If their televisions were only capable of receiving BBC2 one certainly might sympathise, but most of us can receive four channels and even if the other three are not offering programmes that appeal, does that mean we have to pester the poor schedulers with our fatuous prejudices?

That style of complaint is one thing, howling insane certainly, but relatively harmless: the BBC are not such donkeys as to take notice of the few hundred who complain when weighed against the fifteen million who watch. But unfortunately the corporation is not always so restrained. In radio especially, television's fragile parent, management has a fatal tendency to disregard that arithmetic. The fallacy is to argue that if, out of two hundred calls and letters logged, seventy per cent register a dislike then the programme must be unpopular. But it is imperative to remember that *at least* ninety per cent of that two hundred could instantly be sectioned under the various mental health acts that exist to protect society from the damage that the boilingly mad can inflict. How is it that the views of the disturbed can hold sway over those of the balanced?

There was once a decent and jolly sort of radio sit-com called *After Henry*. My only worry was that the language, for something as well conceived and performed, was a little unrealistic. Too many 'golly's' and 'goshes' for my taste. The odd 'Christ' and 'bloody hell' popped up, but too infrequently to suggest the reality of intelligent British speech, which as we know, uses blasphemous, coital and cloacal expletives as a matter of course. But even those few Gods, bloodies and hells were too much for the average Radio 4 listener. The senior executives in radio around this time started to issue terrifying edicts about language which have all but strangled the medium. Radio writers are now in the position of painters a few hundred years ago. If there are pudenda, let them be provocatively swathed in gauze. Single entendre is proscribed, but double entendre is acceptable. Another generation of children will be brought up to regard sexuality as a sordid adult world of guilt and fear, to be protected from them until they commit the crime of growing up.

It is time television management stopped regarding letters received as a sample of anything except the tortured ravings of those requiring urgent help. Normal people are too busy getting on with their lives to bother with writing to their family and friends let alone to broadcasting companies, and until this is realised and letters of complaint are automatically incinerated unread we will continue to be dictated to by the disordered.

How I Wrote This Article

Tut, tut . . . the man's struggling. Only a few weeks after he wrote Absolutely Nothing At All he's scraping the bottom of the barrel with an article about how to write an article . . . dodgy, distinctly dodgy.

I know it reeks of navel contemplation of the worst kind, but I thought it might interest you to know how this article was written. As a child of the communications revolution, the information technology boom and all the other electronic explosions that have taken place over the last few years I think I can justify such distasteful auto-omphalic scrutiny by stating that this article could not have been composed, proof-read and dispatched to *The Listener* in the way that it has been without the help of the kind of technological splendour which people claim, in a brow-clutching sort of way, they abominate much as a vegetarian abhors a veal chop.

The more banausic details of the piece's composition are that it has been typed on a word-processor and delivered over the telephone *via* a fax machine. It is more interesting perhaps to concentrate on the parallel programs that operate with the word-processor and assist the harassed journo in his headlong rush towards the deadline. Let me talk a little more about my 'kit' as they would say in the army. I have a sound digitiser which enables me to talk into a microphone and have the computer welcome me when I turn it on. 'Hello Stephen, good morning!' it might say in my own voice or perhaps 'Go on, make my day' in Clint Eastwood's. It is hardly a productive tool to anyone but a musician or radio producer, but how much better it is to have a monkey-screech or car-horn reminding you that you have mistyped than a dull computery sort of 'beep'. I have available dozens of type-faces or 'fonts' as they are called in the trade. These range from the simple but elegant Times Roman, to the more elaborate Tiffany and Trump Medieval fonts, by way of Galliard, Garamond and Helvetica. There are thousands of colours available too, I have complete control over saturation and hue to achieve precisely the blend that most satisfies me. That takes care of the simple anal priorities, the sound and the look. These are equivalent to the feel and smell of the paper and the colours of inks and width of nibs with which writers used to be obsessed.

As well as footnote, table of contents, automatic hyphenation and indexing facilities, suitable for longer works, I have an ingenious option called 'Smart Quotes' which works out whether I want opening or closing quotation marks. Thus in the phrase 'Smart Quotes' I type the same inverted comma key and the clever machine knows how to handle the direction of curl. Similarly the ligatures 'fi' and 'fl' for 'f i' and 'f l' look after themselves (I hope the typesetter for *The Listener* is able to reproduce them or the foregoing sentence will be meaningless to you). Again these are anal concerns, but the output on a 300 dots per inch laser printer is of impressive quality and this fills one with confidence.

Now to the handling of the document itself: I have an on-line Thesaurus which enables me, when desperate, to find synonyms. Let's try it on 'desperate': 'Acute, critical, crucial, major, pressed, somber and unhappy' are offered *inter alia*. That American spelling of 'sombre' leads me to tell you about the spelling checker. If I pass the text of this article as written so far through the on-line lexicon, the following words are queried: omphalic (quite understandable, why should it know such a pompous, sixth-form sort of a word?), banausic (ditto), fax, computery, harrassed (which it correctly told me should be spelt with only one 'r') and, amusingly, 'somber' (this is an English spelling checker).

So, the article is pretty, correctly spelt, and full of blisteringly accurate synonyms. But what of style? There is software for that too. 'MacProof: The Macintosh Style-Checker' can trawl my document for infelicities of style: sexist, racist and inelegant uses of language. It cleverly spotted that I had written 'which which' (a common double-typing easy to miss when proof-reading) earlier on. It frowned on the use of the word 'per' in the phrase '300 dots per inch' saying it preferred 'a', 'for each' or 'for every'. It accused me of too much of what it called 'nominalization', turning verbs into nouns: offering as general advice that the sentence 'The re-creation of Paul Revere's ride by the Historical Society was beautifully done' is better rendered as 'The Historical Society re-created Paul Revere's ride beautifully.' Otherwise I was cleared of sexist or racist usage and the text was positively vetted as free of vague or overworked expressions.

I turn next to perhaps the most indispensable aid of all: the Word Count. I find that I have typed 887 words so far. Too much: I shall have to go back and prune. I am allowed 830, at a pinch 850.

Well there you have it. One fresh, stylish, clear and bouncing article, now reduced to 842 words. Boring though, isn't it?[1]

---

[1]Yes, ed.

Tear Him for his Bad Verses

If Salman Rushdie is still alive by the time this article emerges from the print-room, and I do hope he is, I wonder if he is considering how fortunate he is not to have written a novel in medieval Britain which contained any criticism of Christ. If certain members of the Islamic faith are a little overzealous in their protection of the good name and offices of their Prophet, then they are as kittens compared to an affronted Christian of the old school. A mad Mohammedan might riddle you with bullets and scream a lot, but at least he won't tear the skin from your body, slowly draw out your entrails and preach you a homily on your soul's purity while doing so. Not, I appreciate, that this is much of a consolation to the beleaguered Mr Rushdie, who would rather stay alive than be a martyr to artistic freedom any day of the week, I should imagine, but the thought might take his mind off the more terrible daily anxieties. He might also chat to his armed body-guards, in between games of Pass the Pig and Crambo, on the subject of Cinna. He was the Roman, you remember, who was *not* Cinna the Conspirator, one of the assassins of Julius Caesar, but was Cinna the Poet. The mob decided he had better die anyway: 'Tear him for his bad verses,' summed up the popular feeling at the time. I dare say in Bradford this very day there is a Salman Rushdie the Pastry-cook who is going about the place in fear and trembling lest he might be torn for his bad biscuits.

I am about to embark on a novel myself next week, writing one that is, I'm not ready to read one yet, and I have been puzzling over what subject I could possibly treat which would have me walking in fear of death. I can't think of many. But it is interesting and, frankly, not unworrying, to think that I could endanger myself, my publishers, and all good booksellers, just by making a few flippant remarks about the Prophet.

We cannot underestimate the enormity of what has happened to Salman Rushdie. He is forty years old. He knows that for the rest of his life he is under a sentence of death. This year he will probably escape the bullet, and next I expect. But in five years' time? Will the police continue to protect him: would the expense be considered justifiable in the year 2000? To the Islamic fundamentalist there is no statute of limitations. They do not forget or forgive. We've all seen movies about the Mafia informer who is given a new identity after shopping his boss and moves from city to city, never settling, never making friends. The contract is out and he cannot sleep easy. The contract is out on Rushdie now and there are in Britain alone, it is thought, a thousand who would want to honour it for their eternal soul's sake. Quite simply can you imagine the horror of seeing a life of fear stretch out in front of you? I really believe that the Rushdie Affair constitutes one of the most extraordinary international incidents of the decade.

We are forced to examine every idea we think permanent and unchallengeable. Try to imagine persuading a Moslem fundamentalist that Rushdie has a right to live. 'But he insulted the Prophet, he must die,' is the response. 'But tolerance,' you protest, 'if he insulted Christ there would be a lot of fuss, a few apoplectic bishops would appear on *The Late Show*, but he wouldn't be killed.' 'But Mohammed is the Prophet, Christ is not.' That is the crux. The Islamic fundamentalists do believe, are sure, that there is only one prophet and his name is Mohammed and they do not accept that everyone has a right to a point of view if it is going to be a wrong one. 'If we are actually right, then it is absurd to be tolerant of those who are wrong.' They are not interested in freedom of expression, they are interested in correct expression, they cannot be argued into thinking their point of view shameful. *We* can see the difference, or think we can, but our own faith in tolerance prohibits us from being as intolerant of Islam's point of view as Islam is of ours. But we can't sit by and let a novelist be murdered just because it would be intolerant meddling to fight for his right to say anything. Can we?

We must recognise just how little we have succeeded in exporting the revolution in enlightenment, tolerance and freedom that has been going on in the West, in fits and starts, for the last two or three hundred years and now have to wonder whether our revolution, by definition passive, is going to endure the violent passion of that in the East.

I think my novel is going to be about a dormouse called Clive and a hedgehog called Timothy and the adventures they have together in the forest. It's safer. Mind you the Animal Rights activists these days . . .

Oh dear, I'll play safe and set it in South Kensington.

The following appeared in the Christmas 1987 issue of The Listener:

The literary editor, when clearing out her office preparatory to the move to *The Listener*'s new quarters, discovered a bundle of papers wedged at the back of a drawer. The find appeared to be an autograph manuscript of a previously unpublished Sherlock Holmes story. Uncertain of its authenticity, she asked Stephen Fry, a noted Sherlockian, to edit the text and reflect on its provenance.

Hand-written on nineteenth-century foolscap the document certainly appears to be genuine. According to Edinburgh University's pioneering 'particle method' a quick count of prepositions, final clauses and image clusters tells us that the balance of probability is that the text was indeed written by Watson. Three or four strange inconsistencies, however, which do not become apparent until the very end of the story, throw some doubt on this conclusion. Alert readers will detect these anomalies and draw their own inferences. Apart from trimming back the typically profuse growth of commas and semi-colons familiar to scholars of the canon, I have left the body of the text unedited. I should be interested to hear the opinion of enthusiasts everywhere. In my view, if the story is not genuine then it ought to be.

The Adventure of the Laughing Jarvey

The year 18– saw my friend Sherlock Holmes at the very height of his considerable powers. On leafing through the journals for that year my attention is caught by a number of cases; some startling, some macabre, some seemingly commonplace, but all demonstrating to a great extent Holmes's remarkable gifts of deduction. The Affair of the Stranded Macaw, for which he received the Order of the Silver Myrtle from the hands of His

Majesty the King Miroslaw himself, presents several peculiar features of interest but in the more delicate of its details touches too many figures in public life to allow me to retell it here. The Tale of the Punctual Railway Clerk, while remaining one of Holmes's favourite triumphs, is perhaps of too technical a nature to be of interest to the general reader. The Case of the Copper Beeches I have chronicled elsewhere and the Story of the Tooting Schoolmaster and the Harness, while displaying as perhaps no other the extraordinary meticulousness and patience that characterised my friend's methods, has no place outside specialist journals.

Towards the very end of that year however, when it seemed to us that London had given up on sensation for the winter and was content to prepare itself comfortably for the festive season without throwing up those *outré* mysteries that were as oxygen to Sherlock Holmes, there exploded upon us a case which wrenched him from the indolence and melancholy to which that great mind was prey when there was nothing to engage it and hurtled us into as extraordinary an adventure as any we had known. Although it is his oft repeated assertion that this problem tested his reasoning powers only to the smallest degree, there can be no doubt that its solution yielded to Holmes the richest fee he ever earned in the course of an illustrious career.

I remember that one evening in mid-December I was engaged in the task of decorating our bachelor lodgings with some seasonal sprigs of holly and mistletoe, enduring the while some tart criticisms from my friend.

'Really Watson,' said he, 'is it not enough that Mrs Hudson must come in laden with mince pies and indefatigable good cheer every hour of the day? Must we also deck ourselves out like a pagan temple?'

'I must say, Holmes,' I returned with some asperity, for the effort of standing upon a chair and reaching for the picture rail was taking its toll on the old Jezail bullet wound, 'I think this uncommonly poor-spirited of you! Christmas used to mean something, I remember. Do you not recall the Blue Carbuncle? *That* adventure saw you as full of Yuletide charity as any man.'

'Watson you are confusing the real facts of that affair with the gaudy version of it that you were pleased to set down before a gullible public. Pray do not start upon the course of believing your own fictions. As I remember it, the case was a matter for calm analysis.'

'Really, Holmes,' I ejaculated, 'you are most unfair!'

'You must forgive me Watson. But the infernal *dullness* of it all! A spreading canker of bumbling good cheer seems to infect everybody at this time of year, even the most hardened of scoundrels, who are as likely to give money as they are to abstract it. Here is the *Evening News*. What foul murders or daring larcenies are there here to engage the interest? A woman is injured in a derailment at Lewisham, some one has stolen a statue from Charing Cross, a horse has bolted in Hoxton. I despair, Watson. Let us have an end to this sickening season of good will and peace, I say.'

'Holmes, I will not allow this assault on Christmas! You know perfectly well that – '

But my strictures were interrupted by a wild jangling of the bell downstairs.

'Ah,' said Holmes, 'I am spared your homily. Perhaps a mistaken address, perhaps a client. Such extravagant pealing denotes some urgency at any rate. Well, Billy?'

Our honest pageboy had entered the room, but before he had time to make any formal announcement there burst in like a tornado the most wildly agitated man I think I have ever laid eyes upon.

'Mr Sherlock Holmes? Which one of you is Mr Holmes?' gasped the unfortunate creature, looking wildly from one to the other of us.

'I am he,' said Holmes, 'and this is my friend Dr Watson. If you will be seated he will pour you a glass of brandy.'

'Thank you, a little brandy, yes indeed. That would be most . . . really Mr Holmes, you must forgive me, I am not given to . . . thank you, most kind, no seltzer I beg! Just so. Let me catch my breath . . . splendid rooms, most snug. Charming holly . . . so festive. I congratulate you. Ah! that is much better, I am obliged to you, Doctor.'

Despite the pitiable distress of the man I could not forbear to smile at this twittering and inconsequential monologue. I had seen physical pain induce such loquacity and delirium in wounded men and knew it to be a common sign of mental anxiety also.

Sherlock Holmes sat deep in his arm chair, touching together the tips of his fingers and running an expert eye over the extra-ordinary gentleman seated opposite him. Our visitor was dressed fashionably for the evening, but I could not set him down as a Society figure. Prosperity gleamed in the refulgent shirt and hand-made boots, for all the fresh traces of mud upon them, but too lively an intelligence shone in his piercingly blue eyes to suppose that he did not use his brain for a living. His thin face, in its rare moments of repose, seemed of a melancholy cast, but when it became animated the features fairly quivered with movement, a wiry beard wagged and jerked in time to his speech and the wild, disordered locks upon his head tossed about as if in a tempest.

'Such *very* good brandy . . . oh dear, oh dear, oh dear. Whatever am I to *do*, Mr Holmes?'

'Well, when you have caught your breath, you had better lay your problem before us,' said Holmes. 'To have come from at least as far as Gray's Inn all the way to Baker Street on such a night would take its toll on any man.'

Our visitor started visibly. 'But how on earth? Oh dear me, that is most extraordinary! I have indeed run all the way from Gray's Inn, though how you could know that is beyond me.'

'Tush, sir, it is as clear as day. That you have been running a child could tell from your breathlessness alone. The line of the splashes upon the toes of your boots could not be caused any other way.'

'Well,' chuckled the other, momentarily diverted from the cause of his peculiar worry, 'I see *that*, but how the deuce can you read Gray's Inn in my appearance?'

'I was there this morning,' said Holmes. 'They are painting the iron railings that fence off the north side from the pavement. The palings themselves are painted black, but the tip is gilded, in your hurry you have brushed your left arm against the wet paint. See upon your sleeve, black topped with a smudge of gold. It is possible that there is another railing freshly painted in like manner somewhere in London, but it is highly unlikely.'

'Remarkable, remarkable. A capital game! What else, sir? What else?'

'I am afraid,' said Holmes, 'there is very little else to tell.'

'Ah, I am freshly changed into my evening clothes, after all. Every clue starched over, I fancy.'

'Beyond the obvious facts that you are a writer, that you suffered deprivation in your boyhood, that money is a little harder to come by for you than it once was and that you are fond of conjuring tricks, there is certainly very little to be seen,' said Holmes.

Our visitor started up. 'You know me then! This is a pretty trick to play, sir, upon my word! It is unworthy of you.'

'Be seated, I beg' said Holmes, 'I have never set eyes upon you before. When I see a man with so pronounced an indentation upon the inside of his middle finger it is surely no great matter to assume that he is a writer?'

'A clerk! I might be a clerk!'

'In Lobb boots? I hardly think so.'

'Hum, the deprivation then?'

'Your face is lined beyond your years, but not, I perceive, by the trouble that has brought you here. That is too recent to have yet written itself across your brow. I have seen such marks only on those who grew up knowing misery and want.'

'True enough, Mr Holmes – but the money, the conjuring tricks?'

'Those fine boots were made some three or four years ago, I fancy. The excellently cut coat you are wearing dates from that time also. The sudden burst of prosperity that their purchase betokens has receded a little into the past, therefore. As for the conjuring, you will have noticed, I am sure, Watson, the small metal cone that protrudes a little from our visitor's waistcoat? Flesh-pink in colour, it is called a thumb-tip: an essential part of an illusionist's apparatus.'

'Bravo, Mr Holmes!' cried our guest, applauding with great energy. 'Miraculous!'

'Meretricious.'

'And a happy new year, my dear sir. Meretricious and a happy new year! Dear me,' said he, sinking in spirits once more, 'you quite take my mind from the purpose of this visit. Such a calamity, Mr Holmes. Such a dreadful calamity. I am beside myself!'

'I am all attention Mr – ?'

'Oh! My name? Yes. Ah, Bosney, Culliford Bosney, novelist. You have heard of me perhaps?' He scanned our bookshelves eagerly.

'I am afraid, Mr Bosney, that with only a few exceptions I do not have much time for novels. Dr Watson is the literary man.'

Culliford Bosney turned his lively gaze upon me. 'Ah yes, Dr Watson – of course. I read your works with great interest. Accept the compliments of a fellow scribbler, I beg.'

'Thank you,' said I, 'I am afraid Mr Holmes does not share your good opinion of my efforts.'

'Nonsense, Watson! As exotic romances they stand in a class of their own,' said Holmes, filling his briar.

'You see what I have to contend with, Mr Bosney?' said I, with a rueful grin.

'Oh, Dr Watson!' answered he, with a pitiable return to his former woe. 'You will understand my misery when I tell you that it is lost! It is lost, and I am at my wits' end!'

'What is lost?' I asked in bewilderment.

'The manuscript, of course! It is lost and I am sure I shall lose my mind with worrying over it.'

'I think,' said Holmes, leaning back in his chair, 'that you had better favour us with all the facts of your narrative, Mr Bosney.'

'Of course, Mr Holmes. Omitting no details, however trivial they may seem, eh?'

'Quite so.'

'Well, you must know that I have been labouring now for some six weeks on the manuscript of a story. I was due today to deliver it to my publishers – it is necessary that they publish it within the week you understand, for it has a Yuletide theme. I have high hopes for this story, Mr Holmes. I will not palter with you, my last novel did not take at all well and I have been at great pains to do something which will in some way recoup my fortunes and restore the good opinion of the reading public. I have not been on the best of terms with my publishers for some time and I am hoping that this newest work will earn me enough by way of royalties to enable me to leave them and seek a more congenial firm.'

'Are they aware of this ambition?' asked Holmes.

'No, Mr Holmes, I do not believe that they are. I have great hopes of this story however. *Had* great hopes, for I am sure I shall never see it again!' The agonised novelist sprang up from his seat with a gesture of despair. 'Mr Holmes, it is useless. How can one find a needle in a haystack?'

'Given a strong enough magnet, Mr Bosney, it is an elementary task. Put me in possession of the relevant facts and who knows but that we will not be able to find just such a magnet?'

'Yes, yes. I must beg your pardon gentlemen, but I have been tried these past few hours, sorely tried. Well then, at half past four this afternoon I had finished reading the story back to myself and was satisfied that it was ready to be printed. Rather than have the manuscript collected I thought that I would deliver it myself, on my way to the theatre. I also wanted to give some last-minute instructions for the printing. I wished the book to be lavishly presented, Mr Holmes, in gilt and red. I thought that would be appropriately festive.

'I changed into evening clothes, tucked the manuscript under my arm and went out into the street to hail a cab. My street runs into Theobald's Road, Mr Holmes, just opposite Gray's Inn. There is usually no difficulty in finding a hackney carriage on that thoroughfare. To my surprise, however, there was already a hansom standing right outside my house. I called to the driver to ask if he were waiting for anybody. He seemed startled but replied that he was not. I opened the door, put the manuscript onto the seat and was on the point of climbing in, when I noticed that the seat was already occupied. Mr Holmes, I am not a fanciful man, but the sight of the figure sitting in the corner of that hansom made my blood run cold! A deathly pale countenance, with blank unseeing eyes. I shudder at the memory of him.'

'You recollect how the figure was dressed?' asked Holmes sharply.

'I do indeed, it was most striking. I recall a many-caped driving coat buttoned up to the throat, a billycock hat and a woollen scarf. There was something so incongruous about this strange apparel and those inhumanly blanched and spectral features that I could not help but step backwards with a cry. No sooner had I done so than the jarvey whipped up his horse with a shout and rattled down the street, disappearing into the mist.'

'Really?' said Holmes, rubbing his hands together. 'Most intriguing. Pray continue, Mr Bosney, I beg.'

'I must own, Mr Holmes, that I was at first relieved that the vision had fled so fast. I stood trembling upon the pavement, wondering at the meaning of so horrid a sight. Perhaps I had imagined it, perhaps I was still in the grip of the fever of imagination with which I had finished my story. But then I remembered that my manuscript was still lying on the seat of the vanished cab and I became quite mad with fright. I ran down into Theobald's Road and stared about me. There were dog-carts and broughams and hansoms by the dozen rattling in both directions. But which was my hansom, I could not tell. I have sent my servants out to the cab companies offering large rewards for the safe return of the manuscript Mr Holmes, but so far with no success. I am at my wits' end!'

'A piquant mystery,' said Holmes, looking dreamily up at the ceiling. 'Can you describe the jarvey to me, I wonder?'

'I cannot Mr Holmes!' groaned the other. 'I usually have an excellent memory for faces, but this man was so muffled up against the chill that I had no opportunity to read his features. I have an impression from his voice that he was a young man, but I may be wrong. Also – '

'Yes?'

'Well, it may only be my fancy, but I could swear that as the cab hurtled away from me I heard laughter. I attributed it to the medical students who have just moved in to lodgings next door to me and are rowdy at the best of times, but thinking back I am sure it came from the jarvey himself! What can that mean, Mr Holmes?'

'A laugh you say? Now, that is really most revealing.' Holmes rose and began to pace about the room. 'You have mentioned students, Mr Bosney, what other neighbours do you have?'

'For the most part we are a quiet lot – solicitors and stockbrokers in the main. The street is handy for both the Inns of Court and the City of London. I am not on especially intimate terms with any of my neighbours, however. Colonel Harker, whose house adjoins mine, has recently returned from India and staffs his household with native servants, at whom he bellows with immoderate choler. I do not think that I have ever exchanged above two words with him. He is away in Hampshire for Christmas in any case, so I do not think he can have any bearing on the matter.'

'Well, Mr Bosney,' said Holmes, buttoning up his cape, 'I will look into this little problem for you.'

'Thank you, Mr Holmes!'

'Come Watson, let us all take ourselves to Gray's Inn and see what we can discover.'

*

As the three of us were whisked through the dark London streets, Sherlock Holmes and Culliford Bosney looked out the window at the fog-wrapped streets and alleyways of the great capital, the former keenly, the latter with comical anxiety. Holmes, drawing heavily on his most pungent shag mixture, noted off the street names as we flew down the Euston Road. I have remarked before that his knowledge of London streets was profound, from the lowest and vilest alleys in the east to the broadest and most fashionable squares and avenues in the west. I was surprised to discover that Mr Bosney too was possessed of an exact acquaintance with the capital. The pair of them talked enthusiastically of their love for the great city, Bosney even contriving to surprise Holmes on occasion with some obscure fragment of history or local anecdote.

'Yes indeed, Mr Holmes!' cried he, 'London is alive, believe me. Every citizen is like a cell of the great organism, connected to every other. The meanest tapster in Limehouse and the grandest duke in Grosvenor Square are bound together and give life each to each! You think me fanciful perhaps?'

'Not at all, sir,' replied Holmes, 'my work largely depends upon that fact. What is a crime but a disease? My work is largely diagnostic: just as Watson here might see a deficiency of iron in a swollen elbow, so I might detect a suburban murder in a frayed cuff. A death in Houndsditch may leave the inhabitants of Belgravia unmoved, but they mistake the matter if they do not believe themselves involved.'

'Mr Holmes, you are a man after my own heart,' said Bosney warmly. 'And is this not the season for just such reflections?'

'As to that, Mr Bosney,' said Holmes with a wry look towards me, 'I must confess that what with the weather on the one hand and the false civilities on the other, Christmas leaves me quite cold.'

'Why then,' returned the other in some surprise, 'you are a perfect – ah, here is Gray's Inn. See how they have now put up signs warning the unwary of the fresh paint upon the palings. Good cheer, Tom!' This last remark was addressed to a young crossing-sweeper who had stepped smartly up to open the door for us as we drew up, and to whom Bosney tossed some pennies.

My heart sank as I looked at the tide of traffic roaring past us and crossing the Gray's Inn Road. How could Holmes hope to recover one lost bundle of papers in such a vast confusion of humanity?

As always when Sherlock Holmes was engaged on a case, his reflective lassitude gave way to an extraordinary vigour and his demeanour took on the keen expression of a greyhound loosed from the slips.

'This is your street down here, I take it?' he inquired of our companion. 'John's Street, I think it is called.'

'Exactly so, I inhabit one of the houses further down, where it changes its name before joining Guildford Street,' replied Mr Bosney, scampering to keep up with Holmes as he strode down the well-lit thoroughfare. 'Here we are, allow me to invite you in for some warming negus, I beg.'

'Thank you. Later perhaps. Now the cab stood here, I perceive? Quite so. No rain has fallen this afternoon, that is good.'

Holmes whipped out his lens, dropped onto all fours and began to scramble about on the ground outside Culliford Bosney's house. To one so well acquainted with Sherlock Holmes and his methods, the minuteness of the scrutiny and the animal energy with which he conducted it held no real surprises for me, but the novelist watched with frank astonishment as Holmes, with blithe disregard for the knees of his trousers, crawled in the mud of the cobbled kerbside, now scooping tiny objects into a fold of paper produced from an inside pocket, now measuring invisible marks upon the ground with a tape.

At last, Holmes rose to his feet. 'Now, Mr Bosney, this house here that adjoins yours, this belongs to the Colonel from India, or to the medical students?'

'To the students. That house there, all shut up, is Colonel Harker's.'

'As I assumed. We must make haste if we are to recover your manuscript. I think now I will go into the house.'

I followed Mr Bosney to his front door, but turned in surprise to see Holmes proceeding down the front path of the neighbouring house.

'Why Holmes!' I cried, 'this is the house.'

'On the contrary Watson. You were a medical student once, you should be aware that *this* is the house.' So saying he pulled at the door bell. 'Read the ground, gentlemen, it is the skin of the great organism we were discussing and bears battlescars that can testify to many a strange history.' The door opened and a maid admitted Holmes into the dwelling.

'Well!' said Mr Bosney. 'Most extraordinary! What can these students have to do with the matter?'

'I think we should wait,' said I, 'Holmes very rarely makes a mistake. If he thinks that they have some connection with the mystery, then you may depend upon it that they have. Come, let us look at the ground and see if we cannot follow his reasoning.'

The pair of us spent a fruitless quarter of an hour examining the mud of the street with the aid of a lens that Bosney brought out from his house. Whatever code was printed there was too cryptic for us to decipher, however, and we were just climbing the steps of Mr Bosney's house to partake of a hot posset when the door of the students' lodgings opened and a young man shot out, clutching a hat to his head and running at breakneck speed down the street. He was followed a few moments later by Sherlock Holmes, who eyed the retreating figure with benevolent amusement.

'An elementary problem, Mr Bosney. Appropriately frivolous for the time of year. If you would be so good as to return with us to Baker Street, I think I may be able to shed a little light on the matter.'

'But . . . but Mr Holmes!' cried the other. 'The manuscript! You mean you have found it?'

'Unless we are very unfortunate, it should be in your hands within the hour.'

*

Not a word would Holmes vouchsafe us, on our homeward

journey, save the observation that were all cases as simple as this one, life would soon become insupportably dull.

When we were ensconced in the comfortable warmth of 221B Baker Street, Holmes plucked a book from the shelves and left Culliford Bosney and I to complete the festive decoration of the rooms while he read. Of a sudden, Holmes closed his book with a laugh.

'Well, Watson, perhaps this will turn out to be a case for your memoirs after all. Most remarkable. I should have known, of course.'

'What should you have known, Holmes?' we cried in exasperation.

'We were remarking earlier, Mr Culliford Bosney,' said Sherlock Holmes, with an uncharacteristic twinkle, 'that all things in this great capital interconnect in surprising ways. The observers of life, such as ourselves, must place ourselves like spiders at the centre of the great web, and train ourselves to interpret every twitch upon the gossamer, every tremble of the fibre. As soon as you mentioned to me that you lived next door to medical students I registered just such a quiver on the web. Perhaps it meant something, perhaps nothing, but I filed it away just the same. Watson may remember my remarking that the only notable crime London had to offer today was the removal of a statue from Charing Cross. You may be aware, Mr Bosney, that it is the habit of medical students to play pranks upon each other. The rivalry between the students of the two great hospitals at Charing Cross and Guy's is legendary.'

'Why, that's true!' I cried, 'I remember in my day that we – '

'Quite,' said Holmes, always impatient of interruption. 'I had therefore already set down in my mind the theft of the statue as an incident of just such festive exuberance. Your mention of medical students, Mr Bosney, while conceivably immaterial, prepared me for some connection. As soon as I came upon the scene of your meeting with the spectral hansom the true facts of the matter became clear to me. To the trained eye the tracks in the kerbside were easy enough to interpret. I saw at once that the cab had been waiting outside the *students'* house, Mr Bosney, not your own. The signs of movement and restlessness on the part of the horse also told me that no professional London jarvey had been at the reins. It had been all the driver could do to keep the horse still while the statue was loaded into the cab.'

'A statue!' Culliford Bosney clapped his hands together. 'Of course! The awful fixed stare and the ghostly pallor!'

'You were an excellent witness, Mr Bosney, but you failed to interpret your own evidence. Your senses had already told you that you beheld something inhuman, but you refused to make the logical inference.'

'Ghosts were much on my mind, Mr Holmes. I had after all just completed a fiction and was perhaps still dwelling in the world of the imagination. But what of the manuscript?'

'I called on the students, as you observed. They were most communicative. They revealed to me that for the purposes of the jape one of their number had hired a hansom for the day and bribed the cabbie to stay away. He had purloined the statue and brought it straight to your street, Mr Bosney. There the other students came out and dressed it up. I already knew that something of the sort had taken place from the disposition of footprints outside. The students had then gone back into the house, leaving their ringleader in charge of the cab, while they changed into builders' overalls. It was their mad intention to climb Temple Bar and place the statue in a prominent position overlooking the traffic. The young gentleman who had played the part of the cabbie related to me how you had accosted him while his friends were still inside. You took him so by surprise when you hailed him, that he did not think to say that he was engaged.'

'The young hound!' exclaimed Culliford Bosney.

'He is most penitent I assure you,' said Holmes. 'I think I may say without conceit that he was a little startled to find Sherlock Holmes on his trail.'

'A hammer to crack a nut, to be sure . . . but the manuscript, Mr Holmes?'

'Ah the manuscript! Your cabbie took advantage of the moment when you sprung back in amazement from the cab to make good his escape. He contrived to smuggle the statue into Charing Cross Hospital itself and put it into a bed where, as far as he knows, it remains still. He returned the hansom to the cab company who had hired it out to him and had reached his lodgings next door to your house not half an hour before we arrived upon the scene.

He has a vague memory of seeing a bundle of papers in the back of the cab, but he paid them no attention. When I made it plain to him that the loss of that manuscript would result in the story of his adventures being made known to the dean of his hospital he rushed from the house to recover it. I think I hear his tread upon the stair now.'

Just at that moment the door opened to admit a flushed young man carrying a large bundle of papers.

'My manuscript!' cried Mr Bosney, leaping to his feet.

'Allow me to present Mr Jasper Corrigan,' said Holmes. 'This is my good friend Dr Watson, and this gentleman, whose manuscript you appear to have found, is your neighbour, the novelist.'

'Well sir, I believe I owe you an apology,' said the medical student, holding out a hand. 'I'm sure Mr Holmes here has told you everything. Believe me when I say that I had no intention of doing you such a wrong.'

'My dear fellow,' said Mr Bosney, warmly shaking hands, 'think nothing of it! If the manuscript is complete . . . let me see . . . ' He took the bundle of papers and examined them eagerly. 'Yes, it is all here. I will take it to the printers this instant. Will they be open at this time of the evening? But they have a night staff. Yes, this very instant! Mr Corrigan, I hope you will do me the honour of coming with your friends to my house tomorrow night. We shall have a party! Yes, with chestnuts and games and all manner of fun. A man should know his neighbours. It is disgraceful that I have not invited you before. Marshmallows too, and a hot punch! Please tell me you will come.'

'Sir, we should be honoured. We . . . I do not deserve such generosity.'

'Pooh! Is it not Christmas? As for you, Mr Holmes, I am sure I do not know where to begin . . . such brilliance, such – '

'Really, Mr Bosney, you are too kind,' said Holmes, smiling a little at the author's exuberance. 'I am happy that your story is saved, but I think on reflection that you will see that it was not a testing problem. Indeed it is probable that it would have solved itself without my aid.'

'That I cannot allow,' replied Mr Bosney, 'I insist that you name your fee.'

'As to that,' said Holmes, 'I *will* ask a fee from you.'

234

'Name it, Mr Holmes, name it!'

'I have a fancy to own that manuscript of yours. When it returns from the printers, I wonder if you will send it to me?'

Mr Bosney blinked slightly. 'Really Mr Holmes, you do me a great honour. You told me you have no time for fiction.'

'Some fiction I have all the time in the world for, Mr Bosney, and I have an idea that I will enjoy your story. I think it is you who are doing me the honour.'

'Shake my hand, sir!' said the other. 'You are a remarkable man. A remarkable man.'

★

Mr Bosney was as good as his word and the manuscript arrived a week later through the post. Holmes took it up immediately and for the next two hours sat reading it. When he had finished, he looked up and I saw that there were tears in his eyes.

'Really Watson,' he said at last. 'Couldn't we have more holly about the place? It is Christmas, you know.'

'But Holmes!' I expostulated.

'Read it, Watson,' he said passing the manuscript over to me. 'Just read it.'

I took it up and looked at the cover page. 'But . . . but . . . Holmes!'

'Quite, Watson.'

I looked at the manuscript again. On the cover page was written, 'A Christmas Carol, by Charles Culliford Boz Dickens.'

'And a merry Christmas to us all!' said Holmes.

FINIS

Section Four

The Telegraph

Extra Sensory Deception

I was flicking through the quarterly journal of the Committee for the Scientific Investigation of Claims of the Paranormal the other day – I don't know if you're a subscriber? No? But you should be, you really should – and I found myself laughing aloud so much that the waiter had to rally round with a cloth, a glass of water, a disclaimer form and a moist lemon-scented cleansing square. I should have explained that I was in a Taiwanese restaurant while reading this inestimable work, whose proper title is the *Skeptical Inquirer*. It specialises in disposing elegantly and ruthlessly of the rubbish of ESP, astrology, ghosts, UFOs, spoon-bending and similar tommy-wash and hog-rot. There is a British publication too, called the *Skeptic*, spelt thus in honour of its American counterpart.

I find it very hard to conceal my contempt . . . no, contempt isn't the right word exactly . . . to conceal my mixture of distress, anger, pity and revulsion at the huge industry of the paranormal, and the irrational mélange of mystery and pseudo-science that is attached to it. On the one hand astrologers and similar charlatans tell us that 'science doesn't know everything; there are more things in heaven and earth, sucker, than are dreamt of in your philosophy' and on the other, they hasten to assure us that their fatuous cabalistic charts are worked out in accordance with scrupulous scientific principles and that 'a lot of very important academics and politicians (unnamed, always unnamed) are one hundred per cent convinced by them'. Working often in a profession like acting where one is constantly exposed to the shivering madness of vitamins, wild-flower essences, homeopathy, crystals, zodiacs and holistic balancing, I find it very difficult sometimes to respond to some of the claims made while retaining that soigné, chivalrous old world courtesy that wins hearts and avoids Unpleasant Scenes.

It is refreshing, therefore, to find a magazine that thinks as I do. I feel as some poor lonely old deviant must feel when first he discovers the existence of *Bin-Liner Fantasy Weekly* or *Nipple-Piercing News*. I am not alone.

The *Skeptical Inquirer* will never outsell zodiacal and UFO magazines; there is no market for what might be considered the negative or closed-mind approach of rational scepticism. In fact there is nothing at all closed about the minds of sceptics. The list of physicists, psychologists and philosophers who contribute to the magazine is awesome indeed, but they are surely more open to the miraculous mystery of the universe than those who believe that the cosmos could be so capricious and nonsensical as to enable for instance telepathy, which would contravene the second law of thermo-dynamics, a principle far more beautiful, mysterious, yet demonstrable, than the hazy guff of ESP.

Last quarter's *Skeptical Inquirer* contained a magnificent counterblast to the drivelling of those who think that the new Chaos physics casts all in doubt and proves that anything is permissible in a random universe. An article by Isaac Asimov on the Relativity of Wrong blows away the fallacy that everything scientists think now will one day be disproved.

The funniest feature, however, contained news of a side-splitting American television show called 'Exploring Psychic Powers – Live!' At stake was $100,000 which would be given, there and then, to any psychic, astrologer or similar contestant who could prove their 'powers' under conditions which they themselves had agreed to. Uri Geller appeared, naturally, but did not subject himself to testing: every trick he performed was instantly duplicated by the Canadian magician and conjuror, a great hero of mine, James Randi. As the *Inquirer* so succinctly put it: 'Randi was on the firing line. It was he, using all his knowledge and skills as skeptic, magician and thinking human being, who defended reason over bunkum and presented the case for a questioning, skeptical attitude toward paranormal claims.' Randi opened the show by levitating a human being, bending spoons with no apparent effort and making the time change on the spectator's watch while it lay on the table, all Geller favourites.

Then came the real fun: the first contestant was an astrologer 'famous' for being able to tell at a glance people's star signs. He had interviewed twelve people, all within three years of the same age, all with different star signs. If he could attribute ten of the star signs correctly he would instantly win $100,000. He got none right. Statistically improbable that anyone could be *that* incompetent, I know, but he got zero out of twelve. Zilch. Diddley-squat.

An ESP challenger was then offered $100,000 if she could get 82 out of 250 correct calls using Zener cards (those wavy-line/plus-sign/circle/square/star chaps). She got fifty, precisely as the laws of probability would predict. The 'psychometry' challenger had to match keys and watches belonging to the same person by 'feeling' the psychic resonances of these objects. By prior agreement nine out of twelve would have given her the prize. She got two. The $100,000 remained unspent that evening and common sense prevailed.

Ah, but if only it would in real life. Nonetheless I remain optimistic, like all good Sagittarians.

This Sporting Life

Twenty years ago, life was tough. The oil crisis was looming, the Vietnam War raged on and the human race still hadn't come up with a washing powder that could prevent stale odours while ironing. Horrific as these international crises were, they loomed not at all large in my little life. My twelve-year-old soul was consumed by one problem only: How to Get Off Games.

You, I know, are to a man and woman upright, clean, fresh, decent sprigs of ruddy health and sappy vigour. You were never happier than when thundering down the three-quarter line or mobbing about in the changing rooms playing Flick the Flannel with the Captain of the Colts. I, however, was a Sensitive for whom a game of cricket was an opportunity to make a daisy chain and who, with Kipling, had little respect for 'the flannelled fools at the wicket or the muddied oafs at the goals'. Like the hero of Vivian Stanshall's 'The Odd Boy', I would lie in the long grass with a volume of Mallarmé listening to the distant shouts. Well, if we're honest, more likely Dornford Yates than Mallarmé, but the principle's the same.

Your honest English faces are already purpling with disgust. 'I thought men like that shot themselves,' you are thinking. Don't worry. I am not about to write a revenge piece casting myself as the embittered and embattled Aesthete and the games players as crude, bone-headed Philistines. Far from it. What is exercising my mind at the moment is the fact that I now love all forms of sport so very much.

What would my young self say if he could see me now, six-pack at my side, ingesting every form of sport that television can offer? He would draw himself to his full gangling height and sneer. Fry, the Spazzo of the Fourth, watching every stroke of the Open Golf? Fry, the Weed who once wore furry gloves and a scarf while playing rugger, roaring 'that was *never* off-side!' Fry, who would give himself an asthma attack by burying his head in laburnum bushes just to get off cricket, wangling an introduction to Denis Compton so as to talk about the relative merits of Miller, Hadlee and Botham? It's inconceivable.

But I do love sport. Cricket first, by miles, but soccer too, and rugbies league and union. I love darts, bowls, snooker, baseball, motor-racing and badminton. I even work out. It's true. Twice a week I grunt and sweat under the eye of a physical trainer. I used to faint at the sight of a jock-strap and now I babble of deltoids and anaerobic toning. What is going *on*?

I certainly don't want to present myself as the all-round Hemingway-style hero, both manly and sensitive. You know the sort of thing; up at six, brisk ten rounds of wrestling with one's drinking companion of the night before; light breakfast of mescal and roast stag with a volume of Swinburne sonnets propped up against the pepper-pot; an hour of real tennis while dictating an article on Danish enamelware followed by a lunch of absinthe and raw fillets of narwhal to the accompaniment of a string quartet playing late Couperin. That's not quite me. Nonetheless I have betrayed the adolescent self who swore that one day he would get even with the swaggering hearties.

Unlike most sports lovers I do derive a perverse kind of pleasure from the behaviour of the *Hooligani Inglesi*, repellent as it is. It is the pleasure of anticipation. Every time I see footage of the Italian police coping with our disgusting compatriots I try and imagine what will happen in 1994 when the World Cup is held in the USA.

The American police and National Guard weren't notably sympathetic in their treatment of Vietnam War protesters. Given the opportunity to express themselves properly with some Category One English football fans, the like of which they will never have experienced, I feel sure they will surpass themselves.

The spectacle of some scarlet-faced oaf draped in a Union Jack looking up at the grim, unforgiving features of Inspector 'Dirty' Harry Callaghan of the San Francisco Police Department is one to which I look forward eagerly.

'I know what you're thinking, punk. You're thinking, did he fire six shots or only five? Now, to tell you the truth, I've forgotten myself in all this excitement, but being this is a 44 magnum, the most powerful hand-gun in the world, and will blow your head clean off, you've got to ask yourself a question. "Do I feel lucky?" Well do you, punk?'

''Ere we go, 'ere we go, 'ere we go. Eng-er-land!'

Kerboom!

Even my young, sensitive self could have learned to love a sport like that.

A Question of Attribution

The story is told of how F.E. Smith used to stroll to work each day from his lodgings in St James's. The walk would take him along Pall Mall, past the row of gentlemen's clubs that have made that thoroughfare such a hissing and a byword, into Trafalgar Square, through the Strand and thence to the Law Courts which were his natural domain and fiefdom. Being a regular sort of fellow, diligent about his matutinal ingestion of prunes and unswerving in his dedication to oats, he found it necessary every morning to stop off at the Athenaeum, for all that he was not actually a member, and make use of the excellent lavatories that are such a feature of that remarkable institution.

One lynx-eyed porter, after several years of painstaking observation and deduction, came to the conclusion that he only ever saw this august gentleman on those occasions when he came in for what Lord Byron would have called his morning supplication at the shrine of Cloaca, goddess of the bowel. The brave porter plucked up courage one day and actually stopped F.E. as he attempted ingress. 'Excuse me, sir,' he said, 'but are you actually a member of this club?' 'Good lord!' said Smith, 'don't tell me it's a *club* as well.'

I was reminded of this remark when I visited Wimbledon last week as the guest of the BBC, whose frankly and openly Marxist coverage of the tournament has no doubt incensed so many right-thinking people over the last fortnight, but which I, sunk in sin as I am, find so commendable and efficient. There were many there thronging the corporate marquees and measuring out the afternoon in champagne flutes, who would have been as staggered as Smith to learn that somewhere in that vast tented village there were actually games of tennis afoot; genuine matches of what my cricket master at school used contemptuously to describe as 'woolly balls'.

I don't mean here to rehearse the common moan of those who find corporate entertaining vulgar and demeaning, enough ink has been spilt on that subject already. The point is that I repeated the F.E. Smith anecdote to a companion that afternoon and they replied: 'Yes, but it was Churchill, actually, wasn't it? At least, that's what I heard.'

I have already steeled myself to the possibility that I will soon be bobbing helplessly in a swollen torrent of letters informing me that in fact the gentleman in question was neither Churchill nor Smith but actually Sir Thomas Beecham, or 'my uncle, the late Dean of St Paul's', or the fourth Duke of Bassingbourne, or Joad, or Porson, or Marcus Aurelius, or Jael, wife of Heber. This is the difficulty of approaching what Disraeli called one's 'anecdotage' – it *was* Disraeli, wasn't it? Or was it Dr Johnson or Sidney Smith? – stories seem to accrete to a chosen cast of people. In medieval times when the milk soured or the chimney caught fire it was convenient to blame Robin Goodfellow, later to achieve world fame as Puck. We know that mud sticks, but it seems that cream sticks also. Sam Goldwyn, Dorothy Parker and Groucho Marx on the other side of the Atlantic and Churchill, Wilde, Shaw and Coward on this; they have all been credited with other people's *bons mots*, simply because it is more convenient to attribute to the known than to the unknown.

But who are the epigrammatists of today? If one wants to repeat a story which involves a word-processor and a Post-It Note one can hardly lay it at the door of Mark Twain, can one? I believe a modern wit should be nominated, whose duty it would be to take the credit for all the anonymous sallies and unattributed one-liners that are thrown up in modern life. Such a person can hardly be a politician, I think. When you consider that the most thigh-slappingly brilliant gag heard in the chamber in the last twenty years is Denis Healey's remark about being savaged by a dead sheep, it is clear that Parliament is no longer a repository for wit of any kind. I feel we should elect our new Quipmaster-In-Ordinary in aleatory fashion. Someone chosen entirely at random, someone like, say, Ian McCaskill the popular and charming weatherman. 'Wasn't it Ian McCaskill . . . ' conversational gambits would begin. 'Well it's fine, as McCaskill once said about Cajun food, but it's nothing to fax home about.'

I think the name has the right ring. Which reminds me of McCaskill's splendid aperçu on the subject of Wagner's great *Nibelung* tetralogy. 'It's splendid,' he once remarked over a brandy sour, 'but I don't think the *Ring* has the right name.' What a man.

Carefree Panty-Shields and Intimate Wipes

We live in dangerous, uncertain times. Dame War, her mean, pinched features cracking into a ghastly smile, threatens to enGulf us in a molten river of desolation and ruin. The Harlot Inflation is pulling up her petticoats and allowing us a peep of her huge, swollen thighs. That surly footpad, Recession, rubs his brutal blue beard-line threateningly between finger and thumb and leers down with grim delight at the prospect of poverty, squalor and homelessness. At such a time it's good to know that people are coming up with television advertisements for Carefree Panty-Shields and Intimate Wipes.

Now I am not quite sure what a Panty-Shield is; something, one might wildly hazard, that shields a panty. The identity and purpose of an Intimate Wipe is something I know even less about and I am content to go to my grave that way. They are a closed book, or at the very least a closed wipe, to me. There are some mysteries, I feel, best not enquired into; some depths that are better left unplumbed. Besides, I have a powerful intimation that I am not the target audience for Carefree Panty-Shields and Intimate Wipes; my ignorance as to their function, appearance, packaging, availability and price is not, I reckon, going to cost the manufacturers, marketers or advertisers a moment's sleep. Somewhere in the back of my mind I have a dim feeling that Intimate Wipes are in some loose way connected with Personal Freshness, a subject I am appallingly hazy about. I seem to remember that I had German Measles when we covered it at school and I've never quite caught up.

But that is not the point at issue, or at tissue, here. What puzzles me is that there are men and women who are paid real cash money

248

to sit round tables and come up with this kind of calamitous drivel. I bored you all a few months ago with my puzzlement at the phrase 'Serving Suggestion' or the title 'Moist Lemon-Scented Cleansing Square' but Intimate Wipes? Surely there has been some ghastly mistake somewhere. I mean, lawks.

I am told that when a new product is to be launched, marketing people have what they are pleased to call Brainstorming Sessions which decide brand names and product descriptions. How I wish I could have been present at the Carefree Panty-Shield and Intimate Wipe brainstorm.

'Well,' says Tom, 'let's face it, these little beauties shield your panties and leave you totally free from care, don't they? Well, why in hell don't we call them Carefree Panty-Shields?'

Large measures of Jack Daniel's all round (marketing people like to be thought of as American) at this inspired piece of left-field thinking.

'Tom's cracked it! Tom's cracked the son of a bitch,' everyone agrees.

'Wait a minute,' says Jacqueline. 'What about . . . what about Carefree Panty-Shields *and* . . . '

'Yes? Yes?' Everyone is breathless with excitement, Jackie has a proven track record. She, after all, was the marvel who came up with the catch-line for Moists, the revolutionary new moist lavatory paper, 'Moists, they're a bidet in a box.'

'What about,' says Jacqueline, 'Carefree Panty-Shields and Intimate Wipes?'

Now if you or I had been there, reader, we would have called for a nurse at this point. A once talented marketing mind in ruins. With the best possible care in an up-to-date rest home and a great deal of quite violent electric shock therapy perhaps one day Jacqueline would again be ready for the outside world. But that is not what happened. Instead of someone being deputed to keep her talking while Tom called for an ambulance, Jacqueline was cheered to the echo, the printers and packagers were informed, the advertising agency briefed and the whole package presented to the British public.

The English language, in all its glory, can be pressed and pummelled and scrunched and squeezed into many shapes and configurations. It is capable of wonders like 'Goodnight, sweet prince, and flights of angels sing thee to thy rest,' 'Yet a little sleep, a little slumber, a little folding of the hands to sleep,' and 'How strange the change from major to minor, every time you say goodbye.' It is also, of course, capable of horrors like 'heritage care' and 'family values' but I never thought the day would dawn when someone would be allowed to ransack the dictionary and force a shotgun wedding between the innocent, blushing adjective 'intimate' and the strange young noun 'wipe'.

There are hundreds of thousands of words left in our language that will in time be conjoined in beautiful, ugly, coy, obscene and bizarre ways that we cannot guess at. Let us all fervently pray that with the invention of the Panty-Shield and Intimate Wipe we are over the worst.

The Stuff of Dreams

I am a foreign correspondent today. Fate has found me coming to America, to the badlands of Los Angeles, California. The grand hotel from whose bright balcony I write these few faltering words is in the Avenue of the Stars, just off Santa Monica Boulevard and Constellation. It's hard not to drop such splendid sounding street names, harder still not to drop the names of the big motion pictures that have been made in this remarkable country. My task today therefore will be to include as many film titles as I can think of in the course of writing this communication; your task will be to find them buried in the (of necessity) rather torrid prose that follows. Not a shatteringly fascinating programme for the day, perhaps, but no more harmful a way of killing 10 minutes during the incredible journey you take to work than doing the Agatha Christie book titles game or counting satellite dishes. You will need a pencil or similarly low-tech implement of scripture with which to circle the titles. Full titles only will count, with proper conjunctions and definite or indefinite articles. In this opening paragraph, for instance, you might have spotted *Foreign Correspondent*, *Coming to America*, *Badlands*, *The Incredible Journey*, *Agatha* and *Grand Hotel*, but you may have missed *Country*, *10* and *Big*. It doesn't matter, none of them counts; the competition starts from the next paragraph. A Californian present for the first person to send me more than 112 different titles. Be warned, American films only.

Welcome to L.A. This above all is a place stranger than paradise. Being there, with Sunset Boulevard around the corner, one cannot help but run the gauntlet of emotions from intolerance to suspicion and fury. It's a wonderful life, to live and die in L.A., but I confess to feeling that I am an alien amongst aliens in an alien nation. It is angel city and I'm no angel.

From sunrise to sunset the blue skies shelter people carefree, rich and famous, or at least rich and strange; they shelter scenes of notorious wealth and power, interiors and estates where even the gardeners wear livery. But the awful truth is that there is a different story, for the sun also rises on ordinary people, the misfits scarred by poverty; on loveless, violent streets and on the men and the women who find themselves cornered like the rats they are treated as. They are the outsiders, missing out on the real glory.

Call me indiscreet, but I wake up screaming and breathless when I think of how this deranged bedlam teeters on the edge of sanity: pet perfumeries, bra museums, outdoor air-conditioning, a wedding for dogs, all done without a trace of irony, by the beautiful people of this over the top heaven.

When the adventurers of the past, the gold diggers, first decided to go west to the promised land, the general idea was to find the motherlode. Things change: the descendants of these explorers still share this frantic greed, but it has turned into an indecent obsession with the mirage of fame. They are given over to it hearts and minds, body and soul, flesh and blood. Los Angeles is not of this earth; it's a boom town for dreams that money can buy. Everyone believes with the burning frenzy of the moonstruck that they too can make a splash and become a giant legend, if only fortune deigns to smile. The conversation you pick up from the starstruck lounge lizard and the beguiled barfly always revolves around hitting the big time or the struggle of keeping up the desperate mask of pretence that they have already jumped on the bandwagon of easy money and easy living. Family life, security, every normal impulse is sacrificed one by one in this ruthless quest for miracles.

It's not a safe place; the crazies and ruthless people who run it show no mercy, they hire and fire with caprice and in cold blood. They hold nothing sacred but the sweet smell of success. The verdict of future generations will probably be harsh. I could go on singing the dispraises of Los Angeles for ever, but I'm on dangerous ground because, bananas as it may sound, I love this magic town.

I forget who first exposed the natural truth that if you look hard enough beneath the surface tinsel of Hollywood you find . . . more tinsel, but he overlooked the city's saving grace. In the end, the real genius of Hollywood is that the tinsel is perfect tinsel. The producers at work in the glitter dome may only turn out trash, but it's model trash. They have turned alchemy inside out and discovered the formula for the most important of secrets: taking real gold, dull and useless as it is, and transforming it into the shining dross that millions like us need: the stuff of dreams.

Answers to The Stuff of Dreams

Bold type indicates a film title. There are probably more than I have shown.

Welcome to L.A. This above all is a place **stranger than paradise. Being there,** with **Sunset Boulevard** around the corner, one cannot help but run **the gauntlet** of emotions from **intolerance** to **suspicion** and **fury. It's a wonderful life, to live and die in L.A.,** but **I confess** to feeling that I am an **alien** amongst **aliens** in an **alien nation.** It is **angel city** and **I'm no angel.**

From **sunrise** to **sunset** the **blue skies** shelter people **carefree/rich and famous,** or at least rich and strange; they shelter scenes of **notorious** wealth and **power/interiors** and estates where even the gardeners wear livery. But **the awful truth** is that there is **a different story,** for **the sun also rises** on **ordinary people,** on **the misfits/loveless** and **scarred** by poverty, on **violent streets** and on **the men** and **the women** who find themselves **cornered** like **the rats** they are treated as. They are **the outsiders/missing/out** on **the real glory.**

Call me indiscreet, but **I wake up screaming** and **breathless** when I think of how this **deranged/bedlam** teeters on **the edge of sanity:** pet perfumeries, bra museums, outdoor air-conditioning, **a wedding** for dogs, all done **without a trace** of irony, by the beautiful people of this **over the top/heaven.**

When **the adventurers** of the past, **the gold diggers,** first decided to **go west** to the **promised land/the general** idea was to find the motherlode. **Things change:** the descendants of these **explorers** still share this **frantic/greed,** but it has turned into an indecent obsession with the **mirage** of **fame.** They are given over to it **hearts and minds/body and soul/flesh and blood.** Los Angeles is **not of this earth;** it's a **boom town** for **dreams that money can**

254

buy. Everyone believes with **the burning** frenzy of the **moonstruck** that they too can make a **splash** and become a **giant/legend**, if only fortune deigns to **smile**. **The conversation** you pick up from the starstruck lounge lizard and **the beguiled/barfly** always revolves around hitting the **big time** (2) or **the struggle** of keeping up the **desperate mask** of pretence that they have already jumped on **the bandwagon** of **easy money** and **easy living**. Family life, security, every normal **impulse** is sacrificed **one by one** in this **ruthless** quest for **miracles**.

It's not **a safe place**; **the crazies** and **ruthless people** who run it show **no mercy**, they hire and **fire** with **caprice** and **in cold blood**. They hold **nothing sacred** but the **sweet smell of success**. **The verdict** of future generations will probably be harsh. I could go on singing the dispraises of Los Angeles for ever, but I'm **on dangerous ground** because, **bananas** as it may sound, I love this **magic town**.

I forget who first **exposed the natural** truth that if you look hard enough beneath the surface tinsel of Hollywood you find . . . more tinsel, but he overlooked the city's **saving grace**. In **the end**, the **real genius** of Hollywood is that the tinsel is **perfect** tinsel. **The producers** at work in **the glitter dome** may only turn out **trash**, but it's **model** trash. They have turned alchemy inside out and discovered **the formula** for the most important of **secrets**: taking real gold, dull and useless as it is, and transforming it into **the shining** dross that millions like us need: **the stuff** of dreams.

Piles

Round about the middle of the last decade, when Peter York's phrase 'Sloane Ranger' still held sway over the multitudes, the car to be seen in was the Volkswagen Golf GTI. I remember a friend of mine who was Sloaner than the Square itself seeing one parked outside his house. He had sold his own cabriolet version the moment he noticed they were becoming fashionable, such is the game these types play. He looked with contempt at the model that was cluttering up his leafy Brompton avenue and said, 'I hate those ruddy cars. Piles, I call them.' 'Piles?' I enquired. 'Yes,' he said. 'Sooner or later every arsehole gets them.'

Not the finest joke in the world, and almost certainly not original. Nonetheless this remark set me thinking, for I myself had succumbed to my first attack of haemorrhoids that week and they were much on my mind, well, much on another part of my exquisitely proportioned self, of course, but you know what I mean. By the kind of perfectly probable and predictable synchronicity which deluded Arthur Koestler into wasting his time on developing a theory of coincidences, it so fell out that a fortnight after this event my agent was holding a houseparty in Essex. He was a marvellous man, since gathered to God, it grieves me to say, but very much the last of a breed. I remember him as a sort of flurry of cigar, Bentley and Old Etonian tie, with the aspect of a rather cross owl who has just washed his feathers and can't do a thing with them. His obsession, in his later years, was to bring people out on the subject of piles. The particular evening I am recalling was rather formal, possibly it was St Vedast's Day, and the dinner had ended with the women leaving the table and the men clustering around the host's end trying to remember port etiquette.

As soon as the last female had departed this splendid man

rapped the board with the decanter and said, 'Now. With how many here have I had my Piles Conversation?' The confused silence that followed this unusual question revealed that we were all innocent of any such ennobling experience. For the next few hours (until, that is, the hostess had coughed loudly outside the door for the seventeenth time) we proceeded to enact The Piles Conversation, the transcript of which would be fit only for a dedicated journal of proctology or a medical student's rag mag.

The gist, nub, burden, gravamen or thrust of the Conversation was that all men suffer from piles, the same truth upon which the Golf Gti joke depended. Certainly the ten or so men in that room were all chronic sufferers. I use the word chronic in its medical sense here. Freed by our host's brave introductory confessions and flushed with a fine vintage of the Portuguese, out tumbled tales from all of us. What chequered careers our bottoms had all had! Perineal abscesses and haematomas as well as the common domestic haemorrhoid. This was a Damascan Road conversion for me; the scales, as it were, fell from my eyes.

The knowledge that one is not alone is priceless. We know from the poets that we are not alone when we are frustrated in ambition, crossed in love or dumb-struck by Dame Nature in her best designer-wear spring collection, but few poets have understood that we need to be consoled in our more banausic moods as well. Haldane, the great scientist, it is true, wrote a splendid poem about rectal carcinoma, but that is a rarer condition. There was a graffito reportedly scrawled on the lavatory at the Earl of Leicester's Norfolk seat (as it were) which is attributed to Byron.

O Cloacina, goddess of this place,
Look on thy suppliants with smiling face.
Smooth and consistent may their offerings flow;
Neither rashly swift, nor insolently slow.

Only Byron, I think, would describe constipation as insolence. But one has to look all the way back to the epigrammatists of the Greek Anthology to find any comparable poetic consolation.

We are constantly told, or constantly tell ourselves, that we are obsessed by things lavatorial. I beg leave to doubt it. We believe that picturing this politician or that great financier on the lavatory will somehow drain them of their power over us. But this reveals a shame more than an obsession.

In an attempt, therefore, to rid our society of its fundamental pudeur, I would urge all those of you with unwell bottoms to raise them over dinner. You will be doing a great public service. In less than a year all sorts and conditions of men and women will be freed of one area at least of acute social embarrassment. The costive of open conversation can purge us of this and all our ills.

Pass the doughnut-shaped cushion, Alice.

A Friendly Voice in the Polo Lounge

Whose is the last voice you would expect to hear drifting over to your table if you were dining alone in the Polo Lounge of the Beverly Hills Hotel?

The Polo Lounge is celebrated in legend, song and paperback novel as the place where people go to be seen. The thing to do is to get yourself *paged*. 'Telephone call for Herb Buckleman. Herb Buckleman to the telephone please.' These words will ring out from time to time as you sip your Long Island iced tea or crack your Dungeness crabs. It seems that important producers and powerful executives will be mightily impressed to know that Herb Buckleman is somehow, somewhere Wanted. Suddenly Herb Buckleman becomes an interesting person: just the man we are looking for, in fact, to write the seventh draft of that new Schwarzenegger movie.

This bizarre concept leads to the improbable phenomenon of people paging *themselves* in the Polo Lounge, or by the pool. They nip round to a telephone booth, ring the operator of the hotel with a message for themselves to call a certain number *at once*, and then streak back poolside or to the Polo Lounge in time to receive their message. To create an even more favourable impression it is common to give yourself an alias. Thus: 'Will Herb Buckleman, using the name Jerome Lassinger, please contact the operator urgently.' Herb Buckleman is now established as so important that he has to stay at the Beverly Hills under an assumed name, so as to keep the world's media off his back.

As you might expect, this creates a kind of backlash. So well known is the self-paging procedure, that should anyone be summoned to the telephone it is now assumed they have arranged it themselves and are therefore sad, desperate individuals best avoided.

The atmosphere in the Polo Lounge is therefore fraught with tension. I was dining there last night, all of a doo-dah because irresponsible friends back home had threatened to have me paged once every ten minutes, an ignominy I didn't think I could face. This fear made it very difficult to peep through my fingers at Eddie Murphy and Michael Douglas and generally enjoy the fun of being in such a place at such a time. Fortunately my friends did not ring; mostly, I think, because half past seven in Los Angeles is half past three in the morning in England and even the most dedicated ruiner of people's lives needs sleep.

I moved thankfully therefore from the cocktail area of the Polo Lounge into the dining area, ordered a warm tenderloin chicken salad and whipped out a paperback. It is strange to imagine that chickens have loins and that they are substantial enough for their tenderness to be determined; I think the name is in fact part of that amiable American preference for tough, pioneering names for their food. We are satisfied with French as the language of cooking but Americans find it a little sissy. I think they have a point: 'Seared belly of Nebraska hog, with sourdough and cracked Maine lobster claws' does sound more manly and more appetising than, say, *noisettes d'agneau à la Grecque dans un coulis de pamplemousse.*

There I was, cosily and blissfully wrapped in my own world – for dining alone is surely one of the most exquisite pleasures the world has to offer – when a familiar voice, not English, drifted over to my table. A voice more familiar to my generation than almost any other. The voice of a man who has regularly presented his own television programme for twenty-five years, a man who has had many top ten records in England; a man who has been as affectionately mocked and persistently imitated as anyone during that time. For all that, the last voice I would ever have expected to hear in the Polo Lounge of the Beverly Hills Hotel.

It was the voice of Rolf Harris. Quite why his voice should be so incongruous in this setting, I do not know, but a healing wave of homesickness swept over me like a moist mountain wind. I forgot America and its billion-dollar entertainment industry, its strangely named foodstuffs and its recondite hotel etiquette. Rolf Harris was there and suddenly I knew I was English and could never be anything else.

For all that our influence abroad has dwindled to Aston Martins and Mrs Thatcher's hats, the magnetic power of home has a pull with which dollars and avocado salads cannot compete. When you're wandering lost in Patagonia the sight of a battered packet of Scott's Porage Oats in a small *tienda* can tug at your heart strings like nothing else. When you're alone in the Polo Lounge, the fluting tones of Australia's greatest son beckon you home like a lighthouse.

The moment Rolf Harris's wonderful bass baritone voice penetrated my ear, I rose from my seat, hurried to reception and had him paged. It was the least I could do.

Drawing up a Hate List

There was a very silly joke people used to tell in the unreconstructed sixties, around the time when the fruits of the Wolfenden Report were being born, which concerned a Geordie who had visited Australia House, received all the necessary jabs from his doctor, packed up his belongings and sold his house preparatory to making a new life in the Southern Hemisphere. At the airport a reporter is interviewing him and asking why he has decided to give up the old country.

'Well,' says the Geordie, 'two hundred years ago homosexuality was punishable by death in this country. A hundred years later the sentence was two years' hard labour. Fifty years ago it was six months' imprisonment. Now it's legal. I'm getting out before they make it compulsory.'

Not a salubrious joke, nor frankly an enlightening or enlightened; still less an amusing. There is value, however, in reflecting on what changes could be wrought in one's country which would force one to consider leaving. The usual motives for emigration revolve around opportunity, taxes or familial plight, but is it possible to imagine legislation which would cause one to leave Britain, not for financial reasons, but out of disgust?

I was thinking about this earlier in the week, because I have long promised myself that if ever capital punishment was reintroduced here I should have, regretfully (on my part at least), to fold my tents and steal silently into the night. I mean, how too embarrassing it would be to belong to a country that went round putting its subjects to death. How could a fellow hold up his head with any pride as an Englishman if at the back of the mind was the thought that part of his taxes were going towards the cost of rope that was designed to snap people's necks? Simply too unthinkably shame-making. One just wouldn't know where to look when in the company of persons from civilised countries.

Of course the difficulty with such a drastic resolution, that of forswearing one's homeland on a point of principle, is that it can appear so petulant and hysterical. Those who like the idea of hanging would regard my emigration as good riddance to bad pusillanimous rubbish. 'If you can't stand the heat then get out of the kitchen,' would be the nub of their argument. To which I would reply, in that way I have, that I would much rather stay in the kitchen if someone would only be kind enough to turn the heat down, or possibly open the window and let in some fresh air. But democracy being democracy, an Act of Parliament that reintroduced the Death Penalty would hardly be stayed in its course because I, or any citizen, threatened to leave. One's departure would be of no value therefore as a protest, nor as a stunt; it would be a pure act of preference: one would rather not live here any more.

But perhaps this is simply cowardice. Wouldn't a fellow of real principle stay and fight? Is it not better to hold one's ground and campaign manfully than to flee and whinge feebly from the sidelines? I suppose this is true. But the return of the death penalty would cause such an overwhelming weight of weariness and revulsion to descend on me that all my fight would go. The same would happen if those weird anti-smoking fanatics got their way and managed to outlaw God's honest cigarette or Nature's healing cigar. I could try and justify my abhorrence and dread of Capital Punishment and Tobacco Prohibition by recourse to argument, but what separates them from other political or social issues in my case is, in fact, a deep and implacable hatred.

I was in a play once where an actress used to cheer us up during the dull hours between matinée and evening performances by getting us all to compile what she called Hate Lists. Anonymously we would have to compile a list of ten things that we hated irrationally and irretrievably. It could be anything: brass bands, Oxford, Vauxhalls, Wales, vitamins, sherry-glasses, tennis, the novels of D.H. Lawrence . . . whatever sprang from the real depths of one's soul. The lists would then be read out and we would have to guess who had written what.

I would recommend this as a Christmas game, adding perhaps the listing of possible legislation that would force one to emigrate.

Hatred might seem rather unseasonal, but the optimistic results of such an undertaking are that healthy players of the game (if they are really honest) never put *people* in their lists, even truly ghastly people; they only list things, attitudes and actions. This is because people are not capable of *being* evil, they are only capable of evil; that is the crucial difference that allows repentance and forgiveness, which, when all is said and done, is what Christmas is all about.

The discovery that one cannot hate people, only what they do or what they say, is a profoundly important one. It is as good a note as I can think of on which to wish you all, as they used to say in those unreconstructed sixties, a Cool Yule and a Gear New Year.

Blithe & Bonny & Good & Gay

Like many of my discredited generation I am insanely in love with gadgetry of all descriptions. In that dread era of eighties conspicuous consumption, none consumed more conspicuously than I. Even though we are now firmly into the new age of gentle caring, I'm finding it hard to catch up. In moral terms it is as if I am still gelling my hair back and wearing Bass Weejuns (a thing no nineties child would *der-ream* of doing, as you know). Why, only yesterday I caught myself going into a shop in the Tottenham Court Road and buying a CDV player. You don't know what a CDV player is? Shame on you. It's a sort of CD player, only instead of playing just audio laser-discs it plays video, too. So now you can watch your favourite film with crystal clear freeze frames and digital sound. An important step, I'm sure you'll agree.

This means that my snuggarium, den, rumpus-cosy or room-in-which-all-my-equipment-is-kept as I crazily call it, now has five, almost identical, remote control hand-held thingummies in it. One for the television, one for the normal CD, one for the video cassette recorder, one for the CDV and one for the hi-fi. Come to think of it there are six, I forgot the one the burglars foolishly neglected to take when they abstracted my previous video-player. (Next time you're passing, lads, you'll find it on the occasional table near the window, under an angrily defaced edition of *Halliwell's Film Guide*. I know how maddening it is not to have your hand-held, as it were.)

Aside from this lone, selfless attempt to bring down John Major by prolonging the boom in foreign imports (for believe it or not Britain has no domestic CDV laser-disc player manufacturing industry of its own, which is in itself nothing short of a national scandal) and amassing electronic equipment of all kinds and uses, I enjoy collecting (as which newspaper columnist doesn't) the latest, state-of-the-art catchphrases, slogans and buzzwords.

I was there cheering when David Steel made a brave stab at introducing the word 'overarching' into the political vocabulary; there too when British Rail decided that 'passengers' were going to be called 'customers' and chuff-chuffs would be designated 'services'; none squealed with greater delight than I when it was resolved that education and defence were sure to be the 'hot button' issues of the last election.

Few of these phrases come, unsurprisingly perhaps, from Japan. We look to America for our brightest neologisms and euphemisms. On my last visit I leapt like a spawning salmon when, after having bought a ruinously expensive tie from a shop in Rodeo Drive, the not un-mimsy assistant winningly waved his little fingers and trilled by way of valediction, not the usual 'goodbye' or the more usual 'Have a nice day, now' but these immortal words: 'Missing you already!' Well, I mean, what? I mean *what*?

The latest euphemism for disabled, hot from the United States, and I am aware that I am on dangerous ground here, but I'll charge on anyway, the latest euphemism for disabled is 'physically challenged'. The word 'blind', as you may already know, should now be replaced where possible by the phrase 'visually impaired'.

I have never shared the distaste for the word 'gay' which, as the correspondence pages of this newspaper have more than adequately shown, is felt by many. I know it was a nice word and that nothing else will quite do, I know it has been ruthlessly hijacked and shamelessly taken away from us. But we have, let's face it, been given back the equally good and irreplaceable words 'bent', 'pansy', 'fairy', 'faggot' and 'queer'. One good word for the price of five is a pretty good exchange. The word homosexual was fine as a quasi-medical definition, but always to use that would be like having to say 'parturition' every time we meant 'child-birth'. It's good to have a non-judgmental, lay word for a common enough fact. The trouble with the phrases like 'visually impaired' is that they are turning their back on the kind of word gay people (there I've used it!) craved for years, the word 'blind'. It is not a euphemism, nor derogatory, nor complicatedly technical.

I know the blind and disabled lobby is attempting to be 'positive' in its attempts to usher in these new words but I'm horribly afraid that there is a law of diminishing returns here. 'Handicapped' was originally a new 'positive' word, as was 'disabled'; but each one had a shorter currency than its predecessor.

I fear that 'challenged' and 'visually impaired' will be obsolete too very soon. Round about the same time as my new CDV player, I should guess.

I suspect the Japanese will find it easier, however, to design a fun replacement for the CDV than the Americans will to invent a new word for blind.

God Bless Worcestershire

If you are not reading these words, but find yourself gazing instead at a white empty space with room enough for 800 words bearing the legend 'Stephen Fry is on holiday' then you will know that the editorial staff at the *Daily Telegraph* has drawn up its maidenly skirts and decided to exercise its right to suppress and censor, for the article that you are not reading is a fearless exposé of the uses, practices and thinking behind said editorial staff and it is highly probable that they would rather operate behind a veil of secrecy than have their methods ruthlessly broadcast in their own newspaper.

I begin with a question. Do you come from Worcestershire? Some of you reading this (or gazing in wonderment at the white empty space where this should be) surely dwell within the marches of that inestimable shire. I wonder if there is something unusual about you? Are you more than usually prudish? Is there something in the waters of Droitwich, the carpets of Kidderminster or the broad smiling acres of Evesham that lends itself to a missish, puritanical air? It had never crossed my mind, living as I do beneath the wide Norfolk skies, that this might be the case, but it may please you to know that the breadth or narrowness of your minds is a source of constant concern to those whose business it is to supervise the matter that fills your daily newspaper.

Let me explain. I telephoned the features desk this afternoon. You will understand by this metonym or synecdoche that I wasn't so far sunk in sin as actually to attempt to engage a piece of furniture in conversation, but that I was dutifully ringing an editorial assistant to advise her of the contents of my hebdomadal tribute. I employ what my English master at school called such 'sixth form words' as 'synecdoche' and 'hebdomadal' not out of a perverse desire to be sesquipedalian but so as to ready you, especially those of you who come from Worcestershire, for the stunning shock of the obscenities with which I am about to foul the air.

I told the editorial assistant that I was considering a piece on Saddam Hussein and the current agonies in the Gulf. It had occurred to me that there was no word to cover the crime of illegally violating another sovereign state and that perhaps the word 'saddamy' should be coined. The United Nations might enshrine this in an Article expressly forbidding one country wantonly to saddamise another and enforcing strict sanctions against saddamites.

The editorial assistant listened carefully. 'Yes,' she said. 'I'm just a little worried about how the readers in Worcestershire might react to that.'

I jerked like a gaffed salmon and dropped the telephone. Why had no one ever told me about the readers in Worcestershire and their special requirements? I knew how disgusted the townspeople of Tunbridge Wells could be and I was aware that Colonel and Mrs Chichester had no truck with modern playwrights. That Enraged of Minchinhampton is sick and tired of the use of 'target' as a verb is widely understood, as is Simply Livid of Carshalton's impatience with the emergence of the Pacific Oyster at the expense of the good old Colchester Native, but I have to confess that Worcestershire's problems had entirely escaped my notice.

If the features desk's fears are justified, but out of a commendable sense of liberality they have decided to publish this article, it is possible that Worcester General Hospital has already received a number of calls from mauve-faced citizens bellowing for digitalium, that the County Constabulary has formed a highly mobile task-force to deal with crazed villagers from Broadway picketing the newsagents and that the Fire Brigade is overrun with calls to deal with out of control *Telegraph* bonfires started up by outraged *ad hoc* 'Burn The Filth' Action Committees in Dumbleton.

If this is the case I am heartily sorry; sorry enough to eat my hat.

I think it is time the people of Worcestershire let the *Telegraph* know that they can take a great deal more than has been supposed. Time, too, for people of other counties to make their views heard. All these years you have been reading material in this newspaper that has been vetted, yes vetted! Adulterated, bowdlerised, censored, blue-pencilled, emasculated, muffled, repressed, curbed, gagged and stifled and all for the sake of the sensibilities of Worcestershire. You probably did not know that the copy of William Deedes is often so saucy that it has to be written on asbestos, that Worsthorne and Heffer are known as the Gilbert and George of modern letters and that Hugh Montgomery-Massingberd's original submissions can only be read by those who have been passed medically fit by the *Telegraph*'s in-house doctor. Of course you did not know, because their writings have always been sanitised and sieved and filtered, entirely for the benefit of Worcestershire.

Well, bottoms to you, Worcestershire. Some of us refuse to be muzzled.

Back on the Road

The Tuesday that has just passed, unmourned and unshriven like all Tuesdays except the Shrove which, I suppose by definition, is always shriven, was by way of being rather a red-letter day in the Fry diary. Actually my diary these days, like the diary of any self-respecting *flâneur*, runs on batteries and makes no allowances for rubric. In today's theme park world, however, what you lose on the Laser Mountain you gain on the Giant Corkscrew and while my electronic organiser may be ignorant of red-letter days it can tell me the time in Tirana and schedule my day into To Do Lists. Tuesday 21 August was accordingly flagged as the day it became legal for me to contribute once more to London's growing traffic problem.

Three hundred and sixty-five days earlier the bench of Number Two magistrates' court Bow Street, London, to the accompaniment of minatory remarks and austere sniffs, had taken from me five hundred pounds, my driving licence and a good deal of my self-esteem.

A year is a long time in motoring. The thought that haunted me over the last few weeks as the end of the ban hove in view was that I had perhaps forgotten how to drive.

A favourite car, that I have kept garaged throughout the last year, is a handsome Wolseley 15/50 saloon, deep maroon in colour and smelling of Bakelite and a vanished England of glistening pavements, raincoated Inspectors of the Yard and, for some improbable reason, Valerie Hobson and Tide detergent. It is almost precisely my age, having been registered on 23 August 1957. I was born at six o'clock the following day, so today, you may like to note for future reference, is my birthday.

The proximity of our ages has caused a rather voodooistic relationship to develop between me and the Wolseley. If I put on a couple of inches around the waist, its wings and sills seem to bulge slightly too. If I keep slipping and falling over for no apparent reason the explanation will be that the rear tyres are getting worn and need changing. On the rare occasions when I have a bath, I look out from my bedroom window while towelling myself and see that down in the street the old bus is as gleaming and clean as I am.

I was in a play in the West End a couple of years ago and lost my voice. Fellow actors thought I had been over-straining my vocal chords in the now legendary Potato Scene and rallied round with fatuous bottles of vitamins and homeopathic nonsenses but a quick check-up showed me that a connection just behind the solenoid had come loose and was fouling the contacts on the wire that fed out from the steering wheel. This stopped the horn from working. Two minutes with the screw-driver and both of us were in perfect voice once more.

I, as the cruelly honest photograph above this article can testify, sport a broken nose. When researching my car's history I discovered with a thrill that the bent Wolseley mascot on the bonnet had got that way after an incident involving a Home and Colonial Stores delivery van and a librarian from Daventry on 17 January 1962, precisely the day my own proboscis met its fate! These things are meant.

Might this special symbiosis, this marvellous interdependence and mutual reliance, might it be weakened by a year's neglect? That was my fear on Tuesday as I found myself once more behind the wheel.

The Wolseley's transmission system requires a manoeuvre perhaps familiar to my older readers, that of the double declutch. Today's *louche* world of synchromesh and, heaven help us, automatic gears, has rendered such a procedure antique and I feared that after a year's absence, ear, hand and foot might have lost their magic connection with the car's cogs and clutch-plates. I need not have worried. The old bond still exerts itself and we are once more as one.

One thing, however, still concerns me. Should I have the engine converted to take unleaded petrol? If I do what might be the personal consequences? Will it mean I have to drink decaffeinated coffee, or will even more calamitous changes be

272

wrought in my own engine? Is it possible that I will be able to ingest nothing but alcohol-free wine? If the Wolseley isn't going to be allowed to get high on lead it'll be damned if it will let me gorge myself on intoxicating liquors.

Well so be it. At least that way I'll find it easier to cold-start myself in the mornings.

In November I get my poetic licence back. I was banned for taking a caesura too fast and stopping at an enjambment while under the influence of Auden. Never again.

Zoo Time

In my salad days, when I was green in judgment and tossed in a light vinaigrette of faith, I liked nothing better than to put my trusting little hand in that of my mother and toddle to the zoo. The possibility of pandas and the likelihood of woolly monkeys exerted the strongest of pulls. But then, in my pudding days, when I was starchier in judgment and steeped in a heavy syrup of doubt, I found myself wondering dreadfully. Was it not possible that future generations would look back with amazement and distaste at our casual willingness to countenance the imprisonment of animals?

This whole question of the refinement of moral values is an interesting one. Perfectly virtuous, kind and considerate people two hundred years ago kept slaves, owned shares in sugar plantations that used nothing but slaves and wore cotton that they knew perfectly well had been picked by slaves. If you were to tell them that they were participating in, encouraging and prolonging one of the most noxious and inhuman practices conceivable they would have thought you mad.

More recently our grandfathers or great-grandfathers would have snorted with astonishment and distaste if told that the withholding of the vote from one half of the population gave the lie to claims that Britain was a democracy. Those who campaigned for feminine suffrage were hysterical, women didn't understand politics, they should never, never be allowed to vote, the majority of men argued. If you were then to tell them that in sixty years' time Britain's longest serving Prime Minister would be a woman they would probably have gone into spasm.

But our grandfathers were not wicked, nor too stupid to grasp the moral arguments that we now take for granted. Morality after all is custom and we are accustomed to the idea that it is wrong for one human to own another, that it is inimical for women to be denied a vote and, for instance, that bear-baiting and freak shows are disgusting.

What then will our grandchildren wonder at in our world? What practices that we indulge in will turn their stomachs and make them amazed that we could ever have called ourselves civilised? I have a strong feeling that zoos will figure high on the list.

Is it possible, they will ask, that we actually stole polar bears away from the arctic and set them in concrete-floored cages in southern climes to be gawped at? No! *My* grandfather would never have countenanced that, he would have demonstrated, or lobbied Parliament or written to the newspapers; he, kindly old grandpa, would have been ashamed to live in a country which imprisoned animals for show. Wouldn't he?

Human beings, who have imaginations and the ability to distract themselves by remembering poems or writing new ones, or betting on which bluebottle will fly off the window-pane first, find it hard enough to cope with incarceration. Animals, as far as we know, do not gamble or hum tunes to themselves or have an interior life that can make captivity less irksome, they simply turn slowly from rage to despair to neurosis and finally to a kind of numb torpor.

Some zoo keepers claim that seeing animals live and close up teaches children respect and awe for the glory and variety of nature, makes them understand their responsibility to these creatures. That might be so, but I have yet to hear plans to put South American Indians in pens in Regent's Park or Whipsnade, or herd together Kurdistani tribesmen in wild-life parks, thus to better our understanding of *their* lot. I have no doubt that the sight of a trembling Winnebago Indian in a cage, together with a little plaque describing his habitat, diet and ancestry, will encourage millions of British school children to respect the diversity and nobility of humanity and make them better, finer school children, but oddly no one has suggested such a procedure, even though it might save a tribe from extinction.

I don't subscribe to the idea that animals have 'rights'. It is more a question that there are some rights that we do not have. We surely do not have the right to put other creatures in prison, especially for so obscene a reason as for the furtherance of *our* appreciation of them. We do not have the right to tease them or bully them or send them mad. It may be that future generations will believe that we don't have the right to herd them, slice them into tender juliennes and steaks and then eat them. We raise our eyebrows at such a preposterous notion, but then so did our ancestors when it was suggested that small boys might be kept out of chimneys.

When my young nephews next come to London I shall deny them the zoo and take them to Parliament instead, to see Prime Minister's Questions. It's the same as watching gibbons fight over territory and rhinoceroses urinate, but without the guilt.

Trefusis Returns!

Never go back. Those words are written upon my heart in letters of flame. I have gone doubly back recently. Two years ago I was in a play in the West End by Simon Gray called *Common Pursuit*. The BBC are filming it and this week we are in Cambridge, evoking those gilded years of flared trousers, side-burns, collar length hair and stupid waistcoats.

I was up at Cambridge myself a few years after the era we are recreating, but it is nonetheless alarming to realise that, as far as the wardrobe and make-up departments of the BBC are concerned, the mid-seventies constitute Period. Sitting for an hour having strange wefts of human hair woven into one's scalp and ludicrous whiskers stuck to one's jowls to represent what my mother insists on calling 'bugger's grips' is one thing, but to have one's face painted with a strange translucent 'skin tightener' is quite another. I was an undergraduate only nine years ago, surely I haven't wrinkled and sagged so terribly since then?

In an attempt to cheer myself up I spent a morning showing the American member of our cast, Andrew McCarthy, around the colleges. He was as good as gold and never once expressed astonishment at the lack of air-conditioning in King's College Chapel or disgust at the absence of ice machines in the Wren Library. He started to yawn after an hour or so though, so I showed him the way back to Peterhouse, where we are filming, before turning my own steps towards the rooms of my old friend and mentor, Donald Trefusis, Professor of Comparative Philology and Extraordinary Fellow of St Matthew's College.

It was Trefusis who had initiated me into the Disciples, a close, intense sodality of intellectuals, sexual heretics and liberal humanists who toasted marshmallows and copies of the *Spectator* by the fire and read each other papers on intense topics such as the ontology of the flesh and the signature tunes of Jonathan Cohen. Donald had also recruited me for the KGB . . . or was it MI5? He never actually told me and it would have been un-Cambridge of me to have asked. In Cambridge you were on your friend's side, right or wrong. Human relations were the only loyalty.

Trefusis would be able to tell me why a heavy feeling of depression and alienation had begun to haunt me as I had ambled through the courts and cloisters.

The Professor opened his door to me in some surprise.

'So you've finished that essay on the Great Fricative Shift at last, young man?'

I assured him that I had not, but was still pursuing some more lines of research. I begged another nine-year extension, which he gracefully allowed.

'These things take time,' he conceded. 'My article on Slovakian Diacriticals for the *Neue Philologische Abteilung* took seventeen years simply to proof-read. I am persuaded it was worth the effort, however. You read the piece of course?'

'Who has not?' I replied, an evasion he was graceful enough to ignore.

'Dear me!' he cried, rubbing his hands with glee. 'I shook a few people up with that little paper! They tell me that copies of it were publicly torched at the Cornell Convention on Phonemes last year and that a certain lecturer at the School of Slavonic Studies in London hanged himself on account of my strictures on the origins of Croatian verbs of motion.'

We walked together along the Backs.

'Where's it all gone, Donald?' I asked. 'This is not the Cambridge I knew. The buildings are the same, you are the same, and yet . . . '

Trefusis gazed down at the sweetly flowing Cam from which floated up the melancholy strains of a punting tourist in a Gazza® hat singing 'Just one Cornetto' to the tune of 'O Sole Mio'.

'You cannot step into the same river twice,' he quoted, 'for fresh water is always flowing past you.'

'Heraclitus!' I exclaimed.

'Bless you,' he said. 'Your Cambridge was built of people, not of bricks and stone and glass, and those people have severally dispersed into the world. They will never be assembled together again. The circus has long since folded its tents and stolen silently away and you are standing on the empty village green wondering why it looks so shabby and forlorn.'

'You're right,' I sighed, 'as always, you are right.'

'Of course I am. Now pop off out of my sight. You smell of mortality. I don't need you to remind me of my age, I have a bladder to do that for me.'

I returned to the film set in time to be bombarded with more questions from the crew.

'Would a typical undergraduate have hung their Freshers' Photograph on their wall? Did they wear gowns to lectures? Did they leave their doors open?'

'Don't ask me,' I said. 'This is my first time here.'

A Bang on the Head

If the following words seem to you to be senseless wanderings from a tragically disordered mind I must apologise. I have just sustained an extremely violent bang to the head and it is possible that I am in a concussed and confused state.

It is not uncommon for people of my height to bump their skulls against lintels, beams and other projecting members. The usual procedure for me after such an occurrence, once all the effing and blinding has died away, is gingerly to prod the affected area of the cranium and run through a kind of check-list to determine how much my mind has been affected by the shock to its housing.

I ask myself firstly how much two plus two might come to. If I don't arrive at the answer 'yellow' or 'Cardinal Richelieu' I move on to my name, fax number and age. If I satisfy myself on these points I turn over the examination paper, as it were, and question myself closely on the date of Magna Carta, the capital of Uruguay and the name of the currency of Bulgaria. Then I turn to more difficult questions like whether there is a God, the reason men have nipples and the purpose of Geoffrey Wheatcroft. These problems are insoluble in a normal state of mind, but it is always possible that a bang to the head will bring about improvements that offer up previously denied insights.

It is of course an absurd and illogical reaction. If my mind were to be lost through a sharp blow how would I know what questions to ask? And how would I know if the answers I gave were wrong or right?

The surest test of softening or deterioration in the brain after an accident, it seems to me, is a desire on the part of the subject to sue someone or something. I banged my head in a very respectable Cambridge hotel. The blow was so severe that I found myself instantly sitting down. It is possible that I even lost consciousness for a small number of seconds.

As I sat there, nursing the medulla oblongata and embarking on my check-list, I found myself suddenly surrounded by a surging savannah of grey-striped trousers and concerned expressions. The hotel staff had observed the incident and were embarking upon the complex business of apology. The hotel, like almost every hotel in Britain nowadays, is part of a chain and I dare say there are very definite procedures to be undertaken when a guest has an accident within company premises. Procedures more to do with making sure that responsibility is never owned up to than with genuine expressions of sympathy, regret or fellow-feeling. This is in line with what travelling salesmen who frequently use cars are taught. After an accident, whatever the reason for it, never *ever* say 'sorry' to the other party involved. To say 'sorry' admits liability. I find this repellent and nauseating in the extreme. Most English people will apologise to a hatstand if they walk into it, let alone another human being. One would much rather hear a hotel manager say '*So* sorry' and see him go up to the offending beam into which a guest had bumped and smack it crossly crying 'naughty, naughty beam' than hear him greasily ask 'Didn't you see the large well-lit sign saying "Mind Your Head" hung clearly on the beam, sir?'

Of course the sign was there, of course the whole incident was, as it were, my fault. In life, if you are six foot four and a half inches tall, clumsy and occasionally distrait, you will bump into things. All one asks for, when it happens, is a teensy weensy bit of sympathy and just a smidgin of a scintilla of an iota of a soupçon of a shade of a suspicion of a shadow of concern. When it is not forthcoming, one's temper rises with the bump on the loaf and thoughts, strange, un-English thoughts, of civil actions and law suits actually do flit across one's mind. The very care and unctuous deftness with which liability is denied makes one determined to prove it.

With luck, reflection and a finger or two of good Islay malt will restore reason to its throne. There is a sort of absurd reverse Catch 22 that argues that anyone who could seriously sue a hotel or organisation after a simple accident must be so mentally damaged that they have cause.

'M'lud, does not the *very fact* that my client is doing something so preposterous as suing demonstrate how clearly deranged he has become?'

Case proven, *ipso facto*.

Fortunately however my mind is not one whit affected and I retain all my faculties.

I must leave you now, order a nice Pot Noodle from room service and enjoy that marvellous programme *Telly Addicts*. Good night, citizens. Next year your Emperor will be in Moscow. Help yourself to Wine Gums.

Dear Sid

This week filming has begun for a second series of *Jeeves and Wooster*. I'm sorry to spring this appalling intelligence so suddenly upon you but, as with removing old sticking plasters, these things are best got over with quickly. If you managed to miss the screenings last time and have somehow contrived not to buy the videos available at most good stores, you will have no idea what I am talking about, so I shall explain. *Jeeves and Wooster* is a television series about the exploits of the character Jeeves and the character Wooster. We took up five hours of valuable prime ITV viewing time earlier this year with our first series and intend to infest your screens again with six new-minted episodes in the spring of 1991. Book your skiing holidays now.

We have started in the grand old resort of Sidmouth, Devon. Do you know Sidmouth? The silver ribbon of time that is the River Sid twists amiably down through Sid Vale, Sidbury and Sidford until it opens into the south coast at Sidmouth. As you can see there are more Sids to be found in South Devon than at a 1950s dog-track. Here too can be seen large Edwardian hotels called the Belmont, the Westcliff, the Victoria and the Riviera; a long esplanade with a greater concentration of tea-rooms, bun-shops and knick-knackariums than one would have imagined possible outside the novels of E.F. Benson. Cliffs, too, abound. Nobody does cliffs quite like the English, do they? I have never seen anything worthy of the name in Australia or California. The Greeks and Italians seem innocently to believe that they can bung a hill or a rocky promontory somewhere near a coastline and pass it off as a genuine escarpment, but they never even gesture at the great sheer splendours of the classic British cliff as available in Caswell Bay, Cromer, Dover or our own dear Sidmouth.

Sidmouth, like every English resort worthy of the name, is

pleased to tell the visitor that it rejoices in a climate which gives it the lowest rainfall and greatest number of sunshine hours in Britain. The air is uniquely balmy, bracing and healthful; the waters peerlessly sweet, clear and invigorating. This is true of towns as far afield as Bournemouth, Skegness, Morecambe and Scarborough and just goes to show how much God smiles on the sea-side.

Sidmouth caters for the more mature citizen. Bridge not bingo; thin lemon-coloured cardigans rather than T-shirts; a putting-green instead of crazy golf; stay-pressed leisure slacks before Levi 501's. Other, less happier, towns may hurry on a dizzying, madcap, frenzied path to hell with their juke-boxes, frothy coffee and drug-crazed kinemas, Sidmouth has no use for such diabolical distractions. Here the pleasures of promenading before the pre-lunch Amontillado or challenging the Potters to a round robin on the croquet lawn take unruffled precedence. The only coin-operated machine I have so far sighted has been a telescope. The word arcade in Sidmouth means a line of shops and that, surely, is as it should be.

There are an average of four deaths a week in the hotels of Sidmouth, I was told yesterday. It is the usual practice amongst the hoteliers to remove bodies from their hotel rooms at two o'clock in the morning, so as not to unsettle the guests. If you're going to hop the twig in Sidmouth, hop it late in the day or you'll have a long cold wait for your coffin.

Yesterday, the town was transported to the early thirties, not as long a journey for Sidmouth as it would have been for most English resorts. There were no television aerials for us to take down, no yellow lines on the kerb for us to conceal, precious little need for the hair of the local people hired as extras to be cut any shorter.

The Silver Band was dressed up in fancy uniforms and sat in a bandstand on the esplanade playing Maid of the Mountains. Children were popped into sailor-suits and long baggy shorts and given shrimping nets to run around with; donkeys, flannel trousers, bathing togs, bath-chairs, canvas wind-breaks and changing-booths abounded. In the distance Rudge Whitworth motor-bicycles and Morris Cowley automobiles chugged along the coast road. It was heaven, sheer heaven under Roy Plomley sea-gulls and a blue English sky.

Period drama like *Jeeves and Wooster* is sometimes accused of being hide-bound and retrograde in its sentimental evocations of a past Britain lit in glowing colours and dressed in perfect, crisp linens. We are held back, it has been said, by our obsessions with the moribund past of a never-never land. It is all just chocolate box.

That may be so, but I rather like the odd box of chocolates. Just once in a while a chocolate box will make a better present than a set of spanners or a pair of socks. As a diet, emetic; but as a treat, delicious. But perhaps the air of Sidmouth has turned me sentimental. I hope so.

As Mad As Mad Can Be

One of the tasks that faces the writer is the search for the telling simile. It takes one back to the days of the rather 'modern' English master at school (by modern one meant his jacket was green needlecord and sprinkled with scurf instead of a traditional Harris tweed speckled with chalk-dust), who delighted in drawing attention to the 'freshness' and 'originality' of Ted Hughes and his pike or Dylan Thomas and his slow, black, sloe-black fishing-boat bobbing sea.

One remembers with a blush one's own desperate lunges at freshly struck epithets: 'storm-clouds of gym-shoe black' and 'cheeks carved with hell-hot tears' still cause me particular wrigglings of shame, although both at the time won warm approval from young, unconventional Mr Kershaw and a brace of his best alpha double-pluses. It is fortunate that when we arrive at manhood the saving anchor of embarrassment bids us rather face those similes we know (black as night, bold as brass, mad as a hatter) than fly to others we know not of; to mint one's own smacks of verbal dandyism.

Unfortunately, however, man has moved forward in blackness, boldness and madness since the days when our forefathers laid down the law on literary comparisons, and embarrassment must be risked in order adequately to convey the perplexing realities of modern life. Madness is an especial problem. The Blackadder solution is to strive for what one might call repetitive hyperbole: 'as mad as Mad Jack McMad, winner of the all-Scotland Mr Mad Competition'.

Another approach in circumscribing madness is the Disorienting Nonsense Simile, invented by, I think, the comedian Ken Platt, who offered the world his immortal 'daft as a brush', which opens up many endearing possibilities: 'as mad as a pair of trousers', 'as mad as a house', or even perhaps 'as mad as Ovaltine'. The most direct route to a new trope, of course, is to examine modern madness more closely and see what it suggests: 'as mad as an actress', 'as mad as a 'phone-in caller', 'as mad as a train-spotter', 'madder than a man who decides to use the M4 on a Bank Holiday Monday'.

The madness of those who thought it would be a Good Idea to get rid of the old rear-platformed Routemaster buses and the red telephone kiosks needs, of course, special attention, as do the wilder shores of lunacy inhabited by the unfortunate who thought up the phrase 'serving suggestion'.

But what verbal resources are there left to cover the real madness, the madness which in miniature goes like this: 'I know if I just let go and pee in my trousers I'll regret it. They'll go cold and unpleasant and start to stink. Nonetheless I can't be bothered to walk to the lavatory, so here goes.' Followed by misery, discomfort and a fouled pair of trousers.

Who behaves like this? Well, on a larger scale it is the same madness that bids us say: 'I know we're destroying species of tuna, eliminating dolphins, whales, rhinos, elephants; destroying rain forests, poisoning the earth, air and sea, but heigh-ho.' In this second scenario, of course, we're fouling more than a pair of trousers.

Many of you will now be thinking: 'Lumme! More fashionable Greenery, let's turn to the Sports Section,' but I don't intend to rehearse the environmental argument here. After all, we know it already; that is the point.

How do we describe a madness so complete and universal in our species as not to be a madness at all, but a norm? 'As mad as the maddest thing you can think of whipped up into an insane pottiness, psychotically marinated in maniacal unreason and folded into a bubbling bedlam of wild lunacy before being heated under an unbalanced flame of raving derangement. Drain, leave to stand, then section under the Mental Health Act.'

Not strong enough; it doesn't cover even the external symptoms. 'As mad as a human?' Perhaps, but we should be more honest. We all know the way we are taking the world and the most we are doing, like myself, is *talking* about it. The new index of madness is personal. 'As mad as me,' should be the official entry in the *Oxford Book of Similes*.

Young, unconventional Mr Kershaw would have frowned at that one, it lacks concretion and poetic intensity, but he wouldn't have been able to fault it for accuracy. I might have got away with a beta plus, brackets minus, question-mark, close brackets.

The Appearance of Reality

We are capable of seeing only what we want to see. This is a well-documented and widely understood truth. Those unsympathetic to the causes and aspirations of the Left in politics look into the face of a Dennis Skinner, say, or an Arthur Scargill and see ravening ambition and frothing insanity; those from the other side cannot understand how anyone can look at the aspect of a Tebbit or a Thatcher without reading the manifest signs of megalomaniac unreason and deluded pottiness written there. Prejudice or plain knowledge inform what are supposed to be our dispassionate and neutral senses. 'You've only got to look at the eyes,' people never tire of saying of Enoch Powell or Tony Benn. But there is, as King Duncan so wisely remarked, no art to find the mind's construction in the face. Lady Mosley on *Desert Island Discs* last year found herself able to discourse freely on the blueness of Hitler's peepers with the gasping admiration of a teeny-bopper and of course she was perfectly right: Hitler's eyes *were* blue and strikingly so. We would *like* to think that they were blank and pitiless as the sun, savage, heartless and diabolical, but life is never as easy as that. If all wicked people looked wicked to a disinterested observer, things could be managed so much more easily. Can we honestly say Schweitzer looked any more saintly than Crippen? If we showed photographs of Mother Teresa and a Ravensbrück concentration camp guard to a person unfamiliar with the faces of either, would they be able to tell us which was which?

I was once interviewed for a respectable Sunday newspaper by a highly regarded journalist, if there is such a thing. I arrived at the restaurant designated for the meeting, checked in my crash helmet, or skid-lid as we wild leather-boy bikers like to call them, and joined her at the table. I was wearing a goat-skin flying jacket, jeans and a T-shirt. The interview when published opened with the words 'Tweedy Stephen Fry . . . ' As far as she was concerned I was a walking bolt of hand-loomed Hebridean heather-mixture tweed and she was damned if the evidence of her eyes was going to contradict this view.

Sheridan Morley reviewed the first of the television performances of Wagner's *Ring* Cycle earlier this week in Another Newspaper. He described the introduction in which Norman Rodway, as Bernard Shaw, delightfully performed an extract from 'The Perfect Wagnerite'. Morley admired this opening enormously, but it was followed, he said, by the curtain rising, and a lot of fat women singing. After that, in his opinion, the whole thing went downhill. Now plenty of people seem to dislike the music and drama of Wagner; it's a bally shame, but they do. Richard Ingrams reviewing a book in last Saturday's *Telegraph* managed a sideswipe at the Meister's musicianship which one could not have believed of a man who can write so sensibly about Bartok, but there you go, one man's whatnot is another man's thingummy. The strange thing about Sheridan Morley's remark is that none of the women who appeared on stage for the ensuing performance of *Das Rheingold* could, by the remotest stretch of the imagination, be described as even slightly fat, large, rotund, corpulent, stout, of ample proportion, obese, tubby or over-generously endowed with adipose deposit. The Rhine Maidens were willowy; Fricka, Freia and Erda all splendidly proportioned. There are no other women in that work. But as far as Sheridan Morley was concerned female Wagnerian singers are huge and that is that, ocular evidence can take a powder.

The reputation of Wagner's music itself is forever clouded by the knowledge that Hitler liked it. For some the *Ring*, a work as much about the redemptive power of human love and the meaninglessness and destructive madness of power as anything, should only be used as the sound-track for documentaries about Nazi bestiality. Poor Dickie W. is forever damned by association.

There are nine more weeks to go of this television Wagner. Judge it for yourselves. We haven't yet seen Sieglinde, Brünnhilde or the other Walküre Sisters. I'm just praying that they won't be fat, or your worst predispositions will be realised. Even if they do turn out to be grotesquely gigantic I, of course, will probably swear blind that they are thin. No one is exempt from this kind of prejudice. Except you, naturally.

*

There have been a number of depressing revelations lately in the letters page of this newspaper about pointless and insulting changes in pub names. I heard recently that a well-known public school had decided to 'up-date' the title of Bursar. He is now to be known as the school's Financial Manager. God save us all.

What Are We Fighting For?

Like any freedom-loving, red-blooded, vetiver-scented English-man I'm all for giving Saddam Hussein a damned good hiding. I think we are all aware that it's time to open the dusty cupboard, take out the swishy cane and bend the bounder over. The man has it coming to him, that no one can deny. Putting on side, cheeking his seniors, bullying the little sprogs and generally swanking around the place like a peacock, it's more than a fellow can stand. It is therefore appropriate that the masters' common-room of the world should have decided to come down on him good and hard, sending him to Coventry, confiscating his sweets and making sure that it is now against the rules for anyone to smuggle fresh supplies to the little beast until he gives back what he stole. It is also natural that the Americans should have been appointed prefects, entrusted with the job of swinging the cane should that ultimate punishment prove to be necessary.

I have become increasingly disturbed over the years, however, about the behaviour, demeanour and intent of these our prefects. There was a photograph in one of the Sunday magazines this week of an American desert soldier standing in front of a wall on which had been painted the words 'BURN IN HELL, SADDAM'. I know there is a tradition of chalking phrases like 'This one's for you Adolf' and 'Cop this, Fritz' on the noses of bombs and shells, but simply to adorn a wall with such a bald, remorseless curse seems to me to reveal a frightening flaw in the American fighting man.

Jimmy Swaggart, the Christian fundamentalist, claimed that Mother Teresa of Calcutta would burn in hell because she had not been born again. Islamic fundamentalists have insisted that Salman Rushdie be assassinated because of scenes he invented in a novel. On all sides we feel threatened by fanatics and fundamentalists in whom all trace of human fellow-feeling would appear to have been erased. On good evidence we have persuaded ourselves that Saddam Hussein, as commander-in-chief of a million loyal fighting men, represents one of the most dangerous and wicked of these fanatics and that he must be stopped. Leading the concerted global effort to stop him is the United States Army.

As an admirer of so much in and of America I hate to say this, but I really do not feel in the least bit represented by that army. I cannot convince myself that they are fighting for values with which I can identify. The phrase 'BURN IN HELL, SADDAM' comes close to explaining why this is.

It all started I think with the adoption of war-paint and headbands during the Vietnam War. The men had to have rock music, officially supplied drugs like marijuana and amphetamines and they had to be allowed to dress virtually as they pleased.

The forces that subsequently invaded Grenada and Panama looked more like a band of mercenaries than any national army. Coupled with the peculiar willingness on the part of the Pentagon to play along with their fantasies of make-up and bandannas came a ludicrous element of public relations manipulation that led to the packaging of these military adventures with logos and brand-names. Thus the invasion of Panama was dubbed Operation Just Cause. American soldiers gave out free Operation Just Cause T-shirts to the citizenry of Panama. T-shirts. I assure you it's true.

Now poor President Bush has to put up with generals promising him on television that 'they can be in Baghdad inside five days', fantastic claims that an awareness of history and plain common sense must instantly deny. These top-brass soldiers with their unbelievably childish nicknames, 'Stormin' Norman' and so on, are publicly behaving like ten-year-olds, obsessed with 'kicking butt' and 'nuking the sonofabitch'.

I am sure 'our side' needs consolation, encouragement and a little positive propaganda to keep public opinion from going soft, but are the united nations of this earth in this decade at this moment in history best represented by the insane infantile posturing that leads to phrases like 'BURN IN HELL, SADDAM' being painted on walls in military encampments? I like to think that in an English camp in the desert such a graffito would earn the perpetrator one heck of a rocket from his commanding officer.

To be disturbed and frightened by the fundamentalism of this aspect of American military behaviour is not to be anti-American any more than it would be anti-British of an American to despise our football hooligans. The difference is that we are ashamed of our football hooligans. I am not sure how many Americans are ashamed of the image their military seems so keen to foster.

I am aware that many will read this and claim that criticism of any aspect of America's involvement in the Gulf is tantamount to 'giving comfort to the enemy', a crime that prohibits all but the most orthodox opinions on the matter. I admire immensely America's remarkable and courageous commitment. I am sure that the average American fighting man is as decent, brave and civilised a GI as ever he was. They are our allies, we stand with them in the desert, shoulder to shoulder. But I would also like to believe, foolishly no doubt, naïvely for sure, that we are fighting for the same reason – a detestation of fanaticism, fundamentalism and barbarism – and that vengeful ferocity and unfettered machismo will form no part of our strategy.

Let's stand up to Saddam in the name of civilisation, not in the name of our own particular brand of savagery.

Making the Right Moves

We all know that the English tug-of-war team has had unparalleled success in recent decades, consistently winning the world championships in a manner that has left the world gasping with envy. Victory has been more elusive in the sister sports of soccer, tennis and asynchronous breaststroke, but it would be unseemly for us to hog all the great athletic trophies to our manly chests. English prowess in one activity, however – part sport, part game – has gone largely unheralded. For half a century Russia has bestridden the chess world like a colossus, marking it and making it her own. How can it be, then, that the second strongest chess country on earth is England?

Even as Karpov and Kasparov wrestle again for the world crown England, a nation which had never had a Grandmaster fifteen years ago, now has more than any other country save the Soviet Union. It started with Tony Miles, creator of the extraordinary Birmingham Defence, and includes Nigel Short and Jonathan Speelman, two of the highest ranking players ever.

The English Chess Explosion, as it was designated ten years ago, was said to have been the result of young British players being inspired by the monumental Spassky–Fischer clash in Reykjavik in 1972. But this begs the question why weren't *American* players similarly inflamed? It seems extraordinary that the United States should be a weaker chess nation than England; they receive after all the pick of the defectors; they have a population five times as great. English chess is notoriously underfunded, underencouraged and underpublicised and yet it continues to prosper.

My own theory, and I cannot emphasise its worthlessness enough, is that chess is fundamentally a theatrical affair. I first became really interested in the game when I heard about the Smyslov Screw. There was a great Russian world champion, who recently enjoyed something of an Indian summer, called Vasily Smyslov, particularly noted as a master of the end-game. Whenever he moved a piece from one square onto another he had a habit of twisting it, as if screwing it into the surface of the board. Others might drop their man lightly, or bang it aggressively, Smyslov gently screwed it in. The psychological effect of such a move can be devastating. It looks so permanent, so deliberate, so absolutely assured. Kasparov hunches himself over the game, in a brooding, minatory and virile manner that is worth at least three extra pawns. Jonathan Speelman's attitude, lolling and flopping over the board like a benign octopus, is essentially a comic approach, funny without being vulgar, which cannot but put his opponent at a huge disadvantage.

Chess is ludicrously difficult, I choose the word 'ludicrous' with etymological care. George Steiner in his excellent *White Knights of Reykjavik* claimed that there are more possible games of chess than there are atoms in the Universe. I, for one, shall take his word for it; I can't possibly be bothered to count. That being the case, taken with the sad likelihood that a computer will beat Kasparov one day (Karpov has already been defeated by a machine), human chess will have to continue to develop along dramatic lines. The Russians have been amongst the most significant theatrical nations of the modern age, with Stanislavsky, Gorky, Gogol and Chekhov: British theatre needs no such citation of names to prove its illustrious heritage.

The development of modern chess closely reflects the development of dramatic styles; the old classical romantic distinctions were quickly replaced around the beginning of the century by the Modern style of Steinitz, a dialectical, realist mode of playing that might be said to compare with the dramaturgical styles of Shaw and Chekhov. It was no longer the King that counted, but the pawns and the bourgeois minor pieces that controlled the centre. The Hypermodern age that succeeded this had an abstract quality, almost absurdist in its refusal to engage in those central questions, preferring to concentrate on the tensions behind the control of the centre, the language of chess itself rather than engagement in it. This recalls the age of N.F. Simpson, Stoppard, Beckett, Pinter and Ionesco.

Today, in the post-Modern and post-Hypermodern chess age,

things are altogether more ambiguous and mannerist, more 'multimedia'. This is true in drama too, we are without a settled style or voice to the age.

If we wish to achieve real supremacy in chess we must stress those qualities that have given our drama its greatest strength: the eccentric, the bizarre, the comic, the mannered and the elegant; the same qualities we associate with, say, Stoppard or Olivier. We must at all times refrain from the conventional, the orthodox, the pedestrian and the timid. We need chess equivalents of Alastair Sim, Ralph Richardson, Maggie Smith, Noël Coward, Arthur Lowe and Alan Bennett: absolute technical mastery, benevolently disguised.

Chess is indeed like life, for we need people of precisely those qualities in all aspects of our national existence. If the British have any contribution to make to the world that might stave off grey-suited stalemate it is to offer a bouncy, charming, unorthodox and theatrical flair.

Licked By the Mother Tongue

Did you know that the verb 'to buttonhole' is a small corruption of 'to buttonhold'? You probably did. I discovered this truth the other day in Bill Bryson's *Mother Tongue: The English Language*, along with the astonishing intelligence that Shakespeare invented nearly two thousand English words, including 'obscene', 'bare-faced', 'critical', 'leapfrog', 'countless', 'excellent', 'gust', 'hint', 'hurry', 'lonely' and 'dwindle'. Ben Jonson was apparently responsible for 'damp', 'clumsy' and 'strenuous' while Thomas More gave us 'absurdity', 'acceptance', 'exact', 'explain' and 'exaggerate' and Carlyle devised 'decadent' and 'environment'.

How you sit down and invent a word is one thing, but how you get the world to accept it is very much another. My friend Hugh Laurie once invented a word which I have since used unchallenged. You know those strange spongy and – let's not deny it – phallic objects that are placed over microphones? The official name for them is 'pop-shield'; they are supposed to stop the microphone 'popping' on violent plosives. If you say 'Peter Piper picked a peck . . . etc.' closely into a microphone denuded of such an article you will see why they are necessary. Hugh Laurie was sitting in a recording studio once and he said to the engineer, 'There's rather a lot of Ps and Bs in this, hadn't we better have a spoffle on?' Without so much as a raise of the eye-brows the engineer hurried in with a pop-shield and fitted it to the microphone. A word was born; unchallenged, somehow instinctively understood. I have since used spoffle regularly and never found anyone in doubt of its meaning.

Of course there is an onomatopoeic quality to spoffle, and possibly an unconsciously devised portmanteau element, something between 'spongy' and 'muffle', which makes it a much easier word to invent and understand than say 'obscene' or 'strenuous'.

It is also true that the word 'pop-shield' already existed, rendering the neologism, however satisfactory, superfluous. All this demonstrates just how difficult it is to make new words.

There is an old story about an eighteenth-century Irish theatre manager called Daly who wagered that he could introduce a brand new word into the language within twenty-four hours. He then was supposed to have spent the next day and night chalking a four-letter word over every wall and public building in Dublin. Everyone talked about the word and wondered as to its meaning and the bet was won. The word was 'quiz' which came to mean originally a teasing problem or craze, 'What's the quiz?' It then developed into a noun for a teasing person and a verb meaning to twit or scrutinise someone teasingly, often through a quizzing-glass. Now of course it means a game-show. This pleasant story is all very well, but I think most people would accept that the origin of quiz is probably a contraction of 'inquisition'.

The fact is that the initial explosion of English is over. In modern times we have received many new words from other societies, Anglo-Indian, American, Australian as well as our own marginal and regional cultures, but these have provided technical and demotic words; writers, poets and commentators have not contributed, they have decided to make do with the reservoir of verbiage already in place. Today, if a playwright decided, like Shakespeare, to invent hundreds and hundreds of new words, he would simply be sniked at, he would be tredged and impulcated.

A piano key-board may have only eighty-eight keys, but it does not stop new harmonies and melodies being discovered every day. The tragedy of our language is that with a million keys to press we so often come up with the same phrase, time after weary time, endlessly reusing the same tired stock expressions.

I propose a Fresh Phrase Day to be held every year. Any newspaper, writer, commentator or public figure who uses a phrase that can be proved to have been used before will be fined, the money going to the sadly depleted coffers of the *Oxford English Dictionary* whose latest magnificent venture has yet to enter the black. On Fresh Phrase Day 'majorities' may be enormous or colossal, but they will never be allowed to be vast or overwhelming. Coffers will not be described, *ut supra*, as 'sadly depleted' nor will 'ventures' be either 'latest' or 'magnificent', allegations will not be 'wholly unfounded' nor will any phenomenon 'take place against a background' of anything. The new phrases that will be coined to replace the usual clichés will replenish the stagnant pond (or stale pool) of the language for another year until the next Fresh Phrase Day.

This should encourage us to *think* in new ways too. I disgusted myself yesterday when I was buttonheld by a child in the street who hailed me with the familiar cry 'Penny for the guy'. Instead of dropping fifty pence into his palm, which is presumably what he meant by a penny, I allowed myself to look at the feebly half-stuffed pillow case with a badly felt-tip penned face on it and say 'Call that a guy? Why in *my* day . . . ' just the kind of rank, tedious, sententious remark most likely to get a child's goat, the kind of remark you promise never to let fall from your lips when you grow up, and there I was, letting it fall.

Had it been Fresh Phrase Day the child could have fined me, as it was, of course, he punched me in the face.

Let the People Speak

I have been on the streets interviewing representatives of the British public on the subject of the situation in the Middle East. The results have been revealing if not interesting.

'What are your feelings about the Gulf Crisis?' I asked a gentleman in Turnpike Lane.

'Well obviously,' he said, 'I was delighted to see that Sandy Lyle's swing has returned. Let's just hope they can sort out the shenanigans over Ryder Cup selection by next season.'

I moved on to Duke Street, St James', where I waited outside Green's Oysterium to catch the opinions of the great. A leading head of the secret service had views it would be foolhardy to ignore.

'War as such,' he said, 'is currently inevitable. You cannot seriously imagine that President Bush would spend billions of dollars on moving a colossal force of arms to the Middle East, wait a few months and then simply bring it home without the primary concession, unequivocal Iraqi withdrawal from UN agreed Kuwaiti territories, being met. It is therefore probable that hundreds and thousands of young lives will be lost. The sand of the desert, to paraphrase Newbolt, will be sodden red.'

'Is there no alternative?' I asked.

'There is one,' he replied to the accompaniment of a hiccough in which I detected a mingling of Rossmore oysters, Tabasco and, surprisingly, a New Zealand Chardonnay. 'I have a radical solution which will involve the expenditure of one life. One only life.'

'Ah,' I said, 'you are talking about "taking out" Saddam Hussein.'

'By no manner of means. The only event, in my judgment, which will stop war is the precipitate termination of the existence of George Bush.'

I put up my hand to interject but the distinguished spymaster would brook no interruption.

'Before you think I have run howling mad, hear me out,' he said. 'I am talking here theoretically. Imagine if you will for just one moment please the effect on American morale if they thought that their war effort in the Middle East was to be masterminded by Dan Quayle.'

My mouth fell open.

'Precisely. Dan Quayle as Commander-in-Chief, Dan Quayle giving daily press conferences in the White House, Dan Quayle conferring with the British, Syrian, French, Italian, Saudi generals who would be his allies, Dan Quayle trying to temper the ambitions of his generals, Dan Quayle announcing a draft of young Americans – the same Dan Quayle whose family pulled strings to keep him out of Vietnam when he himself was subject to a draft. The idea is preposterous, yet the sudden demise of George Bush would bring it into stark reality. Think on.'

'Are you seriously recommending that an elected leader be assassinated . . . ?' I began.

'The ethics are without my province, I deal in mechanisms and contingencies, good afternoon.'

A pin-prick on a map settled Old Amersham as my next port of call. A florid old buster in a stained REME tie had a well of military experience on which to draw.

'Drew up plans to construct a base camp in a huge bugger of a *wadi* twenty miles from Tobruk. Woke up next morning, *wadi* gone. Sandstorm you see, redrawn the landscape in four hours. Another thing, my sergeant was a Geordie, told him to get the men to work round the clock to remedy the situation. Whole platoon knocked out by exhaustion and sunstroke. Old fool had got them marching for twenty-four hours without stop. Communication, d'y'see? To a Geordie "work" sounds like "walk". Nightmare. Now, picture four tank brigades in the heat of battle in the Iraqi desert, one Syrian, one British, one Yank, one French. All on radio comms. Tower of bloody Babel, I mean what? No, no, won't do at all.'

I moved on.

'Let's get one thing straight,' said a doctor from Long Melford. 'Soldiers are made from flesh and bone and tissue that is, as

Wilfred Owen said, "so dear achieved". It has taken them from seventeen to thirty years to grow into what they are. In seconds it can be a tangle of blood and smashed material that can never be put right again.'

'Whoops!' I said. 'Isn't this conchie talk I'm hearing? Are you in the business of giving comfort to the enemy?'

'No,' he said. 'I'm in the business of repairing flesh. Just be sure, that's all. For God's sake be sure.'

A vigorous lady stocking up on mange-tout in Hexham market had a point of view too.

'I'm sick and tired of hearing the moaners and the appeasers who say that the whole thing is because of oil. These people never seem to have heard of the word principle. If Kuwait had been the lowliest, poorest little country in the world we would have rushed to its aid. Principles and values. I can't say that often enough.'

'What about the hostages?'

'Well that MP had it about right, didn't he? Their relatives are just miaowing and spewing. Shameful.'

'Perhaps you and that MP would like to swap your families for the ones out there? That way our resolve against the oppressor can be strengthened.'

'Don't get clever. It's very easy to be smart, it's far harder to stick to values and principles, principles and values.'

'Righto.'

Playing the Political Game

I don't know whether the Prime Minister (I am assuming that by the time you read this M.H. Thatcher will still be the holder of that great office – this article will take up to three minutes to fax and three minutes, as no one once said rather amusingly, is a very long time in politics) but I don't know, as I say, whether the Prime Minister at the time of this article going to fax has a genuine interest in cricket. I suspect she has not. Her recent remark to Neil Kinnock that he was 'bowling from the Nursery End' suggests that her acquaintance with the game is, at the most, nodding. To a non-cricketer her implication that Mr Kinnock's bowling was childish makes some kind of sense as word-play; a cricketer however would take such a remark to be a profound compliment. To be told that you are bowling from the Nursery End is to be told that you are playing first-class cricket, at the headquarters of the game and at the end of the wicket from which so many of the greatest bowlers in history have chosen to bowl, taking advantage of the famous Hill. Left-handers, of course, have preferred the Pavilion End, notably Hedley Verity in 1934, but left-*wingers* are free to choose either end.

All this is by way of being irrelevant; the notable flurry of cricketing metaphors is however of great psychological interest. The choice of cricket as a frame of reference reveals the deep sense of British solidarity all the personalities involved in this leadership tussle wish to convey. There can be no greater way of showing Europe how private this whole business is than by reverting to a series of images that only an Englishman (in Europe at least) can understand. The Continental press is obviously fascinated by the internal rumblings in the Conservative Party, but it is a private fight after all, however wide its reverberations, and at some subconscious level all the participants have made a decision

304

to eschew the more readily comprehensible soccer analogies that would have allowed Europe access to the subtleties (such as they are) of the debate. As it is even the sub*titles* of the debate would reveal nothing to them.

As a Welshman, Neil Kinnock, I have no doubt, will, when his time shortly comes,[1] introduce the language of Rugby Football into prime ministerial rhetoric, which will confound any but French observers of our political scene.

It all demonstrates that we need never fear for our sovereignty, whosever head is on our coins and whichever bank decides our Minimum Lending Rates, so long as we have mastery of a language that can so effectively bind us together and shut out our non-Anglophone neighbours. However divided we may appear, the sound of our politicians talking a figurative English of stumps and wickets and bouncers and boundaries, even in the heat of internecine party battle, has a strangely unifying effect.

Meanwhile in Australia our touring party is coming under a barrage of assault from the press of the host country. The *Melbourne Age*, a respectable newspaper, speculated on whether this squad is the worst ever to visit Australia. I wonder if, in a spirit of generous reciprocity, Graham Gooch will borrow the language of politics in his defence. 'I have stood at the Despatch Box many times and been asked searching questions by the Opposition,' he might say, 'but I have always been able to deflect them. I am still at that Despatch Box and intend to remain there. It's up to the selectors if I am to remain, it is not up to the media. I would remind you that over-rates and productivity are higher than at any point in the seventies. I am deeply sorry that Ian Botham is on the back-benches, but essentially we are both in full agreement on matters of substance. He and I were part of the team that caused a great and miraculous revival of England's fortunes in the early eighties, it would be madness to lose faith in the policies that we both saw through so successfully, simply because of a temporary blip now.' It might work.

Meanwhile Michael Heseltine is polishing the ball against his trousers and walking back to his mark ready to bowl. It remains

[1]Bad prophecy

to be seen whether Mrs Thatcher can win by an innings or whether she will be forced to follow on.

Whatever one's politics no one can deny that this is entertainment of the highest order. Nothing has happened in Parliament for years that has been half so exciting as the events of the last week. Drama, tactics, occasional longueurs, timing, luck and skill all have played their part. I don't go along with the stuffed shirts who believe that this is bad for the country or bad for our image. The winner, Brian, as always, is the Great Game itself.

My Leonardo

I was given a Leonardo portrait the other day. Despite a great deal of pressure I have resisted the temptation to place the work on the open market. I am determined that it should stay in this country, in private hands. My private hands in fact. It would be catastrophic if this important piece should find its way to the Getty Museum or a Japanese boardroom, both of whose profligacy has swollen the art market beyond what is seemly or proper. I am trying to persuade a friend who owns a delightful Raphael to emulate this selfless patriotism. This portrait is not actually *by* Leonardo, it is more *of* Leonardo, done when he was very young, still a teenager as it happens. It shows him in typical pose, the distinguishing blue bandana wound around his head, his shell quivering with mischievous energy, stomach fairly bulging with pizza, his green skin absolutely glowing with good health. Of all the four Pubescent Morphollactic Ninjitsu Chelonians, or Teenage Mutant Ninja Turtles as they prefer to style themselves, Leonardo is quite my favourite.

The portrait is fashioned from bright emerald plastic rendered against one side of a pure white drinking vessel, the whole cunningly wrought into as pleasing a *bibelot* as one could hope to possess. It was given to me by Neil, my trusty 'stand-in' on the *Jeeves and Wooster* set, who in turn was presented it by the Slough branch of the Blockbuster Video Shop as a reward for hiring a video cassette from them. How it fell into their hands I cannot guess; no doubt the usual trail of blood, ambition, revenge and ill-luck that dogs all fabulous items has pursued it since leaving the factory in China where it was fashioned. Yes, China. Strange, is it not, that the vast wall of Turtle merchandising that is all that stands between the High Street and bankruptcy this recessional Christmas should have given so much work to the manufactories and sweat-shops of the Republic of China whose hideous gerontocracy has been responsible for one of the most obscene and shameless massacres since the war?

The Turtles, for those who do not know, are strange young creatures named Leonardo, Raphael, Donatello and Michelangelo, who live in sewers with a rodent *sensei* and their human friend, April. They are devoted to pizza and the thwarting of the evil plans of their enemy, the Shredder. Such is their phenomenal success with young people all over the world, through television cartoons and a feature film, that there is no item that springs readily to mind that has not been packaged as a piece of Turtle merchandise. Toothbrushes, duvet covers, crockery, jig-saw puzzles, chewing-gum, underpants, hats, coats, gloves, alarm-clocks, lavatory-paper, computer games, tinned spaghetti, wallpaper, corn-plasters, even *books* I shouldn't wonder, all have been turtlised and stacked in the shops. Out of the best possible motives, those concerned have been careful to keep the prices of these itemries just low enough to enable Mummy and Daddy to fork out without too loud a squeak. This means that the factories of the West lie idle as far as the production of these cloacal reptiles is concerned. The underpaid billions who toil under the yoke of the unspeakable old beasts who run the People's Republic of China are given the job of filling our stockings.

We in the West are actuated by motives of the purest altruism in this as in all matters. We Do Not Do Business With Tyrants, naturally, unless they are tyrants who can gear their factories for the production of Turtle peanut butter jars. Disgusted as we were by the carnage of Tiananmen Square we know that Sanctions Do Not Work, unless the sun is in Sagittarius in which case naturally, as civilised people, We Must Implement Sanctions Across The Board. We show our support for the students and liberals of China and their fight for democracy not by cutting China off from the rest of the world but by giving them designs for Turtle pencil cases. This is all part of what we like to call Giving A Moral Lead. A moral lead in the pencil, presumably.

If all objects that we use and own gave off the smells and sounds and senses that went into their production, wouldn't the world be extraordinary? A BMW car would emanate order and crisp efficiency, a hand-made table would smell of a carpentry shop and hours of devoted craftsmanship, a pair of Turtle pyjamas would scream with the cramped, half-lit clatter of a sweat-shop where children and young girls slave away hour after hour for enough money to buy, for instance, a packet of Weetabix containing a giveaway plastic Turtle.

Perhaps, heaven forbid, I am being naïve. But perhaps, heaven forbid even more strongly, it is still more naïve to hope that the people of China might be delivered into freedom for the price of a million plastic Leonardo coffee mugs.

It is probably safest to shut our eyes, stop thinking about where things come from, who makes them and under what conditions, and remember that trade is trade, business is business and that charity begins at home. It is Christmas after all.

A Chatterer Chatters

I am happy to be able today to write as one of an insidious force, part of a self-nourishing coterie of aggrieved nonentities who swirl ill-naturedly in a vortex of their own making. If you recognise the words then you probably read a leading article in the *Daily Telegraph* the other day by someone called Alan Clark MP, writing to praise the qualities and character of John Major. In doing so he singled out Mr Major's 'classlessness'. The old cliques, the grouse moor gentlemen and the union baronies no longer 'have teeth', Mr Clark asseverated, 'a far more insidious force, if only because its members are so committed to their advancement at the expense of everyone else, is that self-nourishing coterie of aggrieved nonentities known as the "chattering classes": dons, actors, television producers, "commentators", playwrights. Their real complaint is that they feel themselves excluded (that is to say from access, consultation, backstairs influence) . . . from government for the last ten years.'

Well now this is fighting talk. As a member of the second profession listed and indeed as someone who has written a play, I feel it incumbent upon me to reply to these freakish charges. Let us try to put names to some of these monsters who are simultaneously so threatening and so impotent. Firstly dons: let me see . . . Maurice Cowley is a don, so is Roger Scruton, both part of the 'Peterhouse Mafia' often credited with the establishment of an intellectual framework for modern Conservatism. Alan Walters, Mrs Thatcher's famous economic adviser, is an academic too. Members of the Adam Smith Institute, the Bow Group and other Tory institutions also qualify. What about actors? There are so many. Let us choose a few at random. How about Sir Alec Guinness? Perhaps we should, according to recent fashion, 'skip a generation' and look at, say, Anthony Hopkins or Paul

Eddington. I know a number of television producers, the first who ever gave me a job was the redoubtable Dennis Maine Wilson, who brought Hancock and the Goons to prominence, or there is Biddy Baxter, the begetter of *Blue Peter*, or Roger Ordish who produces 'Sir James'll Fix It'. In the category 'commentators' I suppose I could suggest Richie Benaud or Brian Johnston, the great cricket broadcasters, but I suspect Mr Clark was referring to the political kind. John Cole of the BBC with his merry Ulster brogue and great gifts of extemporaneous exposition is both efficient and endearing. Playwrights complete the grim elite. Let us choose Sir Ronald Miller, the charming and courteous dramatist whose speeches written for Mrs Thatcher included the celebrated 'You turn if you want to: the lady's not for turning', an arch reference to the title of a play by another wicked dramaturge, Christopher Fry.

What a gang of aggrieved, self-nourishing, insidious, ill-natured, vortex-swirling nonentities is here! How they chatter like all their class; what a threat they pose to democracy. With what ruthless self-interest do they pursue their advancement. How right Mr Clark is to draw our attention to this sinister sodality of embittered and dangerous nobodies.

But perhaps I have picked the wrong names, in fact I will go further: *of course* I have picked the wrong names. Mr Clark, that great and substantial entity, was not thinking of *those* dons or *those* playwrights, he was thinking of other dons and playwrights, men and women who do not align themselves with the Conservative Party. The dangerous ones, as far as he is concerned, are those who have the temerity not to share his political views. It is a marvellous world he inhabits, one in which the dons who write articles in the national press, who counsel and nourish each other in the interest of *his* party, use their influence benignly, with unfailing responsibility and modesty, while those dons who fail to find themselves in whole-hearted support of this government use the influence which, to their frustration, they do not possess, malignantly, chatteringly and insidiously. They are a threat to democracy and our way of life; they must be excoriated for daring to dislike the tenor and thrust of the last decade.

But the government of the last ten years has been popular, some might argue. It must therefore follow that those who do not support it have contempt for the will of the people, are undemocratic and elitist. When a Labour government comes to power shall we expect Conservative dons, playwrights and commentators therefore to hold their tongues? Of course not, in a generous, pluralist society it is acceptable for all those with views to be allowed to express them, whether 'chattering' around a table or writing in a newspaper. What is unacceptable is a denial of this kind of free exchange. All of us who hold strong views can occasionally get things out of proportion and start seeing our political opponents as enemies of society. I, as one of Mr Clark's chattering nonentities, love my country dearly but I reserve the right to my own vision of a better Britain, one in which, for instance, no citizens are ever described by politicians as nonentities. I am happy to accept that dons, actors, commentators and playwrights on the Conservative side of the fence are of honourable and decent intent, surely Mr Clark has the grace to reciprocate?

For a politician, of all people, to accuse such a diversely constituted group of self-advancement at the expense of others demonstrates a special kind of weirdness. Let us trust that the new Prime Minister, whose mind Mr Clark praises as 'cool and rational', has a rather more mature concept of what a democracy can be.

Game Show Heaven

Today marks the last day of the filming of *Jeeves and Wooster* II on which I and some seventy others have been engaged for the last thirteen weeks. The happy routine of being jerked from one's slumbers at six each morning and deposited back at home more or less in time for bed ends today. I am not complaining at the hours; actors like to make a great thing of calling their profession 'work', but it is, thank heavens, nothing more than play. We are players and, as a man who likes nothing more than games, I find no shame in thinking of what I do as ludic, if not ludicrous.

I have had the great good fortune to catch, over the weeks, a great deal of that curious phenomenon, Daytime Television. While film sets are being lit and the furniture and props prepared, technicians prefer that actors, with their cigarettes, their atrocious eating habits and their irritating voices and conversations, are kept in their dressing rooms out of the way, and who shall blame them? In my dressing room there is a television. This has meant that I have been able to satisfy my voracious appetite for trivial and idiotic television game shows, a greater proliferation of which this country has never known. *Daily Telegraph* readers, as important and thrusting men and women of affairs, have, I know, little time for these fripperies. I doubt if one in a thousand of you has ever pulled up a chair for a Four Square. Indeed it is probable that you do not know the origin of that inestimable phrase. This is a pity. I am not sure that one can ever understand this country and its citizens (stroke subjects) unless one knows that there are enough people living in it not only to watch these extraordinary programmes but also (and this is the truly remarkable fact) to *participate* in them as studio audiences and contestants. That the supply of egregious emeritus disc jockeys prepared to host these games has not given out is one thing, but that the stock of members of the public willing and able to sit in a studio and applaud them seems inexhaustible, I find simply awe-inspiring.

On an average day there are at least five quiz-style game shows on offer throughout the day on British terrestrial broadcasting channels. I cannot speak for satellite but I am sure they have much to offer in that direction too. The current season that is about to come to an end as Christmas approaches, includes *Brainwave*, *Keynotes*, *Going for Gold*, *Talkabout*, *Catchword*, *Fifteen To One* and the perennial *Blockbusters*. Each one is broadcast daily on weekdays between 9.00 in the morning and 6.00 in the evening, each one has its own studio audience, and each one runs through a large number of contestants. The prizes on offer range from a modest number of pounds to a safari holiday in Kenya. There is another, even sillier show which takes place on Tuesdays and Thursdays at 3.15 hosted by a highly entertaining man in a full-bottomed wig; the catchphrases here are 'I refer the Honourable Member to the reply I gave some moments ago' and 'Order! Order!' The prize for this one is a square red attaché case stamped with the show's distinctive portcullis logo and a chance to go forward into the grand final chaired by Peter Sissons on Thursday nights.

It would be easy to savage these entertainments as anodyne drivel dreamt up to keep lonely sherry-swigging housewives from going mad, but in fact they characterise the continuing development of one of mankind's best and most distinctive instincts: games playing. It was *homo ludens* who first rose to take his place above the other creatures, not *homo sapiens*.

If you go into a toy shop these days you will find that where once Monopoly had a Scrabble – or is it the other way round? – the shelves now are stuffed with ever more new and remarkable games. Trivial Pursuit, which has given rise to an explosion in pub and club quiz teams, has been joined by hundreds of specialised word games, board games, strategy games and very silly games without purpose or character. It may be that more real pleasure may still be derived from a simple pack of playing cards or a set of dice, but the fact is that playing, as a pastime, is taking more and more precedence over solitary and unsocial pursuits.

If you are sitting at home all alone, then watching others play on television at least keeps the instincts sharp and satisfies, albeit vicariously, one's gamesome instincts.

Even though, as I said, my profession is largely that of a player, nothing will satiate my desire for games. I shall be that tiresome one over Christmas who – as the others clamour to settle back, surrounded by tangerine peel and nutshells, to watch *ET* or the Queen – insists on marshalling the company for games. Long-term studies have shown, as liars always like to preface their arguments, that games players live longer. 'But what sort of life is it?' the quibblers cry. I would echo the response of the WOPR computer in the film *War Games* when asked if what he was doing was real or a game: What's the difference?

A Drug on the Market

At a Conservative Party Conference some years ago there was available to members of the press, the Tory Party and the public the peculiar sight of a man marching up and down in front of the main entrance to the conference hall bearing a placard. On one side of his banner were written the charming and gracious words 'Repatriate all immigrants NOW'.

'Ah,' you might think, 'I've got *his* number. The unacceptable face of unacceptability.' I wonder, though, if you can guess what motto was emblazoned on the obverse of his pennant? If you know something of the weird logic of right-wing libertarianism you might be able to make a stab at it. Put down the paper and have a think for a few moments.

Time's up. If you divined this correctly you either share this man's political outlook or you are a sophisticated and knowledge-able social observer, for what was written on the other side of the conference-goer's banner was this: 'Legalise cannabis NOW'.

The legalisation of cannabis has long been an interesting cause. The report compiled by Baroness Wootton of Abinger at least twenty years ago found nothing wrong with the drug and seemed to recommend its decriminalisation. Speaking as one who grew up bombarded by anti-drug literature, films and homilies, I have long felt that the strategies used by those who wish to discourage the use of prohibited narcotics have been hopelessly misguided. If drug-users are consistently shown to the impressionable young as spotty, vomiting, reeling and incoherent there is, I concede, no doubt that the idea of drugs loses its appeal. The truth however is so much less straightforward. Any young person nowadays is bound to bump into a drug-user of some kind during their life. I can well remember the first time I met someone who, I was told in an excited whisper, was a genuine junky and had been for years. Imagine my surprise when I saw that his skin tissues were clear, his hair glossy, his eyes bright, his speech well modulated and unslurred and his behaviour irreproachable. All those warning films, those stern lectures from visiting policemen and those frightening pamphlets that had been from prep school onwards thrust at one, they had been no more than sensational and hysterical propaganda. The feeling of having been conspired against by a kill-joy older generation was very strong indeed and tended, if anything, to turn one towards the forbidden fruit of the poppy, now that it was clear that it was not as grotesque as we had been warned.

There is a famous story of a television documentary made only a few years ago about a group of heroin addicts. They were in middle age, prosperous and successful. They had been junkies for twenty-two years. Their behaviour, appearance and mode of life was utterly normal, irreproachable and unexciting. The documentary was never broadcast for fear of seeming to show that drug addiction need not be the nightmare that we spend so much money and time assuring our younger generations that it is.

The truth is this: if you want to witness blotchy skin, yellowing eyes, incoherent mumbling, uncoordinated staggering, stumbling and retching then don't look for a junky, look for a drinker. One of the great unspoken secrets of our age and ages previous is the prevalence of alcoholism in public and private life. We allow a few joke drunks to stand as our butts: Oliver Reed, George Brown, George Best and so on, but we ignore the fact that a very large percentage of journalists, politicians, writers, jurists, judges, financiers and civil servants drink to an extent that would lead any doctor to describe them as functional alcoholics. Alcohol is a much more dangerous drug than many that are proscribed. Rich alcoholics, like rich junkies, can last for years on fairly good quality stuff, it is the poor and ill-educated drinkers and drug addicts who stumble down the streets, pick fights, steal, vandalise and decline to vagrancy and degradation.

The ancient Greeks used to say that wine is the mirror of the soul. Only a fool blames a mirror if the image it offers is not to their liking. To prohibit alcohol simply because some can't cope with it would strike most of us as ludicrous and intolerable; to do the same to certain narcotics might be regarded as just as foolish and oppressive. We know that the arguments for decriminalisation are growing amongst doctors and members of the governmental and non-governmental organisations responsible for fighting the vast bandit organisations that profit, like bootleggers, from the illegality of heroin, cocaine and marijuana.

Sobriety is a chemically induced state of mind that many find bearable for only short periods of the day. In heaven, I suspect, they drink well and wisely. On earth we must face up, not to alcohol abuse, but to the abuse of people's lives that leads them to drink badly. To the educated drinker the prohibition of a good Islay malt or a Château Margaux would be a crime against nature's bounty and man's artistry; the same may be said, by the connoisseur, of best Andean Flake Cocaine or Moroccan Gold Cannabis. You don't, unless you are mad, solve the problems of burglary by outlawing possessions.

1991 approaches and I must dash to the shops, as I am sure must you, to get hold of a few hundred units of alcohol with which properly to welcome it in. Your very good health.

The Moustaches From Hell

Eight or so years ago, when I was younger and greener behind the ears, I used to do a weekly five-minute slot on a radio programme called *B15* which was broadcast on Sundays on BBC Radio One. All *Telegraph* readers, I know, are absolute Radio One junkies, never listen to anything else, so you hardly need me to remind you that Radio One's news coverage used to call itself *Newsbeat*. My job each week on *B15* was to do a parody of *Newsbeat* called, boldly and imaginatively, *Beatnews*. About five weeks into this assignment came the invasion of the Falkland Islands. In response to this I hastily assembled a 'character' called Bevis Marchant who was one of those flak-jacket-wearing reporters who like to know all the latest military jargon ten seconds before their colleagues. He always signed off his despatches ' . . . Bevis Marchant, Port Stanley? No thanks, Ollie.' A pretty crummy joke by any standards, I admit. Came the day, however, that the letters and telephone calls started rolling in. 'Doesn't this man realise that there is likely to be conflict? That people are going to be killed? How can he make jokes about it?' I naturally dropped the assignment like a hot brick.

The whole question of the role of comedy during wartime remains a thorny one. I know of no comedians at the moment who are interested in laughing at pain and sacrifice; equally, I know of no comedians who are particularly interested in confining their jokes to making fairly obvious, line-toeing fun of Saddam Hussein.

During World War Two it is notable that the memorable comedy of the time did not centre around laughing at Hitler, but on mocking British bureaucracy, the ration, ARP Wardens, staff officers and the whole panoply of total warfare. Perhaps if this Gulf War drags on, which please God it doesn't, a comedy approach to it will develop. At the moment, however, life is stern and earnest.

I correspond with a number of officers and men of the 7th Armoured Brigade who are out in the desert and they were all frankly amazed to hear that *Allo, Allo* has been taken off the air. It is easy to forget that the most important aspect of comedy, after all, its great saving grace, is its ambiguity. You can simultaneously laugh at a situation, *and* take it seriously. Making jokes is not necessarily a sign of frivolity and insensitivity.

There are those who react very strongly against any joke made at all during a crisis. Their monumentally false assumption is that a comedian who finds things to laugh at in a war is somehow laughing at death and destruction. Those of us who were involved in the last *Blackadder* series, which was set in the trenches, were occasionally sent letters asking us if we did not know how grim and ghastly the First World War was. But we felt that it was possible to realise that the Great War was an appalling catastrophe, filled with horror, degradation, slaughter and sacrifice *and at the same time* laugh at it. The one does not cancel out the other.

In this sad Gulf business there must, I feel, be more to laugh at than David Dimbleby's ridiculous determination to continue his personal round-the-clock commentary on the war despite a bout of laryngitis and flu that would have laid an elephant low, and more to giggle at than Saddam's moustache. It is incidentally fascinating, isn't it, how so many of the wicked characters of this century have been comically moustached? The Kaiser had a perfectly priceless pair of nonsenses that looked as if they were melting. Stalin's moustache, of course, grew bigger every time you turned away from it and gave the appearance, as P.G. Wodehouse used to say, of having been grown under glass. Hitler's becomes especially amusing when you picture him shaving every morning. The point about facial topiary, after all, is that it is deliberate and therefore screams the owner's vanity. Each a.m. Hitler must have got his razor and delicately reaffirmed the boundaries of that silly black thumb-print of bristle with two careful downstrokes. Had his moustache been a freak of nature, like Gorbachev's gravy-stained pate, we would have felt sorry for him, but it was in fact absolutely deliberate.

Saddam, for some reason known only to himself, favours the

Silent Comedy Barman style. Every time he appears on television I feel certain he is about to cross his eyes, haul up his apron, spit on his hands and throw Laurel and Hardy into the street for non payment of a bill.

Well, it may be that the time is not right to start looking for comic angles in this conflict. But when the dust has settled everyone, not just comedians, will start calling to account the simply unjustifiable expenditure that has been going on over the last ten or twenty years stockpiling professors of Strategic Studies, lecturers in Defence Strategy, Middle-East experts and lecturers in Scudology. These people have On Air Superiority, I wouldn't say they have quite achieved On Air Supremacy, but it's getting close. Surely the money that pays their salaries could have been spent on something that would assure peace for all time? Like the manufacture of billions of effective razors and a massive programme of enforced shaving of upper lips worldwide.

She Was Only the President's Daughter

Ladies and gentlemen, I was there. Right in the heart of it. It was the strangest thing. Let me explain.

I don't know if there is a generic term for a group of British actors; a mannerism of actors, a twitter of actors, something like that. Whatever the correct form of words – a mince, possibly – I was part of such an assembly in America this week. There is a remarkable institution in America called Masterpiece Theatre. The fact that this is the usual spelling should give you some clue as to its very English nature. It is a television programme that goes out on the public, non-commercial, broadcasting network, PBS, every Sunday evening at nine o'clock. It transmits exclusively British dramas like *The Jewel in the Crown*, *Tom Brown's Schooldays*, *Bleak House*, *I, Claudius*, *Edward and Mrs Simpson* and perhaps most famously to the Americans, *Upstairs, Downstairs*.

Masterpiece Theatre was twenty years old this week and the 'mother station' WGBH Boston, with the help of the long-term sponsor Mobil Oil, flew out a howling of actors associated with the series to join in celebrations of this anniversary. Hugh Laurie and I were invited as representatives of *Jeeves and Wooster* which is the most recent series to have 'aired in the slot' as broadcasters like to say. With us were a great quantity of fellow screamers: Diana Rigg, Sîan Philips, Keith Michell, Ian Richardson (whose delicious Francis Urquhart in *House of Cards* they are about to enjoy), Jeremy Brett, Geraldine James, Simon Williams, John Hurt . . . shoulders of fine honeyroast hams in whose company Hugh and I were not fit to be seen.

The celebrations took place in two cities; firstly there was a press conference and dinner in Los Angeles, with a speech made by the figure most associated with Masterpiece Theatre in American eyes, Alistair Cooke. The only begetter of the series, a British producer in America called Christopher Sarson, had approached Cooke and asked him to give a small introductory talk before each programme, setting it in context, explaining any unusual references and so on. Initially, I believe, this was because many of the programmes shown came from the British ITV network and would not run to a natural time without commercials. Alistair Cooke's talk would fill up the advertising gaps and make the shows take a proper hour. The sight of Mr Cooke in a large green hide wing chair saying 'Good evening. Welcome to Masterpiece Theatre' became as familiar an American TV spectacle as Richard Nixon's sweating upper lip or the Walton family wishing each other goodnight.

This Los Angeles dinner went well, especially because of a splendid show at the end put on by the company of the satirical revue Forbidden Broadway which they had written especially for the occasion. The second dinner was in Washington DC and this is where life became very exciting.

The dinner was held in the State Department on the eve of the United Nations deadline. The room was filled with classy Washington hostesses, ambassadors, naval and military brass hats and political journalists. At the table where Hugh Laurie and I sat was Ben Bradlee, editor of the *Washington Post*, famously played by Jason Robards in the film *All The President's Men*, the man who stuck with Woodward and Bernstein throughout the Watergate Scandal. I sat next to his wife, better known as Sally Quinn a quondam television anchorwoman. Hugh sat on the other side of Mrs Bradlee and next to a girl called Doro, short for Dorothy. Hugh was telling this charming woman about our day in Washington. We had walked all the way down Pennsylvania Avenue, past the protesters camped outside the White House, which sadly had been closed to visitors, and on to the Capitol, where we had obtained tickets to watch a senatorial debate which, naturally, had consisted of Senator Robert Dole, on his own, talking to Mr Speaker and a shorthand-taker about Social Security. To be fair, the average day in the House of Commons is no more exciting, but we had felt a little let down. Doro suggested that she come round to our hotel the next morning and take Hugh and me on a private guided tour of the White House herself. We naturally thought this kind, but expressed polite scepticism, or – as we were in America – skepticism.

'I don't think there will be a problem,' she assured us. 'You see, the President of the United States is my father.'

True to her word and in the company of a Secret Service agent straight from Central Casting, complete with ear-piece and Burberry, Doro picked us up from the hotel and we sped, to the accompaniment of much radio communication between our car and the White House security staff, to number 1600 Pennsylvania Avenue.

Doro and a White House girl called Lydia gave us a tour that included the kitchens and the flower rooms. At one point we passed a large photograph of a couple standing in front of a Christmas tree. 'The two nicest people in the world,' said Doro. It was of her mother and father and she clearly meant it.

We passed the Oval Office as we walked away. I swear to you I didn't press any buttons. I'm almost sure I didn't anyway. If I did and this whole conflagration is all my fault then I'm terribly, terribly sorry.

The curtains of the Oval Office were drawn shut. One could almost smell the intensity of the conversation going on within amongst the hatchet-faced men helping this girl's father come to a decision that would deploy thousands of aircraft and men and change the history of the world. 'Should I give a little wave?' said Doro. 'He'll be busy,' we said. Indeed, at that moment it turns out that the Execute Order was being prepared for his signature. We waved anyway and passed on.

On the flight back home the Concorde pilot, Captain Riley, invited Hugh and me to the cockpit for take-off and landing.

It is indeed something to have friends in high places.

The Sin of the Wheel

If you want the clearest proof in the world that there are no such things as clairvoyants, you only have to visit a casino. They are temples erected to the Absolute Certainty of Uncertainty. For every person who claims that they once had a vision of the number twelve, that they went up to a roulette table, planked their everything on twelve and then walked away with a fortune in their pockets, there are thirty-six people who had the same vision, planked their same everything and stumbled away broke.

Casinos live on what they call their 'vigorish'. In roulette there are thirty-six numbers. If you place one single chip *en plein*, as they say, on one of those numbers and it comes up, the casino will give you in return thirty-five chips tax free – honest odds of thirty-five to one, you might think. But no, there are in fact thirty-*seven* numbers on the wheel: there is a zero. The house should therefore pay odds of thirty-six to one on every *en plein* bet. That difference of one in thirty-seven is the vigorish. This tiny percentage pays for the croupiers, the furniture and props, the surveillance cameras and all the paraphernalia of a well-appointed casino, leaving enough over in profit to justify government bribes, gang warfare and all the muscle an anxious concessionaire can bring to bear on rivals and authorities to enable him to run his gaming house free from interference.

Casinos do not cheat. There are no magnets under the wheel, no loaded dice, no marked cards. The mathematics does all the work for them. In American roulette, it grieves me to say, there is not only a zero, there is also a double zero. They more than double their vigorish. Americans, as we know from countless Hollywood dialogues, like 'an edge'.

I am full of all this nonsense at the moment because I am currently staying in the South of France, barely a craps roll away from any number of casinos who are more than willing to let me prove the immutability of the laws of probability. In conversation with a number of the croupiers, I have been wondering at the amazing gall of American casinos and their double zeros.

Before the first sortie was flown in the Gulf War, over a month ago, I remember seeing on television a number of street interviews with American citizens. They were nearly all in favour of using force against Saddam. One of the reasons they gave was that they were 'fed up with America being kicked around'. To anyone but an American such an idea is fantastic in the extreme. *Americans* are kicked around? Ask a national from any other country how much they think the most powerful nation on earth has been bullied and coerced like a fall guy on the world stage and you will hear what Americans call 'the horse's laugh'.

We have been there before ourselves. From the first Afghan War to Rhodesia's UDI the British felt themselves ill-used by smaller countries. You only have to read our press comments at the time of the Boer War or Indian Mutiny to see this. It is the fate of a dominant power to feel a kind of paranoia, to see itself as a Gulliver pegged by the hair and fingers to the ground by hordes of squeaking Lilliputians. This is not by any means to say one thing or the other about the justification for the war against Iraq or any war, merely to try and understand the American point of view. As they see it their might and their sense of moral responsibility gives them a duty to police the world and yet they are derided and traduced every time they attempt to do so.

As a dominant power they are used to an edge, a double zero; massive superiority in conventional forces and unparalleled nuclear capability. But it is an edge they can never cash in on. To use nuclear power against a non-nuclear nation would be regarded as genocidal mania; to assemble all their conventional forces in one place would be logistically impossible and leave dangerous gaps in other parts of the world. Their edge disappears and they feel mightily hard done by. Suddenly any punter with enough chips to sustain big losses at successive spins of the wheel looks as if he can come close to breaking the bank. The odds are almost matched and America has lost its vigorish. It complains to the world that it is being kicked around and everyone laughs to hear a giant complain that its ankles are being nipped. Next time, they swear, next time they will come in with a triple zero – SDI, lasers from satellites, whatever they can dream up; next time no one will kick their butts.

But 'next time' is the cry of the irretrievably lost gambler. As the errant computer discovered at the end of the film *War Games*, the only winning move is not to play. Americans may discover this too and next time they may decide to keep their money in their pockets. Who can blame them?

I have to go now – opening time at the casino. I'm rather anxious to try out a new system. If it works Prince Rainier may well be washing my car and calling me 'sir' before the week is out.

Patriot Missive

There have been a number of bracing remarks made about patriotism over the years. I think it may have been Clemenceau, or someone who looked very like him, who gave it as his opinion that a patriot loves his country and a nationalist hates everybody else's. Doctor Johnson is credited of course with having decided that patriotism is the last refuge of the scoundrel, while the poet Roger McGough offered the view that patriots are 'nuts in the head'.

Perhaps the weirdest, wildest and wickedest idea of patriotism, however, comes negatively, through defining what is *un*patriotic. Some have claimed, and you may find this hard to believe, that it is unpatriotic of broadcasters and journalists to use the phrase 'British troops' instead of 'our troops'.

I am immensely fond of this country, its language, its scenery, its eccentricity, its traditions, its customs and its people. It is, after all, home. I cannot claim in all conscience that were I born a Yugoslavian I would fret with dismay at not having been born British – who can? But I do have a genuine love of home, which is what patriotism means. One of the things that I particularly admire about Britain is the measure of free expression afforded its citizens. It is disturbing to note, therefore, that a strange and disturbing heresy has been creeping into public life recently. This takes the form of a crazed belief that any public use of free speech is automatically an abuse.

When the protesters were camped outside Greenham Common the remark could often be heard from politicians and interested observers that 'they wouldn't be allowed to do that in Russia.' The same insight was offered the people who gathered to protest against the Gulf War earlier this month. Whatever one's views about the conflict, British people anywhere do have the right to assemble peaceably in order to express their grievances and disagreements. But the argument was shrieked forth nonetheless: 'You wouldn't be allowed to do this in Iraq, you know,' as if the protesters should therefore get down on their knees, praise God for making them English and vow never again to disagree with anything their government did. The use of free speech was regarded as abuse: but free speech, if it is to mean anything, must surely be taken to be unconditional.

'We all agree that the individual is inferior to the State if the Revolution is to succeed,' the Stalinist argument went. 'Therefore what is good for the State must be right. Therefore anyone who doubts the State must be wrong. Therefore you must be shot.' It was a ghastly logic and it would be something of an old shame if a similar one began to obtain here, for all that it would be more jolly and British and a great deal less Draconian.

'We all agree that Britain is marvellous, it has things like free speech and a jury system. Anyone who starts complaining that governments make mistakes or little confusions with the truth is undermining the good name of Britain. Governments are democratically elected, therefore anyone who argues with the government is arguing with the people. Therefore they are being undemocratic, seditious and subversive. Therefore they should put up or shut up.'

If you love a person, a son or daughter for instance, you are not blind to their faults, you do not stop your ears to any criticism that may come by way of school reports, complaints from neighbours or the evidence of your own eyes; you feel shame and anger and you do your best to correct those faults. You want your child to be better and nicer to know. So let it be with one's country. A patriotism that is blind to faults and deaf to criticism is no patriotism at all.

We can be proud of our protesters. We are not obliged to agree with them, but we are honour-bound to present to them a better argument than one which invites them to relinquish their freedom of speech simply because they should feel privileged to possess it. Our troops, of whom we can also be proud, are not engaged in a jehad for the western democratic way of life; they are not going into battle with cries of 'Freedom!' on their lips; they are not risking their lives for good obedient Britons only. They have no wish to read drivel about 'our heroic forces gloriously breaking through the defences of the satanic enemy'. When they come back they will tell as many stories about hilarious incompetence and puffing majors trying to rescue two-ton food trucks stuck in the sand as they will about courage and sacrifice. I cannot imagine that their morale will be boosted by the thought that we back home descended into a fog of censorship and witless propaganda in order to demonstrate our support for them.

When an important general comes to address the school in Kipling's *Stalky & Co.* he starts beefing on about the flag, the good old Union Jack, how we love it and all it stands for. Outraged, Stalky and his friends begin to hiss with indignation. That's patriotism.

Oops . . .

I have to start with an apology. I feel such a fool. Last week I made a reference to *Stalky & Co.* in which I confused a general with a politician. I am grateful for the letters – the barrage of what one might call patriot missives, some friendly, some frankly vicious – which put me right on this catastrophic error. The only excuse I can plead is that I wrote the offending article in France where I had no access to the works of Kipling. Dame Memory, I am sorry to say, let me down. The actual quotation would in fact have lent greater weight, as one sympathetic letter-writer pointed out, to my argument such as it was, than my mistaken memory of it. The less sympathetic correspondents, I fear, will accept nothing less than my suicide which, for the moment, I am reluctant to offer.

I will never cease to be surprised at the kind of letters it is possible to receive from readers and television viewers. I suppose more experienced journalists than myself think nothing of finding anonymous postcards and strangely printed communications full of dark threats and savage imprecations plopping onto their mats on a daily basis. Bernard Levin, I dare say, thinks the morning a dull one on which he is not traduced and abused in different coloured inks by concerned citizens from all over the country. I am still weedy enough, however, to gape and blink with astonishment when confronted with evidence of the vituperation and apoplectic frenzy into which people can be driven by contrary opinion.

There is an infectious and dispiriting paranoia abroad which causes the Right to be filled with obsessions of a conspiratorially Marxist BBC and a dangerous and unaccountable vortex of chattering classes determined to undermine democracy; it causes the Left to imagine a rampant Tory press determined to smother and ridicule all opposition and monolithic cliques of business and administration wielding dangerous and unrepresentative power over the impotent masses. Nothing new in that, perhaps, but something new in the blind detestation of one side for the other. Those on the Right noted, with wonder and despair, the volume and depth of the dislike that the Left felt for Mrs Thatcher; those on the Left gasped with amazement at the level of contempt in which the Right held Mr Kinnock, or even their old leader, Mr Heath.

I have met many politicians: Tories with consciences, warm hearts and an understanding of the plight of the poor and Socialists with sense, moderation and charm. I have seen Conservative MPs talk amicably with producers of *Panorama* and *Newsnight* and I have seen Labour front benchers sharing vol-au-vents with newspaper editors. Nothing strange there, you might think. Yet why does there exist, ranged behind these largely equable and temperate people, a phalanx of supporters so monumentally angry that they cannot hear a view on immigration or monopolies or read an opinion on patriotism or religion without reaching for the glue-pot, the scissors and the copy of yesterday's *Telegraph*? I am all for passion; we are all, all of us, for passion. Adversarial heat drives the turbines of this great democracy, none can doubt it. Vitriol, however, can only eat through the casing and bring the mighty engines to a juddering halt.

I suppose letter-writers are driven by a kind of frustration. They are given furiously to wonder why this figure or that should be given a public platform for their facile and muddle-headed views. Without such a platform themselves, they have no recourse but to their writing-desks where they can pour out all the bitterness and accreted venom of a lifetime.

They have a point, of course. Why *should* a mere journalist be allowed to give his opinions every week? What qualifies him? Why should an actor or a writer be heard and not a welder or quantity surveyor? What *right* does this chosen few have to expound and express its fatuous ideas? Well now that you come to mention it, I have to admit that I am absolutely damned if I know. All I can observe is that no one challenges the rights of journalists and writers with whom they are in agreement. If we agree, we applaud the stout good sense and the witty disparagement; if we disagree, we froth and fulminate against the snide, graceless tone and the gratuitous insult and we question what business these writers have to be addressing the world in the first place.

'We must love one another or die', wrote W.H. Auden, who did both. Perhaps our new Prime Minister and the tradition of One Nation Toryism from which it is claimed he descends will go some way towards sweetening the sour breath of contemporary politics. It would be a disservice to the Royal Mail perhaps, but that is surely a small price to pay for inculcating such a rare and unfashionable quality as niceness.

Comic Belief

The Ides of March are come. Aye, Caesar, but not gone. Today is the day that sees millions of Britons behaving more oddly than usual – a source of irritation to many, including one writer of leading articles in this newspaper. Comic Relief and its Red Nose Day inspire different feelings in different breasts. In my breast a mild, fluttering panic is beginning to be replaced by horrid fear; this is because there are a number of functions which it is necessary for me to perform at the BBC television centre before the day is done. At round about seven o'clock this evening I have to help deposit a personage into a bath of steaming, viscous gunk, a personage that the young of Britain have voted for in their hundreds of thousands as being the one they would most like to see sploshing helplessly around in something green and nasty. At one o'clock in the morning there is more to do, of a secret and terrible nature. It is the long interval between the two events that terrifies me. How on earth can a person fill six nervous hours without becoming hopelessly intoxicated? I suppose I shall have to take a long improving book and a bottle of Evian to my dressing room and hope for the best.

But these are trivial problems and I should be ashamed of myself for bothering you with them. The most important point about the event is that through the energy of the hundreds of thousands who participate by comporting themselves oddly and by sponsoring others to do so, millions of pounds are raised. Two years ago Red Nose Day raised twenty-six million. There are those who argue that the existence of such events allows governments to abnegate their responsibilities; that the longer we rely on charitable institutions the less we question the parlous state of affairs that allows so many hundreds of millions around the world to depend upon such charity. Events like Comic Relief

334

or Live Aid are described as 'sticking plaster' exercises that cover up the real sores that should be addressed at a global level. This is true, of course, few doubt it. But which of us has the ability to tolerate present suffering in the hope of future justice? If there is pain now our instinct is to relieve it now.

Others find the spectacle of licensed japery so forced and grisly that they want to hide themselves for the whole twenty-four-hour period, terrified of their attention being drawn to yet another larky figure in a red nose bathing himself in custard or eating roll-mop herrings upside-down in the name of spontaneous jocundity. These things are a matter of taste, of course. But those who ask 'Why can we not scrap this day of dreary antics and simply sign a large cheque instead?' rather miss the point. It would be *splendid* if the day could be scrapped, simply splendid: it would save the BBC a great deal of money, it would leave car radiator grills unsullied by red plastic, it would no doubt please millions; but would it *raise* millions? If we were all in the habit of writing out large cheques of this nature there would certainly be no need for Red Nose Day or any events like it. Unfortunately, however, things don't work out quite like that. There are hundreds of domestic charities alone that rather depend upon large fund-raising exercises of this nature to remain in existence.

It would be easy to characterise those who dislike or disapprove of Comic Relief either for aesthetic or political reasons as spoil-sports, skinflints or cynics; I am quite sure that is unfair. It is equally easy to brand those involved as exploiters of guilt – moral blackmailers if you will – show-offs or simpletons; that too is unfair. For the moment, the important thing to remember is that it is happening, it is, for this year at least, a *fait accompli* and there is no point at all in undermining it. If we want a huge debate on the desirability of these events then we should at least wait until the maximum number of pounds have rolled in and gone to the organisations that have asked for them. Then, when the smoke has cleared, it is possible that we may all find that the days of the giant telethon are numbered and that help and funds can be found in other ways, less irksome to those who cannot bear to see a red nose or a funny hat.

Unlike Christmas, Red Nose Day comes but once every two years, and only to one of the four terrestrial television channels.

Many people, otherwise staid and sober, actually *enjoy* wearing soft fruits or dressing as pandas once in a rare while, it gives them enormous pleasure to tap dance on a barrel of dilled pickles or to use the word 'moist' as many times as they can during important business meetings. They do it with gusto, verve and quite often with astonishing imagination and wit. I cannot bring myself to believe that it can be so terribly harmful.

Heigh, ho. Looking at my watch, I see that it is time to take myself off to the television centre. As usual I shall be wearing my amusing Bent Nose which, unlike the red plastic kind, can never be removed.

The C Word

I'm going to do something rather dreadful today and write about one of the most loathed and feared aspects of late twentieth-century life, a greater scourge of our times than cellular telephones and cellular underwear put together.

Celebrity.

Even to write the word causes a small flush of embarrassment. Its worst incarnation as a sort of semi-adjectival describer in phrases like 'celebrity polo match', 'celebrity stock car racing' and 'surprise celebrity guests' tells the whole grim story.

The most awful thing for me about the dread world of the celebrity is that I am a part of it. Without consulting Emily Post or Debrett on the subject, I am pretty sure that it is a very far from done thing ever to discuss one's own level of celebrity; nonetheless I am forced to confess that I do qualify for the term, possibly – and this is the most exquisitely embarrassing of all – even for the deadly phrase 'minor celebrity'. It would be nicer to be thought of as a bloke whose job involved being on the television from time to time, but as far as organisers of strange charity events are concerned one is unfortunately counted as 'one of many hundreds of celebrities who have consented to contribute an article of clothing to be auctioned'.

Lord Reith, the founder of the BBC, banned the use of the word 'famous' as a descriptive adjective in broadcasting. 'If a man really is famous,' he barked, 'the word is redundant. If he is not, it is a lie.' How he would have reacted to the word 'celebrity' the Lord alone knows. I suspect he would have gone into spasm.

No one likes to think of themselves as a celebrity any more than they like to think of themselves as a tourist, but for the purposes of newspaper gossip columns, characters as diverse as Jeremy Beadle,

Sir Peregrine Worsthorne, Russell Grant, Ian Botham, Anthony Burgess, Sir Isaiah Berlin and Felicity Kendall are 'celebrities', kick and squirm at the appellation as they might. They have in common only this: members of the public have heard of them; many thrill to learn of their amatory or social exploits and many more would walk a long distance in ill-fitting boots to see them snip the ribbon at a new supermarket or sign copies of their latest book. The fact that millions more people have heard of Jeremy Beadle than of Anthony Burgess or that Sir Isaiah Berlin's life's work is likely to have a more lasting impact on the human race than Russell Grant's is neither here nor there. That is what is so grisly about the whole business. I once heard a man described on television as 'Mr (Name Withheld Out of Kindness), the famous celebrity.' Well I mean, what?

I have seen people who hate being famous, detest recognition and slink down alleyways rather than meet a member of the public and I have seen others who absolutely revel in the limelight, adore being spotted and positively glow when stopped in the street. I cannot argue that one position is morally superior to the other. The real drawback with television celebrity as far as my own humble share of it is concerned is that it prevents me from ever showing annoyance at terrible service in a restaurant or from tutting with impatience in a supermarket queue. One has to face life's irritations with a benign and foolish grin all over one's face. Otherwise one will be accused of expecting special attention. Gone are the days when one could rap on the counter and demand to see the manager.

I realised that something was psychically wrong with this whole business of celebrity when I first noticed, some years ago, that the hands of an autograph hunter waiting for me at a stage door shook like a blancmange as she handed over her book to be signed. Talking to people who had been longer in the public eye I discovered that this is very, very common. It sounds insane, I know, but there are people who quiver and tremble from head to foot simply because they are in my presence. This is wildly disturbing and disquieting. That the fame which adventitiously accompanies certain professions can have such an effect must be unhealthy. If it were a reaction confined to teenage girls I suppose one could draw bracing and obvious conclusions, but it is not. Our whole culture seems to have gone fame crazy.

In the end quality will out, of course. Fifty years ago Dornford Yates was almost certainly better known than W.B. Yeats; now the reverse is true and it is (rather maddeningly) difficult to get hold of a full set of Dornford Yates anywhere.

Christopher Fry the poet and playwright will be read and admired years after Stephen Fry's last videotape has crumbled in a museum of television curios, and quite right too. The maddening thing is that Christopher Fry, having wisely kept his face off the screen, also gets the benefit of being allowed to lose his temper in Sainsbury's. Sometimes life just isn't fair.

Don't Thank Your Lucky Stars

I have mentioned once before in this space the great Canadian magician, James ('The Amazing') Randi. Randi's renown as a conjuror is only exceeded by his reputation as an investigator of alleged 'paranormal' phenomena. He has just completed a series for Granada television in Manchester in which he concentrates each week on a different field of supernatural endeavour – psychic surgery, dowsing, ESP, astrology, the spirit world, psychometry, graphology and so on. Randi has always claimed that he would be delighted to find himself confronted by evidence of any phenomenon that could not be explained by reason, existing science or the laws of probability. He has never yet, in a long lifetime dedicated to exposing fraud, misapprehension or credulousness, seen a scintilla of evidence that suggests that there is any truth behind any of the claims made for the existence of ghosts, telekinetic powers, clairvoyance through palmistry, the tarot or tea-leaves, mediumship, horoscopy or any of the other fantastic systems the hungry human imagination can devise. The human mind, after all, is remarkable enough in its ability to write symphonies, build suspension bridges, invent a thousand types of cork-screw, predict to the minute the appearance of comets in the sky and devise new daytime TV game-show formats, without us having to pretend it has unprovable, unknowable and untestable powers to receive spirit messages from Red Indians or read character from birth-dates as well.

As a conjuror, Randi is perfectly placed to see how the practitioners of these dubious mysteries achieve their effects. He shares, after all, the same techniques. I do not mean by this that all who claim powers of prophecy or insight are deliberate shysters and frauds, although many are (Randi has shown, for instance, how it is that a spoon may be bent by what appears to be only the gentlest stroking), I mean that conjurors and paranormalists alike rely on human nature to do their work for them. I have often seen someone describe a magic trick in these terms: 'He gave me a sealed envelope, got me to shuffle a deck, choose a card, remember it and shuffle it back into the deck. I opened the envelope and it contained my chosen card which was then discovered not to be in the pack.' Almost no card trick works like this, but that is how the audience remembers them. What is left out is that the conjuror actually put the sealed envelope under a book, for example; *he* shuffled the deck too, before and after the selection of the card, he then gave the envelope to the subject to open after the card had been selected and looked at. These crucial details are forgotten and only the effect is remembered. Conjurors absolutely bank on this selectivity in human memory, this preference of ours for recollecting the miracle itself, not its set-up.

In the same way I have heard tarot readers and palmists saying something along these lines: 'There is evidence here of a hobby, I think it is collecting . . . an enthusiasm? Something beautiful, china . . . coins . . . furniture . . . second-hand books . . . something . . . paintings, drawings . . . prints, is it? . . . yes, prints.' The subject will then babble on enthusiastically to anyone who cares to listen that this extraordinarily gifted reader volunteered out of nowhere the information that they collected prints, ignoring the six boss-shots that preceded the right answer.

There are many books available on the subject of 'mentalism', the branch of magic that deals with apparent mind-reading. They always start with the advice that these effects rely on an understanding of human nature and an ability to read social class and character type quickly and easily. You could try it yourself at a party. You can judge fairly instantly from meeting someone whether they are the kind who collects things, who skis or fishes or hunts or watches sport or reads slim volumes of poetry. You won't always be right, of course, but nine times out of ten one can estimate basic characteristics and likely pursuits with some accuracy. If you have the sheer nerve then to pretend to an understanding of a mystic art and can create the kind of atmosphere in which a stranger will listen to you, you will be able to amaze him. It will never work, however, if you give your 'reading' just like that; people want to believe that there is some system behind your amazing gifts. Take their palm, demand a sample of their hand-writing, ask their birthdate, go into a trance, anything that might lend the bogus authority of a tradition. No one wants to believe that their character or nature is readable from their clothes, accent, linguistic mannerisms or gait, that would seem like impertinence and presumption; people love the idea, however, that those same truths are written in their palm or in the way they cross their 't's.

In America there are 2000 professional astronomers to 20,000 professional astrologers; in Britain quondam sports commentators wear turquoise and babble about resonating streams of Lucifer energy.

Superstition is just not harmless fun. It is in fact bad luck to be superstitious, for the simple reason that in this world it is bad luck to be foolish.

Good Ole Country Boys

'I believe in America.' The opening words of that unrivalled masterpiece of modern cinema, *The Godfather*, will serve as the opening words of this article. I do believe in America; the kitsch phrasing of its constitution, its institutionalised sentimentalism, its madness, squalor and opulence; all that is fanatical and fantastical about the United States appeals, appals and mesmerises. I know only the thin slices of rye at each seaboard; the great stuffing of pastrami in the middle, the 'real' America that voted in Reagan, believed that Nicaragua posed a violent threat to security and reckoned Senator McCarthy talked a barrel of good sense – that America I do not know at all. Its influence, however, we all feel.

I had the pleasure of entertaining my seven-year-old nephew this week and found myself staggered by the depth to which American popular culture had penetrated his language and out-look. An overgenerous helping of baked beans was labelled 'gross'; the prospect of four Bernard Matthews Golden Drummers was regarded as 'mega' and a heap of American oven-chips as nothing less than 'neat', 'wild', 'cool' and 'bad'. Nothing surprising or new in that; the ever-rising level of American influence on our culture this century can be compared to the ever-rising tide of the middle classes this millennium. The popularity of Bart Simpson, the Turtles, American football and baseball caps is not necessarily greater than the 1920s adoration of the Charleston, gaspers, shingled hair, rag-time and Lillian Gish. The great success of the Beatles and the Rolling Stones in the sixties lay not in their home-grown musical originality, but in their submersion in American culture, in Rhythm and Blues and Rock and Roll.

However, what is new today, I think, is the penetration of

America into the countryside. Urban excitement with America is comprehensible: the United States all but invented post-Dickensian urban life. The discos and cinemas that replaced the dance and music halls were American, the fast-food chains and supermarkets that took over from ABC tea-shops and Home and Colonial Stores were American in origin too. Rural England however, that part of our homeland which, despite the industrial revolution, still defined and characterised us as a nation, appeared to be immune. Our cities may have lost their distinctive Englishness but our countryside was still unlike that of any nation on earth.

Look, stranger, on this island now. I grew up in Norfolk, helped in harvests, served in communions, croaked in the choir and bicycled around the hedgerows. Throughout the sixties and early seventies I was a country-boy, a swain, a Corydon. I live in Norfolk again now, when I can get away from the lure of the metropolis, and what a change has been wrought.

The rural youth of today takes as his model the heroes of that American television show *The Dukes of Hazard*. He customises his car with wide Firestone tires (that, naturally, is how he spells 'tyres'), he paints the Confederate flag on the hood and he goes hot-rodding and drag racing, like any American small-town hick. The fact that there is no pot-bellied, Ray-Ban-wearing, baccy-chewing county sheriff to whip his ass into shape when he gets outa line and starts buzzing the neighborhood, must be a source of great and mystifying disappointment to him and the other good ol' boys of rural East Anglia.

The stores that fringe the highways stick up multi-signed totem poles for the garden-centers, gas stations and road-houses that huddle in mini-mart fashion in the lay-bys. Norwich has a drive-in McDonald's these days, there are drive-in movies available too.

If this description sounds bitter, snobbish or resentful, I do not mean it to. Rural East Anglia, within the meaning of the act, exists only in those pretty villages which are part of manorial demesnes or on those parts of the North Norfolk or Suffolk coast that can effectively be called Kensingtons-by-the-Sea, kept villagey and nice by the Londoners who get up there 'as often as they can': Londoners, I suppose, like me. The cultural vacuum left behind by the industrialisation of agriculture and the destruction of village life has been filled by the American small-town. To paraphrase Cassius – the fault, quite brutally, lies not in the stars and stripes, but in ourselves that we are undermined.

Those born in country villages cannot be blamed for seeking role models, archetypes and heroes that justify and empower them. These are not to be found in English rural lore, but can be observed daily in the films and television that sweep over to us from across the Atlantic. If I were a tractor-driver's son from Swaffham I would rather emulate a wild Southern rebel in an old Mustang than a deferential hayseed in a tight-fitting Norfolk jacket.

We want desperately to preserve what we call rural England, just as we want to preserve rural churches. A church, however, is a congregation and services, just as a school is pupils and a curriculum and a nation is people and practices. If the barn has yielded to the aluminium silo (the second 'i' in aluminium is optional these days) and the barn-dance to the hoe-down in just twenty years, what will have happened in another twenty? Morris dancing and preservation orders cannot save it now.

'Ichabod', as the good book says: the glory is departed.

Grammar's Footsteps

The following joke is often heard in theatres throughout Britain during the pantomime season.

UGLY SISTER 1: Whenever I'm down in the dumps, I buy myself a new hat.

UGLY SISTER 2: So that's where you get them from.

Not guaranteed to cause everyone to fall off their seats and writhe around on the floor barking with laughter perhaps, but a perfectly adequate gaglet.

For myself, whenever *I* am down in the dumps I buy myself a new piece of software. I lavish on my computer a love and loyalty that others prefer to expend on their pets, their cars or their collections of erotic bookplates. The latest confection with which I have tried to tempt the jaded palate of my machine is a perfectly extraordinary program called GRAM●MAT●IK™ Mac. Please don't ask me to explain the bullets between the letters, I suspect the tmesis is necessary for copyright reasons, as is the unusual spelling of the word 'grammatic'. 'Mac' refers to the fact that my computer is called a Macintosh, named after the variety of apple, not the impermeable raincoat, of that name.

The purpose of GRAM●MAT●IK™ Mac is to assist the writer by proof-reading his scripts and texts and offering grammatical and stylistic advice. Perhaps the most bizarre feature offered is a 'comparison chart' in which the user's writing is measured against three different prose styles: Lincoln's Gettysburg Address, Ernest Hemingway's short stories and a Life Insurance Policy (author unknown). The writer is awarded marks for readability, according to two alarming criteria known as the Flesch–Kincaid Grade Level and the Gunning's Fog Index. The writer is also told to which High School Grade his writing is equivalent. In common with most Britons I have not the faintest understanding of the

American educational system and wouldn't know a Grade Point Average from a sophomore, so I cannot tell whether the fact that my writing consistently achieves an Eleventh Grade standard is good or bad. It may mean that I write like an eleven-year-old, it may mean that I am Marcel Proust; I think I am happier not knowing.

I have just passed every word of the above through the program to see what the computer would make of what I have already written today. The very first sentence of this article, I am afraid, was challenged. GRAM●MAT●IK™ Mac has a downer on the passive voice. 'Consider revising, using active voice. See Help for more information,' it commanded. I was also told to replace the word 'assist' with the word 'help', the word 'achieve' with the word 'get' and the phrase 'the fact that' with the word 'because'.

On the Flesch–Kincaid level I achieved or 'got' a 12, which means, I am sorry to say, that my prose is 'difficult for most readers'. Averages of 4.66 letters and 1.5 syllables per word, on the other hand, compare favourably with a Life Insurance Policy. At 23.6 words per sentence, I am almost exactly level with Lincoln's Gettysburg Address which has 23.4, but nowhere near Hemingway's sparse 13.5. I can be pleased, apparently, that 12.7 per cent of the total words are prepositions, but must work on my over-reliance on the passive voice.

Monday's leader in the *Telegraph* fared little better. A convincing piece on Mr Hurd's visit to Hong Kong was excoriated for over-use of the word 'unacceptable'. This shows a lamentable unfamiliarity with the correct style of *Telegraph* leaders in general. I, for one, hope the day never dawns when a *Telegraph* leader fails to use the word 'unacceptable' at least four times.

The leader writer's paragraph lengths were also abused. 'Paragraphs may be too long for most readers to follow. Try reorganising ideas into shorter logical units,' was the program's advice.

A Flesch–Kincaid level of 14 means the writing is 'difficult for most readers' and represents a High School level 'above the 11th grade'.

Well, having forked out good money for this program, I am loath to call it a useless and impertinent piece of junk, so I shall go on, for the time being, testing myself against it.

Something may happen over the weeks. My style may change.

It may remind you of Hemingway. He was a great writer. He used short sentences. His writing was good. He knew it was good. He knew it was good because his Gunning's Fog Readability Index was high. He never used the passive voice. He thought adverbs were cissy. He never said 'the fact that'. He preferred to say 'because'. He liked to say 'gotten' instead of 'achieved'.

He has gotten himself a reputation. He was tough. He wore a beard. He drank. He fished for marlin and bonefish. He shot. He even shot himself. Perhaps he shot himself because he thought his life was too long, like a bad sentence.

Perhaps he thought his life was too passive.

Who can say?

Careering All Over the Place

Vermeer is probably the only artist who could successfully have painted my schooldays. Having to depict all those floors in his interiors made him the absolute master of rendering the chequered and you simply don't get more chequered in this world than my unfortunate schooldays.

One of the few schools at which I was allowed to stay long enough to unpack boasted, as well as all the usual staff, a careers officer. This man's job, so far as I could tell, was to get each pupil to fill in a form and, on the basis of the answers given, to tell him what job he was fit for in later life. Like any sinecure of this kind, the post of careers officer was exclusively reserved for retired naval officers. Admirals got the job of bursar, commanders naturally expected the post of careers man.

It was part of the careers officer's duties to maintain an office stuffed with glossy brochures and prospectuses so that those who wished to find out what life was like with Proctor & Gamble or Penguin Books could read all about those incomparable institutions. The office (being deserted for nine tenths of the time and secured with a childishly simple lock) became for me a bolt-hole from which to escape the attentions of authority or in which to enjoy a quiet smoke.

While frowsting in this refuge I used to read the files on those boys, senior to me, who had been sent for to fill in their career forms. It became clear that the job of careers officer was money for the oldest of old rope. To the question: 'What sort of career to you envisage for yourself?' a subject might answer: 'Doctor'. After a few more queries about 'working with other people' and O level results, the careers officer would write at the bottom, 'should be a doctor'. If the applicant had written 'Don't know' in answer to the first question, the officer would scribble instead 'Accountant?'

After my O levels, it was my turn to complete the form. Next to the first question, 'What sort of career to you envisage for yourself?' I wrote, naturally, 'School Careers Officer'. Beside this answer the careers officer, I discovered when I hoicked out my own folder on my next visit to his office for a soothing Embassy Filter, had written 'Comedian, eh?'

I like to think, therefore, that I am one of the very few people in the world who has taken his careers officer's advice.

The great joy about living the kind of life I do, I have always imagined, is in being able to pursue a kind of Bohemian ideal. There is no point in writing and acting for a living, it seems to me, unless you are prepared to smoke in bed, get up late, wear clothes that are comfortable to the point of squalor and be loose in your morals and language. It may be a struggle to live up to these ideals, but whether we like it or not, they go with the territory. I have always therefore been very surprised by those colleagues of mine who have turned themselves into limited companies and taken to producing their own television shows and running offices filled with secretaries, photocopiers and espresso machines. I suppose the word I am groping towards is responsibility. The moment you start hiring squads of assistants and telephonists you are responsible for others. I yield to none in my admiration for managers and the officer class in general, but some flaw in my character has always caused me to be terrified of hiring, firing and giving orders.

Politicians, of course, by the very nature of Parliamentary democracy, have a great deal of responsibility. They cannot be loose in their morals or language; they cannot wear pyjamas until five in the afternoon and for all I know are forbidden by their Whips to smoke in bed.

In some moment of madness I agreed, last week, to appear with politicians, on the BBC's *Question Time*. As the supposedly 'non-aligned' figure on the programme I could not decide whether it is easier to answer a question as an independent soul or whether the strictures of partisan discipline give one a simple line with which to respond. Everyone was hugely nice and jovial and not in the least pompous, off air at least. At one point, however, the audience was accused of being partisan. I noticed a letter endorsing that opinion published in this newspaper.

The BBC get very upset about this accusation. Every audience applicant has to fill in a form full of details about voting habits, jobs, hair length and all sorts of apparently irrelevant factors. Audiences are then chosen to reflect what is designed to be a rigorously representative cross-section of British society. I have the greatest faith in this system. I believe in filling in forms.

It is perfectly possible, after all, that the questionnaires were drafted by the same people who designed the careers forms for my old school.

Tolerance to Disease

Ten years ago (in May 1981) an article appeared on page twenty of the *New York Times*. It reported an outbreak of a rare cancer, Kaposi's sarcoma, in forty-one previously healthy men, aged twenty-six to fifty-one. A Dr Alvin E. Friedman-Kien of the New York University Medical Centre said that he had tested nine of these men and 'found severe defects in their immunological systems'.

By the same time the following year everyone had heard of AIDS, a disease communicated by the infection of the blood by the retroactive virus HIV. In this country, as in America, it became clear that the overwhelming majority of those who had contracted the disease fell into three categories: homosexual men, intravenous drug users and haemophiliacs.

For a time the pestilence attracted the hysterical attention of the press, primarily in the case of the tabloids because of the thrill involved in chronicling the affliction of famous people like Rock Hudson and Liberace. Wild rumours flew around suggesting that the disease originated from Haitian pigs or Central African monkeys with whom disastrously adventurous American tourists had enjoyed unorthodox intimacy. The *Globe* newspaper in America put forward in all seriousness the theory that AIDS was part of the curse of Tutankhamen and that the virus had been released when his tomb was opened in 1922, reaching America when an exhibition toured in the 1970s.

None of these theories, for all their freakishness, can match the appalling truth of the Western world's reception of this disease. It is held by many Christians here and abroad that AIDS is a visitation from God, sent down to punish those whose life-styles the Almighty finds reprehensible. This is one of the most startling and disturbing ideas to have emerged from a species already renowned for its fatheadedness and unwillingness to reason that I have ever heard. We are supposed to imagine a Divine Being who for centuries has gazed down on earth and witnessed daily acts of cruelty, wickedness, violence, tyranny and merciless hatred without ever raising a hand to interfere; a Divine Being who, since the Ark, has vowed never to involve himself in Mankind's affairs, but who, late in the twentieth century, decides that those who roll around with same-gendered friends or who, like thousands of respectable Victorians before them, decide to fill their brains with a distillation of poppy juice, are meet to be destroyed by the most unpleasant, lethal and ruthless plague that ever the earth has seen. What kind of Divine Being could be so capricious, cruel and irrational as to behave like that? Where is the disease that affected only concentration camp guards? Where the virus that strikes down the torturers of children, the corrupt, the murderous and the despotic?

Well, it may be argued that only a fundamentalist fringe can dare hold such desperate beliefs. But there is an apparently less extreme view that argues that those who contracted the disease through blood transfusions, primarily the haemophiliacs, are somehow 'innocent' sufferers. This implies of course that the rest are guilty, and therefore somehow less deserving of our pity. Pity, however, is not subject to computation, qualification or contingency. It, like mercy, droppeth as the gentle rain from heaven upon the place beneath. Certainly one could argue that anyone who becomes HIV positive today must have done so by disregarding simple advice freely available for years and is therefore foolish. But when we begin to divide the world into the deserving and the undeserving, as the Victorians did with the poor, we are turning our backs on every decent human impulse.

How would Christ have behaved in this situation? Would he distinguish and discriminate, would he pronounce judgment? It seems unlikely that a man who touched lepers and befriended sinners would ally himself with those who crow and rub their hands with barely disguised pleasure at the misery and suffering this disease has brought. He might well say 'Go and sin no more,' but he would say that as much to the bank-manager, the priest and the politician as to the homosexual. We are, after all, all of us sinners. Christ is still the man who said, 'Let him who is without sin cast the first stone.'

Ten years into the development of the disease, if the advice of the Princess of Wales that when we meet someone with AIDS we hug them is taken up, then perhaps some actual good may have come of this affliction, something that improves *us* as well as those who are suffering.

For it is sure that even if AIDS lasts a thousand years it will never claim as many lives as intolerance already has and daily continues to do.

A Strange Man

There was a strange man on the wireless the other day. Nothing new there, radio has become more or less a home from home for strange men. When Marconi took his very first working set to the patent office I am sure he listed as one of the advantages of his system the possibility that strange men would one day be taken from the streets and given refuge around a green baize table with nothing but a microphone and other strange men for company. Radio has developed a function, not unlike that of London clubs, in creating safe havens for the deranged and deluded of the realm.

The strange man I am referring to was a 'witness' on the Radio 4 programme *The Moral Maze*. I usually find that my moral requirements are met by *The Archers*, from the ethics of mineral water bottling to the duties of pig-keeping, but there are those who need more, and for them the programmers have provided *The Moral Maze*. This week's episode addressed the subject of censorship. The strange man was brought on to argue that we should certainly censor not just our artistic product, like films and television, but also our journalistic output. What possible interest could be served, he wondered, by covering stories of violence and disturbance in countries thousands of miles away? His children did not need to be exposed to this kind of thing.

On the subject of films, he remarked that the crazed soul who tried to assassinate Ronald Reagan had watched the film *Taxi Driver* and had emulated in his dress and *modus operandi* the film's hero, Travis Bickle. He also maintained that Michael Ryan had been imitating Rambo when he terrorised Hungerford. Anyone with an interest in films would agree, I suspect, that *Taxi Driver* is a superb film, one of the very best ever made, and that *First Blood*, *Rambo* and *Rambo II* are frankly dreadful. Whether this is relevant I do not know, it certainly did not concern the witness.

A point not raised was the circumstance, of which we are all aware, that a great many serial killers, far more than is comfortable, are actuated by motives which spring from a close reading of the Bible. Peter Sutcliffe and many others who went about the place 'cleaning up' the streets, ridding the world of prostitutes and sinners, claimed to have heard in their ears the voice of God and the words of St John from the Book of Revelation. I have not heard a call to suppress the Bible for this reason, nor would such a call be reasonable. Perverted minds have used the Bible as a pretext for antisemitism, violence, tyranny and torture many times in our history. One perverted mind seems to have used *Taxi Driver* to endorse an attempt on the life of a statesman. I am not claiming that *Taxi Driver* is as great an achievement as the Bible, that would be nonsense, but the principle remains the same.

We are suffering, perhaps as a result of the rise of training at the expense of education, from a notable lowering in the understanding of fiction and what it means. There is a character in a West End play at the moment who, preparing her defence in an action brought against her by a Royal Shakespeare Company actress, talks disparagingly about what she imagines to be a typical RSC audience. 'Who goes to the RSC?' she asks. 'Eight rows of ponces on the mailing list and fifteen hundred extremely browned off schoolchildren.' A review of this play in a serious newspaper the following day asked, 'Does the playwright seriously believe that this is an accurate reflection of what constitutes a Stratford audience?' They may as well have said, 'Does Mr Shakespeare really think it is acceptable for people to strangle their wives on the evidence of nothing more than a dropped handkerchief and a few whispered insinuations?'

Perhaps we are to develop into a society in which warnings are pasted onto written works, as they now are on cigarette lighters, penknives and plastic bags. I should say, therefore, that if anyone takes this article as an encouragement to put their hands in their pockets, smoke in the street or slouch yobbishly, I take no responsibility. If this article happens to end all war and strife, I happily take the credit.

Fun With Dolphins

What do you get when you cross a kangaroo with a sheep? A woolly jumper. Everyone knows that. What do you get when you cross a Mancunian with a dolphin? A court case. Perhaps you missed the article in yesterday's *Telegraph* in which it was revealed that a Mancunian (male, 38) has been arraigned for allegedly committing an act of a lewd, obscene and disgusting nature with a dolphin, whose name, gender and age have been withheld to protect the animal and its family from further embarrassment. A lewd act, you might think, would be bad enough; a lewd and obscene act throws into doubt one's whole faith in mankind; a lewd, obscene *and* disgusting act really gives one occasion to wonder what the world is coming to. Only heavy and relentless counselling, one supposes, can save the dolphin from being traumatised, socially damaged and possibly – in that awful cycle that so characterises acts of sexual impropriety – from becoming itself an abuser and forging another link in the chain of degradation that will pass even unto the tenth generation.

I cannot of course comment on a specific case that is *sub judice*, but it may be that acts of this nature can be argued to be consensual. Dolphins, after all, are highly intelligent animals with a language and etiquette all of their own – they even have schools, probably better run than our own. It may be therefore that they like nothing better than a little interspecies congress from time to time. You do not have to be a perverted French Structuralist or a formalist anthropologian to discern elements of the erotic in many of the myths and fables concerning mankind and the dolphins, from Arion to *My Friend Flipper*.

I dare say the details of this case will emerge, but what intrigues me at the moment is the preparation that must have gone into the procuring of this creature for sexual purposes, or indeed porpoises.

You cannot, in my experience, roam the streets, even of Manchester, on the expectation of finding available dolphins. Some careful planning is necessary. A jemmy, wire-cutters, swimming-trunks and an underwater torch would seem to be minimal requirements. For the more romantic sexual adventurer a bunch of plankton and a box of herrings would surely be a *sine qua non*.

Once, through the usual contacts, one has obtained the name and address of a likely dolphin, the chances are that it will be found to be in captivity and therefore already reduced to the awful indignity of having to perform all kinds of futile and demeaning tricks on the promise of a slither of stale cod and a pat on the nose, a kind of prostitution in itself which more and more people are looking on as quite as lewd, obscene and disgusting as any private act of poolside, moonlight passion.

It is not for me to read motives of the purest love into what may, after all, have been a squalid and bungled affair. When animals behave improperly with humans, as stallions and bulls often will, magistrates often take a lenient view; their lusts are excused, ours are not. Perhaps this is just.

On a legal note, I believe one can never be indicted for committing, or attempting to commit, an act which is impossible. A man some years ago was found not guilty of behaving indecently with a duck on the grounds that it is actually a physical impossibility to do any such thing, whether because ducks as a species are generally held to be so lost to shame and so sunk in sin that they are incorruptible or because of the limitations of their physical dimensions I have no idea. In any case it was a startling precedent.

As usual we fail as a civilisation to take into account our heritage. We happily accept from the Ancient Greeks all those principles of logic, mathematics, democracy, architecture and equilateral triangles, thinking we can also escape the inheritance of blood-feuds, incest and barbarism. These things are bred in the bone. Zeus performed acts with swans and heifers that would debar him from every London club except the Garrick or possibly the Naval and Military. We inherit our culture from a people who said 'A woman for necessity, a boy for pleasure and a goat for ecstasy'. Somewhere in that heady spectrum there may well be room for dolphins, ocelots and, given suitable clothing, hedgehogs and spiny anteaters too.

I wonder if history will judge it a worse crime for one man to try to do to one dolphin what we have been successfully doing to the whole species for years.

My Sainted Aunt

It is curious, is it not, how an entire nation can change its habits, its personality and even its pathology, within a generation? Not long ago men wore hats and smoked. It was almost a rule. Look at news-reel of any public meeting, from Ascot to the hustings, and you will see men topped by headjoy of all kinds and cupping cigarettes in their hands as they walk and talk. Cinemas, music halls and theatres had hanging over them a permanent blue mist of smoke. Good news was greeted by a wild up-throwing of hattage; what scrambles for repossession occurred seconds after these impulsive acts, I have no idea. Hats and smoking materials were so universal that no self-respecting comedian would take the stage without being master of hat and cigarette material. W.C. Fields, the master, could do things with a boater, a cane and a cigar that put one in mind of what Mozart could do with crotchets, accidentals and a borrowed treble clef.

I had a great-aunt, now gathered to God, I am sorry to say, whom I used to visit as often as I could. Whenever I crossed her threshold she would sit me down and push towards me a silver box which contained a handful of cigarettes of incalculable vintage.

'No really, Aunt,' I would protest.

'Fudge and fiddlesticks,' she would say, there was always something of David Copperfield's Aunt Betsy about her, 'I like to see a man smoke.' So I would be forced to take one of her monstrously stale gaspers and smoke it, while she looked on, nodding contentedly. All was as it should be: she was sipping sherry, I was smoking. She had never herself smoked, and I suspected that her nonagenarian lungs would, if offered a vote, have rather that I refrain from billowing clouds in their direction, but conditioning is all.

Today conditioning is working in the opposite direction. The circumstance is at its most noticeable in theatres. There are many plays, notably anything written between 1900 and 1970, which call for the consumption of cigarettes. Noël Coward plays have cigarettes written into them at what one suspects were strategically timed moments for the comfort and convenience of Noël himself, as actor.

There is nothing more pleasurable in life than acting in a play set in a drawing-room. Those poor dears who work for our great subsidised theatre companies are always having to perform without legitimate cigarette moments, on abstract rostra, dressed in leather often with (my personal nightmare) bare arms. Those locked forearm Roman salutes that RSC actors are forced to give each other as they march on stage babbling of mighty Caesar's power growing in the north are the very reason that I have always eschewed the great classical roles. That and not possessing the kind of calf that can carry off a pair of tights. Looking back on this last sentence I am given to wonder what a foreigner learning English would make of it, after consulting a dictionary. 'That and not owning the sort of young cow that is able to transport away two drunks,' would be a possible and baffling translation.

However. Coward, Maugham, Rattigan, Orton, Pinter, Osborne, Gray and Stoppard all wrote cigarettes into their plays. What happens today when an actor lights a cigarette on stage? In a picosecond, before the smoke has had the opportunity to travel into the actor's lungs, let alone the lungs of anyone else, dozens of people go into loud, disapproving coughing fits; kind of 'how dare you, did you not know that my doctor has officially told me that I am allergic to smoke?' fits. Those same people, had they been born a generation earlier, would have sat, as a matter of course, in public places swirling with smoke and failed to cough. Today they splutter like a cuckolded water buffalo at the very sight of what is usually only a herbal cigarette anyway, actors like everyone else being abstainers these days. Conditioning again.

With the anti-smoking lobby seriously attempting to force Hollywood to cut smoking scenes out of their past films (imagine *Casablanca* and *Now, Voyager* without cigarettes) and the general and no doubt laudable bans on smoking in public places, one wonders how soon it will be before plays have cigarettes written out of them. Fictional characters can be seen to murder their wives, embezzle from their employers and wear appallingly ill-cut suits and no complaints are heard. Let them be seen with a cigarette dangling between their lips, however, and we never hear the last of it.

Fiddlesticks, as my aunt would say. Fiddlesticks and humgudgeon.

A Simple Backwardsman

Last week I was given a ride in an RAF Jaguar. This week I was at a literary festival in the West Country. From way on high to Hay-on-Wye.

In the company of that very nice Nigel Forde who presents Radio 4's *Bookshelf*, Philip Howard of *The Times*, and Jane Mills a feminist etymologist who will need, I know, no introduction from me, I had been invited to talk about 'The State of the Language'.

There was a great deal of unanimity on the panel. We all thought that language was alive and well. It is, as Philip Howard pointed out, the only true democracy, changed by those who use it. The audience was less sure, many felt that it was degenerating. Hopefully, disinterested, different to, different from, different than and many other bugaboos were raised. It is, of course, hard sometimes to be confident about the future of the language when the President of the largest English-speaking nation on earth is capable, as George Bush is, when opening a museum extension in Houston, of saying 'this wonderful institution of which we are all so proudful'.

I was able to lower the standard even further by contributing a sentence that ends with seven prepositions one after the other. Perhaps you know it? You must imagine a young child whose mother has gone downstairs to find a book for the bedtime story. She comes up with a volume about Australia. The child cannot understand such a monstrous choice. 'Mother, what on earth did you bring a book to read out of about Down Under up for?'

While we are on the subject there is a sentence of perfectly good English which contains the word 'and' five times in a row. Again there is a scenario to be imagined. I want you to picture two cheerful sign-writers; we shall call them Miroslav and Neville because we are in that sort of mood. Miroslav is

363

doing the lettering for the Pig and Whistle's new pub-sign in a small village just outside Nailsworth, whose name I forget. Neville looks on. He cocks his head to one side, then to the other. He takes a step back. He is worried about the spacing between the words. Neville is very much the perfectionist of the pair. Miroslav is sometimes a disappointment to him. Miroslav looks anxiously as Neville continues to gaze at the sign. At last Neville speaks.

'It's all wrong, Miroslav. The spacing. It's all wrong.'

'How is it wrong?' asks Miroslav, stung.

'You want a bigger gap between "Pig" and "and", and "and" and Whistle,' says Neville.

I suppose such games and puzzles are frivolous but I have to confess that I adore them and, at the risk of turning into the Gyles Brandreth of the party, for whom everyone tiptoes silently away, I will offer a palindrome for you. Palindromes, words or phrases that read the same backwards and forwards, are usually interesting only if they make good sense. The first words ever spoken were of course a palindrome, 'Madam, I'm Adam'. Not many other palindromes that I know are especially coherent. 'Niagara, O roar again,' and Napoleon's lament, 'Able was I ere I saw Elba', have a charm of course, but my favourite palindrome, while being a true sentence, makes very little sense at all, I am sadful to say. It has the compensating distinction, however, of including the word 'oscillate'. I don't know about you, but I think there is something uplifting, ennobling almost, about a universe which allows for the possibility of a palindrome which contains the word 'oscillate'. I will reveal the sentence in about the only context in which it can make sense in a moment.

The Dog Days are upon us, so I am holding a competition. Whoever comes up with what is, in my opinion, the best new palindrome, will win a cassette of the recently departed Wilhelm Kempff's recording of three Beethoven sonatas, numbers 8, 14 and 15. This recording has been digitally remastered onto the best quality metal tape. This is not inconsequential detail, but highly relevant, as you will see. In order to qualify, the palindrome should be a proper sentence: the more sense it makes the better. The closing date for entries will be Friday 21 June.

The proudful winner will be in a unique, or an unique if you prefer, position. He or she will be able to place his or her prize cassette on a table, draw the curtains, light candles and offer up this prayer to the Evil One: 'Satan, oscillate my metallic sonatas.'

Goodbye, Fat Owl

So Billy Bunter bites the dust. Banned from the shelves of Lincolnshire school libraries (*Telegraph* 10 June) because he is 'old hat'. Of course, as every schoolboy knows, Bunter was never new hat. Frank Richards his creator was not a public school man nor were most of the readers who followed the exploits of the Fat Owl and his tolerant contemporaries, Nugent, Wharton, Mauleverer, Cherry, Quelchie and the rest. For a time Richards occupied, and may still, the pages of the *Guinness Book of Records* as the most industrious writer that ever was. The Bunter written about at such breakneck pace lived in a fantastically implausible world, shorn of credible social or local detail, a world which revolved solely around stolen cakes, common rooms in which to frowst, expected postal orders from Bunter Court and cellars filled with tuck-boxes. To call such pleasingly ludicrous drivel 'old hat' is itself foolishly outdated and comically inappropriate.

There are embarrassing emendments in the current Penguin editions of the two great P.G. Wodehouse school stories, *Mike* and *Mike and Psmith*. These noble pearls on the necklace of literature were produced in 1909 and originally contained references to contemporary cricketers of the Golden Age. As a result of some lamentable rush of blood to the head on the part of the publishers these references were updated in the 1950s. The language was not, nor the mention of servants, nor the description of a retired soldier who had served on the North-West Frontier: only the references to cricketers. The editions available in bookshops today contain therefore the anomaly of a credible Edwardian world that inexplicably features Trueman, Sheppard, May and Compton. This is not old hat, it is odd hat: the kind of hat that even Gertrude Shilling would baulk at wearing. It may occur to the present publishers that the neatest solution to this problem would be to update once more and replace Trueman with de Freitas, Sheppard with Ramprakash, May with Gooch and Compton with Hick. Should they decide to do so I swear, here and now, on the souls of my grandchildren as Don Corleone used to say, that I will devote the rest of my life to hunting these publishers down like animals and stabbing their softer parts with the sharp end of a cricket stump.

It is the mark of a confident and prosperous society that they adhere to the great American adage 'if it ain't bust, don't fix it'. Nothing could prove more to the world how hesitant and unsure of ourselves we are than our futile interference with things that would be best left alone. Telephone boxes and Routemaster double-decker buses are an obvious, indeed hackneyed, example: stamps and currency notes another. It is a rule that the larger, bolder and more fluorescent the postage stamp, the more fragile and uncertain the society. When I collected stamps as a child I was entranced by those vast, triangular Day-Glo nonsenses with 'Polska' or 'Uruguay' written in large letters across them. When it got to the point that you could barely fit two to a page, you could be certain that there was about to be a bloody *coup d'état* or a more than usually merciless purge in that particular nation state. Britain continued on its gracious course of small, dull-coloured oblongs with discreet cameo-style busts of the reigning monarch until the dread arrival of those hideous Christmas stamps painted by four-year-old children. There followed a succession of horrors depicting Great British Monuments; Shakespeare, the GPO, Churchill, antiseptic surgery, vaccinations and all the rest of it. Proud achievements all, but how lowering it is to realise that we have become so paranoid and insecure that we have to *crow* about them.

America, supposedly the land of the brash and vulgar, sees no need to put Bogart and Edison on the back of its dollar bills, indeed it is happy to let its currency worry along as it has done for most of this century; green, grave, modest and positively vibrating with power and assurance. We sad British have repeatedly to squeak the word 'heritage' and swank to the rest of the world, but chiefly to ourselves, about our former glory, indulging in pitiful squabbles about whether it should be Shakespeare or Faraday who 'makes it' to the back of our twenty-pound notes.

Bunter was the walking, or at least bouncing, embodiment of greed, indolence, dishonesty and whining vulgarity. If I weren't in such a good mood after Monday's victory at Headingley[1] I would be inclined to suggest that he would be the best candidate yet for a brand new British twenty-pound note.

[1]England had just beaten the West Indies in a Test Match at home for the first time in twenty years.

And the Winner is . . .

In a spirit of cautious enquiry I wondered, two weeks ago, whether any *Telegraph* readers might be able to come up with some original palindromes. The response has been awesome. For the simple reason that God decided to put a measly twenty-four hours into a day and no more than seven days into one week it is sadly impossible for me to reply to every one of the hundreds of letters I have received on that, and related, subjects.

Over a hundred wrote with variations on the 'Smith, where Jones had had had . . . ' scenario, which contains eleven hads in a row, and many readers offered sentences containing seven consecutive ands, as well as other word puzzles of intriguing diversity and ingenuity, for all of which I am very grateful.

It was pleasant to learn of W.H. Auden's facility with palindromes; I suppose it is natural that so great a logophile and prosodist would have had a natural turn at all verbal tricks. His view of T.S. Eliot is worth reprinting here. According to Mr Phillips of Hampshire and others he cabled a friend this opinion: 'T. Eliot, top bard, notes putrid tang emanating, is sad. I'd assign it a name: "Gnat dirt upset on drab pot toilet." ' Auden is also credited with 'Sums are not set as a test on Erasmus' and this rather neat summing up of the rival claims of photography and art from the point of view of a resentful painter. 'A limner, by photography dead bent in competition, thus grumbled: "No, it is opposed, art sees trades opposition." ' According to Mr Phillips the first sentence of a romantic novel by Auden entitled *I Can't Have Norm* begins, 'Norma is as selfless as I am, Ron.'

As far as the Great Telegraph Palindrome Contest is concerned, I apologise unreservedly for the sleepless nights that this competition has caused; readers have been vigorous in their curses and imprecations on that head, and I cannot blame them.

Words and letters spin around the brain in endless cartwheels in the attempt to avoid inelegancies like ' 'e did, Nora, wot 'e . . . ' and so forth. I think it fair to say that the classics 'A man, a plan, a canal, Panama', 'Sex at noon taxes', *et al.*, can rest easy. This is not to disparage the colossal resourcefulness and mental muscle that went into the submissions.

Some of the entries are nonsense: nonsense frankly and cheerfully confessed to: of this category my favourite, because of the extraordinary words it manages to include, is Mr Blackmore's ludicrous telegram from a Mr Crow. "Worcester Five lose. Pats TUC law on EMI time not new. Desk law defies O. Levi. TUC executive lose if Ed walks. Ed went on EMI time. Now Al cuts tape so Levi frets. E. Crow.'

Attempts to involve my name include 'See Fry tot yr fees', 'Stephen is not narrow? Oh rot, to row or rant on sin, eh, pets?' and 'Oh, sod 'em! Reviled desk-satyr Fry tasks Ed: deliver me dosh-o' and many other shamelessly crawly ventures.

The world of sport offers 'Now did Seles's "tennis yell" overawe? Beware volleys in nets: Seles did . . . won!', ' "Wonder" Everton – not revered now,' 'Anne's dog "Spot" stops "God" Senna' and, still with motor-racing, 'Senile distaste begins, as races use cars, as Nige bets at sidelines.'

A subtle and silly one which appealed to me was 'Rettebs, I flahd noces, eh? Ttu, but the second half is better.'

Smaller offerings include a description of a perforated eardrum as a 'noise lesion' and the Harlem fruiterer's cry 'Yo, banana boy'.

My topical favourite is from T. Evans of Cheltenham. 'Drat Saddam, a mad dastard' (what a pity his name isn't Sabdam . . .) For *Darling Buds of May* admirers the dread scenario that the actress Catherine Zeta Jones had backed out of the second series drew this from Rodney Barnett of Budleigh Salterton: 'Degenerate Zeta Reneged'. Hope for the nineties was offered by B.V. Blomper of Colchester. 'Are we not drawn onward to a new era?'

But the palm goes to Mr V. Miles of Bracknell, for his many submissions (which included 'Marge let Evadne send a VE telegram') and for the sheer bravura of the name-dropping winning palindrome: 'It's Ade, Cilla, Sue, Dame Vita, Edna, Nino, Emo! Come on in and eat; I've made us all iced asti.' The inclusion of a phrase like 'Come on in and eat' finally swung me to Mr Miles, but to all of you, to those mentioned and to those criminally ignored, many, many thanks.

I shan't mind if I never see the words detartrated, kayak and redivider ever again.

Taxi!

While filming an episode of *Jeeves and Wooster* last year I was idly flicking through, as one does, some of the old magazines that the prop department scatters around the sets to create that authentic period look and feel. I found myself inexplicably entertained by a cartoon printed in a 1934 edition of *Punch*. It figured a man leaping into a taxi and shouting to the cabbie, 'The Royal School of Needlework, and drive like hell.'

The cartoon came into my mind this week when I was driving along the Marylebone Road in London, humming a Cole Porter tune to myself and trying to be stoical about the monstrous queue of traffic in which I was irretrievably wedged. The calm of my reverie was shattered and the notes of that tricky middle section of 'In the Still of the Night' froze on my lips, when a rear door opened and a man sat down with a crisp, 'Pimlico, and don't dawdle.'

Rather an embarrassing moment, as you can imagine. As far as I know this kind of social situation is not covered in Debrett's *Handbook of Etiquette*. It was entirely my own fault, of course. In London, you see, I drive a black taxi-cab. It has always been an ambition of mine. Hardly an original idea, I know; Nubar Gulbenkian, the financier, had the notion first. 'It can turn on a sixpence,' he said proudly of his own cab, 'whatever that is.' I am pleased to be able to report that the taxi steering-lock has not deteriorated in any particular since the great Armenian's day. There have however been, in show-room catalogue jargon, numerous improvements: power steering, automatic transmission and central locking are now fitted as standard. Many versions even have an electric window.

For most people, central locking is at its most useful when leaving a car; one turn of the key or one touch of a button and the car is locked: you can kiss goodbye to the misery of fumbling for rear-window locking studs. In my case, however, central locking is activated by a switch *inside* the car, thus ensuring that people do not jump in shouting 'Pimlico, and don't dawdle', while I am humming to myself in traffic-jams. It was this locking switch that I had neglected to depress the other day.

I have gone to some pains to make my taxi look authentic. There are owners who spray their cabs yellow and fit them with ermine seat covers, leatherette head-rests, Wilton carpeting, burr-walnut picnic tables and expensive speaker systems. To me this defeats the purpose of owning a taxi in London, which is to be taken for the real thing. Genuine cabs seem to be allowed to push out into traffic without signalling and they are extended every courtesy of the road by other cabs. I would not, naturally, stoop so low as to use bus lanes or to park in taxi-ranks: heavens, no. Good lord, what do you take me for? Nonetheless I am happy to enjoy the legal benefits.

All properly licensed cabs have a small white plaque on the back with a number and the words 'Licensed to carry 4 passengers, Metropolitan Police' written on it. I went to the trouble of having a special one made up which said 'Not licensed to carry any passengers. Neapolitan Police'. You would have to inspect it very carefully to tell the difference. Thus equipped, all the excitements of real cabbying are open to me, without the drawbacks of having to interface with irate members of the public or develop bracing views on repatriation and the traitors who stabbed Mrs Thatcher in the back. Until, that is, the other day.

Now, as it happened, I was going very near Pimlico and knew the street the gentleman sitting in the back required. The embarrassment only began after I had dropped him off.

'Can't see your meter,' he said.

'Um,' I said.

After a fraught pause I hit upon a happy notion.

'It's free,' I said. 'Today's the first day of rear seat belts. I promised myself I would drive for free the first person I didn't have to remind of the new law. You strapped yourself in without prompting, so it's a free journey.'

'Good Lord,' he said.

As he moved away a woman approached and leant in the window.

'Chelsea Arts Club, Old Church Street,' she yelled above the roar of a very quiet engine and no particular street traffic at all.

What the hell? It was sort of on my way as well.

'Hop in, love,' I said.

Another Question of Attribution

There is a scene in *Ulysses* where Stephen Dedalus, working as a junior schoolmaster, sits in the study of Deasy, his headmaster. Deasy, who is somewhat sententious, is handing over Dedalus's pay and a homily about money. 'But what does Shakespeare say? Put money in thy purse.' Dedalus, unheard by Deasy, murmurs in reply, 'Iago.'

It is all too easy to offer up a quotation from Shakespeare as if its provenance is a guarantee of its worth. Dedalus has spotted that it is not necessarily worth trusting the advice of Iago, a malignant manipulating murderer. Every word of Shakespeare, in his plays, is actually said by a character, not by the playwright. Shakespeare the man said absolutely nothing. Well, in one sonnet alone of course, he came up with Summer's Lease and The Darling Buds Of May, but aside from providing a title service for novelists the world over, Shakespeare personally offers little in the way of proverbs, axioms or mottoes by which we can live our life. He was an artist, after all, not a philosopher or an advertising copywriter.

This does not stop people wagging fingers at their juniors and intoning, 'Neither a borrower nor a lender be', with that smug addition, 'Shakespeare', as if to say, 'so there!' This rather overlooks the fact that the speaker of that phrase is the comically absurd figure of Polonius, whose understanding of what goes on around him, even the most partial critic would agree, is limited. The advice is being offered to his son: all parents are desperate that their children do not run up debts; it is the parents, after all, who end up paying. In dramatic context it is an amusing line, but it could hardly be said to represent Shakespeare's own views.

The inconsistencies of those who use Shakespeare to support an argument when in reality they are using Macbeth, Iago, Oberon or Polonius are nothing to the peculiarities of those who offer select quotations from the Bible. There are, for instance, a couple of passages from Leviticus where it is explicitly stated that it is 'an abomination' for a man to lie with another, as with a woman. This is eagerly seized upon by those who wish to demonstrate the wickedness of homosexuality. Neighbouring passages which state, with equal fervour, that thou shalt not wear a garment made of two different kinds of stuff, nor round off thine hair at the temples, nor mar the edges of thy beard, nor make any tattoos upon thyself, nor breed one kind of cattle with another, these are cheerfully ignored. Yet Leviticus states that *all* the statutes must be obeyed, from kosher food to the sacrifices of a lamb (or two turtle doves if you cannot afford a lamb) made by a woman who has purified herself after giving birth. In the case of bearing a male child, of course, a mother is unclean for seven days; if the baby is female she is defiled for two whole weeks. One is not given the option of picking and choosing between these eccentric commands.

For sure, quotation is a dangerous business. Nonetheless I found myself saying, the other day, 'There is a tide in the affairs of men, which taken at the flood leads on to fortune.' I was standing on a pair of bathroom scales and resolving that I had to take myself in hand before it was too late. As someone who was described at school as 'skinny' it has taken me a long time to rid from my mind an image of myself as a scrawny, lanky, gawky individual. The odd interview I have done of late has started to refer to me as 'substantial', 'generously girthed' and, in one memorable article, 'squashy'. My stomach's journey from concave to convex has been beastly quick. My body now resembles, in sight and sound, a bin-liner full of yoghurt and it is time to do something about it. Some of you will be reaching for your Bibles and that passage about vanity and the preacher and I suppose I cannot deny that you have a point. I have no spur to prick the sides of my intent save only vaulting ambition. The ambition for people not to shout 'fatty!' at me in the street.

I am about to embark on five weeks of rehearsals and recordings of a television programme, so I shall be relinquishing this column for that time. When I return I hope to be slimmer, trimmer and not so very like a whale, as Polonius might say. No one could describe my will power as awesome however, so please – don't quote me.

The Tracks of my Tears

Peter Cook, one of the funniest men ever to bite a biscuit, once considered founding a self-help group for comedians which would be called Melancholics Anonymous.

From Roscius to Roscoe Arbuckle and beyond, the image of the dismal comic has persisted throughout history. Coloured-chalk drawings on black velvet of clowns with big tears falling down their cheeks and splashing off their ruffs can be seen for sale every Sunday along the park-side railings of the Bayswater Road. The aria *'Vesti la giubba'* from *I Pagliacci* still runs *'Non, je ne regrette rien'* as a close second as a *Desert Island Discs* favourite year after year. The comedian's red nose, we like to think, is red from weeping or from whisky, never from *joie de vivre*.

Why? What right have comedians got to be miserable, you might be excused for asking? A large number of them are overpaid, overadulated, overexposed and overcourted. They are seen in the first circles these days; they mill about in the Stewards' Enclosure at Henley and are allowed to roam unmolested in the Long Room at Lord's; they count crowned heads and world statesmen as their intimates – why, some are even given weekly platforms in reputable newspapers. Charlie Chaplin in his day was more famous than Lloyd George or the Tsar; Bill Cosby is one of the richest men in America; Leslie Crowther has perhaps the second finest collection of enamelled snuff-box lids in the Home Counties. Fact.

So again I ask, why the whining and kvetching? It is not simply a baseless myth. I am forced to admit that a great many comedians of my acquaintance really do conform to this 'heartache and tears behind the laughter' nonsense. In a foolish, syllogistic sort of way I used to worry that my general cheerfulness and optimism were enduring proof that I would never truly cut the mustard as a comedian. For a time I considered alcoholism; perhaps the misery

377

of hangovers, gin-blossoms and vomit-flecked trousers would lend me the authentic blue-note accidie and *Weltschmerz* that marks out the true funnyman and thus pole-vault me effortlessly across the gulf that divides the reasonably entertaining from the pricelessly, hysterically amusing. It didn't really work: I just used to fall over a lot and giggle.

One explanation for the universal glumness of comics may well be their frustration at having to explain to interested parties that British television does not use canned laughter. A large number of people, what is called a vocal minority, likes to make a fuss about 'background appreciation' on comedy programmes. Canned laughter, it should be explained, is a specific and rather dubious technique whereby off-the-shelf tapes of general audience laughter are dubbed onto *soi-disant* amusing programmes. This is at its most peculiar in American cartoons where it is perfectly obvious to the meanest intelligence that Scooby-Doo and Fred Flintstone cannot perform in front of live audiences.

Comedy shows in this country, from *ITMA* to *Yes, Prime Minister*, have been and continue to be recorded in front of studio audiences. Most comedians will tell you that imponderables like confidence and timing are best served by having live spectators: scientific studies have shown that it is easier to be romantic in the car-park of an edge-of-town Do-It-All than it is to be even faintly amusing in an empty television studio.

In the case of an acknowledged masterpiece like *Fawlty Towers*, the viewer at home doesn't mind laughter at all – he is probably too busy laughing himself even to notice. I once had a contretemps with someone who claimed there was no laughter track at all on *Fawlty Towers*; an argument settled only by entering a shop and buying the video. Even then this person didn't believe me and insisted that the laughter had been added on for the cassette version.

In the case of a more run-of-the-mill situation comedy or sketch show, the sound of a sycophantic audience is, no doubt, infuriating to a degree. I can assure you, however, for what it is worth, that such laughter is not canned, it is as fresh and dew-picked as the jokes may be rotten and stale.

A difficulty, perhaps, arises from the fact that those individuals who comprise studio audiences are, perhaps properly, determined to make an impression. They have developed a habit, therefore, of screeching with laughter at improbable moments so that when, weeks after the recording, the programme is broadcast, they can nudge their spouses and friends and say, 'Hear that weird scream? That was me!'

Nonetheless, I still favour studio laughter. It would be fairer on comics, however, if their serious counterparts reciprocated. To that end I am lobbying for weeping tracks on news programmes.

The Mouse that Purred

Working with white mice must be enormously rewarding. Scientists proved recently that white mice, like humans, are devoted to pleasure. It is possible to implant a small electrode in a mouse's brain which the mouse himself can activate by pressing a button with his or her nose. This electrode releases large quantities of enkephalins into the bloodstream of the rodent. These enkephalins, or endorphins, give pleasure – great washing streams of pure, thrilling joy. Endorphins are loosed into us when we eat, when we follow the instructions carefully set out in magazines like *Cosmopolitan* and manage to achieve orgasm, when we look into a baby's eyes, when we are tickled or groomed by a friend. They are the complement of pain and spur us on to eat the right food, mate with appropriate partners, protect vulnerable infants and be nit-picked in Nature's approved wholesome fashion.

Alcoholics feel a rush of endorphins when they sip their first gin of the day; I expect Lord Hanson gets a decent buzz when he buys his opening 15 per cent of a vulnerable corporation and no doubt editors of tabloid newspapers hit huge endorphin highs when they see spread out on their desks photographic evidence proving that a test cricketer's wife has turned to prostitution. Others of us are afforded similar tidal waves of delight attending Motley Crue concerts at the Castle Donnington Monsters of Rock festival, beholding Brancusi sculptures, watching Alastair Sim's eyebrows in full flight or, my particular poison, listening to Wagner.

The only true equivalent to these euphoric peptides that mankind has been able to devise is extracted from the poppy. Opiates have an identical capacity to give pleasure and the same ability to suppress pain – they bind, as doctors put it, to the same receptors in the brain. Scientists have been working for years on a means of synthesising our own endorphins chemically to produce a drug which avoids the frankly undesirable side-effects, or 'contra-indications' as medical men prefer to euphemise, of heroin and morphine. The white mice, however, teach us that this may be a bootless line of research.

For, given a choice between a button that releases endorphins on demand and a bowl of nutritious food, the white mice will opt for the button every time. They will sit there triggering their electrodes, dreaming, wriggling and frothing with pure pleasure until they quite literally starve to death.

Puritans might interpret this as proof that man's ability to create new pleasurable entities like wine, art, drugs, sport and position number 42 from the Kama Sutra is a perversion of Nature's pleasure reflex that is so far removed from its function as a survival mechanism as to constitute Devil's Work. The day will come, they warn us, their brows beetling under highly conical and highly comical Puritan hats, when we will make buttons not for white mice, but for ourselves, and *we* will be the creatures frothing about with pleasure at the expense of toiling, spinning, praising the Lord and eating potatoes. The white mice meanwhile, our arching and purring backs being turned, will make good their escape and get on with the business of running the world, which the writer Douglas Adams always maintained they did anyway.

Perhaps this is the reason for the furious dislike of the BBC that is expressed by our masters. A television set, after all, contains buttons that many feel are in danger of transmitting far too much passive, morphinous pleasure. When strange politicians and bears of very little brain froth about the BBC calling the Soviet old guard 'right wing' or 'conservative' it is, of course, nothing to do with an argument that is already lost: they cannot be that stupid. After all, President Bush himself called the Kremlin coup of last week right wing: American, French, German, Italian and, most importantly, Russian newspapers use the words 'conservative' and 'right wing' of the reactionary element in Soviet society too. No, this simulated stupidity is actually part of a plot to undermine television itself. Hence the new ITV system, devised specifically to reduce the pleasurability of independent output. The franchise bid system, the most inefficient and disastrous 'in corporate history' as the financial house of James Capel put it, the attacks on the BBC and the advent of satellite are all designed to reduce our pleasure and keep us working. It's puritanical, it's unkind, it's unethical and it's sneaky, but Nanny knows best. This, of course, must also be the reason why arts and sports are massively underfunded. I can think of no other.

Any white mice who are bothering to wear shirts in this warm late summer weather must be laughing up their sleeves.

A Game of Monopoly

Some years ago, when the world was more innocent and anything seemed possible, I remember somebody at a dinner party asking the question, 'Have you ever been to a party where the conversation didn't eventually get round to the subject of the property market?'

For younger readers, this is a reference to a period long ago when Estate Agents still roamed the land, conquering, seeking whom they might devour, jingling keys, revving Peugeot 205 GTI engines and generally making the metropolis unsafe for the citizenry. Then something happened. Nobody quite knows what. How a dominant, confident species could be wiped out in what, geologically speaking, was only a millisecond, seems inexplicable. Were they *too* successful? Or did, as some believe, their warm fruitful habitat recede before an encroaching economic ice floe and was it this recession that made them extinct? Perhaps their endless recycling of phrases like 'well-presented', 'increasingly desirable' and 'realistically priced' created so much specious methane that the oxygen of credibility was snuffed out and they died. Or were they simply, like Bunbury, 'quite exploded'? At any event, divers *memento mori*, the imprints of their existence, are still with us in the shape of disused High Street premises and fossilised To Let signs. *Et in Acacia Avenue ego*, they seem to say.

Back to the dinner party. To the question above, another guest offered as a reply, 'Has anyone been to a dinner party when someone hasn't asked the question "Have you ever been to a party where the conversation didn't eventually get round to the subject of the property market?" ' This is how endemic the problem then was. The fact that property was such a pervasive topic was itself a pervasive topic. In more sophisticated circles that fact itself was a pervasive topic too. And so on.

There was another popular subject, however: science. The publication of provokingly entitled books like *A Brief History of Time* and *The Man Who Had No Endorphins* caused subjects like Chaos Physics, Morphic Resonance and Schrödinger's Cat to compete with property for table-talk attention. One of the most widely read books, perhaps as much for its title as anything, was Dr Oliver Sachs's *The Man Who Mistook His Wife For A Hat*. The eccentric behaviour of the dysfunctioning human mind provided pleasing anecdotes and opportunities for speculation that offered a change from discussions about Victorian bathrooms, coving and original ceiling roses – at least until the cheese course.

The *New Yorker* magazine last year invited a comparison between one of Doctor Sachs's patients from his case-book *Awakenings* and wider international events. Sachs was called out to a household in the 1950s to examine a young girl who was behaving hysterically. It was an unexceptional case, but Sachs couldn't help noticing an old man who had been sitting quietly in a window seat throughout the examination. Sitting quietly? Sitting entirely without movement or noise of any kind. Intrigued, Sachs examined the man, who had apparently been in that condition for years: he never moved, barely ate, never spoke. His body temperature was astoundingly low, his heart-rate fewer than forty beats a minute. Sachs also noted an insignificantly small stomach tumour, which was not the cause of this almost cryogenic state. Some kind of hormonal shortage was diagnosed and a compensatory serum injected. Within a very short time the man was back on his feet; bouncy, talkative, aware and cured of his Rip van Winkledom.

Three weeks later he died of stomach cancer. The sleeping tumour had been awoken too.

The *New Yorker* suggested that the great Soviet Bear, bound in the ice of inefficient political hegemony, catatonically slowed by bureaucracy, a command economy that didn't work and channels of distribution that were clogged beyond hope, was in a similar case to this man. The cancers of nationalism had been long frozen with the rest of the system. Once the serum of democracy and freedom had been injected, these malignant growths would awaken with the whole body. That is no reason, of course, the magazine argued, not to make the injection, but my goodness, we had better keep our fingers crossed.

How apt and prophetic an argument this has transpired to be. In a short time Slovenes and Croatians, Slovaks and Serbs, Armenians, Azerbaijanis and Georgians, Siberians and Kamchatkanis, Anatolians, Letts, Pomeranians, Bosnians and Herzegovinians, Russniaks, Ruthenians, Ukrainians, Byelorussians and Moldavo-Wallachians will all be competing for space in central London to erect their embassies. The Estate Agents will emerge from the ice to welcome them, house-prices will soar and London dinner party conversation will revert to the subject of Property.

And so the world turns.

Education is a Wonderful Thing

When I was young and the world was green and squeaky as an iceberg lettuce, I found myself addressing the question of what to do between school and university. Should I tread in the footsteps of Waugh and Auden and offer myself to a prep school as a junior master, or should I bravely venture forth, like others of my generation, to Australia with only twenty pounds and some sheep shears in my pocket? Perhaps I should tread grapes in Bordeaux or poke such cows in Wisconsin as needed poking? With the fine, brave blood of the Frys coursing in my veins I naturally chose a prep school.

I found that things had moved on since my own schooldays. Parent Power was rearing its ugly head, and believe me, heads do not come any uglier. The traditional Open Day in which parents would be ushered around form-rooms as suddenly spotless as High Streets on the day of a Royal Visit, forced to admire grotesque artwork on the walls, given tea and wet cucumber sandwiches in the gym and the opportunity to ask masters a few questions, had been replaced by parent governorships, regular PTA meetings and the free run of the place to every parent.

Today, Parent Power has become an important electoral counter. In a political world which has seen a proliferation of more charters than Heathrow Airport in July, Parents' Charters are being given much podium space this Conference Season.

The principle of charters, as I understand it, is to give rights and powers to the consumer, the 'users' of any given service. The Patients' Charter allows you to tell doctors what to do, the Chocolate Charter gives you redress if your Mars Bar causes you indigestion, the Weather Charter grants you the right to sue God if your roof is blown off in a gale. Strangely there is no Charter Charter that allows an elector to mulct a government for pestering us all with ludicrous legislation and replacing common sense and decency with flattering pamphlets and grandiloquent gestures.

But it is Parents' Charters that remain the most nonsensical of all the diplomas and twenty-eight-day warranties with which politicians are inviting us enrich our lives. For it does not seem to have occurred to anyone that it is *children* not parents who are the users of the education system.

I have not been blessed with progeny so far, but when in due course my line is propagated I am certain that I would not wish my issue to come home full of the same nonsenses, prejudices and half-baked ideas that clog up my own mind. The idea that children should be trained to respect their God, their country and their political 'heritage' seems to me to be repulsive. If you want a system where religious values, patriotism and a respect for law and order are pushed into the young then go and live in Iran or Saudi Arabia.

I am not advocating that children should be pumped full of rebellion, dissidence, anarchy and hatred of their country. They should be educated. Being educated does not mean being told what your parents want you to be told, being soaked in your parents' values or learning a syllabus that your parents approve. You can get all that at home.

The generation of sixties figures that some despise for their 'trendiness' and over-ripe liberal values were educated at grammar schools and secondary moderns along the rigid lines and disciplined paths that are now being sought by so many. The product of *their* teaching is the old-fashioned, sober and conservative (with both 'c's) younger generation of today. If parents really want their children to share their perceptions of the world they should insist on teachers who hold an absolutely opposite point of view. Pupils do not buy their teaching wholesale, they are not empty vessels into which prejudice and attitude can be poured.

So to those parents who want schools to teach the supremacy of the British way of life, the dates of our Kings and Queens, the glory that was Empire and the superiority of Tennyson over Pound, Turner over Pollock and Mozart over Motorhead, I strongly advise that you do not use whatever powers a Parents' Charter may grant you to choose a school which reflects your point of view, else your young sprigs will grow up believing in the wickedness of

Empire, the splendour of rock and roll and the triumph of trade unionism over capitalism: they will go on to read Sociology and Peace Studies at Essex.

The Children's Charter that I am drafting will recognise that in a pluralist society education helps make you singular.

Role Credits

I have heard many complaints recently about the increasingly long list of credits that roll at the end of a film. If every tube of Smarties, some argue, were to include the names of the colour-blender, the packer, taster, chocolate-stirrer, conveyor-belt-oiler, lid-affixer and picker-up-and-duster-down-of-the-odd-bean-that's-fallen-off-the-production-line-and-onto-the-floor, then just where the deuce would we be? Smartie tubes would be seven foot long and small children's satchels would be even more expensive than they already are.

Well, I am not prepared to enter that argument. On the one hand, credits where credits are due; on the other, a credits squeeze might be in order.

Work began last week, you will be distressed to know, on a third series of *Jeeves and Wooster*, and I thought that for those of you who find credits confusing I would offer a small glossary of film terms.

Actor insufferable layabout with opinions and a ludicrous faith in horoscopes and crystals. Actors do the least work and the most talking on any film set.
Armourer responsible for fire-arms and weaponry on set. Disturbingly disordered psyches.
Best boy second in command after the *gaffer*.
Boom operator holds up the large woolly sausage of a microphone. Big biceps.
Chargehand (aka **property master**) head of props department.
Chippy carpenter.
Clapper/loader operates the clapper-board or 'slate', loads the camera with film, checks its batteries, attaches the filters, polishes the lenses and wears the T-shirts.

Director of Photography (aka **cinematographer** or **lighting cameraman**) like a cricket umpire, a man who stands around with a meter and consults about the light. His lamps are called brutes, pups, misars, zaps, blondes, redheads and kittens and have attachments like barn-doors, scrims, trace, gel, flags, egg-crates, snoots and Charlie bars.

Director wears a woolly scarf. No other discernible function.

Dolly a large trolley on which the camera sits, sometimes on railway tracks (hence 'tracking shot'). The dolly is looked after, polished and protected by the . . .

Dolly grip a man, necessarily of much muscle, who pushes and pulls the camera and *operator* backwards and forwards, lays tracks with the *riggers* and bends down, like a roadmender, to reveal posterior cleavage.

Dressing props dresses the set with furniture and props.

Featured artist acceptable name for what Americans call a 'super'. *Never* use the word 'extra'.

First assistant director known as The First. The lynchpin of the whole enterprise. Sort of sergeant-major, adjutant and aide-de-camp all rolled into one. Does most of the shouting and all of the work.

Focus puller responsible for operating the focus and zoom on the camera. Hopes one day to be an *operator*. Secretly plays with the camera during lunch-breaks.

Foley artist responsible for post-production sound effects like footsteps and explosions.

Gaffer *capo di tutti capi* in the world of *sparks*

Grip one who totes or 'grips' the camera or related equipment, erects tripods and takes on the main burden of jean wearing.

Jenny driver drives and operates the generator lorry.

Key Grip (Amer.) chief *grip*.

Make-up hides the bags under *actors'* eyes, but thoughtfully returns them at the end of the day.

Operator operates the camera. The only member of the crew who actually sees what the audience will see.

Producer one who visits the set round about lunchtime.

Riggers erectors of scaffolding and layers of track

Runner gambols about; ferries cups of tea and coffee hither and thither.

Script supervisor (aka 'continuity girl') checks continuity between shots so that cigarettes don't suddenly jump from one hand to the other and hats don't disappear off heads between shots.

Second assistant director looks after the *featured artists*, helps with holding up traffic. Only capable of speaking through the medium of a walkie-talkie.

Sound recordist holds up filming by pretending to hear aircraft overhead.

Sparks electricians responsible for the powering, operation and installation of the lights. Frequently burn themselves.

Stand-in doubles for an *actor* (who is relaxing in his caravan or writing foolish articles) while the scene is being lit. Assists with crowd control and lays *actors'* table for lunch.

Stand-out a stand-in who has wandered off and can't be found.

Standby props responsible for the care of props used in the action of the film.

Stuntman drafted in to double for actors in love scenes, nude scenes and other dangerous work.

Third assistant director mufti traffic policeman. Has the unenviable task of asking motorists if they would mind waiting while a shot is completed.

Wardrobe responsible for costume. With so many socks to wash and shirts to iron, they get up the earliest and go to bed the latest. Flick invisible specks of dust from the *actor's* cuff two seconds before a scene begins.

Writer see *producer*.

The Analogizer®

Three years ago the world was a very different place. We were young and everything seemed possible. Our absurd, youthful ideals had not yet been hammered against the anvil of experience, nor been muddied in the lake of circumstance, nor yet had they had a hole torn in them by the CFCs of disappointment and the exhaust fumes of compromise . . . oh lor, I'm afraid I am being got the better of by 'Analogizer™' the new on-line metaphor-generator ('Spruce up your similes and reanimate your metonyms'), compatible with all popular makes of word-processor.

Three years ago, computer-enhanced figures of speech notwithstanding, we stood hopefully on the brink of a new era. Did we *really* wear shirts with collars like that? Was our hair gelled *quite* so smarmily? Did we *honestly* imagine that Rik Astley was going to change the face of pop music? It is easy to mock the Class of '89, no doubt . . . the hair, the taste in sushi, the designer trousers, that credulous belief in the free market, but this was BF, let us not forget. To Aldous Huxley, B.F. meant Before Ford, to us those initials stand for something quite different.

For, holding that image of a hopeful, innocent 1989 BF for a few seconds, let us dissolve to this September. We are in the Sultan of Brunei's sumptuous new-look Dorchester Hotel. A dinner is being held by the Writers Guild of Great Britain. Lord 'Ted' Willis is about to introduce the winner in the category 'Best Children's Book'. He makes a graceful, apposite and very funny speech. The *paparazzi* allow smiles to wreathe their bored countenances; they still feel they would have been better off attending Mel Brooks's party down the road, but this speech has at least perked them up a little.

Finally Lord Willis comes to the envelope bearing the winner's name. 'I think it unlikely that this man will be present,' he says, 'for the winner is Salman Rushdie, for his book *Haroun and the Sea of Stories*.'

Suddenly a Roman Tortoise of grey Special Branch suits starts to roll towards the podium. From within the worsted carapace of this formation emerges a man, pale as manuscript paper. It is Year 2.7 After Fatwah and so the *paparazzi* flutter like the butterflies they were named after and the whole assembly rises uncertainly to its feet.

We all stare at Mr Rushdie with open mouths, awestruck. We are not awestricken by his courage or even by the sight of an Asian complexion now white from withdrawal from the sun. We stare instead, if we are honest, like those who drive past the aftermath of a car-crash, like those who gawp at photographs of AIDS victims in the press.

Just as Mr Rushdie's skin is blanched from years in the shadows, so his case now has been deprived (if you will pardon Analogizer™ once more) of the ultra-violet of public attention. It is rickety with neglect.

Whether you have read his book or not, whether it is a consummate work of art and the imagination or pretentious opportunistic nonsense, whether he is right wing or left wing; whatever our national policy on 'normalisation' of relations with Iran, whatever our views on fiction, religion, politics or race the simple truth remains that Mr Rushdie is a hostage in his own country. The cell he inhabits is as real and as horrible as those that imprison Jackie Mann and Terry Waite: more real and more horrible perhaps because it appears more permanent and less open to negotiation. He is, according to the laws and usages that make us proud of our country, as innocent of crime as the most blameless citizen among us.

Yet his Japanese translator was murdered this year and his Italian translator was beaten to death by assailants who wanted to know his address. The day will come when some will start begrudging the expense of the policemen detailed to protect him, when the Rushdie Affair will be incapable of earning so much as a 'News In Brief' couplet in a newspaper, when we forget the awful simplicity of his case.

It may be that it is impolitic to raise the Rushdie case internationally until the Lebanon hostages are finally released. Then perhaps we might be free to remind the world of the outrage done and the insensitivity shown by the mullahs towards *our* religion, a religion of free speech and tolerance.

Today is no particular anniversary of the Fatwah, it is just another day of imprisonment and fear for Mr Rushdie and therefore a day as meet as any other for us to remember it.

Analogizer™, if it existed, would allow the man at least one or two days of sunshine a year.

A Signing of the Times

Take this business of books. As it happens, heedless of the protesting screams of the populace, I have just plopped out a novel. Now, I am deeply sensible that it would be most atrociously bad form to use the space entrusted to me here as some kind of platform from which to peddle this frightful effusion, so let me say as clearly and boldly as I can that my book is dreadful nonsense, stearine bilge, as the Master would say: you simply must not even dream of contemplating the idea of considering the thought of entertaining the notion of putting yourself in the way of wondering about the vaguest possibility of expending a suspicion of a scintilla of a particle of a hint of an iota of a smell of a vestige of the smallest part of a fraction of your fortune on such ineffable hogwash.

The experience of being published is a remarkable one, however. The arrival on one's kitchen table of an early copy, complete with cover, is quite as exciting as you might suppose. 'Lordy,' you think to yourself. 'There it is. I mean, there it actually *is*. Complete with ISBN, copyright notice, Library of Congress Catalog number and *everything*.'

You prop it up against the mantelpiece and walk backwards to obtain the effect, as it were, in longshot. You place it on its side and squat down to peer at it on its own level; you toss it casually on a sofa; you insert it between *Ulysses* and *The Looking Glass War* on your bookshelf; you squint at it through half-closed eyes; you smell it, lick it, prod it, stroke it and poke it; you address it shyly; you open it up and bestow a reverent rabbinical kiss upon its title page; you offer it a glass of sherry and a biscuit; you take it for a drive; you balance it on your head, tuck it under your arm and stuff it in your pocket; you do everything, in short, but dare to read a single word of it.

Then, after publication, begin the furtive visits to the bookshops to see if anyone can be spotted actually buying it. This is rendered more difficult for me by having a face that has been more whorishly put about than that of proper, respectable authors. If a bookseller sees you he might easily suspect you are there to complain about the inadequacy of the display – something writers are notoriously given to doing – or he might press you into signing his stock. Equipped, however, with some kind of hat, a pair of dark glasses and a false moustache borrowed from a friendly make-up artist, one can loiter around a Picador carousel for hours observing the habits of the book-buying public. The alternative for me is to replicate exactly the clothes I was photographed in for the embarrassingly gigantic cut-outs that currently infest many of the bookshops, stand stock still next to a dump-bin (as the display receptacles are disrespectfully called) and pretend to be made of cardboard. I think, however, that this stratagem only really works in Abbott and Costello films.

I had such difficulty in deciding to whom to dedicate the fruit of my novelistic loins that I hit upon the notion of having 'To .... (insert full name here)' printed on the first page so that each reader becomes the dedicatee. This has had the unexpected benefit of making signing sessions a simpler matter than otherwise they might be.

Signings are potentially minefields of embarrassment. Kind, decent people line up in front of a desk and you sit there, pen in hand, ready to inscribe to order. Some customers, collectors probably, have very firm views about what must be written: ' "With every good wish" and then your name please,' they demand. 'Nothing else.'

'With every good wish' is not quite *me*, somehow. It smacks of a Christmas letter from a coal merchant thanking you for your very esteemed good favour. But better a wilderness of 'with every good wishes' than some of the personalised inscriptions requested. 'Could you just put, "To Martin, Up yours, fatso, and the devil take the hindmost," and then sign it please?' Or, 'Put "This'll teach you to laugh at my melamine surfaces, you slag. Yours till hell freezes over." ' One is happy to oblige, naturally. As the Master also observed, the poet's eye may well be in a fine frenzy rolling, from earth to heaven, from heaven to earth, but the other is always firmly fixed on the right-hand royalties column.

But I must catch a train to East Anglia, where I am signing tomorrow.

With every good wish.

Good Egg

I think of myself as an optimist, almost a eudæmonist; cheerful and sanguine to the point of Pollyanna-ism. This is not an achieved state, a point of view arrived at by thought or principle, it is an attitude inculcated by experience. If you were to fling a sachet of non-dairy coffee-whitener in a busy high street I contend it would be likely to fall at the feet of a good egg, a decent, kind, tolerant and likeable soul, someone, roughly speaking, on the side of the angels.

Perhaps this is because I grew up near Norwich, a city long renowned for being the politest, most affable settlement in this here United Kingdom. A daily newspaper once sent a journalist there specifically to test the courtesy and amiability of the average Norvicensian. This hound of hell tried barging to the front of queues in shops and bus-stops to see if he could elicit outrage and impatience. The reaction was always the same, 'That's all right, go you on ahead, my man . . . that's clear you're in a hurry.'

In Norwich, I suspect, you could still try out P.G. Wodehouse's method of posting mail. He used, in the London of the thirties, after writing his morning letters, to throw them out of the window into the street. He reasoned that the average Englishman, on seeing a sealed, stamped and addressed envelope on the pavement, would pick it up and pop it in the nearest post-box. He claimed never to have had a single letter go astray using this method.

People today like to claim that we have become a ruder, more selfish nation: they believe that if you were to collapse in the street the populace would simply ignore you, possibly even crossing the street in disgust. The ritual repetition of this belief is as hackneyed and universal as going on about how winter always catches us by surprise or swapping eulogies on the magnificence of Marks & Spencer's. But if *everyone* expresses revulsion at the growing callousness of the British, who then are those Britons who actually evince this callousness? Or are we to believe that the same people who ventilate their contempt for others' indifference are the very ones who, at the drop of a pedestrian, will themselves pass by on the other side?

It is true that there is not a driver alive, including you and me, who has not said, 'Tut! I was on the motorway the other day in thick fog and you should have *seen* the speed at which people were driving! Maniacs, simply maniacs.' You can guarantee that those castigated by the judiciary the other day for the dreadful driving in appalling conditions that caused the tragic M4 crash earlier this year had said more than once in their lives, 'I cannot believe how some people drive in motorway fog . . . maniacs, they are. Maniacs.'

So perhaps we are all hypocrites. We damn others for what we fear as faults in ourselves. We rehearse the shortcomings of 'people' as a means of warding off the evil spirits that threaten us. It is certainly observable that those who most notice another's excessive drinking, for instance, are those most worried about their own habit.

But by projecting our own fears, inadequacies and self-loathing onto others we perpetuate those failings. Any doctor will tell you the first step to the cure of an addiction is to confess out loud, to others, that you have it.

So let it be with other problems. Paradoxically, the moment you tell others what a lousy driver you are, you cease to be a lousy driver at all. 'I must be careful here,' you say to yourself, like any good driver, 'it's rather foggy and I'm a hopeless driver.' Any workaholic will tell you he drives himself hard because he is so terribly lazy.

G.K. Chesterton, the modern master of the paradox, realised this when he ended a long newspaper correspondence on the subject 'What Is Wrong With This Country' by writing, 'Sir, I know exactly what is wrong with this country. It is me.'

If everyone had written to say that it was *their* fault that the country was in a mess, rather than blaming it on the young, the rich, the parents, the poor, the teachers, the experts, the media, the politicians and anyone but themselves, there would have been nothing wrong with the country in the first place. A nation of Chestertons, a country whose citizens blame themselves and not others, would be a Utopia or, possibly, the Kingdom of God.

Mind you, Chesterton would probably add that the best way to ward off evil spirits is to drink them.

Mad as an Actress

I hope one day to edit the next edition of *Roget's Thesaurus*. This is not because I would enjoy the hours of grind and research it would involve, nor because I fancy myself as having any particular insight into the English synonym. There is only one reason to take on this job, chore, work, post, position, function, office, situation, duty, task, assignment, vocation, profession, calling, discipline, labour, line, livelihood, occupation, role, pursuit. The opportunity would allow me finally to clear up a long-standing omission in standard editions of the great work. For my first task would be to include in the category Madwoman the word 'actress'.

How previous editors from Roget himself onwards have neglected to set their official seal on the indelible ink between those two sorts and conditions of person, I have no idea. My editorship would at least give me the chance to do that service for scholarship and science.

No longer, after the arrival of my edition, need anyone say, 'I met an actress the other day, she seemed to me to be absolutely potty.' Such a statement would be as redundant as 'Extraordinary thing! Went dark last night. Sun simply disappeared in the west,' or 'Saw a chap in tinted spectacles yesterday: frightful tick.'

One would not want to make the falsely syllogistic claim that all madwomen are actresses. That would, of course, be nonsense. It is nonetheless hugely, beautifully and entirely true that all actresses are madwomen.

I have absolutely nothing against the mad at all. Anyone who has been watching Jonathan Miller's excellent programme on the mentally excited will see that, throughout history, they have been given the rawest of raw deals. If they're not being restrained in tight-fitting waistcoats they're having electricity forced through them or being trepanned. I would wish none of this on actresses, who are for the most part charming, generous and good. Daffy to the eyebrows, of course, but utterly enchanting.

But why do I say actresses are mad? It is not because so many of them believe in astrology: that is not a sign of madness, merely of stupidity; a condition afflicting the sane and insane alike. Nor are they mad in that dreary sense of 'Hah! You have to be crazy to do this job!' We all know there is no one on earth more depressingly sane than the person who has a sticker proclaiming 'You don't have to be mad here – but it helps!'

In my experience there are many more good actresses around than there are good actors. Being mad in no way conflicts with or militates against good acting. Quite the reverse. The madness springs from the very way they approach their work.

In the rehearsal room most actors are, quite properly, highly embarrassed. Picture the initial read-through of, say, *Oedipus Rex*. The actor playing Oedipus comes to that mighty passage where he realises he is a parricidal mother-snogger. Sophocles demands a scream. A great scream, a monumental 'Aieeeeeeeeeee', a keening, shrilling howl of agony. Any British male confronted with this moment out of costume, with only cast and general support staff for audience, will, quite naturally, blush, grin and shuffle his feet, muttering 'And then there's the scream, er, we'll come to that later, um, obviously,' and get on with the rest of the reading. The actress playing Jocasta, however, in the cold of the rehearsal room, confronted with her big scene will, a polystyrene cup in one hand, the script in the other, let out such a heart-rending, naked wail as to make the soul of the beholder quiver. No embarrassment. If there is a definition of madness that satisfies it is the complete absence of any sense of social embarrassment.

English male actors, like the characters they play, are highly embarrassed creatures. Irony, self-hatred, shame, guilt and embarrassment are the qualities of which the English actor is the acknowledged dramatic master. Macbeth wailing about Duncan and daggers, and Hamlet hiding behind wit and feigned eccentricity, they both are shown by Lady Macbeth and Ophelia to be remarkably sane. Lear is an exception of course, but then, as we all know, Lear is unactable, at least by a British actor. That's the point.

Naturally the embarrassment, resistance to emotion and spiritual constipation that are the hallmarks of the British male might, viewed through the other end of the telescope, be shown to be the truly insane properties and it could, with some justification, be shown that it is all actors, like me, who are howling, barking mad, while the unembarrassable, emotionally open actresses are as sane as teaspoons.

The thesaurus will have to decide.

Motor Literacy

A friend of mine once showed me a feature in a 1930s *Boy's Wonder Book of Science* which speculated, with the appropriate style of boyish wonder, on the new phenomenon of electric motors. Electric motors, the article claimed, were set to change the world. Soon everyone was going to have to accustom themselves to their magical properties. A large pen and wash illustration depicted the House of the Future: the attic was shown with a gigantic electric motor, off which ran a system of belts driving water pumps, lawn-mowers, salad spinners, washing-machines, mousetraps, food blenders and the lord knows what else besides.

The article was right in one respect: electric motors *have* changed our lives. What the authors failed to foresee, however, was that we would not need to accustom ourselves to them, they would need to accustom themselves to us. Instead of a vast controlling electric motor in our attics, we have today dozens of little ones all over the place, each working invisibly. Every video player, dishwasher, garden strimmer, electric shaver and cordless instrument for personal recreation and massage has one. We are, as a civilisation, no more electric motor literate than were the Phoenicians.

Dire prognostications were made when the home computer took its stand in the market-place. 'Oh my lordy,' people cried, 'the home computer has taken its stand in the market-place and I'm too old ever to be able to catch up. VCRs are bad enough – I have to get my four-year-old daughter to programme mine – but computers . . . '

Everyone imagined that the population would be divided into the computing and non-computing classes and that those in the former would flounder hopelessly in a world they could not understand.

These pessimistic forecasts were as unfounded as those made for the electric motor. Most electronic appliances today contain chips that, functionally speaking, are computers, working transparently in the background.

We should remember that when we find it difficult to get a video recorder to record or a computer to compute, it is not our fault, but the machine's. A steam iron, for instance, that required an alphanumeric keyboard, monitor and programming language to be able to function would be ridiculous. It would be badly designed, primitive and useless. A computer that requires a flashing cursor at the command-line, a low-level operating system language and a thick user's manual is ridiculous too. Those monstrous IBM PC's that flooded the market a few years back were like the early motor cars, primitive and noisy; requiring enthusiastic amateurs to do the equivalent of putting the bonnet up every six miles to fiddle with the magneto.

A group working at the Xerox Palo Alto Research Centre (PARC) in the seventies posited the existence of a device which they called the Dynabook: this would be a computer about the size of a paperback which had no keyboard and which could be used by anyone, intuitively and simply. The PARC team never expected to produce the device itself, it was a Platonic paradigm towards which they could work. On the way they devised a system called WIMP, standing for Windows, Icons, Mice and Pull-down menus. This was a Graphical User Interface which allowed a computer user to treat a screen as an analogue of a desktop. We humans work best with analogues. Which of us would not rather tell the time by an analogue watch which shows us a representation of time as existing in three hundred and sixty degrees, enabling us at a glance to see time elapsed and time to come, than be told in bald terms by a digital display that the time is 19.38:07? Thus, when Apple Computers took over the WIMP technology and brought out the first Macintosh computer in 1984, it was clear that, as their advertising blurb ran, 'the computer for the rest of us' had arrived.

Big Blue, as IBM are called, has slowly caught up: their biggest software developer has brought out an operating system for the IBM which apes the Apple style closely. As the speed and capacity of computers increases and the cost comes down, even the astonishingly friendly and productive Macintoshes will seem cumbersome and primitive before long. Voice recognition, which depends on huge memory and processing speed, will be with us in a few years. Dedicated computing machines in offices or homes will be as unnecessary as single electronic motors.

All this will leave those who revel in their technophobia and computer illiteracy with the problem of what aspect of modern life to worry about next. The correct level for the PSBR in the current cycle, possibly. 'I just can't get this dratted new-fangled economy to work . . . you don't happen to have a five-year-old son, do you?'

Vim and Vigour

In my family, as in millions of households throughout the land, we made use of the scouring powder Vim. This was a result of no politically or socially significant purchasing strategy on our part, Vim was simply the brand we used. If, visiting another family, I discovered a different powder there, every feeling would be revolted.

'Mummy!' I would hiss, 'they use *Ajax* here!'

As far as I was concerned, whatever we used in our house was proper; variations were inferior and faintly embarrassing; I accepted no substitute: if other households used Omo rather than Persil, took Quaker Oats instead of Scott's, or brushed with Colgate not Gibbs, they were beyond the pale and pity was the only emotion I could muster.

So it was with politics. For years I tried to imagine how it was that anyone could be so lost to shame as to be able to vote Labour without blushing. It was almost as frightful as buying Dixcel rather than Andrex.

The year I turned from a disgusting twelve-year-old into a repellent thirteener there was held a general election. This was a source of great excitement in North Norfolk, as you might imagine. While our domicile could not in truth be compared to the great political households of the past, there were certainly plenty of comings and goings at home during that giddy and exciting time, of a kind to put one in mind of Cliveden in its heyday. Why, on any given Tuesday the Conservative Party agent for North Norfolk himself could be found deep in conversation with the treasurer of the Aylsham (incorporating Cawston and Yaxham) branch, discussing matters that touched the highest in the county. Sometimes the Member himself would be there. On such occasions, let me tell you, the Vim flowed pretty damned freely. Many was the time I would be sent down to the cellar for a fresh supply. I would enter the dining-room, brush the cobwebs from my hair, plank the canister down on the table and listen, round-eyed with awe, to the matters of state being settled in that room. How many telegraph poles on the Cromer road would have blue posters attached to them, whether the public address system on the electoral Morris van was loud enough to wake up the inhabitants of North Walsham and who would undertake to ferry the elderly to the Booton and District polling booth.

It is a matter of record that the issues decided around that table by the men and women of the North Norfolk Conservative Association, giddy with good Vim as they may have been, flushed with Scott's Porage Oats and maddened by Andrex as they undoubtedly were, swung the destiny of this nation. As a result of our efforts, Edward Heath was summoned to Buckingham Palace and we good East Anglians and true bumpered his health with fine Gibbs SR into the still watches of the night.

Next came a referendum on Europe, what today we would no doubt call a Euroferendum. It was around that time, for some reason that I still cannot fully understand, that I decided on open mutiny. While still loyal to the Party, I came to the conclusion that I was fanatically anti-European.

It was, no doubt, a foolish teenage pose; an effort to show independence, to set, as we would say now, my own agenda.

My heroes became Barbara Castle and, of course, Enoch Powell, whom I forgave for making every schoolboy's life a misery with his edition of Thucydides: I even went so far as to write him an incoherently adoring letter of support.

Twenty years on, while I may no longer care what lavatory paper I employ or toothpaste I eat and my political affiliations have swung to the Labour Party, on the question of Europe I change my mind daily, running, like an hotel-room shower, alternately too hot and too cold. Sometimes I worry about faceless Eurocrats and then I realise that when you come down to it there's nothing notably facey about our masters in Whitehall. Government by diktat can emanate as easily from Westminster as from Brussels, I think. It's not as if there are no European elections. And, if the current recession is part of a world downturn, how can the concept of economic sovereignty have any meaning? But then I consider the possibility, acutely highlighted by Martyn Harris in the *Telegraph* last week, that Brussels will bar children from making newspaper delivery rounds and I come over all ridley.

In the end, the clannishness that begins with judging by scouring powders and ends with the bombarding of Dubrovnik is not an energy with which one can happily ally oneself. Other people's houses have good qualities too.

A Critical Condition

A few days ago a reasonably well-known dramatic critic retired, to the jubilation of all those who work in and love theatre. His fame was a result more, I suspect, of longevity than anything else, for his paper was a London evening sheet, and those of you who live outside the capital will not be familiar with or interested in the career of a local journalist.

Why this jubilation? You may fear that I am about to use my column inches as a whetstone on which to grind a very private axe, but I can assure you that, so far as I can remember, I have no personal reason to dislike this ludicrous figure, who is as much 'a man of the theatre' as Attila the Hun was a federalist, nor any other particular member of his ghastly profession.

Yet there *are* personal feelings at stake. As a child I saw on television a film starring Alastair Sim called *The Green Man*. Like almost any picture featuring that incomparable genius it contains moments of as absolute a joy as one is ever permitted on this sublunary plane. There is one scene, in which he attempts to bustle a female palm court trio out of a room that he needs to be vacated, which remains as funny as anything ever committed to celluloid. Watching that made me wriggle with delight, but more than that, it made me want to have something, *anything*, to do with a world where such pleasures were possible. The film was shown again recently on television. In the listings column of a Sunday newspaper the other week it was described as 'a thin, ultimately unsatisfactory vehicle for Sim'. Now, I would never claim that my liking for the film is definitive, *de gustibus* and all that, but look at the *style* of this remark. How typical it is of everything that must displease and revolt about critics. The vile, possessive impertinence of this jumped-up hack referring to the man by his surname, the *ex cathedra* dismissal, the cold contempt, the complete absence of anything approaching enthusiasm or love; not a hint of fondness for the medium, of pleasure, of any of the emotions that are so recognisable in those who love film, who love comedy, drama, performance or narrative in any form.

It is a truism that if these absurd people could actually *do* any of the things they spend their days judging, then they would.[1] That posterity has the last laugh is obvious too. Who will ever remember or be inspired by the trashy bile of such as Martin Cropper, Michael Coveney and Lewis Jones? 'Steady on, Stephen,' you may say here, 'no need to be gratuitously offensive.' Well quite. My point exactly. But even the pain critics inflict is perhaps irrelevant. Yes, people are wounded by their barbs; certainly, people cry. Sir John Mills told me a story this weekend of how he sat in front of a dressing-room mirror and burst into tears when he recalled one remark by a critic whose name he has now completely forgotten.

'Ah, diddums,' you will perhaps exclaim, 'and did the nasty man make him all upset, then? Actors are paid enough, aren't they? If they can't take the bitching why don't they get out of the heat?' This may well be true. It may be true also that critics perform a *service*, that actors and writers and artists need their egos deflating, that the public needs to be advised about how, where and when to spend their money on artistic activities, that 'standards' must be maintained.

All the foregoing may be fine and convincing reasons for the existence of critics. The point is that no one would volunteer for this dreadful trade but the kind of worthless and embittered offal we do, by and large, get. What decent person would *want* to spend a life picking and cavilling? How would they sleep at nights?

Picture this scene. A critic arrives at the gates of heaven.

[1]Oddly, when Milton Shulman, the critic referred to in the opening paragraph, wrote about my article in the *Standard*, this paragraph was the only one he quoted. He gave his small band of readers the impression that I had set great store by the observation that critics can't do what they talk about, neglecting to tell them that I had only mentioned it in passing as a truism. He then went on to list great writers who had been critics. A false syllogism, of course. I never imply that great writers can't be critics. It's professional critics who can't write that I am talking about. The rest of my argument he conveniently ignored.

'And what did you do?' asks Saint Peter. 'Well,' says the dead soul. 'I criticised things.' 'I *beg* your pardon?' 'You know, other people wrote things, performed things, painted things and I said stuff like, "thin and unconvincing," "turgid and uninspired," "competent and serviceable," . . . you know.'

I think we can guess Saint Peter's reaction.

Criticism is like corporal punishment: it may be considered good for the victim, but the prospect of encouraging the kind of person prepared to beat children is more appalling than a world full of unflogged youngsters. 'Standards' in the arts may be considered low today, but as low as standards of criticism?

Heartbreak Hotels

I am feeling like a hydra with several sore heads this morning. This is not the result of a hangover. A hangover would be welcome. As Frank Sinatra liked to say, 'I feel sorry for people who don't drink: when they wake up in the morning, that's as good as they're going to feel for the rest of the day.' A hangover, frankly, is a good, clean, healthy pain compared to the mournful discomfort I am suffering today.

As we approach the final weeks of filming on *Jeeves and Wooster* 3 ('they're back . . . and this time they're angry') our days are getting longer and longer. This has meant overnights. Last night I stayed in a hotel which was once a coaching inn, a proud caravanserai that offered beers, wines, spirits, freshly aired sheets, shoulders of mutton, stuffed capons and as able a team of ostlers as ever ostled in the county of Buckinghamshire. It is now, naturally, part of a chain and serves as a tragic emblem of this unhappy land. It might as well be called the Albion Hotel and exist between the covers of an allegorical satire.

It is almost possible to detect in the sad demeanours of its mostly young employees, under the woundingly foul polyester liveries in which they are costumed, under the layers of false and greasy group management training and staff protocols that cake them like cheap make-up, under the heavy burden of drudgery and dull adherence to company rules which prescribe their every move, traces of the features of once cheerful, rude, bouncy and hopeful school-leavers: the echoes of the playground must still ring in the ears of these unfortunates who have, like Leonard Bast in *Howards End*, 'given up the glory of the animal for a tail-coat and a set of ideas'.

Such hotels survive, in the classic paradox of the enterprise economy with its watchwords of 'choice' and 'competition', by buying up small independent hotels and even medium-sized or large rival groups and by observing and replicating to the minutest detail the style and customs of their competitors, thus ensuring that all their 'outlets' offer identical 'product'. They are residential supermarkets now of course: breakfast is largely a help-yourself ceremony which no amount of lighting or descriptive copy can elevate to a country house breakfast. Coffee-making apparatus is supplied 'for your convenience' (not, banish the thought, for the hotel's) complete with non-dairy creamers and coffee-whiteners; small fridges contain stocks of drink and peanuts: there is even a form which one has to fill in oneself detailing the raids made on this fridge. In America the system has led to minibars being called 'honor bars'. I look forward to the first sighting of such a nomenclature in this country . . . extra points if American spelling is used.

Service, therefore, is reduced to an absolute minimum, largely provided by the client himself who is paying eighty-five pounds for the privilege of spending a night in one of these gehennas, with its preposterous carpeting, decor and fitments. What the hotel provides is limited to a standardised horror of 'detailing': some grotesque bounder in the senior management of the Forte Group decides it would be just ace to fold the leading edge of the lavatory paper into a coy and provocative peak and a fortnight later this lunatic practice is repeated by the Crest Group and the de Vere group and every other in the land. One night a small bar of soap, misleadingly labelled 'goodnight chocolate', appeared on pillows in a hotel in Newport Pagnell: a fortnight later the practice was universal.

A recent custom, and the one which has caused such a welling tide of misery to sweep over me this morning, is that of placing the guest's morning newspaper in a small plastic bag on which is printed 'Your morning paper' and hanging it on the door knob. Is it less likely to be stolen than a paper folded and left in the corridor? Or one pushed under the door? No. This is simply another grisly attempt at a personal touch. Another phenomenal waste of money and world resources, another grotesque smirk from the leering and dishonoured prostitute that is the international hotel trade.

It is not that the American hotel style is impossible to achieve with some degree of salubriousness: Holiday Inns (ironically British owned these days) continue to do the thing rather well in largely purpose built premises. But the sight of cheap bright carpet overlaying and deadening good varnished oak floorboards, and cheap bright management orthodoxy overlaying and deadening good British spontaneity, stabs the heart.

Better Fawlty than Forte, I think.

Mercury, Messenger of the Gods

Some things in this world make me want to tear my clothes off and jump up and down, ululating wildly. Lavatory seat covers, corn dollies, ceramic plates by 'leading and internationally renowned British artists' depicting woodland voles snouting for blackberries in our native heritage woodlands in an heirloom edition you'll want to keep for ever, *Gardener's Question Time*, people who say 'would you like an eggy?', ribbons on Yorkshire terriers, tea towels with the Desideratum printed on them, gift ideas connected with golf and school choirs singing 'Lord of the Dance': these are a few of my favourite things. A desire to pollute the air with industrial strength obscenities when confronted by such itemries sweeps over me like a simoom.

This is as nothing to the wild, giddy and Bacchic storm that engulfs my whole being when I stumble across letters like those published on the subject of Freddie Mercury in last week's *Telegraph*. One woman described the late rock star as a 'monster' whose 'lifestyle' was 'disgusting'. Suddenly, on reading this and other articles and letters condemning the man's life, I was gripped by an overwhelming urge to behave disgustingly myself: all at once I wanted to be a monster. I realised that the real divide in Britain is not between rich and poor, between Labour and Conservative, between male and female, between North and South, but between the merciful and the unmerciful. In the name of 'protecting our children' any unchristian condemnation, any greasy judgment, any canting anathema is permissible.

The deep cruel corruption of a Frank Beck in leafy suburbia is the real threat to children, not the Dionysiac licence and liberating excess of a rock concert. Murder, abuse, suffocating oppression and mindless cruelty are preponderantly found, as any newspaper will show you, in the home, nestling deep in the welcoming bosom of the Great British Family.

Those who sent half an acre of flowers to carpet the road outside Mercury's house; the girls who travelled halfway across the world to bid him farewell; the quarter of a million South Americans who attended one single Queen concert a few years ago in Rio; the millions upon millions for whom he was the Judy Garland, Pagliacci, Falstaff, Don Giovanni and Dionysos *de nos jours* . . . were they depraved by him? Did he lead them astray? Did he lecture them? Tell them how to live? Urge them to narcotic riot and anal impropriety? Incite them to rebellion, degradation or crime? Of course not. He entertained them. He did so wittily, stylishly, outrageously and with a gigantic Grand Guignol spirit that may as well be called genius.

'A billion flies eat excrement,' you may say; 'that does not ennoble the practice.' Perhaps. In as much as it does not rally the masses, a revolutionary might call rock music a capitalist bread and circuses sop; in as much as it is 'wild and warm and free' a latter-day puritan might call it sinful. But for millions it is *their* music, *their* world, *their* answer to the panic and emptiness of traffic jams and mortgages.

What a phrase is 'family values': yet what does it mean? What are the virtues it offers? It has nothing to do with Christianity, certainly. Would Christ confuse bourgeois smugness with moral strength or judgmental bigotry with neighbourly love?

Don't get me wrong. I love families. Parenthood, children, Christmas, security, nurture, mutual love, all these make for a safer, better, friendlier world. I love my own family and many individual families I know. But 'a family' is a very different entity from 'Family'. Just as Swift loathed and detested that creature called man, but loved John and Peter and Andrew individually, so I loathe and detest that creature called family life and the smothering, leaden, twee, false, moribund, time-serving attitude to existence that is espoused in its name.

Our children *should* be protected, naturally: from ignorance, convention, the inheritance of parental prejudice, the denial of a youth of experiment and freedom and from the clannish intolerance that really threatens mankind. Of course we should urge them not to inject themselves with poisonous narcotics or mix bodily fluids with strangers – Bohemia has its slums after all; but who could condemn a child to a world of heritage porcelain and ruched Dralon without first allowing them a glimpse of art and surprise?

Setting a good example? What does that mean? Churchill drank too much alcohol, his father died of a sexually transmitted disease. Kennedy was an adulterer. King George V swore. Gladstone met prostitutes. I am far from perfect myself. What about you?

Freddie Mercury went to perdition in his own way: *en route* he made a difference to millions of lives; he amused, delighted, entranced and enriched. It is right to mourn him. If Britain cannot have diplomatic relations with Bohemia then truly we are damned.

Thar's Gold In Them Thar Films

Imagine, if you would be so lovely for just one minute of your exceptionally valuable time, the following scenario. A group of people has discovered oil in Britain. They are entranced. They dance with joy, weaving their enraptured steps towards the doors of venture capitalists in the City of London.

'Please!' they cry. 'Only lend us the money to buy drill bits and soon the oil will be pouring from the wells and we will all be rich beyond the dreams of avarice.'

The venture capitalists rub their chins. 'When will we see a return?' they ask. 'Will *all* the wells bear? What is your collateral?'

Surprised, hurt and a little daunted, the prospectors head towards Downing Street.

'We've discovered oil,' they say, a little less jauntily. 'Can we please have some money for drill bits?'

'Oh lordy lord,' says the man from the Treasury, 'but drill bits are expensive aren't they?'

'You don't understand,' our heroes whimper. 'Oil . . . we've got oil, *here*, in Britain. It will make us millions. We just need money for the actual drilling . . . '

'Oh gracious heavens,' mutter the ministers. 'Oh my good night, oh my beer and whiskies . . . but drills are expensive aren't they?'

The geologists and prospectors shake their heads in wonder and leave, only to be heard of next in America, where they are helping to divert oil out of gushers into the coffers of the American Treasury.

It sounds absurd, doesn't it? After all, we *did* discover oil in our territory and British companies took advantage of it.

There is more than one kind of oil, however. More than one substance that can lubricate humankind, fuel a nation's prosperity and energise society.

Examine the extraordinary success of the United States. They are no longer the great manufacturing power they once were, yet there are more nations on earth being penetrated by the sacred American names now than there were twenty years ago: names like Levi, Zippo, Harley-Davidson, McDonald, Coca- and Pepsi Cola, Apple, Disney, Marlboro, Häagen-Daz, Budweiser and IBM. Why?

You may cross the planet from end to end without meeting a soul who has heard of Daks, Bryant & May, Rover, Wimpy, Vimto, Sinclair, Ealing, Woodbines, Lyons Maid, Double Diamond or ICL. Why?

The answer is simple. Films. Movies. American cinema, and the lifestyle – to use a loathsome but necessary word – that it reflects, promulgates, examines and disseminates, reaches every corner of this cornerless earth. America is not the trading nation that Japan is, yet Japanese culture, save a Hokusai exhibition here and a Sumo tournament there, has never influenced or pervaded us in the way American culture continues to do.

British people crowd into pubs drinking Budweiser and smoking Marlboro because of movies; they wear what they see worn in movies, they aspire to a life, a slang, a vocabulary and *modus vivendi* that is shown them in seventy millimetre Eastmancolor and Dolby stereo. This doesn't make them weak, pusillanimous or ovine. Many of those who mock this apparent fashion slavery are themselves living in a style borrowed from an Evelyn Waugh novel, drinking drinks drunk by John Buchan protagonists or speaking a language culled from Trollope and Macaulay. It is not people who are weak, it is culture that is strong. That is why tyrants burn books, ban films and imprison artists.

Whether American films are artistically on a par with Waugh, Buchan or Trollope is another question. What is indisputable is that we, as a nation, have lost our cultural influence and, more importantly for our government and industry, with it we have lost our power and authority as manufacturers of icons.

We have no voice in the world. The only voice we could have is cinema, allied with pop music and television. The Japanese, wise as they are, realise that, although they make almost all the machines that enregister, reproduce and rediffuse the product, they cannot generate the product itself. Therefore Sony has bought

Columbia, and other Japanese hardware companies continue to buy the studios, the backlists, the 'intellectual copyright' as it is known, and the creators of all this popular culture.

Britain, from time to time, chugs out a film revelling in its past – beautifully photographed and acted, no doubt – but hardly a showcase for a nation and its wares.

Yet we retain acres of studio, thousands of the most talented film technicians in the world, hundreds of remarkable actors and actresses, scores of potentially brilliant film writers and, crucially, the native advantage of being born, by definition, Anglophones.

We have oil. But no one, in the public sector or the private, seems to understand that once the drill bits have been paid for and the oil is gushing, the benefits for our entire nation will be incalculably great. Fish and chip shops in Rio, cricket in Tokyo, Marks & Spencer in Moscow.

Valete

It is with heavy heart that I take up my keyboard and fully integrated multi-tasking word-processing software to write these words. It is not post-festal tristesse that weighs me down, nor yet a dyspepsia occasioned by the acid admixture of cranberries, Taylor's 1966 and BBC1's Christmas *Birds of a Feather*. *Ich weiss* dashed well *was soll es bedeuten, das ich so traurig bin*, as Heine would have said (a poet, incidentally, from whom I am descended on the distaff), or as Shakespeare preferred, in truth I *do* know why I am so sad.

I weep because this is the last column I shall be writing in the *Telegraph* for a while. I shall not burden you with the why-the-hecks and the what-on-earths. Suffice to say my work takes me out of circulation for some months; it is possible, before you start standing on your seats and cheering fit to make the welkin bust, highly possible that I shall return ere the blossom withers on the bough. It may just be that when the fields are white with daisies, I shall, like Psmith, return. Your jubilation may be premature.

It has been a remarkable experience leaking out a hebdomadal eight hundred words for this newspaper over the last two years. Let us suppose that I had been columnising during the period 1986–1988. What great events shook the earth then? This or that company was privatised, this or that minister resigned, this or that royal baby was born.

But from '89 to '91 . . . how the twin pillars of the world shook then. Gorbachev and Thatcher ceased to be, we went to war against Iraq, the hostages returned, the political map of Europe changed more than at any time since Hitler and faster too, Maxwell died and was revealed to be what *Private Eye* had always said he was, John Major arose from out the azure mainstream and the

Labour Party, even in the eyes of its enemies, became electable.[1]

We always believe that the age we are in is the age of real change. I have always felt that as I have lived, so the world has undergone its most profound mutations . . . that I was born just too late to have experienced things as they had been since time immemorial. It was while I was at school that prefects were no longer allowed to beat; it was while I was at university that my college, after six hundred years, went co-educational, it was while I was learning to drive that seat-belts became compulsory, it was while I started doing things with the BBC that it was forced to go all modern and competitive. I don't suppose any of these changes are significant in themselves, indeed they are, for the large part, admirable improvements. I do not even believe that this impression of living through change is any greater in me than it would have been in someone writing in other epochs.

No one can deny, however, that the global contortions of the last two years have been gobsmacking, snoutspanking and face-walloping.

How am I going to live with myself, therefore, when I look back over my writings for the period and see that I have, while all about me walls came tumbling down and empires fell, failed to predict a single one of the huge events of the period? I do not suppose that I was hired for my geo-political acumen nor my profound insight, yet it is lowering to consider that I did not even have the gumption to see that Gorbachev was only a doomed transitional Kerensky figure, and that Saddam would still be in power a year and a half after the might of the West was sent to meet him in the field of battle.

What then dare I suggest will happen next year? Will China's wicked leaders finally be ousted? Will Yeltsin be assassinated and South Africa go up in flames?

The only predictable fact in this world is that nothing is predictable. However close together and however deeply the seismic sensors are planted and however sensitive they are, earthquakes still take the geologists by surprise. However many foreign correspondents we send out, however close to a fax machine they are, still each political upheaval astonishes us.

[1]Ho hum . . .

423

So farewell then readers and farewell 1991. I have been simply overwhelmed by the support and interest shown by the many hundreds who have written to me over the last two years. If I have not always been able to reply with as much care and concentration as your communications have warranted, I apologise and plead the usual pleas. I have, at the risk of sounding greasy, at least come to the conclusion that the readership of this newspaper is wider, better informed, wiser and more tolerant, wittier and less conservative (with whichever sized 'c' you prefer) than its reputation might give out.

Thank you all so very much for bearing with me.

Ring out, wild bells, to the wild sky . . . ring out the old, ring in the new. *Valete.*

A Matter of Emphasis

The very nice Max Hastings asked me to write a leading article one week before the General Election explaining why I would be voting Labour. Very kind of an unashamedly Conservative newspaper. Didn't make much difference, did it? Or perhaps it did . . . in the wrong direction.

Bernard Levin once wrote that, while his politics had often changed, one position had never altered, his 'profound and unwavering contempt for the Conservative Party'. I cannot claim such admirable consistency. Indeed, I remember a boy at school whose life was made a living hell because he let slip the dreadful admission that his father voted Liberal. With the unrelenting clannishness of boyhood we were horrified at one of our number being less than truly Blue. How is it then that I find myself to be, twentysomething years later, a passionately keen supporter of the Labour Party, an institution the very pronunciation of whose name, to my younger self, was akin to words like 'toilet', 'serviette' and 'portion', and the very sight of whose leaders, Wilson, Brown and Jenkins, inspired a revulsion in me not unlike that provoked in a vegan confronted with raw steak? Whence this apostasy? It is not as if I have rejected, along with Conservative loyalties, all the other characteristics of my caste. I retain a love of country that, while not jingoistic, a cruel man might call sentimental; I remain as emotionally reserved and spiritually constipated as any proud Briton; I share a love of sport, the countryside, pageant and all the tweed, twaddle and Twinings tea tweeness that one associates with traditional England. I have not embraced that repulsive shibboleth Political Correctness and all its sanctimonious vileness; I am more or less agreed that today's tunes are not as good as yesterday's, that Browning was a better poet than Pound and that discipline and good manners have declined regrettably and deplorably; I firmly hold that ignorance, lawlessness and dishonour are evils; I believe that virtue should be rewarded and vice not go unpunished; I have no quarrel with fox-hunting, Ascot, the monarchy or Bernard Manning; I prefer the *Daily Telegraph* to the *Independent* and I go a bit funny when I think of Churchill, Nelson, Shakespeare, the Authorised Version, Celia Johnson, Jack Hobbs and Richard Hannay.

I do, however, draw the line at the Conservative Party.

There is an element here of what I would call a British sense of fair play, allied to a natural sympathy for the underdog. The almost daily and universal vilification of Neil Kinnock throughout the eighties in the public prints made me feel that there must be good there. How can one not be fond of something that the *Daily Mail* despises? I defy it to be done.

The Labour Party has changed: to associate it with the wilder shores of unreason it once inhabited would be like associating the Tory Party with its historic opposition to the Welfare State. Even if he were never to become Prime Minister, Neil Kinnock would stand as one of the most remarkable politicians of recent times on the record of his rehabilitation of the British Labour Party alone. To damn this rehabilitation as unprincipled when it has effected the changes everyone agreed were necessary to render Labour electable is madness. Would we damn the Tories for attempting to scrap the Poll Tax? Of course not, we would damn them for attempting to stand by it, when it is so clearly out of tune with the electorate. Only bad politicians stand still. Margaret Thatcher, for instance, served the Heath government ably, supporting mixed-economy measures, pragmatism, consensus politics, high taxation and interventionism. She moved away from these throughout the seventies, a move Conservatives saw as the sign of a developing political mind. What's sauce for the goose is sauce for the gander. Thatcher shifted from the centre ground to an extremer, more doctrinaire ideology; Kinnock has moved the other way, as it were from dogma to pragma. I know which direction I believe more sound and more in tune.

Politics in Britain is about what surfers call catching the wave. The Tories caught a great big roller in '79 but it is now, if not on the ebb, certainly fizzling and frothing itself out on the sands. The Labour Party has caught a new wave, less dramatic, more of a swell perhaps, and all the less precipitous and perilous for that.

Modern Conservatism was founded on the principle of an atomism that denied society and perceived humans as discrete autonomous individuals with no dependence on or connection to a holistic, organic whole. Margaret Thatcher actually stated the case when she remarked that there is no such thing as society. A natural result of this thinking has been the division, vulgarity, loutishness, aggression, intolerance, heartlessness, decay and Brownian chaos that have characterised Britain lately.

In the meantime industry has lost twenty per cent of its capacity, our roads, fabric, health and education services have fallen into a state of disrepair and the crime rate has rocketed like a startled pheasant. As a nation we have started to desertify, like any terrain that has been exploited for cash gain without the expedience of management, plough-back and husbandry.

If we discount the inevitable guff about 'vision' emanating from both sides, we are left with choices (the Lord be praised that we have arrived at a general election where this can at last be said) of *emphasis*.

The choices are not between massive state interference, inter-ventionism and government meddling on the one hand, and complete untrammelled market freedom on the other; nor between the total abolition of taxes under one government and the malicious imposition of punitive rates under the other. The Conservatives would, as they always have done, continue to impose taxes and to intervene in industry, finance and family life, both through fiscal policy and through direct action. Nor will enterprise be hampered by a Labour government. It should be remembered, when John Major's own journey from Brixton to Chequers is cited as an example of Tory virtues, that he rose from failed bus conductor to banking high-flier and MP under successive Labour governments. For every economist who sees a higher rate of taxation as an obstacle to enterprise and economic growth you will find another who believes it (especially in time of recession) to be legitimate economic kindling. For every businessman who loathes interventionism, you will find another who craves a more planned economy that encourages investment.

I am not Marxist: my known peculiarities and preferences make me, I suppose, a member of what one might call the Millicent Tendency; so, not just a Champagne Socialist, but a Pink Champagne Socialist to boot (and to boot very hard, no doubt). Some wearisomely still seem to see hypocrisy in the idea of a rich socialist, as if socialism were, like Christianity, a doctrine that demanded the giving away of private alms. They would have it that the rich have a duty to vote Conservative and that only the envious, slovenly and undeserving sections of the poor be excused for voting Labour.

I cannot imagine being deterred from working if my taxes go up: nurses, teachers, ambulance workers and firemen, when they demand higher pay, are told that they have a vocation and cannot hold the public to ransom; *their* incentive to work is their calling. With high earners, it seems, a different logic is allowed to apply: they can threaten to leave the country (an equivalent of strike action if you like) without being excoriated in the public prints.

I do not claim a moral high ground, I am happy to be thought of as a Labour supporter because I am greedy. Greedy for a Britain that is fairer, kinder, more tolerant, better educated and more genuinely prosperous than it has managed to be for many years. But let's not fight about it: it is, as I said, a matter of emphasis. I don't regard all Tories as evil, foolish or damned; the least Conservative supporters can do is understand that the Labour Party has no wicked secret agenda either. Whatever happens the White Cliffs will stand and the rain will fall in Wimbledon fortnight, God bless it.

Section Five

Latin!

Programme note

The following was written for a production of Latin! *(a double bill with* Aunt Julie . . . *the programme cover read in bold letters 'A Double Bill of Strindberg and Fry' which caused me much delight) mounted in 1989 at the New End Theatre, Hampstead, produced by a good friend to the play, Richard Jackson.*

Now *Latin!* has come back to haunt me. It is very difficult for a chap trying to make his way in the world, earn the respect of his peers, the affection of his friends and the hard cash of his paying customers suddenly to be confronted by the deeds of his wild youth. It is almost like meeting yourself as you once were. I am making the play sound like the most precocious juvenilia there ever was: in fact I wrote *Latin!* when I was twenty-two and, you may think, in a position to know better.

Two friends of mine at Cambridge, Caroline Oulton and Mark McCrum, were setting up a new theatre, or 'space' as we rather oddly called them in those days. It was an L-shaped room to be called The Playroom, new plays were required for it and at the instigation of these two undergraduate impresarii, *Latin! or Tobacco and Boys*, to give it its full title, was written during the long vacation of 1980.

Strangely enough, the subject matter of the piece was the least of my concerns. I had long ago decided that it would be interesting to start a play in which the audience were addressed as if they were fictional characters and then, suddenly, with no more than a lighting change, to have the 'third wall' of theatrical distance erected in front of them – to change them from participants to spectators in a flash. In choosing the subject of an English prep school, I followed the simple maxim of algebraic problem-solvers and novelists everywhere: 'Write down what you know.' Prep schools I knew. I had started boarding at one such, now since sadly closed, when I was seven and later on, a year before going up to university, I had taught at another.

I would hate any of you to run away with the idea that Chartham School, the *locus* of *Latin!*, was in any way 'based' on either of those estimable and weird establishments. No such thing. The writing of *Latin!* was much more an experiment in the techniques of theatre and comedy, combined with a not entirely disgraceful undergraduate desire to shock. Death, homosexuality, incest, sadism and Thatcherism had all been proudly paraded on stage for years and the senses of the theatre-going public were quite anaesthetised to any of the horrors that those topics could engender: pederasty on the other hand could still, I hoped, set a few ganglions quivering.

If you would like to contemplate the carefully crafted subtext of the piece for some essay on theatre or art that you may be preparing for your parish magazine, you might like to relate the name Dominic to the Latin *dominus* (or Scotch *dominie*) and note the anagrammatic connection between Rupert and the Latin *puer* from which, appropriately enough you may think, we derive our word 'puerile'. You may also notice that Rupert's initials are 'R.C.' and that it is a Dominican who detects Dominic's forgery in the second half of the play.

Perhaps it is fitting in these hysterical times that the play appears to constitute an apology for Islam, as well as for some of the more sensational practices that still abound in Islamic countries. These are things I do not know. I only know that I had the most terrific fun writing the play and acting in it in Cambridge and Edinburgh: I wish you a quarter as much pleasure in watching it. *Valete.*

Latin! or Tobacco and Boys

A Play in Two Unnatural Acts
by Stephen Fry

DRAMATIS PERSONÆ

MR DOMINIC CLARKE, *schoolmaster in his middle twenties*
MR HERBERT BROOKSHAW, *schoolmaster in his late fifties*
BARTON-MILLS
CARTWRIGHT (*Deponent*)
CATCHPOLE
ELWYN-JONES
FIGGIS
HARVEY-WILLIAMS
HOSKINS (*Absent*)
HUGHES
KINNOCK
MADISON (*Bound for Eton*)
POTTER
SMETHWICK (*Ugh*)
SPRAGG
STANDFAST
WHITWELL (*Bumpkin*)

The action of the play takes place in Chartham Park Preparatory School For Boys, Hampshire, England. The time is the present. The play may be divided by an interval into two Acts. Running time without interval ≈ 1 hour.

For those not acquainted with the prep-school system, it is worth pointing out that a prep school is a private school for children of the ages 7–13 and is used to prepare these individuals for public school (which means, of course, a *private* school for older pupils: Rugby, Winchester, Eton etc. are called 'public' schools). At the age of thirteen, prep-school boys take an examination known as Common Entrance, CE, a general exam the results in which determine acceptance by the public school. Some public schools demand a high score in the CE (65 per cent upwards), some are satisfied with less intellectually able boys. Ampleforth, mentioned in the play, is a famous Roman Catholic public school in Yorkshire.

Act One

A school form-room. The stage is the master's dais, the auditorium serves as the form-room proper, where the pupils, played by the audience, sit. The stage is set simply. A desk Centre. Behind it a chair, behind which is the blackboard. Another chair is set somewhere. There is one entrance, a door, Left or Right, it doesn't really matter which. On the desk there is a pile of exercise books, a box of chalk, a board-rubber, a mark-book, an ash-tray and a packet of Sobranie 'Jasmine', or some other, rather effeminate brand. It would be a good idea to cook up a quantity of boiled cabbage and fried liver with onions in the auditorium some hours before the performance is due to begin, in order to introduce immediately to the nostrils the echt *smell of school. Any other stage properties or means of affecting the atmosphere of a slightly decaying, traditional English prep school would be useful.*

DOMINIC CLARKE is sitting at the desk before and during the admission of the audience. He is marking exercise books rapidly, impatiently and with the use of three different-coloured biros. He is a young man, lean and effete. He wears grey trousers, a russet V-neck pullover and a green needle-cord jacket, which is hung on the back of the chair he sits in. His voice is clear and sharp when teaching, but younger when engaged in normal conversation. He is only able to operate his arms with any fluency from the elbows downwards, the upper arms being almost permanently clenched against his side, in a twisted, gnarled sort of way.

When the time comes for the play to begin, which DOMINIC checks with his own watch, he stands and speaks. The houselights remain up. Any late-comers may be regaled impromptu, or as indicated below with POTTER and STANDFAST. The audience are his pupils, and the actor must judge pauses and deliver his lines entirely in accordance with what he feels is right for each audience. Ideally, no two nights will ever be the same. The actor may add and subtract lines from the opening scene with 6B ad libitum, so long, of course, as it ends with the right cue for BROOKSHAW's *entrance.*

DOMINIC. Right, settle down now. Hughes! Face the front, boy. Silence at the back! Harvey-Williams, what did I just say? 'Silence, sir!' Well belt up then! Drip. So . . . Potter and Standfast, where have you been? Well, *we* all heard the bell perfectly, what's the matter with you? . . . *(Quietly)* Well perhaps your hearing will improve if I YELL at you. Sit down. Yahoos. Elwyn-Jones, sit up straight, you're a slob. And if I catch you looking out the window again this period, you'll get a Minus. All right then – Cartwright, what have you got in your desk that's more interesting than me, hm? 'Just stuff, sir'? Well, I'll 'just stuff' you if you're not careful. Don't snigger, Standfast, it's unsightly. Now, let's have a look at . . . Figgis, I hope that's not a Sherbert Fountain you're vainly trying to conceal in your pudgy fingers. Remove it from my steely gaze at once, boy, or I'll have it confiscated and sent to Oxfam. I'm not paid to teach Sherbert Fountains – though they'd probably learn more than you wouldn't they Hughes? Catchpole? Potter? Yes, I've just been marking your prep and I'm not . . . that's two Demerits, Smethwick. You know very well why, and don't forget to wash your hands before break, repellent object that you are, Smethwick. Now, silence, all of you. I've just spent an appalling morning marking the corporate insult to Rome that you choose to call your prep. And I'm afraid it's not good enough. Yes, Barton-Mills, I'm talking about *your* prep, and yours, Figgis. Shambolic, sham-ruddy-bolic. When do you think Common Entrance is, hm? A year's time? Because it's not, Madison, it's in two weeks. Two weeks, Standfast, Whitwell and co., two weeks and you can't remember the simple fact that *pareo* takes the dative. Two weeks, Spragg, and you still think *gradus* is second declension. Well it's not good enough, I'm afraid. 4A can do better than this and they've got two years until their exams. And it's no use sneering, Elwyn-Jones, you graceless oik, they may be just squits to you but at least they've got the mental muscle and the moral

438

guts to come to terms with the most basic – and sit up *straight*! If I have to tell you again you will suffer. Boys who rub me up the wrong way, Elwyn-Jones, come to a sticky end. No need to smirk, Cartwright. Let's just take a look at these, shall we? You might as well have them back I suppose.

DOMINIC *goes to the audience and starts to hand out exercise books, looking for the face to fit the name, giving some, throwing others to the end of a row, in typical schoolmaster fashion. He can tap some individuals on the head with exercise books as he admonishes them, if he dares.*

DOMINIC. Barton Mills? Cartwright? You're an idle oaf, Cartwright. Catchpole? Butterfingers. Elwyn-Jones? Yes, well I told you to use a fountain pen, didn't I, Elwyn-J., hm? 'Yes sir.' Well, I simply do not accept Day-Glo felt-tip, I'm afraid. I want a fair copy from you, you can do it during detention this afternoon. Don't argue, boy, I don't care if you've got a test match at *Lord's* this afternoon, elegantly written Latin is of more consequence in this world than cricket. I don't think I'm interested in Mr Grey's view of cricket, thank you Elwyn-Jones, you've heard mine. When they start to present candidates for CE with a paper on cricket, then you can argue, but it won't be with me, because I will have resigned when that day comes. Until then, you'll do as you're told. And stop scowling, or you'll be in on Saturday afternoon as well. *(Consults next book)* Yobbo. Now. Figgis? Figgis? Oh, do get up off the floor, Figgis, stop groping about between Standfast's legs, there's nothing there. Never you mind how I know, Cartwright, just face the front. Well, you wouldn't have dropped it if you hadn't been fiddling with it, would you? *(Sighs)* Can anyone lend Figgis a spare contact lens for this lesson? Well, I'm afraid you'll just have to look at the board with one eye, Figgis. You lost the other one yesterday. How? Well, you could have retrieved it from your custard, couldn't you? Oh. That was a stupid, greedy act, wasn't it Potter? Well, I'm sorry Figgis, you'll just have to follow Potter around for a few days and exami – and hope it comes out in the wash. And be quiet the rest of you, don't be so puerile. Here you are then Figgis, catch. *(Throws book)* Sorry! Oh, don't be such a baby, it's just a gash. Harvey-Williams? Hoskins? Hoskins? Does anyone know where Hoskins is? Oh,

I see. Oh dear. Does anyone know *how* he died? I see. I had no idea. No, you may *not* have his desk, Barton-Mills, stay where you are. Poor old Hoskins. I suppose I'd better keep his book then. (*Slips the exercise book to the bottom of the pile.*) Now where were we? Hughes. Yes, where are you Hughes? What is the third person singular imperfect subjunctive active of *moneo*? Mono*ret*. Exactly. You see, you *know* it, but as soon as it comes to writing it down, you fall apart. Not bad otherwise. Kinnock? Yes, very clever, Kinnock. Madison? Complete rubbish, Madison. Potter? Catch it, boy! Smethwick? Ugh! (*Hands it out at arm's length*) Standfast? Moron. Are you sucking your thumb again, Harvey-Williams? That's detention. I warned you, didn't I? If you need a nipple substitute, go and see Matron and she'll give you a rubber dummy. And you can do *your* detention *after* games, yes I thought that would shut you up. I know Elwyn-Jones is doing his during games, but he's disgustingly developed enough, whereas you, on the other hand, are an underdeveloped little weed, who needs all the exercise he can get. What? I don't think the prospect of your mother writing to the headmaster frightens me at all, Harvey-Williams, just wipe your nose and shut up. (*To himself*) Little wet. Whitwell? Yes, well, you're a bumpkin, aren't you, Whitwell? What are you, boy? 'Bumpkin, sir.' Precisely. (*He comes to the last book in the pile*) And Hoskins? Oh yes, poor Hoskins. Now, settle down all of you, let's get through these, we've wasted enough time as it is.

DOMINIC *sits at the desk. He notices that the flowers in the vase on his desk have died. He drops them into the bin, one by one.*

DOMINIC. *Sic transit*, boys, *gloria*, as you will all too soon discover for yourselves, *mundi*. Now, let's get on and make some sense out of these sentences shall we? Number one: 'The master set out to capture the slaves.' All right then, read out what you put will you . . . (*Surveys the form*) . . . put your hands down . . . Madison!

As MADISON *supposedly calls out his answer,* DOMINIC *writes it up on the blackboard.*

DOMINIC. '*Dominus . . . progressit . . . ut capere servos est.*'

(*Laying the chalk down*) Yes, well, that's just arrant nonsense, isn't it Madison? I don't know what it means to you, but I'm afraid it bears no relation at all to the Roman tongue, which would appear to have you licked. It's not that funny, Potter. You're an idle and irritating oaf, Madison. Cartwright'll tell you where you went wrong, won't you Cartwright? Cartwright? (*sing-song*) Hell-o! Cosy naplet? Good. Now, tell us the answer please, we're all agog. Well, what sort of clause is it? Precisely, a final clause. *Ut* plus subjunctive, Madison, not *ut* plus infinitive. Put your hand down, Smethwick, I'm not interested. No, wait until the end of the period. You can hold out until then. Just keep a firm grip on yourself. I speak figuratively, Smethwick, disgusting reptile. So, copy this down everybody, neatly. What you all should have written is this. (*Writes it up as he speaks*) 'Dominus profectus est, ut servos caperet.' 'Dominus' note, Standfast, not 'magister'. 'Magister' is a schoolmaster, and schoolmasters don't keep slaves. It isn't a matter of opinion, Potter, it's a matter of fact. And no, Figgis, I can't write any bigger, and do stop blubbing, it stopped bleeding ages ago. We can all do without your *pluvia lacrimarum* flooding the form-room. Parse *pluvia lacrimarum*, Elwyn-Jones. Oh, never mind, go back to sleep. Ignoramus. So. Number two. 'With Caesar's forces having been . . . '

There is a knock at the door.

Come in!!

The houselights go down the moment BROOKSHAW *enters. A much older man than* DOMINIC, *and much more of the school. He wears Harris tweed, bechalked cavalry twill trousers and impossible spectacles. He smokes a very old pipe, which gurgles.* DOMINIC *is marking as before the lesson. The pupils are not there.*

DOMINIC. Oh, it's you.

BROOKSHAW. Yes, I hope I'm not disturbing you, Clarke.

DOMINIC. No, no. Come in. I'm just marking for third period. Sit down, won't be a tick. (*Crosses something out*) I've marked most of them.

BROOKSHAW. Have you marked but the fall o'the snow,
Before the soil hath smutched it?

DOMINIC. (*Absorbed*) Hm?

BROOKSHAW. I've just been talking to Jane, Dominic.

DOMINIC. Really?

BROOKSHAW. Yes. She tells me that you and she are (*blows nose*) engaged.

DOMINIC. Yes.

BROOKSHAW. To be married.

DOMINIC. Yes.

BROOKSHAW. So it's true then?

DOMINIC. Yes.

BROOKSHAW. I see.

DOMINIC. But she really shouldn't have told you. (*Looks up*) It was supposed to be a secret, until my position here is more – secure. And that all rather depends upon CE results, so I'd rather you didn't tell anybody just now. (*Goes back to marking*) Oh, Potter, you stupid boy. T! (*Vicious crossing out*)

There is a pause, during which BROOKSHAW *lights his pipe.*

BROOKSHAW. Tell me, Dominic. Do you think I can't see what you're up to?

DOMINIC. Eh?

BROOKSHAW. I know perfectly well why you're marrying that poor brainless disease.

DOMINIC. Mr Brookshaw, have a care, you're speaking of the poor brainless disease that I love.

BROOKSHAW. In a pig's arse, Clarke. I am speaking of the poor brainless disease who is also the headmaster's daughter.

DOMINIC. So?

BROOKSHAW. Oh do credit me with a little intelligence. You are marrying the girl out of an . . . admirable . . . sense of ambition. When the Old Man dies, you will inherit the school. Perfectly simple, I'd do the same in your place, if I thought there was an outside chance of the girl accepting me. But I shall do the next best thing instead, and stop the marriage.

DOMINIC. Really? How?

BROOKSHAW. God, in His infinite mercy and wisdom, has seen fit to place in my path certain useful pieces of information. Information concerning you, Dominic.

DOMINIC. What information? What are you talking about?

BROOKSHAW. Tell me Clarke. (*Beat*) What house is Cartwright in?

DOMINIC. Cartwright? Cartwright? What's that got to do with anything? Er, he's an Otter, isn't he?

BROOKSHAW. Dominic, you know perfectly well that Cartwright is a Kingfisher.

DOMINIC. Is he? I still don't . . .

BROOKSHAW. That makes you his housemaster, does it not?

DOMINIC. Ye-e-s.

BROOKSHAW. I was merit-adding for the fortnightly orders last night, Dominic.

DOMINIC. You? Merit-adding? But that's the Old Man's –

BROOKSHAW. The Headmaster's illness has advanced rather too far for that, I fear. It is difficult for him to keep numbers in his head any more. Naturally as Senior Master I was asked to take over this time.

DOMINIC. You lucky . . .

BROOKSHAW. It is a privilege I have earned by thirty years of patience here, Dominic. You're still a new boy, you'd do well to remember that. In the same way, when the Old Man finally goes, it will be my turn to be head. That is why I cannot allow you to marry Jane. Still, if you wait around for twenty years, I might just let *you* do some merit-adding. If you've been good. You never know.

BROOKSHAW *turns to address the audience.*

For those of you ladies and gentlemen here tonight who do not know Chartham Park School, I suppose I ought to explain to you precisely the nature of merit-adding. What is it? How does it work? Is it efficient? Its origins lie deep in the soul of the Chartham Ethic, an ethic method not spun by some politico-educational theorist at the LSE, not gleaned mindlessly from some scholastic tract, but an ethic method learned from years of understanding the average English boy. The average English boy is, at bottom, open, generous and malleable. Mould that material at the right time and you've created a man who will serve his friends, his country and his God in the manner that they have *always* been served by Englishmen, with integrity, decency, respect, truth. How then do we at Chartham realise the potential of all this formless, but malleable, material that is sent to us? Well, the Chartham method is, not surprisingly, governed by the age-old principles of reward and punishment. The qualities that you recognise in the Chartham boy who goes on to stock the finest schools in the kingdom, are qualities achieved by means of the three basic incentives and three basic – um – *dis*incentives, which form the backbone of the Chartham System.

BROOKSHAW *goes to the board and writes as shown in Figure 1.*

The Chartham Method

✔ **Points**   ✗ **Points**

<u>M Merit</u> = 5	<u>DM Demerit</u> = −5
+ <u>Plus</u> = 10 3+ = *free fuck*	− <u>Minus</u> = −10 3− = *VD or no fuck at all*
* <u>Star</u> = 25 +£5.00 *fuck foken*	● <u>Black hole</u> = −25 *offender eafs crap, is caned; rifually Licked ouf by HM every morning*

<u>No fuck if you fail fo score</u>

<u>Fig. 1</u>

Firstly, we have the Merit.

He divides the blackboard neatly into two columns. He places a tick in the L/H column and a cross in the R/H. He writes 'M Merit' under the tick.

Then there is the Demerit. (*He writes 'DM Demerit' under the 'X'*) The Merit is worth 5 points and the Demerit −5. (*Writes '=5' and '=−5' respectively*) The Merit is given for a helpful act, a good piece of work or an able performance on the games field. The Demerit is given for an unsocial act, a poor piece of work or a moronic performance on the games field. Three Demerits in one day disqualifies the boy concerned from tuck in that week.

In the right hand column BROOKSHAW writes '3DMs = tuck off for one week.' The 't' of tuck is lower case and ambivalent; it could easily be taken for an 'f'.

A higher unit of currency is the Plus. This is worth ten points (*writes in the L/H column: [See Fig. 1] '+ Plus = 10'*) or, in the case of the Minus, minus ten points. (*writes in the R/H column: '− Minus = −10'*) The Plus is awarded for excellent behaviour, excellent work, or excellent games playing. Three Pluses in one day qualify the recipient for an extra ten pence worth of tuck on Tuck Day. I should add that for Otters, Tuck Day is Monday, for Coypus, Wednesday, for Kingfishers, Thursday and for Eelcatchers, Friday. (*He writes '3+ = Free tuck', again with an ambivalent 't'*) Three Minuses, however, automatically mean *either* what is called Voluntary Detention for three hours *or* no tuck for the rest of term. It is the boy's decision in either case. Voluntary Detention or No Tuck. (*Writes: '3− = VD or no tuck'*) Lastly we come to the top awards, Stars. A Star is awarded to a boy only for work of outstanding brilliance, gallantry and initiative beyond his years, or for a quite remarkable athletic achievement. It is worth 25 points and a £5.00 tuck shop token. (*Writes: '* Star = 25 & £5.00 tuck voucher'*) The miscreant's counterpart, the

Black Hole, is rarely bestowed. It is minus 25 points and is earned only by committing the grossest breaches of school rules such as armed robbery, genocide and masturbation. It also results in an immediate beating; the boy concerned is only allowed to eat scrap from the kitchens for the rest of term and he is publicly and ritually kicked out of assembly by the headmaster every morning. *(Writes: '● Black Hole = −25 Boy to be caned, eats crap ritually licked out by HM')* Those are the points and that is how they operate. The member of staff who awards these marks signs them into the House Book, and every fortnight the headmaster or myself calculates the individual and house scores. If any boy should be found to have scored no points at all, he is also put off tuck. It is far from our aim to produce boring, middle-of-the-road boys at Chartham. *(Writes underneath both columns: 'No tuck if you fail to score')* The aggregate winning house at the end of term is called the Cock House and enjoys a House Outing, usually to the kinema or the sea-side. The losing house cleans out the school swimming pool, which gives them ample opportunity to contemplate their failure to contribute to the community. They are also banned from the end of term film, as a rule the very exciting *Guns of Navarone*. The system is fair, psychologically sound and simple to operate. If any of you would like to use it in your schools, or in college, office, factory or home, I would be most happy to talk to you about it after the show. Thank you for your attention.

BROOKSHAW *rubs out the blackboard.*

Which brings me to my point, Dominic. *I* was merit-adding last night, when I stumbled upon a most curious and suggestive discovery.

DOMINIC. Well?

BROOKSHAW. It was Cartwright's fortnightly score.

DOMINIC. Oh ah.

BROOKSHAW. Because of that boy's total, Kingfishers are certain of the House Outing this term.

DOMINIC. He's done well, has he, this Cartwright?

BROOKSHAW. In two weeks, Clarke, he has managed to accrue eight hundred Merits, seventy Pluses and twenty-four Stars! Shattering the school record into a million pieces.

DOMINIC. Ah.

BROOKSHAW. With the exception of two Merits, all those awards were signed in by you, Dominic. That is 5,266 points, boy! More than Coypus and Eelcatchers put together. Well? What have you got to say for yourself?

DOMINIC. Look here, Brookshaw, I hope you're not suggesting that I fiddled the books so that Kingfishers win the Cock House Cup, because I can assure you . . .

BROOKSHAW. *(Chuckling)* Good heavens, Clarke, I'm not suggesting that!

DOMINIC. Oh. Well, that's all right then.

BROOKSHAW. No, my accusation is far graver.

DOMINIC. Oh.

BROOKSHAW. Yes. My first thought, you see, was that Cartwright himself had forged the signature against his name in the House Book. So I went along to see the boy myself. He's a nice lad, this Cartwright; open, frank features and a good set of teeth, I trusted him. I've done enough schoolmastering to know when a boy is trustworthy or not, and I was soon convinced that he knew nothing of this colossal score. So I enquired more deeply into the matter. In short, I asked him how he thought he had earned all these Stars and Pluses. At this point, Dominic, the boy simpered. I do not lie, the boy actually simpered!

DOMINIC. Look, I'm not . . .

BROOKSHAW. And what he told me was the most bizarre and horrifying story I have ever heard in thirty years' schoolmastering. Thirty years which I thought had immunised me from . . .

DOMINIC. Well, what *did* he say?

BROOKSHAW. Mr Clarke, I will tell you. With tears brimming in his large, curiously blue eyes, he confessed all.

DOMINIC. Oh.

BROOKSHAW. 'Oh' indeed.

DOMINIC. *All?*

BROOKSHAW. All.

DOMINIC. My God. Er, what exactly *was* all?

BROOKSHAW. That for two terms you have been giving him extra Latin periods in your rooms late at night and that during those periods you have carnally violated that boy in ways too vile, too diverse, for the sane mind to grasp. Cartwright informed me, at first with pride and later, when the seriousness of these events' possible repercussions had been impressed upon him, with shame, that there is no part of that boy's body, and indeed your own, that has not been employed in these riotous acts. Acts that have included, Clarke, and here I am still frankly incredulous, that have included the rape and laceration of . . . of . . . the back of the knees. Well, what have you to say?

DOMINIC. (*Quietly*) Yes. It's true. It is true. We have used the back of the knees. More than once actually.

BROOKSHAW. Is that all?

DOMINIC. With some success I'm glad to report. Though we did have to use a little . . .

BROOKSHAW. Now you listen to me, Clarke –

DOMINIC. No. You listen to me –

BROOKSHAW. I baggsed first.

DOMINIC. Don't care. Just you hear me out. As you know, Brookshaw, I'm a young man with little chance in life and little to lose. At school I was always bullied, you probably didn't know *that*. I tried, you see, to stand up against the Philistines there. It was my plan to represent the aesthetic against the athletic. But one of the advantages of being athletic has always been physical strength, and so I suffered, rather badly in fact. As well as being a physical coward I am in many respects rather weak and uncoordinated and it seemed to give the Barbarians pleasure to padlock roller-skates onto me and then retire to a safe distance to watch the havoc. On one horrible occasion involving a fire-extinguisher they neatly contrived to fracture my pelvic girdle. I forgave them that, but I never forgave them for fracturing my spirit. I vowed revenge on the whole pack of them. Revenge by indoctrination and propaganda directed at their very source. I decided to become a schoolmaster.

I thought, God knows why, that at Cambridge things might be a little easier for me, that there might be a set which shared my aims and interests, which like me loved and understood Swinburne and Elizabeth Barrett Browning. I was shattered to find, however, that the prevailing artistic wind blew from Paris, post-Modernism and the American Novel, and that things that I held dear were looked at in that same cold, hard, muscular light that had always frightened me. I was officially told that Swinburne, my belovèd Algernon, was slushy and lacked concretion. Even in Cambridge, then, I was a sensitive in a world of literary rugby players. In the land of Rupert Brooke, watered by his river, tented by his Cambridge sky and shaded by his chestnuts and immemorial elms, but surrounded by people who sneered at what he found precious and pronounced Grantchester to rhyme with Manchester. I struggled through Cambridge and emerged a bruised and faded violet. Pleasure for me lies between the thighs of a young boy, under fifteen, blond and willing, or between the pages of a romantic poet, sighing in verse for lost love and lost beauty. Cambridge offered me neither of these: I understand that it does so now, but for me it is too late. And so I came here, partly to plant the seeds of those pleasures in the minds and thighs of the boys in my charge, partly to escape from a world that I could no longer understand. Instead I am given Common Entrance Latin to teach and cricket to umpire. It was bitter, bitter. But I came upon my Halcyon days though – I discovered Cartwright, the Kingfisher. He is delightful, Brookshaw, delightful. A shining sun, whose very smile ripens fruit and opens petals. I cannot begin to describe the outstanding hard work, initiative, flair, dedication and conspicuous gallantry he displayed in order to earn those House Points. I crept down into the staff room on Sunday night in my dressing-gown and slippers just to sign them in. I suppose I knew that I'd get caught, but I had to do something. (*Breath*) Jane was down there. Slightly drunk and smelling of Germolene. She'd just come off duty and still wore her matron's white celluloid cap. She sat in an arm-chair, it was *your* arm-chair, I think, with a glass of gin and Gee's linctus in her hand. She noticed that I was trembling – I was trying to work out how to sign all those points into the House Book in one go without attracting her attention – and then suddenly, quite without warning, she burst into tears and out it all came. She revealed that ever since my arrival at Chartham she has delighted in the idea of my body and craved intercourse with me. She is dark and lustrous, and she smothers, Brookshaw. I don't know what it was that came over me, the heat or the fumes of Gee's linctus or something, but I started quoting Byron at her. 'She walks in beauty, like the night Of cloudless climes and starry skies; And all that's best of dark and bright Meets in her aspect and her eyes.' Well, it seemed a natural step from there to propose. If she turned me down I could always withhold my body from her on the grounds of religious principle, and if she accepted I could endure sexual congress in the knowledge that this was the price I had to pay for inheriting the headmastership when her father died. It seemed a neat way out. But now you know about my . . . indiscretion with Cartwright. It *was* stupid of me to sign those points in after all, I don't know why I didn't stop myself . . . and Cartwright is leaving at the end of term. Six weeks left, six weeks!

Look, it doesn't seem to me that you're in much of a position here. Hadn't it occurred to you that if I don't marry the girl somebody else will, somebody from outside. You're an old man, Brookshaw, you'll never be headmaster now. If the next headman isn't me then it'll be someone you don't know, and that someone may just have a friend to replace you as Senior Master. Spare that a thought before you start getting too carried away with yourself. Well?

BROOKSHAW. You're a cunning bastard, Dominic, but I still have the initiative, remember that. I can always ring the police at any time.

DOMINIC. Of course.

BROOKSHAW. (*Sighing*) But I'm afraid you're right. I can never be headmaster now. It's too late. I suppose I've known that for some time. (*Ponders*) This is what you will do, if you wish me to remain silent about your little adventures, Dominic.

DOMINIC. Blackmail is illegal, you know.

BROOKSHAW. (*Temper rising slightly*) Scant though my knowledge of the criminal law may be, I've a fairly good idea that it's not exactly the done thing for a twenty-six-year-old schoolmaster to commit genital acts with a thirteen-year-old boy to whom he is in loco parentis. Yes, Dominic, in loco parentis.

DOMINIC. You can't get me for incest as well.

BROOKSHAW. !

DOMINIC. I'm sorry. All right then, how much?

BROOKSHAW. Excuse me?

DOMINIC. How much do you want?

BROOKSHAW. It's not a question of money, you silly boy.

DOMINIC. Well, what *do* you want, then?

BROOKSHAW. I shall tell you what I want. Now, listen carefully, Dominic. You will do exactly as I tell you. (*Consults a notebook or diary*) As you know, only the Old Man or myself, as Senior Master, are allowed to beat boys for bad behaviour. You have an infuriating habit, if I may say so, Dominic, of sending your miscreants to the Headman and not to me. This nuisance must now cease. In future, you will do your level best to ensure that all bad boys are sent to my study, where *I* shall beat them. The administration of the cane is one of the few pleasures in life left to me, and you will not deny me it.

DOMINIC. W . . . w . . .

BROOKSHAW. Now the second thing you will do for me is visit my bedroom twice a week – Tuesdays and Thursdays will do very nicely I think, at midnight. There you will beat me for half an hour with a clothes hanger or a wet towel and afterwards run up and down on my bottom in cricket boots. I should like that. Quite clear there?

DOMINIC. Y . . . y . . .

BROOKSHAW. If you are a good boy and follow my instructions, I will allow you to marry the headmaster's daughter. I think you are right, if you don't marry the wretched girl, a worse may well come in your place. You will probably be made headmaster. I hope that you will be a good one. I rather think you will. You have all the right qualities.

DOMINIC. A wet towel? You're absolutely sick.

BROOKSHAW. Now, I really must ask you to make up your mind, Dominic. It's first period any minute, and I see that you haven't finished marking yet. So. Do I telephone the police, or will you perform those little odd jobs I mentioned?

DOMINIC. *(Hastily)* No, no! don't ring the police. I'll . . . I'll do as you say.

BROOKSHAW. Splendid! I knew you would. Well that's capital. Now I must rush, Sixth Form Confirmation class.

DOMINIC. But Tuesdays and Thursdays are my extra Latin nights with Cartwright!

BROOKSHAW. Well, I'm afraid you'll just have to rearrange them . . . there's six weeks left after all. I shall expect you tomorrow night then, for the first session. Until then . . . *(Stops at the door)* . . . oh, and bring some peanut butter with you, would you? Crunchy. Bye!

Exit BROOKSHAW. *The moment he goes, the Houselights come up and we are back in the lesson, which is nearing completion.* DOMINIC *is writing up the Latin for the last sentence. So it is important that, during the last exchange with* BROOKSHAW, *he puts himself in the best position to start writing immediately, discreetly getting chalk in hand etc. to make the change as rapid as possible.*

DOMINIC. *(Writing and calling out simultaneously) Ne desperarent neve . . . progredi nollent . . . Hannibal militibus . . . quietem . . . dedit.* Very well, who hasn't had a turn? Hands down. Figgis, the blackboard's over here. Fingers out of noses, Spragg. Well, if Elwyn-Jones wants to pick it, he can pick it himself, can't he? But not during the lesson, Elwyn-Jones, tiresome individual! Now, Barton-Mills, read out what you put for this would you please? 'Aren't you willing to despair or go forward Hannibal asked his quiet soldiers.' Yes, well, we seem to have made a bit of a bish of that, don't we, Barton-Mills? Kinnock, I think you got this right, give us the answer please. Yes, very clever, Kinnock, the prose version will do splendidly, thank you.

DOMINIC *rubs out* BARTON-MILLS's *answer and replaces it with: 'Lest they should lose hope or be unwilling to go forward, Hannibal gave his soldiers a rest.'*

Ne, Barton-Mills, means what *ut non* would mean if you could use *ut non* in final clauses, but you can't so you use *ne*, clear? *(Rising)* One thing I want you all to notice is that the English has twice as many words in it as the Latin, which – as the mathematicians amongst you, Madison, will realise – will mean that the Latin has in it half as many words as the English, showing . . .

Bill rings off.

. . . the beautifully compact nature of – yes thank you, Potter, I heard it. I may be stupid, but I'm not deaf. Just close your desk and belt up, you can go when I say and not before. Now, where were we? Oh yes. Latin is a beautiful language, intense, compact and poetic. None of you seems to have grasped the idea of it yet, which is why you seem to have so much trouble with the execution. Look.

DOMINIC *goes up to the blackboard and writes up the following. He speaks as he writes.*

Magister amat puerum	Puer amat magistrum
Puerum amat magister	Magistrum amat puer
The master likes the boy	The boy likes the master

Now, if I write *Magister amat puerum*, it's perfectly obvious what it means, isn't it . . . Elwyn-Jones? Yes, I think 'like' is a perfectly adequate translation, thank you, Elwyn-Jones. The master likes the boy. But if I write *Puerum amat magister* it means . . . ? *Precisely the same thing*, 'The master likes the boy.' 'The boy likes the master' would be *puer amat magistrum*, or *magistrum amat puer* or any combination of those words. The English rely on word order to change the meaning of a sentence; the only way to change meaning in Latin is to change the word itself, which is why Latin is a better and truer language. So, when in twenty years' time you're all plump executives, whose only contact with Nature is the walk to the Squash Club, don't think you're successful just because you've got a fast wife and a beautiful car. Remember, there was a race who spoke a language that you could never master and who invented the word civilisation. And from their Greek cousins they inherited a word to define the English and all red-necked balding tribes for whom Converse With The Infinite means a chat with the company chairman, and that word is Barbarian, gentlemen, and it describes you all: *ab ovo, ad sepulcrum*, Barbarian. (*He holds a pause, then resumes in a very rapid and business-like manner*) For prep learn the principal parts of all the deponent and semi-deponent verbs on your sheets for a test during double period on Friday. Smethwick, don't forget to wash your hands before having your break, Potter, help Figgis find his contact lens, and Cartwright . . . see me in here after break Cartwright, would you? Very well. Go and suckle.

Exit DOMINIC.

Stage lights BLACKOUT.

INTERVAL, during which milk and Chelsea buns are served.

End of Act One

Sir's Patent Latin Football Game

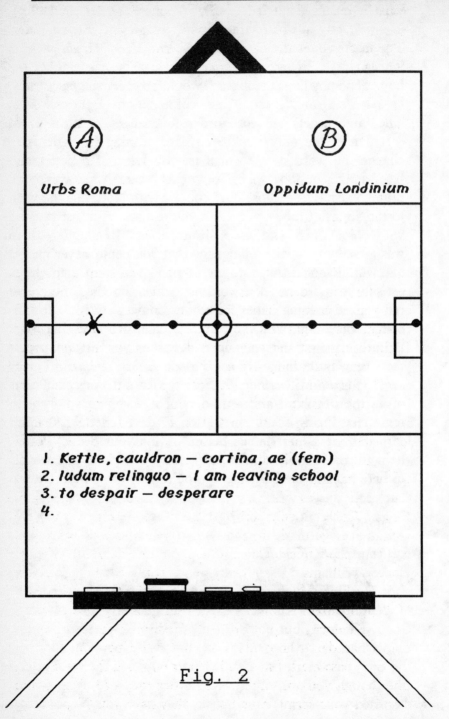

Urbs Roma   **Oppidum Londinium**

1. Kettle, cauldron — cortina, ae (fem)
2. ludum relinquo — I am leaving school
3. to despair — desperare
4.

<u>Fig. 2</u>

Act Two

Enter DOMINIC. *The houselights remain up.*

DOMINIC. Right, settle down 6B, I've got some important news for you, so be quiet and listen. Turn round, Hughes, and you, Spragg. Your CE results arrived today. Yes, I thought that might shut you up. I'm going to give you your Latin results first and your overall results after that, that way you'll keep quiet longer. So, Common Entrance Latin, Form Six B. Barton-Mills, 48 per cent; that's 3 per cent off the Rugby pass-mark, Barton-Mills, cretin. Cartwright, 97 per cent. That's a brilliant result, Rupert, well done. I had a look at your paper before it was sent on, actually, and I thought then that you'd done pretty well. Congratulations, Cartwright, and be quiet the rest of you, envious mob. Now, Catchpole 39, yes well. Elwyn-Jones 52, surprisingly adequate. Figgis? They sent your script back as illegible, Figgis, and gave you an average mark instead, which is just as well, since you had your paper upside down throughout the exam. Silly Figgis. Harvey-Williams 72 per cent, good work. Hoskins, ah yes, poor Hoskins. Hughes 42. As I expected, Hughes, the work of a chimpanzee. Kinnock 71 per cent. *(Smiling with pleasure)* Good, Kinnock, but not brilliant. Madison 4 per cent, better than I had dared hope Madison, but still 2 per cent short of the Eton pass-mark I'm afraid. Potter 69, good for you Potter, tike though you are. Smethwick? After they had cleaned and sterilised your script, Smethwick, they gave you 78 per cent, that's excellent. (*But cannot resist a shudder and an 'ugh!'*) Spragg 51 per cent, stunningly mediocre, Spragg. Standfast 38 per cent, *I'm* not excited about that mark, Standfast, and I don't think you should be, put the fire-bucket down and face the front. Newt. And Whitwell, 22 per cent, yes well, you're a bumpkin, aren't you, Whitwell? What are you, boy? 'Bumpkin, sir.' Precisely. Now, as to your overall results, I'm glad to be able to report that by some extraordinary miracle of misjudgment, folly and misdirected generosity, every single one of you has been passed overall by your respective public schools and will be able to start there next term. Your parents have been informed and are naturally delighted and staggered at the staff's skill. You're all going to good schools, except Madison, of course, and I wish you well. So, it would seem that I have nothing left to teach you, you all know as much Latin as you need and my job is over. So what shall we do to fill in this great gap of time between now and break? Any ideas? Something to do? No, Smethwick, not nice. Anyone else? Yes, Spragg? Sir's Patent Latin Football, eh? Good idea. Right, we'll have two teams.

DOMINIC *starts to draw as shown in Fig. 2, talking as he does so. The game is self-explanatory. Each time a member of team A or B answers a question correctly, a cross is put on a spot in the opposing team's half. Thus, the state of the game when* BROOKSHAW *enters is as shown in Fig. 2.* FIGGIS, *in team B, is about to take a shot at A's goal, the cross having moved to a spot nearer the goal-mouth each time* CARTWRIGHT *and* FIGGIS *answer correctly.*

DOMINIC. Barton-Mills, Elwyn-Jones, Spragg, Whitwell, Smethwick, Catchpole and Potter can be team A: Urbs Roma, and Cartwright, Figgis, Standfast, Harvey-Williams, Hughes, Madison and Kinnock can be Team B: Oppidum Londinium. You all know the rules by now, right answer keeps possession, wrong answer gives it over to the other side and the right answer takes the ball towards the opponent's goal. So Urbs Roma and Barton-Mills to kick off. (*Speeds up voice throughout the game*) Right Barton-Mills, give me the Latin please for a kettle. A kettle or cauldron. Have to hurry you . . . no?

And possession goes over to Oppidum Londinium and Cartwright. Cartwright, a kettle or cauldron? Is the right answer! Wonderful tackle, Cartwright, simply great tackle. *Cortina*, *cortinae*, feminine, kettle or cauldron, should have remembered that, Barton-Mills, Book One stuff. So, Cartwright, still in possession, give me the English for *relinquo ludum*, or *ludum relinquo*. Yes? 'I am leaving school' is the right answer! So Cartwright still battling forward towards the goal in brave possession, give me the Latin for despair. To despair? No? You don't know despair? And possession goes over to Urbs Roma and Whitwell. To despair, Whitwell? No? Bumpkin. Back then to London Town and Figgis. To despair, Figgis, is . . . ? *Desperare*, good boy. Figgis in possession then with a shot at goal – calm down, you lot *(He himself is wildly out of control)* Now, Figgis, give me the Latin, and this has to be a hundred per cent right for a goal shot, give me the Latin for . . .

There is a knock at the door.

DOMINIC. Come in!

Enter BROOKSHAW.

No, not *intrate*, Figgis, you silly boy, I was talking to . . . oh, Mr Brookshaw.

BROOKSHAW. Sorry to disturb your lesson, Mr Clarke. Sit down, boys, but I wonder if I might have a word with you, it's rather urgent.

DOMINIC. Certainly. Um, all right boys, I'll let you go now, we'll call the game a draw. Well life never is fair, is it, Figgis? Free time until break then, but don't play around indoors, remember there are still other lessons going on.

DOMINIC *watches them leave, houselights slowly down as the last stragglers supposedly quit the form-room.*

Might as well let them go now, nothing left to teach them any more.

Pause. Houselights now fully down.

Well, what can I do for you?

BROOKSHAW. Which do you want first, the bad news or the bad news?

DOMINIC. Oh dear.

BROOKSHAW. I think I'll give you the better bad news first. Jane went up to tell the Old Man about the CE results this morning.

DOMINIC. Was he pleased?

BROOKSHAW. Delighted. Sat up in bed for the first time in months.

DOMINIC. That's the spirit.

BROOKSHAW. Then Jane went too far. She told him about your engagement.

DOMINIC. God. What did he say?

BROOKSHAW. Nothing really. He just died.

DOMINIC. DIED?

BROOKSHAW. I'm afraid so.

DOMINIC. But why?

BROOKSHAW. Heart attack. The shock was too much for him, I suppose.

DOMINIC. Oh dear. *(Slight pause)* Is Jane upset?

BROOKSHAW. Relieved really. At least he went quickly.

DOMINIC. Yes, that's true. Well, well, so the Old Man's gone.

BROOKSHAW. It seems he left all his property, including the school, to Jane. Which must make you, as her fiancé, the new headmaster, Dominic.

DOMINIC. Yes, I suppose it must. Ha, just as well the school's not a trust, eh? No governors to go through.

BROOKSHAW. (*Drily*) Quite.

DOMINIC. Though I'd like you to take over until the end of term, Brookshaw. Do that, would you? I'm going to use the summer holidays to have a good look at the place, where it's going, that sort of thing. There are going to be some changes around here, I can tell you that.

BROOKSHAW. As you wish. (*Rubbing his hands*) Now we come to the less palatable bad news.

DOMINIC. Oh yes? (*Miles away*)

BROOKSHAW. Ampleforth telephoned a few moments ago. The Classics master there has been re-checking the scripts to decide on streaming for next year's new boys.

DOMINIC. (*Back to earth with a jolt*) Oh yes?

BROOKSHAW. He was mystified to notice, he tells me, that Cartwright's script appears to have been written in two, slightly different coloured, blue inks.

DOMINIC. Oh God.

BROOKSHAW. What is even more astonishing is that all the mistakes, and only a very few of the correct answers, were written in one ink, and all the crossings-out and corrections, which were originally taken to be end-of-exam revisions, were written in the other. Now isn't that extraordinary?

DOMINIC. (*Between clenched teeth*) Shit.

BROOKSHAW. Brother Aloysius was summoned from the Abbey. He is manuscript illuminator and a renowned handwriting expert.

DOMINIC. He would be!

BROOKSHAW. And he pronounced, indeed swore by St Dominic . . .

DOMINIC. Ha!

BROOKSHAW. . . . that there were two entirely different hands at work on the paper. Before disqualifying Cartwright entirely and instituting an official IAPS enquiry, they telephoned me to see if we could proffer any explanation. I said that I would tell you to ring back. (*Slight pause*) Well? Is there any explanation?

DOMINIC. Well, that's that, I suppose, isn't it? God, how ridiculous of me. I just couldn't resist altering one or two silly mistakes . . . well, you know how it is Herbert, and then I went a bit potty and just corrected and corrected. Oh, coitus! This is the end, Herbert. There'll be a scandal. I can't possibly be Headmaster after this, the parents would complain, IAPS wouldn't allow it . . . and anyway, Jane'll break off the engagement now, so it doesn't really matter. Oh God. This is it, Herbert, I'm done for.

BROOKSHAW. (*Tenderly*) Will Cartwright's parents sue, do you think?

DOMINIC. Didn't you know? He's an orphan.

BROOKSHAW. Really? Well, how could he afford to come here, then?

DOMINIC. (*Distracted*) Oh, there's some trust for him, it's all very odd. Rupert . . . er, Cartwright himself controls it . . . (*Voice changes*) . . . he controls it himself!

BROOKSHAW. Dominic, are you all right? What's the matter?

DOMINIC. (*Pulling himself up*) What? Nothing! Nothing at all. I was just trying to work out what to do for the best, that's all.

BROOKSHAW. Do you want my frank view?

DOMINIC. I should value it greatly.

BROOKSHAW. Then I'm afraid I think it would be best for all concerned if you were to leave Chartham immediately.

DOMINIC. Yes. I think you're right, I think that would be 'best'.

BROOKSHAW. I can deal with Ampleforth, if you can break the news to Jane, and Cartwright himself . . . I'm afraid we're going to have to find him a new school. Pity really, he would have gone down rather well at Ampleforth. Well, the sooner this is over the better, we don't want Chartham to start a new era with a scandal. This way we should be able to avoid one. After all, we still have some term left to run.

DOMINIC. Yes. I'd prefer it if you could handle Jane as well, honestly Brookshaw. I'm really not very good with women. When I try and talk to them they either cry or bare their breasts at me. Jane does both and I really don't think I could cope with that at the moment. All right?

BROOKSHAW. As you wish. I must say, Dominic, you seem to be taking this very well . . .

DOMINIC. I don't know what kind of a headmaster you will make. A bit of a drip I should have thought. You're very good at controlling boys, but what about the staff? You'd rather be told what to do really, wouldn't you?

BROOKSHAW. Well, I don't know about that. I may not be very good at expressing myself, but . . .

DOMINIC. I would have been good, Brookshaw, I really would. Not like you. I'm not gross and deformed like you. I just . . . misbehave from time to time. I think basically you disgust me, Brookshaw. Failure always does. I'm sorry but there we are.

BROOKSHAW. Now, you look here, Clarke . . .

DOMINIC. Oh, shut up. What are you going to do, now that there isn't anyone to beat you any more?

BROOKSHAW. I think you'd better go and pack, Dominic.

DOMINIC. Yes. (*Taking a long look round at the audience*) Keep those desks full, Brookshaw. There's normally more tuck in there than text-books. (*He empties his own desk of confiscated water-pistols, plastic animals, sweets etc.*) And find something useful to do on Tuesdays and Thursdays. Which reminds me, you had better keep the peanut butter. I don't think I could find a use for it, really. Scarcely edible any more.

BROOKSHAW. *(Stiffly)* Thank you. And you may keep the toasting-fork.[1] *(Pause)* Well, I'll go and ring Ampleforth then . . . er, goodbye and . . . you have my sympathy, Dominic, but I'm afraid . . .

DOMINIC. No, Brookshaw, you have mine. Now run along.

BROOKSHAW. Er, yes.

Exit BROOKSHAW, *puzzled. Blackout. A spotlight opens out on* DOMINIC *behind his desk. There is a suitcase behind him and a small tuck-box, initialled 'R.C.'*

DOMINIC. When I was a boy, I behaved like a boy: thought, ate, slept and played like a boy. Then Nature began to drop hints about a change in status: a cracking voice, hairs about the buttocks, acne. But I continued to think, eat, sleep and play like a boy. This is where school moved in and took over, and soon they made sure that I was thinking, eating, sleeping and playing like a *man*. One of those painful steps towards manhood was my first smoke. It was behind the Fives courts of my house at school, with a boy called Prestwick-Agutter. I can remember it as if it were five minutes ago. Prestwick-Agutter opened his packet of Carlton Premium and drew out a short, thin, round cigarette. As my lips rounded about the tip I began to feel panic. I could hear my boyhood being strangled inside me and a new fire awakening. Prestwick-Agutter lit the end, and I sucked and inhaled. The ears buzzed, the blood caught fire and somewhere in the distance my boyhood moaned. But I ignored it and sucked again. But this time my body rejected it, and I coughed and expectorated. My boy's lungs couldn't take the filthy whirl of smuts I was so keen to introduce to them and so I coughed and kept on coughing. Despite my inner excitement and my great coughing fit, I managed to maintain

[1]Or bicycle-pump or photograph of the Queen Mother or whatever strikes as outré.

a cool, unruffled exterior, with which to impress Prestwick-Agutter, who was amused by my coolness and pluck. British Phlegm and British Spunk flowed freely in me and out of me, and the Public School Spirit was born. After about an hour, it began to rain, so we dashed into the nearest Fives court and leant against the buttress. It was an afternoon of rare agony. It was later that evening, when a horde of uncouth Philistines was raiding my study, Prestwick-Agutter amongst them, that my voice broke. Really quite suddenly. I was nearly seventeen, rather embarrassing really. So after a few years of behaving like a man, while my boy's body slowly creaked into a man's shape, I actually became a man, am one now to the satisfaction of the world, but to my own resentment and annoyance. I never asked to be a man. I never wanted to be a man. Don't misunderstand me, I don't want to be a *woman*, I've an idea that that would be even nastier, I could never think of being a woman. No, I am, you see, what doctors call a disgusting pervert. I want to be a boy. I never should have grown up in the first place. I want to be a boy. Sometimes I try on boy's clothing, small and tight as it is, and it pleases me. It would be delightful to be a boy, to find again that acute balance between soft passivity and complete idiocy. *(Getting excited)* If a boy could be stopped from thinking and behaving like a man, if, when Nature starts thrusting pimples and hairs through the skin, a boy could be kept from school and the world of men and just carry on behaving like a boy, then perhaps Nature would give up and the pimples and hairs would recede. The permanent boy would be found. It's worth a try. Hh. *(Pause)* When I came here my aims were simple. I came on the one hand out of sheer pæderastic longing and on the other hand, as I told Brookshaw, to stop the Barbarian rot at source. But I also came to escape the responsibilities of manhood. Here, after all, I'm just a senior prefect. But I went too far, twice. Now I've nearly wrecked a perfectly respectable school, I've scotched a boy's chances for Ampleforth and I've lost myself a headmastership: just by imitating a boy's handwriting, an act which also, curiously enough, gave me a certain amount of sexual excitement. God knows what would happen if I stayed on here. Or if I went further. *(Pause)* But that's just what I intend to do. I see only one way out of this sorry mess and I shall take it. Remember the old saying, 'The boy across the river has got a bottom like a peach, but I can't swim'? Well *he* can swim, it's just another of those things that all boys can do. (*Picks up tuck-box and suitcase*) 'He walks in beauty like the day, Of endless fields and summer hymns, And all that's fresh in golden hay, Floats from the movement of his limbs.'

Exit DOMINIC. *Blackout. The Stage and Houselights go up as* BROOKSHAW *enters, be-gowned and dog-collared, puffing at his pipe. He has an air-mail envelope in his hand. He motions downwards for the form to sit. He clears his throat, pacing up and down a little at the beginning of his speech.*

BROOKSHAW. Sit down, boys. Now. It is my custom, as you know, to address the leaving form at the end of the summer term, usually on the subject of Religion, Sex and Public School Life. I shall keep to those themes today . . . POTTER, whatever it is, SWALLOW it! . . . but through the medium of another topic. This term, as you are well aware, has been an unusual one. Two deaths, those of the headmaster and young Hoskins, have acted as acute reminders that God may choose any one of us, at any time, young or old, to join Him and His Heavenly Host. I have been acting as a kind of makeshift Headmaster for this term, and Miss Puttenham has asked me to stay on in the capacity for as long as I wish. I have consented, readily and gratefully. It will not affect you much, as you scatter to your fresh woods and pastures new, but I feel that you should know that Chartham is in old hands and will not change so long as I am at the helm, with God and His Host of Cherubim and Seraphim at my side. (*He nods genially to his left*) Another development this term was the startling disappearance of Mr Clarke and your form-mate Rupert Cartwright, both on the same day. The police have been unable to trace either of them and we were all at a loss as to their whereabouts (*Dramatic pause*) until yesterday morning, when I received this letter from Mr Clarke. A letter that I am going later on to read to you gentlemen. Otherwise this summer term, all things being equal, has been like many another. We've had our fair share of disappointments on the cricket-field but we've had our fair share of victories, too. Potter's hat-trick against the Old Charthamians is worthy of mention, as is Kinnock's diligent fifty against Gauntstone Manor. Cricket does not quite approximate to Art or the Infinite, boys, but for most of us it is as close a glimpse of either as we are ever likely to be permitted, so I mention these achievements as honourable accomplishments of which Chartham is proud. Well done all. Academically, the year has been a resounding success. 6A-ites have collected between them four exhibitions, two bursaries and a remarkable three scholarships, as our recent crop of half-holidays has testified. All praise to 6A, and of course to the Angelic Hordes and Ministers of the Almighty who so generously supervised their efforts. And nor have you, 6B, been neglected by the Celestial Multitude. I have not a single failure to report. This means that for every one of you, this is your last week at Chartham, and next September will see you strewn by the four winds all over the Kingdom, as far flung as Sherborne and Fettes, King's Canterbury and King William's, Isle of Man. You will emerge from these seats of learning as men and . . . *with* the exception of Madison! . . . the sort of men of whom Chartham will be proud. The England into which you will step is one about which I freely admit I have no more knowledge than you, but you will, as generations of Charthamians before you, emerge as firm and solid members of it, and you could ask for no higher privilege nor no finer fortune than that. And remember that as an Englishman you have a perfect right to treat God as a social equal and the Devil as an inferior, that way lies Salvation. To that I would add my usual advice to leavers. Under no circumstances strike a woman who is wearing spectacles, don't call writing-paper 'note-paper' and always keep your handkerchief in your sleeve, never in your pocket. I don't think I can offer you any more than that: remember it, obey it, and your lives will be infinitely the easier for it. Now, as to the business of the letter I have received from Mr Clarke. After a good deal of heart-searching I have decided that you ought to hear it. It is not the kind of letter frankly suitable for boys, but I think I can now do you the honour of treating you as men, not boys. I know you all loved Mr Clarke and respected him, and will find his tragedy a severe moral lesson. The letter was post-marked a week and a half ago in Tangier. That, for the sake of you who, despite my efforts, managed to fail Common Entrance Geography, is in Morocco, which, for the benefit of Madison, is in North Africa. The big bit below the Mediterranean, Madison! Now, let me read it to you: 'Tangier, 6th July. Dear Herb . . . hem! . . . Dear Mr Brookshaw, I am writing this overlooking the casbah. Rupert is by my side drinking a rather snazzy cocktail through a straw. Well, we have settled at last, here in Morocco. We managed by some careful baksheesh . . . ' That means bribery in plain English, boys. ' . . . to obtain Moroccan nationality in a hurry, which meant becoming Muslims as well, which is rather decent fun. My new Islamic name is Ghanim Ibn Mahmud and Rupert, whom I have now officially adopted, is Abu Hassan Basim: whizzo, eh? His money is very useful out here, we have bought a decentish villa by the sea, just outside Tangier, and we spend most of the day making love–' *(turns over the page hurriedly)* '–ly sandcastles on the beach and swimming. The air is amazing out here, I hardly have to shave any more and my voice is cracking into a treble. It must be all those ice-creams. We're becoming quite well-known locally: they call Rupert "Young Hassan of the Blue Eyes and Million Gold Pieces" and I am known as "Ghanim whom Allah has blessed with a Son and No Wives". Well I must go now. Lots of luck in your headmastership, buckets of love to Chartham and do come and visit us in the hols. Meanwhile, Praise be to Allah, the Beneficent King, the Creator of the Universe, Lord of the Three Worlds, Who stretched out the Earth even as a Bed. Blessings be upon our Lord Mohammed, Lord of all Men, and upon his Companion-Train. Prayer and Blessings enduring and Grace which unto the Day of Doom shall remain, in the Name of Allah, the Compassionating, the Compassionate, Amen!' The letter is signed: 'Ghanim Ibn Mahmud and Abu Hassan Basim, with much love and kisses.' *(Folding up the letter)* Well, boys, that is a sad letter. Between the lines even you could probably detect the loneliness, despair and anguished misery of an Englishman who has lost his nationality and his religion, in other words his actual and his spiritual identities. The tone is unmistakeable; they have lost the only things that made them remarkable and pity is all one can feel for them. In a little while I'm going to ask you to join me in a prayer to God and his mystic Host of Angels and Archangels, Ministers and Servants, Saints and Martyrs, and we shall together beg the Sacred Company to return our lost friends to the faith. To have been born British, it has rightly been said, is to have drawn first prize in the Lottery of Life. To have been baptised Christian, I might add, is to have drawn first prize in the Lottery of Life After Death, a remarkable investment. These two unfortunates have thrown both their tickets away and are now lost. They think, boys, that they have found freedom and happiness, but as we all know, as they must know in their heart of hearts, they have found only dissipation and ruin. Money, sun and sensual pleasure, that is all they have, and these are hollow things, boys, hollow. Cartwright, or Hassan, or whatever he now is, has even been permanently deprived of the best education a Catholic is permitted in this country. Let the example of this unlucky pair be a lesson to you all . . . yes, Elwyn-Jones, what is it? Well, how can I possibly know the price of a child air-fare to Morocco? Cartwright could afford it as you know, to the detriment of his immortal soul . . . stop whispering over there . . . and so, when you start at your new school next term, spare a . . . where do you think you're going, Potter? I haven't finished yet. Figgis? Elwyn-Jones? What are you . . . ? Kinnock? Whitwell? All of you! Where are you going? Come back! I haven't finished yet. Come . . . back . . .

The houselights fade down.

I was going to tell you about God's . . .

Silence. BROOKSHAW *looks in despair around what to him is now an empty form-room. He takes out* CLARKE's *letter, looks at it and turns to the desk. He starts to write a letter, speaking as he does so. The audience should notice fully for the first time that the blackboard is covered with childish scrawl:* 'Puer magistrum amat. Magister puerum amat. *The boy loves the master loves the boy loves the master. Dominus rupertum amat. Rupert dominum amat. Brookshaw fucks figs. Matron eats smegma. etc. etc.*'

BROOKSHAW. To Ghanim Ibn Mahmud and Abu Hassan

Basim, from Herbert Brookshaw M.A., Greetings! Thank you for your letter. I hope you are well. You mentioned that you were able to obtain Moroccan nationality in a hurry . . . *(Continues writing as the lights fade)* . . . I would be most grateful if you could send me details of how I might do the same. I have a not inconsiderable sum saved against . . .

Fade to BLACKOUT. *The sound of a* SCHOOLBOY *singing the Nunc Dimittis turns into the Muezzin's Call to Prayer.*

CURTAIN